CARD

SHARKS

HOW UPPER DECK TURNED A CHILD'S HOBBY INTO A HIGH-STAKES, BILLION-DOLLAR BUSINESS

PETE WILLIAMS

MACMILLAN ■ USA

To the memory of Wendy Williams
and Andy and Linda Smith

MACMILLAN
A Prentice Hall Macmillan Company
15 Columbus Circle
New York, NY 10023

Library of Congress Cataloguing-in Publication Data
Williams, Pete
    Card sharks : how Upper Deck turned a child's hobby into
a high-stakes, billion-dollar business / Pete Williams.
        p.   cm.
    Includes index.
    ISBN 0-02-629061-8 (alk. paper)
    1. Baseball cards—United States—Marketing.   2. Upper Deck (Firm)
3. Baseball players—United States—Finance, Personal.   I. Title.
GV875.3.W55   1995
769.49796357'0681—dc20   95-4183
                                                              CIP

Manufactured in the United States of America
10 9 8 7 6 5 4 3 2 1

CONTENTS

This book has its origins in the summer of 1976, when I purchased my first baseball cards at the gift shop of Lowery's Seafood Restaurant in Tappahannock, Virginia.

I remember very little about the cards, a three-deck, "rack-pack" of Topps baseball cards wrapped in cellophane that allowed the customer—in this case, me—to see the cards on the top and bottom. I do remember that one of the visible cards was of Jim Palmer, the star pitcher for the Baltimore Orioles, who in 1990 was inducted into the Baseball Hall of Fame.

If I still had that card in 1994, and if it were in "mint" condition, it would be worth between $3.50 and $7, according to one of the many baseball card price guide magazines that now exist. Palmer may be buried in a shoebox somewhere, all dinged up and dog-eared. If he is, he's virtually worthless. But I don't lose sleep over it. Back in 1976, I was not concerned with maintaining the card's fresh-off-the-press look, let alone its "investment value."

As an adult, I came to realize that the hobby I pursued as a youth in the late 1970s had grown into a billion-dollar business. Cards now were traded like penny stocks and hoarded by investors who dreamed of cashing them in down the road. How, I wondered, had a simple children's pastime been transformed into a cut-throat industry dominated by adults?

USA Today Baseball Weekly gave me the opportunity to find out. When I joined the two-month-old, spinoff publication of *USA Today* in June of 1991 as a general assignment reporter, I found myself writing stories about the booming business of sports cards and memorabilia. Even though card collecting had become a major industry, its insiders still referred to the field as "The Hobby." One card manufacturer seemed to dominate The Hobby: a young, innovative firm called the Upper Deck Company.

Over the next three years, in a column called "Collectibles Beat," I chronicled this odd phenomenon of people investing in slabs of cardboard depicting professional athletes. I got to know the card manufacturing companies that had joined veteran Topps in the business, firms such as Fleer, Donruss, Score, Pro Set, Action Packed, and Pacific—all of whom, including Topps, seemed to be trying to catch up with Upper Deck.

This is the first book about the Upper Deck Company. It is also the first major book to chronicle the meteoric growth of the sports cards and collectibles industry in the late 1980s and early 1990s. Though Upper Deck has emerged as a household name and the company itself has plastered its image on television, in sports arenas, and through advertising in countless magazines, it has remained an intensely private business. In these pages, Upper Deck is exposed to public view for the first time.

Upper Deck was formed by the personalities of the men who built it, many of them colorful characters. This is a book about these men and how they took the simple idea of making a better baseball card and revolutionized an entire industry, transforming a children's hobby into a business that by 1991 accounted for an estimated $2 billion in annual sales.

This book is based primarily on interviews with more than 150 people in the sports card and collectibles business, many of whom I interviewed multiple times between June of 1993 and September of 1994. I felt strongly that the story of Upper Deck had to be told in as in-depth a manner as possible. Toward that end, I interviewed sixty-one current and former employees, as well as dozens of the company's competitors, consultants, distributors, and licensors.

Upper Deck initially cooperated on this project when I began work on it in June of 1993. But by October, 1993, after I interviewed company president Richard McWilliam by phone about allegations of unscrupulous company activity made in a lawsuit by one of Upper Deck's founders, the company retreated. Interviews dried up and Upper Deck's senior corporate counsel and McWilliam himself wrote threatening letters to my editors at *USA Today* and *USA Today Baseball Weekly*, complaining about my zealous efforts to interview company sources, while at the same time expressing a desire to cooperate with the book. During a phone conversation with me in April of 1994, McWilliam became very angry, saying that if I talked to certain individuals he "would become very upset." I was told on many occasions by current and former employees that they feared retribution if they spoke with me.

Despite the company's apparent efforts, only a handful of current or former Upper Deck employees refused to talk with me for this book. Because of the access I received as well as the extraordinary amount of material available on the company through court documents, I have been able to reconstruct dialogue extensively. This, of course, requires drawing on often selective memories. But in many instances I was able to interview every person who sat in on a meeting or was part of a deal. As big as Upper Deck has become in a short time, it's easy to forget that for much of its first year it had less than twenty employees.

Memories are not perfect, especially when dealing with events that happened years ago. But I felt that to eliminate dialogue from the tale of a company known for its colorful personalities and creative minds would strip the Upper Deck story of much of its vibrancy. The conversations recounted in these pages are based on the recollection of at least one person who was present at the time the discussions took place. Many lines were so memorable people swore they remembered them verbatim years later.

When initially approached in June of 1993, McWilliam was very receptive to this book, sitting for two hours in his office at Upper Deck's headquarters in Carlsbad, California, and offering to show me his extensive memorabilia collection at his home in Encinitas. After canceling several scheduled in-person interviews over the next six months, McWilliam insisted that I provide him with a list of questions before he would agree to sit down with me again. I expressed reservations, wondering if he would not just respond to my list of questions with a prepared list of answers. McWilliam assured me that he would not and invited me to his office on Friday, April 8, 1994, on the condition that he received the questions beforehand.

I faxed a list to his office, and within hours his secretary informed me that McWilliam would not be able to see me. Several days later, I received in the mail a list of brief answers to my questions. Over the next four months, McWilliam continued to insist that he would agree to an interview provided I give him another list of questions beforehand. I sent him a list on August 16, 1994, after Upper Deck's director of communications told me no in-person interviews would be allowed. The list included detailed questions concerning some of the allegations made by former employees in this book. I received no comment. Instead, I was sent a brief letter from Steven Mitgang, Upper Deck's president of sales and marketing. The letter answered my twelve paragraphs of specific questions as follows: "Concerning your request for more information about The Upper Deck Company, I will remind you that we remain, and plan to remain, a privately held company. We hope you are able to understand the information you are seeking is proprietary and confidential. We believe that with the amount of information covering The Upper Deck Company already in the public domain, along with your own empirical research, you already possess all the information we can provide to you."

It was during this period, August of 1994, that McWilliam stepped down as president of Upper Deck, although he remained chief executive officer. Mitgang, formerly senior vice president of marketing, and Brian Burr, formerly the senior vice president of operations, were promoted to president of sales and marketing and president of operations, respectively.

Mitgang and Burr would not be interviewed for this book, although, like McWilliam, they expressed a willingness at various times in this project to talk with me. In the end, like McWilliam, they canceled scheduled interview times and refused comment.

Wherever possible, I have portrayed McWilliam's views. In addition to the two-hour interview he did grant me in June of 1993 and several brief telephone conversations, I relied heavily for his thinking on an extensive deposition and subsequent testimony in a 1993 court case, along with dozens of memos, board meeting minutes, published articles and internal documents that either became public record or were acquired in researching this book. Also, many men who were close to McWilliam felt comfortable recalling his comments because they came from common discussions. It must be stressed, however, that this is not a biography of Richard McWilliam. It is the story of a group of men who built a wildly successful company.

As this book neared its completion in the summer of 1994, Upper Deck publicly addressed some of the issues reported in these pages. In an article that appeared in the August 12, 1994, issue of *Sports Collectors Digest*, Upper Deck's director of communications, Camron Bussard, said Upper Deck went public with a response because people who had received product in the past kept threatening to go to the media with their stories.

Bob Brill, a former UPI sportswriter who wrote the *SCD* article, asked Bussard what impact this book had on Upper Deck's decision to make a public announcement. Bussard replied: "I think if you put Pete in the context of everyone else, he becomes a small thread in this whole fabric. He certainly becomes a thread, but it is the same stuff. If the only thing out there were Pete's book then we probably wouldn't worry about it."

I had far too much material to include in one book. Because of the approach I took, focusing on the principal players at Upper Deck, I did not highlight the contributions of the many behind-the-scenes people at Upper Deck who so graciously granted me interviews, sitting through hundreds of hours of sessions that included reliving an often unpleasant past. To these people, the secretaries, security guards, plant workers, and underlings who helped build Upper Deck, I send my heartfelt thanks, and hope they realize that although their stories are not mentioned specifically, their input can be seen throughout this book.

In addition, a number of books were essential resources for me in portraying the early days of the card business, including *A Whole Different Ballgame* by Marvin Miller, *A Collector's Guide to Baseball Cards* by Troy Kirk, *Hager's Comprehensive Guide to Rare Baseball Cards*, and *The Great American Baseball Card Flipping, Trading and Bubble Gum Book* by Brendan Boyd and Fred Harris.

This book would not have been possible without the strong support I received from Macmillan's publishing team, including Scott Flanders, Alan Oakes, Natalie Chapman, Patty Shaw, and, of course, my editor Jeanine Bucek. Brian Zevnik's fine work as a freelance editor is reflected in every paragraph in this book.

Card Sharks owes its existence to Rick Wolff, the former director of Macmillan sports titles. Even after he left Macmillan, Rick remained supportive of this project.

As a research assistant, Chris Boynton proved once again that he's a great sportswriter masquerading as a lawyer. I'm also grateful for the help of Bob Ivanjack, who sent me a steady stream of information he uncovered through his own research, and John Ale of Richard's Computer, who brought a dinosaur back to life to produce this book. Thanks also to Jeff Caddy of Caddyshack Sports Cards in Alexandria, Virginia.

I received generous contributions from several individuals who have covered the sports collectibles business, particularly Kevin Allen of *USA Today*, Bob Brill of UPI, and Bill Madden of the New York *Daily News*. I'm also grateful to Paul White, Tim Wendel, Rick Lawes, and Greg Frazier of *USA Today Baseball Weekly* and Phil Wood of WTEM radio in Washington, D.C.

Then there are the people who provided support and kept me focused on this book. To Ron Williams, Teresa Williams, Katherine Williams, Chris and Tom Doberneck, Tim Mossman, Suzy Smith, Eric Brown, Bruce Greenbaum, Missy Mikolajczak, Greg Mand, and Roxanne Elliott, I can't say thank you often enough.

Pete Williams
Alexandria, Virginia
September, 1994

Baltimore

July 12, 1993

Baltimore's Oriole Park at Camden Yards was the home of the 1993 Major League Baseball All-Star Game. The blue-collar city by the Chesapeake Bay was suffering from image problems and an increasing homicide rate, but its new ballpark with the old-time atmosphere had proven to be the perfect setting for baseball's showcase event—even if the suffocating heat was threatening to drive everyone indoors.

But nothing would keep fans away from Camden Yards. The All-Star game was still a day away, but 47,891 ticket-holding fans had begun lining up at 10 A.M. for a chance to see a pair of home run contests and a player workout. Without tickets to the game itself, this was the closest most would get to the 64th annual All-Star Game. Even workout day was sold out, with scalpers selling tickets for $50. Tickets for the game itself started at $500.

By mid-afternoon, the stadium was full. Inside the clubhouses, players prepared for the home run contest that would crown the slugger of sluggers. Behind the batting cage, a small group of celebrities gathered for their own homer competition. There was basketball star Michael Jordan, who brought fellow Olympic Dream Team member Patrick Ewing. There were actors Tom Selleck, Bill Murray, and Jim Belushi, Olympic sprint gold medalist Florence Griffith-Joyner, and football star turned broadcaster Ahmad Rashad. Selleck, the former star of the *Magnum P.I.* television series, wore a uniform of the hometown Baltimore Orioles, abandoning for the day his beloved Detroit Tigers. Jordan, in his pre–minor league baseball period, donned a No. 23 uniform of the Chicago White Sox, a team owned by his basketball boss, Chicago Bulls owner Jerry Reinsdorf. In place of a White Sox hat, Jordan, like the rest of the celebrities, wore a black cap that read "Upper Deck."

Upper Deck. The logo was everywhere during All-Star week. It was on billboards, programs, and souvenirs. Giant Upper Deck baseball cards loomed on rooftops and sidewalks. Two blocks from Camden Yards on Pratt Street, an

1

oversized card of Baltimore Orioles shortstop Cal Ripken towered three stories above pedestrians, casting a shadow for nearly a block. As Jordan stretched, thirty former big leaguers wearing Upper Deck hats waited in the dugouts to play in an Upper Deck "Heroes of Baseball" game. Sitting with them were a dozen Upper Deck vice presidents and public relations officials, who had flown in from corporate headquarters in Carlsbad, California.

The company, it seemed, had taken over the All-Star Game. Only five years before, Upper Deck was just one of thousands of sports shops that had popped up in strip malls across the country as the baseball card and sports memorabilia business exploded. The store, located just a tape-measure home run away from Anaheim Stadium in California, had a measly 600 square feet of space. Its owner, Bill Hemrick, had grown increasingly frustrated over counterfeit baseball cards. Once, he had spent $4,000 on a batch of Don Mattingly rookie cards, only to discover later they were fake.

In 1987, Paul Sumner, a printing company executive and a former member of an academic team that had developed the "white light projection hologram"— the device now used to deter credit card counterfeiting—told Hemrick they could apply the same technology to baseball cards. The two men organized a company with the belief that they could make a better baseball card, and in 1992 the Upper Deck Company recorded sales of $263.3 million from its sports cards. The company's logo was all over the sports world: in stadiums, on hockey rinks, and, most importantly, on television. It hired football star Joe Montana as its football card spokesman and hockey great Wayne Gretzky to pitch hockey cards. For its basketball cards, the company signed up Jordan, perhaps the most famous face in the country.

Jordan reportedly made $25 million a year from shoe giant Nike. But on this day, the Nike logo was restricted to his feet. His familiar shaved head belonged to Upper Deck, which had paid $400,000 to Major League Baseball to sponsor the All-Star Game. The money included the right to host the home run contest and an Old-Timers' game featuring Hall-of-Famers and Baltimore Orioles greats. Most importantly, from Upper Deck's standpoint, it meant the rights to All-Star FanFest, a giant baseball retail store thinly disguised as a baseball-related carnival. Located two blocks away at the Baltimore Convention Center, FanFest was expected to draw 100,000 fans over a six-day period ending with the final out of the game itself.

That, however, was still thirty-two shopping hours away. Behind the batting cage, Jordan stopped his warm-ups. The steady stream of attention had shifted away from him to the Upper Deck executive in the gray flannel Upper Deck baseball uniform outside the first base dugout.

"Reg-gie! Reg-gie!" the crowd chanted. "Reg-gie! Reg-gie!" it continued, until Reggie Jackson took off his Upper Deck hat and waved. With broad forearms and a boyish expression, he looked like one of the major league All-Stars who would come out momentarily for the home run contest, an event that had grown almost as popular as the All-Star game itself. Jackson wiped the sweat off his brow. Lost to age was the familiar Afro, but in truth, the 46-year-old who retired from baseball after the 1987 season had never looked better physically. He gazed up at the B&O warehouse that towered over the right field fence at Oriole Park at Camden Yards. The writers had told him it would take a shot 460 feet to hit the 100-year old building, a feat no player had accomplished since the stadium had opened 15 months before.

The same writers who had endured a tumultuous relationship with Reggie during his 21-year career had made him a first ballot Hall-of-Famer six months earlier by a near-unanimous margin. Reggie loved and performed the best under the solo spotlight, so it seemed only appropriate that he would not share his up-coming Hall of Fame induction at Cooperstown, New York. He was the only player elected by the Baseball Writers Association of America for 1993. The Vet-erans Committee, which could have named two candidates whose names had appeared on the ballot for years, had chosen no one.

The writers might have despised the way Reggie treated them at times, but they respected 563 home runs and five World Series championship rings. They also, for the most part, enjoyed his candor. In 1976, during his one season playing for the Baltimore Orioles, he remarked that "the only trouble with Baltimore, is that it's in Baltimore."

That was all forgotten now, as the chants of "Reg-gie! Reg-gie!" continued. He had planned to just serve as a batting coach for the celebrities, but wore his Upper Deck Heroes of Baseball uniform, because, heck, he never knew when the spot-light would wander back his way. And he always wanted to be ready.

The home run contest ended with Jordan defeating Selleck, even though Selleck had sent a ball out of the park and Jordan had only lofted a few lazy drives to center field. Jordan, however, had accumulated the highest average distance, mak-ing him the winner of the Upper Deck home run contest, even though he had not hit the warning track, let alone the upper deck.

Now it was Reggie's turn. He motioned for Hall of Fame pitcher Bob Gibson to stay on the mound. Gibson, who beside playing in Upper Deck's Heroes of Baseball games also had a contract to autograph baseballs for Upper Deck's cata-log sales, threw a pitch high and inside. Both players smiled. As a pitcher for the St. Louis Cardinals from 1959 to 1975, Gibson was one of the most intense players in baseball history. He never talked to opposing players and, with his 95-mile-an-hour fastball, was one of the most feared pitchers of his time. Jackson, who as a player had faced Gibson only in the 1972 All-Star Game, would see no fireballs. Gibson, playing to the crowd, threw Jackson a soft, batting practice fastball. Jackson swung, lofting the ball to shallow right field. Gibson threw nine more pitches. Each time, Jackson took his familiar home run swing, but could not reach the fence. Finally, Jackson stepped out of the batter's box. He again wiped his brow.

The crowd wanted a homer. Out on Eutaw Street, a walkway between the refurbished warehouse and a wrought-iron fence that keeps fans from entering the right field stands, a group of young boys waited for a souvenir. Several youngsters positioned themselves at the base of the warehouse, poised to catch a carom off the building. Inside, the chant continued. "Reg-gie! Reg-gie!"

Jackson stepped back in. Gibson lobbed a pitch knee high. Jackson swung and watched his drive arc toward the warehouse. As he had done 563 times before, he waited at home plate for the ball to clear the fence. It did, but stopped well short of the warehouse. Moments later, the man who held the title of assistant to the president of Upper Deck and a seat on the company's board of directors was circling the bases, with a big grin. There would be many big moments leading up to his Hall of Fame induction three weeks later, but this one was special.

The crowd stood and the chorus grew even louder.

"Reg-gie! Reg-gie! Reg-gie!"

Jackson was mobbed at the plate. He high-fived players, celebrities, and his fellow Upper Deck executives. He took off his cap and waved to the crowd. The moment was perfect. But when he stepped down into the dugout, he noticed something missing. Someone had stolen his glove, the same mitt he had used for 17 years. The same glove he had worn in the 1977 World Series, when he hit home runs in three consecutive at-bats in Game Six. The same glove he ended his career with as an Oakland Athletic in 1987. It could never be replaced. Jackson, who had a $500,000 salary and a million-dollar contract to sign autographs for the largest manufacturer of sports cards and memorabilia in the world, shook his head at the irony.

His most prized piece of sports memorabilia had just become the pride of someone else's collection.

■ ■ ■

As Reggie touched home, Doug DeCinces sat at a booth in the Baltimore Convention Center signing autographs. Above his table was a banner that read "Upper Deck Heroes of Baseball."

Upper Deck. The same company that was suing his sports marketing firm, DeCinces Sports Productions, for $760,000 had offered him $3,000 to sign autographs and play in a Heroes of Baseball game as part of the week-long festivities in Baltimore. He didn't want to come, but figured he owed it to the Baltimore fans. He had played nine years at Memorial Stadium, covering third base for the Orioles, mostly between the time Brooks Robinson retired and Cal Ripken arrived as a rookie. He was a bridge between two Hall-of-Famers, to be sure, but he was still a name. After all, he had hit 237 home runs during a 15-year career that ended in 1987 with the St. Louis Cardinals.

The year after DeCinces retired, Upper Deck started producing baseball cards. His business partner, sports memorabilia dealer Mike Berkus, had suggested early in 1992 that they join forces with Upper Deck. Among their projects was a plan to open kiosks at shopping malls throughout southern California to sell Upper Deck sports cards and memorabilia. Put Upper Deck in the mall mainstream, Berkus had said, alongside Waldenbooks and Orange Julius.

The kiosks failed miserably, never getting off the ground in time for the Christmas shopping season. Berkus, who stayed on as a consultant for Upper Deck, split with DeCinces, telling his colleagues at Carlsbad that DeCinces was to blame for the kiosk fiasco. A month before the All-Star game, Upper Deck filed suit against DeCinces, claiming breach of contract. He filed a countersuit, contending that Upper Deck had not paid him for services rendered. But he knew he might have to settle out of court—his contract stipulated that disputes were to be settled through arbitration—and might end up paying a lot of money in legal fees.

So here was DeCinces, signing autographs for Upper Deck, while being sued by Upper Deck, which still employed Mike Berkus, the man who was at least partly responsible for a bad marketing scheme that the company blamed on DeCinces. Seated next to his former Orioles teammate Paul Blair, DeCinces just kept signing. It was good to be back in Baltimore, where he had spent some of his best years, 3,000 miles away from Carlsbad. He continued to sign, wishing he had never heard of the Upper Deck Company or met Mike Berkus.

Next to the autograph signing table, Upper Deck employees were stationed at a booth selling "certificates of authenticity." The autographs were free; the certificates were five dollars. A sign at the booth read: "If it's not authenticated, it's just a souvenir." Fans who had just witnessed a former major leaguer signing an autograph lined up to pay five dollars for a piece of paper that assured them that, yes, the signature was indeed real.

Even though Upper Deck invited DeCinces to FanFest, promising him the standard $3,000 that the rest of the ex-players would receive, he would get nothing. When DeCinces returned from the All-Star game, he was told by Upper Deck that he owed them money and would not see a penny for his trip to Baltimore.

■ ■ ■

Five hours after Jackson's "home run," Mickey Mantle was surrounded. In 10 minutes, the New York Yankee legend would go on the QVC home shopping channel to hawk sports memorabilia to a national television audience and nothing was going right.

In a back room at the Baltimore Convention Center, just 50 yards from where DeCinces signed autographs earlier in the day, producers and public relations flaks huddled. "How's Mickey going to make it through the mob?" one asked frantically. "How's he going to make it back here?"

"We'll take care of it," Mike Berkus said, dismissing the flaks and patting Mantle on the shoulder with one motion. After he had split with DeCinces, Berkus formed a new company, All-Sport Hobby Sales, and remained a consultant to Upper Deck. Berkus had a second reason for being in Baltimore; he also provided cards and memorabilia to QVC and the Home Shopping Network. Plus, he had experience. He had worked on Home Shopping's "Sports Emporium" program as a guest host, commuting between California and Clearwater, Florida, twice a month.

Wearing an expensive gray suit, a white shirt, and pastel tie, Berkus looked like the man in charge. He sat down across from Mantle, and pointed at his ring. "See this, Mick. It's an Angels' ring. Rod Carew gave it to me. We go way back. He and my wife went to school together. I even bought his house."

Mantle nodded his approval. Dan Wheeler, the host of the program, stepped over a flak and gave Mantle a list of the products that would appear on the show. "Mick, is it all right if I ask you a few questions about you and Roger, you know, Maris? Is that all right, Mick? O.K., good. And how about Joe, I mean, DiMaggio. You and Joe played together, right Mick? Yeah, good. O.K., we'll see you out there in five."

Mantle placed his bottled water down, atop Wheeler's product list. He laced his fingers behind his head, cracked his neck, and yawned. "I'm getting too old for this," he said. It was the night before the All-Star game and the last place he wanted to be was up on some makeshift bleachers at something called Upper Deck All-Star FanFest answering the same old questions about his career. *Hey Mick, remember that shot at old Griffith Stadium? Hey Mick, what was it like back in '61 when you and Maris were chasing the Babe? Hey Mick, remember that time you and Billy Martin shot that cow?*

Mantle took a swig from the Evian bottle. A small ring of water was left on the QVC product list. "Two minutes, Mick," someone yelled.

Plus, he'd have to talk about all that autographed stuff in the Upper Deck Authenticated catalog. Bats he'd signed were selling for $1,750. Photos for $449. Balls for $119.95. He'd have to take calls from Ethel in Erie and Dave from Duluth. *Mickey, this is the highlight of my life. I grew up in Brooklyn in the fifties and even though my dad and my brother Bobby were big Dodgers fans—you know what, Bobby's probably watching right now. He lives in Sacramento now; it's still early over there. Could you say hello to Bobby for me, Mick? Oh, thanks so much, Mick. . . .*

Sitting on those bleachers for two hours wasn't going to be comfortable for a 61-year-old with knees that felt 100. Couldn't they have done this back in some television studio in West Chester, Pennsylvania, where QVC was located? What about Carlsbad, where Upper Deck was? No, they told him. It was in the contract he had signed with the Upper Deck Co. a year earlier. In addition to signing memorabilia, he had to make twenty-six appearances a year on behalf of the company. Man, those bleachers were going to hurt. But $2.75 million a year can buy an awful lot of aspirin.

It wasn't a bad way to make a living. It sure beat doing card shows, sitting at a table for three hours signing autographs, although that was good money too. Who'd have thought people would stand in line for an hour to pay $40 for his autograph? Where would he be—where would all of the ex-players be—if baseball memorabilia hadn't become big business?

His top salary as a player was $100,000 in 1968; a modest figure then and hardly proportional to the routine $5 million deals today. Still, not long after he retired in 1969 he was in financial trouble. His bowling alley near his Dallas home had closed after years of financial losses, and an attempt to capture the young fast-food market called "Mickey Mantle's Country Cookin'" also failed. Without a steady income, he accepted a $100,000-a-year contract to do sports promotions work for the Claridge Hotel and Casino in Atlantic City, New Jersey, an arrangement that prompted then baseball commissioner Bowie Kuhn to ban him, along with Willie Mays, from baseball in 1983.

Peter Ueberroth, who succeeded Kuhn as commissioner, reinstated Mantle and Mays in 1985. By then, the sports memorabilia industry was being fueled by investors, and Mantle's signature was commanding a premium. Now Mantle was sitting in the bowels of the Baltimore Convention Center, making seven figures a year, waiting to go on a nationally televised show where people would call in and gladly spend $1,750 on a bat he signed but never used. Still, the memories of the hard times lingered.

"I was used to making $100,000 a year and all the sudden, I'm there in Dallas with nothing to do, rotting away. I was thinking 'Where the fuck is Mickey Mantle going?'" Mantle said, moments before going on QVC. "Then in 1975, the bubble gum craze started and all of a sudden, I'm real popular again. I'd do these card shows and guys would come by and say 'Mickey, I've been waiting 30 years for this; this is the biggest thrill of my life. You were my idol, man.'

"It was flattering as hell. I hadn't played in years and to have people still act like that, it builds your ego. And I needed it at the time. I was worried about what was going to happen. We had a house in Joplin, Missouri, and a house in Dallas that were both paid for. It wasn't like we were going to starve, but I was used to living pretty high on the hog and all of a sudden I was wondering what the hell was going to happen. Then, cards and autographs get big. It just seems like everything has fallen into place. I can call my own shots."

The door opened. "It's time, Mick," said Dominic Sandifer. Among his duties as manager of operations for Upper Deck Authenticated, Sandifer traveled with Mantle, serving as part publicist, part confidant, and part bodyguard. He brushed a hair off Mantle's black windbreaker, as if preparing a child for school.

"All right, Mick, you got your earphone plugged in? Good. Got your water? Good. Listen, Mick, while we got a minute. There's a Heroes game coming up in Louisville next week and a card show that takes place with it. The folks in Carlsbad want to know if you can do it."

Twenty-six appearances a year. Mantle's knees made it impossible to play in a Heroes game, but he could suit up and go on the field as a coach. The card show would be a pain, but he'd only have to sign Upper Deck Authenticated catalogs. "The card show and the game counts as two appearances, right? Yeah, I'll do it."

For his troubles, Mantle received $2.75 million a year from Upper Deck. He could have made more from the card show circuit—by now, he could get $70,000 a weekend—but it wasn't worth the trouble. Too many planes. Too many hotels. Too much time on the road. All he had to do now was sign thousands of balls, bats, jerseys, and photos for Upper Deck. They'd even bring the stuff to Dallas if that's what he wanted. Except for the twenty-six appearances a year, he never had to leave home to collect his $2.75 million. Easy money. Still, Joe DiMaggio made more. The Yankee Clipper collected a reported $3.5 million from The Score Board, Inc., a Cherry Hill, New Jersey, memorabilia company, just for signing baseballs and photos. He had another deal that paid him an estimated $2 million to sign bats. DiMaggio hadn't played in more than 40 years, but he was the six-million-dollar man.

It was time for Mantle to make his money. Five twenty-something males appeared in the doorway, all clad in khaki trousers and white Upper Deck knit shirts. Along with Sandifer, they were to run interference for Mantle, serving as a human wall against the mass of baseball fans gathered at the set.

"It's weird, though," Mantle said. "Right now, I'm more popular than when I was playing for the Yankees. I used to ride the subway to games sometimes. Hell, now I'm afraid to walk outside my hotel room."

Outside in the Convention Center, baseball was everywhere. Thousands of fans, many wearing officially licensed clothing of their favorite teams, scrambled in all directions. Upper Deck All-Star FanFest was open until 10 P.M., meaning they had less than two hours remaining. Although the building looked like a baseball stadium, it was one part carnival, one part theater, and two parts department store.

Fans entered through a clubhouse and walked past a dugout into the ballpark. If they walked down the first base line, they would see "The Making of the Game," exhibits showing the manufacturing of caps, bats, gloves, and uniforms. Along the third base line, they could try any of a half-dozen carnival games. At the pitcher's mound was the entrance to the Cooperstown exhibit, a miniversion of the Baseball Hall of Fame that had display pieces on loan from the real museum. In right field, fans could have their pitches clocked by a radar gun and take batting practice against a video pitcher. The batter stood at home plate, facing a widescreen television, which showed one of six major league pitchers standing on the mound. As the pitcher released the ball, a real baseball came toward the batter through a slit in the screen, giving the fan the impression he was hitting against a live pitcher.

In center field, fans entered a major league baseball product store where they could purchase caps, T-shirts, jerseys, bar stools, fish tanks—anything with a logo of one of the twenty-eight major league baseball teams. Twelve cashiers worked frantically to get through the lines, each of which had twenty people waiting. Security guards stood outside the store, letting new customers in only when others departed.

Between the store and the video batting cage, the camera crew and the bleachers waited for Mantle. A small crowd had gathered, but they didn't know who would be on the show. Ropes separated them from the bleachers, which were speckled with popcorn and trash. Host Wheeler and guest Mantle would sit on the top row and talk for 30 minutes before taking a break. Hall-of-Famers Harmon Killebrew and Rollie Fingers would go on later, but Mantle was the star attraction.

Upper Deck officials hoped Mantle's presence would help sell hundreds of bats, balls, jackets, and jerseys that were taking up space in the Upper Deck Authenticated warehouse. When the Authenticated line was created in June of 1992 by Upper Deck and McNall Sports and Entertainment, company officials figured collectors would rush to pay top dollar for replica memorabilia signed by the likes of Mantle, Jackson, Ted Williams, and Joe Montana. Five hundred dollars for a Jackson jersey? They'll sell out in hours. A mere $1,750 for a bat signed by Mantle, who had refused to sign bats for years? They won't be able to make them fast enough.

What the company overlooked was that most sports memorabilia collectors look for material with a direct tie to sports. They'll gladly pay thousands for an autographed bat that Mantle actually used in a game. But $1,750 for a bat manufactured in 1993 was a tough sell. Five hundred for a Reggie Jackson jersey that had never been within 30 miles of a baseball stadium was an even tougher one.

But that was not the only problem. Upper Deck Authenticated had guaranteed enormous salaries to the athletes and agreed to pay licensing fees to Major League Baseball, the National Football League, the National Basketball Association, and the National Hockey League. Thus, Upper Deck had to price its merchandise higher than the going rates seen for similar products at sports card and memorabilia shows.

To help move the Upper Deck Authenticated merchandise, Berkus and Upper Deck president Richard McWilliam enlisted the help of QVC. With its barkers singing about the "investment potential" and "limited edition quality" of the memorabilia "exclusively available through Upper Deck Authenticated and QVC," thousands of viewers would light up QVC's toll-free phone lines. At least that's what they hoped, especially with Bruce McNall, owner of the Los Angeles Kings hockey franchise and a half owner in Authenticated, and probably Upper Deck's board of directors, too, wondering why this "sure thing" wasn't selling as many things as expected.

As Mantle and his entourage emerged from the back room, the crowd surged forward. "It's Mickey Mantle," someone yelled, and the scramble for autographs was on. Mantle kept his head down with his hands on the shoulders of a young man wearing a white Upper Deck shirt, looking like a boxer on the way to the ring. Sandifer and the other four Upper Deck employees cleared the path, pushing away fans wielding pens and baseballs. Mantle reached the bleachers and slipped through the gate, where Wheeler slowly ushered him to the top. Mantle sat down with a grimace, and two minutes later, they were on the air.

For 30 minutes Wheeler and Mantle talked. But mostly it was Wheeler, stressing that Upper Deck Authenticated had only made a limited number of each item, and that viewers would want to call in *right now* and order these products because they were available for a *limited time only*, and only through QVC. Occasionally he stopped to talk to Mantle, asking about DiMaggio several times. Yes, Mantle said, it was a real honor to play with a guy like DiMaggio, even though they only played together for a short time. Joe was something else, he said.

Together, they sold Mantle autographed baseballs and Mantle autographed jerseys and jackets. They even sold, according to Wheeler, some of the Mantle bats for $1,750. They took calls from around the country from viewers who all agreed that calling Mantle was the highlight of their life and that they couldn't believe what a great deal they were getting. Wheeler asked Mantle about his career, and he responded as if he were hearing the same questions he had answered for 30 years for the first time. On screen, a toll-free number was positioned beneath the image of Mantle and Wheeler. The name of the product and its price was printed to their right. At QVC headquarters in West Chester, Pennsylvania, operators took orders and patched certain collectors through to the on-air line.

The crowd, sensing Mantle's segment was coming to a close, pushed forward again. Fans jockeyed for autograph position. At the foot of the bleachers, Bill Ginn smiled. As an Upper Deck Authenticated executive, he knew that his future and that of his company depended on the success of programs like these. And this one had been a success. Soon they could clear out some space in the warehouse. With any luck, they might break even on their $2.75 million annual investment in Mickey Mantle.

Sandifer reappeared, this time with eight young men dressed in matching white Upper Deck shirts and khaki trousers. The trip back to the dressing room was going to be much more difficult than the walk in. Fortunately, Mantle had signed a stack of four-by-six-inch photos earlier in the day. Sandifer never went anywhere with Mantle without carrying a supply to give to zealous autograph seekers. The trick was to always keep Mantle moving. If he stopped, Sandifer knew, he would be surrounded, and the only way out was with a pen.

They got Mantle back to the room in under two minutes, but that was the least of their worries. Inside, with only Sandifer, Berkus, two Upper Deck publicists, and this reporter in the room, Mantle exploded. "Does that asshole up there realize that Joe DiMaggio has a contract with fuckin' Score Board? I'm up there for only a half hour and that shithead mentions DiMaggio six fuckin' times. I ain't going back out there until someone tells that asshole not to mention fuckin' DiMaggio again."

Sandifer and Berkus tried to calm Mantle down, but he was livid. The publicists assured him they would talk to Wheeler, and there would be no more talk of DiMaggio. For now, they had to occupy Mantle for an hour before he went back out for his second segment. Fortunately for them, there was a knock on the door and in walked Killebrew.

"Harmon!" Mantle exclaimed, rising to greet a fellow member of the 500 home run club. "They got you doing this shit now?"

■ ■ ■

As Mantle calmed down in Baltimore, a white limousine drove up Pennsylvania Avenue past the White House. Upper Deck president Richard McWilliam leaned over his female companion and pointed at the Oval Office. It was there, he told her, that he and Reggie had met George Bush back in January. McWilliam had flown in to be with Reggie, who was doing *Larry King Live* a few days after his election to the Hall of Fame. Reggie had put in a call to the White House, and just like that they were in the Oval Office. Reggie and Bush talked politics. Then he and Reggie gave the ex-president-to-be some Upper Deck baseball cards. Bush said he would share the cards with his grandchildren.

"It was way cool," McWilliam told his companion.

McWilliam instructed the driver to head back to Baltimore. He would attend the All-Star game the next day, check in with Reggie, but probably leave early. He had been in the Baltimore/Washington heat for three days, and San Diego's 75-degree temperatures beckoned him home. There was work waiting, anyway. Upper Deck FanFest had been a coup. Only $400,000 for the right to be the exclusive sponsor. What a bargain. Plus, Upper Deck had the rights to next year's All-Star game, in Pittsburgh.

Pittsburgh, he thought. *Why couldn't they have the All-Star game in San Diego every year?*

McWilliam had invested $2.4 million in cash and letters of credit in the Upper Deck startup. He wasn't involved at the very beginning, but it was now his show. In five years, he had made over $50 million in salary, dividends, and bonuses from Upper Deck. His 27.08 percent stake in the company was probably worth $70 million. Most importantly, he was in control. Bill Hemrick, whose Upper Deck card shop had been the inspiration for the company, was gone, although he retained 4.2 percent of company stock. Paul Sumner, who had come up with the idea of making a better baseball card, owned 14.6 percent of the company, but he had limited involvement in Upper Deck. Very limited. Except for his appearances at board meetings, he was apparently content to stay out of the day-to-day affairs, collect his seven-figure dividend check, and shut up. Sure, the company was their idea, but where would they be now without McWilliam's money? Reggie didn't have an ownership position in the company, but he was on the five-man Board of Directors, meaning McWilliam and Jackson represented 40 percent of any board vote.

The 39-year-old accountant-turned-entrepreneur was single and had Reggie Jackson as his best friend. McWilliam's company produced the most popular sports cards in the world and was worth, by his estimate, $250 million. He had even appeared on *The Sporting News*'s annual list of the 100 most powerful people in sports. Funny how life had worked out for a guy who was never much of a sports fan. The limousine turned off Pennsylvania Avenue, and headed back toward the 64th All-Star Game.

■ ■ ■

Back at FanFest, four fans huddled around a blank television screen sitting on an Upper Deck platform in the "Making of the Game" section. They each jumped when a loud jingle started and a teenaged spokesman appeared on the screen. This was the "making of a baseball card" film.

The long-haired teenager on the screen wore an Upper Deck T-shirt. Like the celebrities and players at workout day, he had a black Upper Deck baseball cap, although his was worn backwards.

"Five years ago, the boss had a really great idea," he told the fans.

McWilliam appeared on screen, wearing a green Upper Deck knit shirt and sitting at his desk in Carlsbad. As the narrator talked, McWilliam mouthed the words "Let's make a better baseball card."

Now Upper Deck had become the dominant player in the $1.8 billion sports card industry. The company had become so interwoven with sports that it was easy to forget that Upper Deck was only five years old.

While Upper Deck had transformed the baseball card hobby into big business, it had many predecessors to thank for creating the market that it had come to dominate.

1

The First Players in the Card Game

Baseball cards had existed for more than a century when Upper Deck launched its first cards in 1989.

One hundred years before and 3,000 miles away, the baseball card industry was born on a tobacco farm near Durham, North Carolina, not far from where Duke University now stands. There, in the heart of what is now known as Tobacco Road, the growing industries of tobacco and baseball intersected. The result was a successful marriage that benefited both parties and gave birth to baseball cards.

The farm was owned by Washington Duke, a Confederate soldier who returned to Durham at the end of the Civil War and resumed his life as a tobacco farmer. While money was scarce following the war, the region's fertile soil provided Duke and other tobacco farmers with a strong crop. Soon Duke found that he needed a means to sell his tobacco, so he created Washington Duke Sons & Company, enlisting the help of his sons Buck, Benjamin, and Brodie.

James Buchanan "Buck" Duke, more than his brothers, saw a bright future in the tobacco business. His goal was to dominate the market just as John D. Rockefeller had come to control the oil industry. Tobacco, Buck felt, was an industry ready to explode. Since colonial times, the product had carried the economies of North Carolina and neighboring Virginia, but had truly peaked in popularity since the end of the war. Part of the problem, Buck thought, was that there was no cost-effective means of packaging tobacco. Rolling a cigarette from an expensive tin not only was too time-consuming for many would-be smokers, but also beyond their financial means.

By 1885, Duke had succeeded his father at the helm of W. Duke, and a man named James Bonsack had created the "Bonsack machine," which cranked out 200 cigarettes at a time and reduced production costs by 40 percent. Duke, now 31, bought the rights to the machine, made mechanical improvements, and soon was able to produce as many cigarettes as he could sell. To recruit new smokers, Duke conducted a huge advertising campaign using variations on his claim that "Cigarette and tobacco use is here to stay!" A shrewd marketer, Duke was the first tobacco man to include elaborate graphics and advertising on packaging. By 1887, W. Duke had parlayed its production capacities into a 40 percent stake of the cigarette market. In 1889, the company accounted for 940 million of the 2.1 billion cigarettes purchased in the United States.

Duke did away with the expensive tobacco tins, packaging tobacco in paper and cardboard instead. When he discovered that many of the packs were crushed in shipping, Duke came up with the idea of placing a cardboard insert to stiffen the pack. Not only would they prevent damage, but the "cards" would serve as advertising pieces and premiums to boost sales. While Duke was not the first to produce baseball cards—he included cards of actors and actresses in cigarette packs in the late 1880s—his idea inspired competitors to place baseball cards in their products.

In 1886, the Goodwin Company of New York, the parent firm of Old Judge Cigarettes, issued a twelve-card set (one per pack) that included future Hall-of-Famers Roger Conner, Buck Ewing, Tim Keefe, Monte Ward, and Mickey Welch. Sized $1^1/_2$ by $2^1/_2$ inches, they fit neatly into cigarette containers. In 1887, the Richmond, Virginia, based Allen & Ginter Company released a 50-card "World Champions" set that included ten baseball players along with "sports" figures such as Annie Oakley, Buffalo Bill Cody, and John Sullivan. Between 1887 and 1890, Goodwin issued a comprehensive series as inserts in Old Judge and Gypsy Queen cigarettes. The card line or "set," known as "N172," pictured over 500 baseball players in various poses, totaling thousands of cards. All told, about twenty-five card sets were issued from 1886 to 1890, many from the four companies that dominated the tobacco market before the rise of W. Duke: Allen & Ginter, the Kinney Tobacco Company, Kimball, and Goodwin & Company.

With the cards came card collecting, which presented a challenge since the cards came just one to a pack. Collecting became something of a family affair, as young boys would obtain the cards from their fathers and urge them to buy more tobacco products. Non–tobacco users who wished to collect had to pick up the tobacco habit—as the companies hoped—or find a user willing to part with the cards.

In 1890, Duke convinced the four major tobacco manufacturers to join W. Duke and form the American Tobacco Company. With a virtual monopoly on the market and hundreds of thousands of Americans now smoking, Duke raised prices and slashed expenses, particularly in advertising. One of the first casualties was baseball cards.

As American Tobacco grew over the next decade, only a few baseball card sets were produced. The company moved to New York and expanded into the cut plug (chewing) tobacco business. Before the Civil War, chewing tobacco had been more popular than cigarettes, but had lost customers to the growing popularity of cigarette smoking and American Tobacco. In 1898, Duke formed the Continental Tobacco Company by bringing together many of the leading producers of cut plug. Among the members of Continental Tobacco was Mayo Tobacco Works of Richmond, which was largely responsible for the few baseball card sets of the 1890s.

As Continental Tobacco came together, R. J. Reynolds fought to keep his Reynolds Tobacco Company of Winston-Salem, North Carolina, from being absorbed. Reynolds vowed that if Buck Duke tried to swallow his company, he would have a "bellyache the balance of his life." But rather than risk bankruptcy, Reynolds traveled to New York in 1899 and sold two-thirds of Reynolds to Duke for $3 million.

Next, Duke branched out into the cigar business by forming the American Cigar Company, giving him a foothold in all three areas of the tobacco industry. In 1901, he expanded into Europe, setting up production plants and retail outlets. The colossal tobacco empire run by Duke became known as the "tobacco trust."

The trust dominated the tobacco industry, so much so that, in 1907, the U.S. government sued to dismantle the monopoly. Four years of trials followed before the Supreme Court ordered the trust dissolved. Government officials tried to come up with a plan to break up the trust, but the structure of the organization had become so complex that it was decided that the only one who could do the job was, ironically, the man who had put the monopoly in place: Buck Duke.

During the court case, an air of uncertainty settled over American Tobacco, and it was during this time that baseball cards reappeared in cigarette packaging. Between 1909 and 1911, American Tobacco issued cards in cigarette boxes and pouches of tobacco. The set, known as "T206," contained 524 cards and was distributed in three printings. The front of each card pictured a color lithograph of a player in a studio or action pose, while the backs listed the names of thirty-six different tobacco brands. Shortly after production began, Honus Wagner of the Pittsburgh Pirates objected to the use of his photo and threatened legal action if his card was not removed from the set. American Tobacco complied, but not before a quantity of Wagners had been printed and shipped with tobacco. (At $300,000, the complete T206 set today is the most valuable of twentieth-century baseball sets. The Wagner card alone sells regularly for over $100,000.)

In 1911, American Tobacco was divided into four different companies. Of the four, R. J. Reynolds emerged as the leader in the new tobacco industry. Since its purchase by Duke 12 years earlier, Reynolds had remained in control of the day-to-day operation and built a powerful company behind the success of Prince Albert tobacco. In 1913, Reynolds unveiled Camel cigarettes. On the back of each package, Reynolds alerted consumers not to look for baseball cards or any other insert.

"Don't look for premiums or coupons, as the cost of the tobaccos blended in CAMEL Cigarettes prohibits the use of them."

The message, which remains on the back of some Camel products today, was a death blow to the tobacco card era. Reynolds's competitors, not wanting their customers to think that money that could best be used to improve the product was going into baseball cards, removed the cards too. Tobacco cards appeared sporadically into the 1920s, but the industry-wide practice of using baseball cards to sell cigarettes and tobacco was over.

Buck Duke retained stock in each of the four companies that had made up American Tobacco, but his active tenure as the Rockefeller of the tobacco industry was over. Not ready to retire, Duke turned his attention to hydroelectric power, where he made a second fortune building the Southern Power Company, which later became Duke Power. In 1924, a year before he died, Duke and his family created a Duke endowment "to make provision in some measure for the needs of mankind along physical, mental and spiritual lines." The chief beneficiary of the $40 million dollar fund was Trinity College, which was reorganized to become Duke University.

The void in the baseball card market was not quickly filled. Although a number of candy companies issued cards as part of one-time promotions with caramel and chocolate, it was not until 1928 that baseball cards found a marketing partner to replace tobacco. That was the year a 23-year-old employee of the Fleer Corporation in Philadelphia invented a sugary concoction called bubble gum.

■ ■ ■

That the Topps Chewing Gum Company of Brooklyn, New York, would become the largest manufacturer of sports cards is somewhat appropriate. The company's origins go back to 1890, when Morris Shorin created the American Leaf Tobacco Company, an importer and wholesaler of tobacco for independent cigar manufacturers. Though American Leaf did not manufacture tobacco goods, and thus did not have the need to produce baseball cards, a portion of the tobacco that passed through the company's Brooklyn headquarters inevitably found its way into packages that contained some of the earliest baseball cards.

American Leaf was a moderately successful company, and Morris and his wife Rebecca enjoyed a comfortable living in Brooklyn with their four sons, Abram, Ira, Philip, and Joseph. But the company was hit hard by the Great Depression and struggled to keep up with the automated technologies of the 1930s. Realizing that diversification was the only way to save the business, the four brothers considered going into produce, but thought better of entering a market that, in any given year, could be destroyed by bad weather.

Instead, they decided on bubble gum. Invented in 1928, it was a growing market with few manufacturers and required little in startup costs. It had broad consumer appeal and, most importantly, used the same distribution channels they had in place with American Leaf. In 1938, the brothers created Topps Chewing Gum, Inc. The name Topps evolved from the Shorins' goal of making the company "tops" in its field, with the extra "p" added for distinctive identity. That same year, Topps released its first chewing gum, a fruit-flavored cube that cost a penny and served as a popular change maker at variety stores and drugstores.

Topps made its headquarters at 254 Thirty-sixth Street in Brooklyn's Bush Terminal, a six-story warehouse located along the waterfront of Narrows Bay. Visitors to the administrative offices encountered the sweet smell of bubble gum and left with pink dust on the soles of their feet.

The brothers and their families settled within a ten-block radius in the Crown Heights section of Brooklyn. Sundays were spent at the home of one brother or with the grandparents. Joseph E. Shorin, the president of Topps, had a precocious son named Arthur. One afternoon in 1939, four-year-old Arthur sat down at the piano alongside his older sister Alita, who was practicing a piece by Chopin. At one point, Alita took a break and Arthur—with no musical training—began playing the same piece, only with fewer mistakes than his sister.

Naomi Shorin, Joe's wife, heard the music from upstairs and called down to Alita, "You're sounding good, honey."

"It's not me, Mom," Alita said. "It's Arthur."

Naomi rushed downstairs. There was Arthur, sitting at the piano, his tiny legs dangling off the bench as he casually played the Chopin piece from memory. Naomi let out a piercing scream, then called Joseph—known as J.E.—at the office. Arthur stopped playing. *Did I do something wrong?* he wondered.

J.E. was home within minutes, and by the following week the young prodigy was taking piano lessons. At the age of seven, Arthur was practicing his scales four hours a day. Soon he was performing for the entire Shorin clan on Sundays. Naomi even had him wear special gloves to school to protect his hands.

The inevitable taunts Arthur endured at school, however, were nothing compared to the ridicule he took from his brother Joe, Jr., who, like most older brothers, did not like to see his younger sibling getting all the attention. On evenings when J.E. and Naomi had company, Arthur would pretend to be asleep when J.E. called him down to perform.

"You go down there," Joe, Jr., would say. "And I'll beat the crap out of you."

Then J.E. would barge in and take Arthur downstairs to play. As he finished, realizing he would have to now face his brother, tears would form in his eyes. "Look how emotional he gets with his music," guests would remark to the Shorins. "You must be very proud."

The tears, of course, were not from the music but from fear of his brother. Arthur would politely excuse himself, then proceed upstairs to take his medicine. As the guests raved about Arthur, J.E. beamed. Arthur clearly had a future in the music business.

Topps, meanwhile, was growing. During World War II, the company marketed its gum under the slogan "Don't Talk, Chum, Chew Topps Gum," a variation on the wartime theme, "Loose lips sink ships." The Topps motto became a catchphrase among American soldiers and civilians working in defense plants. Since Topps was one of few companies which managed to obtain an adequate supply of sugar during rationing, its gum seemed sweeter than that of its competitors, who had to decrease sugar content in order to maintain production levels.

After the war, Topps developed its first bubble gum. Originally offered in a five-cent size, "Bazooka" took its name from the shape of the humorous musical instrument that entertainer Bob Burns had constructed from two gas pipes and a funnel in the 1930s; the same contraption that was the namesake for the armor-piercing weapon developed during the war.

Released in 1947, Bazooka became an immediate hit. But over the next three years, as the bubble gum market grew and competition increased, the Shorin brothers looked for a way to distinguish their products. For Bazooka, Topps, beginning in 1953, included a small comic strip featuring "Bazooka Joe," a loose parody of president J. E. Shorin. Still, the brothers knew they could not count on Bazooka to carry the company. They remembered the lessons of American Leaf and the dangers of relying too heavily on one product.

The solution came from a young employee from the promotions department, who suggested that Topps include baseball cards as a premium item in packages of Topps gum. The idea was hardly a novel approach; for decades, companies had inserted baseball cards to spark sales of tobacco, candy, and gum products. Most recently, the Goudey Gum Company of Boston had issued baseball cards with gum between 1933 and 1941. Between 1939 and 1941, Gum Incorporated of Philadelphia included "Play Ball" cards with gum. The company stopped production during World War II, returning in 1948 with a set under the brand name Bowman.

The Shorin brothers had no idea how to get into the baseball card market, but the employee insisted he could make it happen. Although Bowman owned the rights to the players, he said, Topps could enter the market.

"All right, see what you can do," J. E. Shorin told the young man.

And with that, Sy Berger went to work.

■ ■ ■

Seymour Berger was born in 1923 and raised in the Bronx. The son of a custom furrier, young "Sy" would rush home from school and run eleven blocks from the Berger home on 172nd Street to Yankee Stadium in time for 3 o'clock games. Other days, he would wander over to the Polo Grounds to see the New York Giants.

Berger graduated from DeWitt Clinton High School and enrolled at Bucknell University in Pennsylvania. There, he met a baseball player named Bob Keegan, who would later go on to pitch for the Chicago White Sox, and joined the Sigma Alpha Mu fraternity and became good friends with a brother named Joel Shorin, nephew of Topps president J. E. Shorin.

After graduation and a stint in the army, Berger was hired as an assistant buyer for the B. Altman Company. It was enjoyable work, paying $40 a week, but Berger longed to get a job in advertising and promotion. But because his degree from Bucknell was in accounting, his job offers usually came in accounting or sales.

Berger stayed in touch with Shorin, who had joined his father and uncles at Topps. Shorin mentioned the difficulties he was having running a promotion called Goldrush Jamboree, where salesmen were awarded prizes based on the number of cases of Topps gum they sold. For each case sold, a salesman received a certificate. The certificates were placed in a drum and each month the salesman whose certificate was drawn received a prize ranging from RCA televisions to fur coats to Chevy automobiles. But what had started as a bonus program to increase sales, Shorin said, had become a major production requiring more time and resources than he had available.

"I need somebody to help me with this," he told Berger.

Shorin arranged a meeting between Berger and his uncle, J. E. Shorin. J.E. could guarantee only five months' work, the amount of time left in Goldrush Jamboree. Berger accepted, with a bump in salary to $45 a week, becoming part of Topps's three-man promotions department. Within 18 months, the other two men were gone and Berger had become the assistant to the promotions manager.

By the time Berger proposed the baseball card idea to the Shorin brothers, he had established himself in baseball circles. His father-in-law, Jerome Kurpf, a New York newspaper editor, had introduced him to Arthur Mann of the Brooklyn Dodgers. Mann worked as an assistant to Branch Rickey, the Dodgers general manager who helped break baseball's color barrier by signing Jackie Robinson. Another colleague of Kurpf's, former New York sportswriter Gary Schumacher, worked in the N.Y. Giants publicity department. Soon, Berger had access to both the Giants and Dodgers clubhouses and went to work on signing players for Topps's 1951 baseball cards. The access was significant because locker rooms were not yet open to women and Joan Crosby, who worked for an agency that negotiated the contracts for Bowman, had to wait outside for players. Meanwhile, Berger was inside talking with players and trying to discover a way to get around Bowman's exclusive player contracts.

Larry Wien, a New York attorney and real estate investor, set up a company called Players Enterprises with J. E. Shorin to market baseball players. While such a relationship might seem like a conflict of interest today, no one objected in an era when player endorsement opportunities consisted of a few commercials for star players. A few months later, Berger discovered an advertising agency that had produced stickers of major league players. An employee of the agency gave Berger copies of the contracts that he had negotiated with the players to produce the stickers.

Berger took the contracts to Shorin. "I'm not a lawyer, but I think we can hang our hat on these," he said.

Shorin looked over the contracts and kissed Berger on the forehead. "You're a smart kid," he said. "Let's make some cards."

■ ■ ■

Topps combined the language of the advertising agency contracts and Players Enterprise agreements, being careful not to infringe upon Bowman's rights. The company did not want to repeat the mistakes of Leaf Gum, Inc., a Chicago gum company that had issued baseball cards between 1948 and 1949 before ceasing production amid threats from Bowman. As a precaution, Topps would not include gum. Instead, the cards would be issued with taffy.

Topps's first baseball cards looked more like playing cards than trading cards. Issued two to a pack with a piece of taffy for one cent, the 1951 cards measured 2 by 2 5/8 inches and contained a game situation (ball, strike, out) which allowed the cards to be used as a game. The cards were issued in two versions, with either red or blue backs.

The problem came in the taffy. The varnish used to coat the cards rubbed off on the taffy, giving it a chemical taste and rendering it inedible. The set (limited to the players from Players Enterprises) contained only a fraction of the superstars in the Bowman card line. Still, it was a start, and Topps heard no objection from Bowman. Berger moved quickly to build Topps's stable of athletes. As teams came to New York during the 1951 season, he attempted to sign players to nonexclusive contracts. While most players graciously accepted Berger's offer of $125 for a one-year, exclusive contract or $75 for a nonexclusive deal, Berger had a difficult time with the New York Giants. Horace Stoneham, the owner of the club, had a long social relationship with Art Flynn, whose public relations agency, Art Flynn and Associates, handled the player negotiations for Bowman. Stoneham urged his players not to sign with Topps. But the contracts were too good to resist, and when Giants infielders Bobby Hofman and Bill Rigney ignored Stoneham and signed with Berger, the rest of the team soon followed.

In 1952, Topps issued a 407-card set, the largest since the 1909–11 T206 tobacco set. Topps increased the size of the cards to 2 5/8 by 3 3/4 inches and employed color "art photographs," unlike Bowman, which used color paintings. Berger acquired black-and-white photographs from the clubs, then sent them to Solomon and Gelman, a Manhattan art studio owned by Ben Solomon and Woody Gelman. Using *The Sporting News Baseball Register* as a guide, Berger instructed the artists on what complexion each player had and how to color their eyes and hair. The artists then painted over the black-and-white photos in color. Berger wrote the card backs himself, toiling at home after work well into the night.

While the financial impact of the 1952 407-card set was minimal for Topps, the cards were a hit among collectors. While some collected both brands, others split into two camps, passionately supporting one company and despising the other. The situation mirrored the New York baseball scene, where families were divided between the Yankees, Dodgers, and Giants. Bowman, meanwhile, filed suit claiming that Topps had violated its exclusive right to use player photographs. The U.S. District Court for the Eastern District of New York ruled in favor of Topps but, on appeal, the U.S. Court of Appeals supported Bowman.

In its ruling, a three-judge panel stated that Topps could enter into contracts to use player names in conjunction with the sale of a commercial product so long as the agreements did not go into effect until after Bowman's contracts expired. Topps had violated this rule, the court found, by acting on its new rights while the Bowman deals were still valid. In its defense, Topps contended that the Bowman contracts were no more than releases by the ballplayers to Bowman of any liability that might have been incurred from using player photos. The court agreed, stating that the contracts gave Bowman no "property" right that Topps's conduct could have invaded. But, the court ruled, Topps had ignored the fact that Bowman's contracts included a promise by the players not to give similar releases to other companies.

Topps, stripped of its rights to many of the players it had included in 1952, issued a smaller set in 1953. While there were cards numbered as high as 280, the set actually included only 273 cards; the remaining seven—which Topps mistakenly thought it had the rights to—were pulled shortly before production. For the next two years, neither Bowman nor Topps could produce a complete set of major league baseball players since neither held rights to all of the players.

Berger, meanwhile, continued to work the clubhouses. In addition to the $75–$125 contracts, he gave each player a $1 check as a signing bonus. "What am I supposed to get with a dollar?" one player asked.

Berger shrugged. "What do you want?"

"I want a steak."

Berger reached into his pocket and handed the player a five-dollar bill. "Here, go buy yourself a steak."

From that point forward, the Topps bonus checks—increased immediately to five dollars—were referred to among players as "steak money."

By 1955, because of Berger's hustling, it had become apparent that Topps was winning the battle of the baseball cards and, as a consequence, hurting Bowman's gum sales. Late in the year, Topps went into negotiations to purchase Bowman. Topps had no interest in Bowman's gum manufacturing operation, but wanted the baseball card contracts held by Bowman so it could produce a complete set of cards. As part of the deal, Topps would receive the rights to Bowman's "Balony" bubble gum.

In January of 1956, the sale was completed and Berger led a group of Topps employees to Philadelphia to see what was left of Bowman. The Topps contingent arrived as conquering heroes. Berger sat down at a desk and called J. E. Shorin, feeling like a victorious soldier relaying news to the general. "We made it," he said. "There's not much here, but it's ours."

As Berger sat back in the chair and surveyed the room around him, he noticed an IBM electric typewriter, the first one he had ever seen. He used the machine to write a simple telegraph, which he sent to Topps's salesmen out in the field.

"Gentlemen," he wrote, "we now own Bowman."

It was a wonderful moment for the 31-year-old Topps employee. But even as Topps defeated one Philadelphia gum company, a second was rising to challenge Topps in the gum and card market. Unlike Bowman, the Fleer Corporation would prove to be an enduring opponent.

■ ■ ■

The Fleer Corporation was founded in 1914 by Frank H. Fleer, but its roots go back before the Civil War. In 1849, Otto Holstein, the future father-in-law of Fleer, founded a company to produce flavoring extracts. Fleer, who was born in 1860, took over the company in the 1880s and by 1885 was producing chewing gum. In the early 1900s, the company invented the first bubble gum and marketed it as Blibber-Blubber. The product did not sell well because the bubbles stuck to the chewer's face and were difficult to remove. The company achieved its greatest notoriety when Frank's brother, Henry, invented Chiclets. Fleer sold the company in 1909 and it later became part of the American Chicle Company.

In 1914, Fleer started a second gum company, the Frank H. Fleer Corporation. Fleer died in 1921 and the company was taken over by his son-in-law, Gilbert "Bud" Mustin, and Bud's brother, Frank Mustin. For years, the company had tried unsuccessfully to invent a better bubble gum. But in 1928, a 23-year-old employee named Walter Diemer—who had no training in chemistry—stumbled onto an effective combination of ingredients. The gum produced huge bubbles and peeled easily from the chewer's face. When Diemer made the gum, the only available food coloring was pink. Fleer named the new gum Dubble Bubble, the first of many pink bubble gums. The gum was an instant success for Fleer, so much so that the company did not follow its competitors into the baseball card market until 1959.

That year, Fleer signed Ted Williams to an exclusive card contract and produced an 80-card set chronicling his life. From 1960 to 1962, Fleer issued a line of "Baseball Greats" depicting stars of the past. The sets included the likes of Babe

Ruth, Ty Cobb, and Walter Johnson, but the product experienced only limited success without current stars such as Mickey Mantle and Willie Mays.

In 1963, Fleer attempted to enter the card market with a set of current players. Even though Topps held contracts with virtually every player in the major leagues, as well as with thousands of minor leaguers, Fleer officials felt they could produce cards so long as they did not violate Topps's exclusive right to market cards alone or with gum. But Topps's rights included all confectionary products, meaning other card manufacturers could not include cards with gum or candy.

Just as Topps had tried to circumvent Bowman's exclusive rights a decade before, Fleer attempted to enter the market through the back door. The company packaged its cards with a cookie so low in sugar content that it could not qualify as a confectionary product. (During the subsequent court battles between the two companies, a Topps executive testified that the cookie tasted like a "dog biscuit.")

Fleer needed help in obtaining permission from the players and found a willing ally in Maury Wills. In 1958, Topps representatives signed virtually every player in the minor leagues but Wills, who they believed had no chance at reaching the majors. In 1960 Wills hit .295 for the Los Angeles Dodgers and led the National League with 50 stolen bases in his first full season in the majors. Topps rushed in with a card contract, but Wills remembered how the company had slighted him two years before and refused to sign. (Wills carried his grudge until 1967, when he finally signed with Topps after the company purchased his rights from Fleer.)

Fleer paid Wills $1,500 to sign players for the 1963 set, serving as Fleer's head player agent. Other players, such as the well-traveled Jimmy Piersall, were hired for $750 to serve as team representatives.

Fleer released a 66-card set in the spring that included Wills and Piersall along with Brooks Robinson, Willie Mays, Carl Yastrzemski, Vada Pinson, Don Drysdale, Sandy Koufax, and Warren Spahn. The set was to be the first of several series to be released over the course of the season. But Topps, like Bowman in the Fifties, threatened legal action, and the 1963 Fleer set ended with the first series. Topps contended that Fleer's "dog biscuit," while hardly a confectionary item, did nonetheless violate Topps's exclusive rights and that the players—except Wills—had no right to enter into a contract with Fleer because they had signed with Topps.

Topps, with its exclusive rights to active players, appeared to have an unfair stranglehold on the baseball card manufacturing business. In 1965, the Federal Trade Commission (FTC) filed a complaint against Topps, alleging that the company had "completely foreclosed competitors from the . . . baseball card market by entering exclusive picture card contracts with almost all major (and minor) league players." In effect, Topps had "created and effected a monopoly in the manufacture and distribution of baseball picture cards."

The FTC's hearing examiner found that Topps had monopolized baseball cards in violation of the Sherman Antitrust Act. The full FTC reversed the examiner's finding of liability, ruling that Topps had not monopolized the market because baseball cards could be sold in combination with a variety of low-cost items without violating Topps's exclusive rights. One sentence of the ruling sums up the general consensus on baseball cards in the 1960s: "Plainly, the real commercial significance of such cards is as a promotional device" to bubble gum.

While Fleer backed down, it did not give up its hope of entering the card business and, over the next three years, it signed more than 3,000 players—mostly minor leaguers—to nonexclusive contracts. Still, the company found it impossible to compete with Topps. Each Topps contract with a player gave Topps the exclusive right to sell that player's name and picture "alone or in combination with chewing gum, candy and confection, or any of them," for the first five seasons in which that player was in the major leagues, no matter when those seasons occurred. Topps renewed its contracts with players every other year by offering a two-year deal at $125 a year plus a $75 signing bonus. The renewals were offered during spring training whenever a player had less than five years remaining in his contract. As a result, at any given time, half of the players were bound to Topps for five years, the rest for six.

By signing minor leaguers to nonexclusive deals, Fleer officials hoped they could assemble a stable of players large enough to manufacture a quality set. But after three years of soliciting players, Fleer did not have enough major leaguers to issue a set that would rival that of Topps. Frustrated by the situation, Fleer effectively gave up its hope of manufacturing baseball cards when it sold its 3,000 player contracts to Topps for $395,000 in 1966.

Before the ink dried on the terms of Fleer's surrender, a new Topps opponent arrived on the scene. This time, the adversary was not a company but a person, a former union official of the United Steelworkers of America who had just been hired as the first executive director of the revamped Major League Baseball Players Association. Topps would not be able to dominate Marvin Miller as easily as it had dealt with Bowman and Fleer.

■ ■ ■

For nearly 15 years, gum manufacturers had fought one another over the rights to use baseball players on cards. While there was controversy between Topps and Bowman, and later Topps and Fleer, about whose rights to which ballplayers were being violated, the one group which clearly was being taken advantage of—the players—had remained silent.

As far as the players knew, they were getting a great deal. As minor leaguers, they were flattered to sign a contract with Topps. Players dreamed of the day when they would see their picture on a baseball card. As much as a uniform and paycheck, a card gave the player official status as a big leaguer. The fact that Topps had sent representatives to the minors to sign them to card contracts appeared to mean they must be close to making it to the majors. Sy Berger's $5 "steak money" and the promise of a whopping $125 was an added bonus for fuzzy-cheeked youngsters who gladly would have signed for free.

For major leaguers, Berger's tour of spring training clubhouses and subsequent visits throughout the season were akin to Santa Claus coming to town. Along with free cards, Berger distributed catalogs that contained everything from kitchen utensils to lawn furniture to television sets. The players had the option of selecting items from the catalog instead of receiving their $125 checks. The products were shipped to their homes, much to the delight of their wives, and the players felt as if they were getting something for free. Berger, who had unlimited access to baseball clubhouses, became very popular, cultivating personal relationships with players. He lent players money, took them to dinner, and became a confidant to many. Players knew they could rely on Berger for favors. Your kid wants a tour of the Topps factory? Call Sy. Your RCA television from the Topps catalog broke? Call Sy. Need additional tickets? Call Sy.

Berger had become so much a part of baseball that once he was crowned "King of Baseball." The title was given to a popular baseball figure each year during baseball's winter meetings. No one was sure what the title meant or how it came about. But as part of the tradition, the King wore a crown and robe at the meetings' major banquet.

Berger's relationship with players became more personal than professional. With a gregarious personality and an uncanny ability to remember names and faces, Berger's network of baseball people was enormous. He even knew many player wives, who frequently called him about merchandise in the Topps catalog. Players did not think twice about renewing their card contracts, in the process keeping themselves bound to Topps for a minimum of five years. While players sifted through the catalogs and opened the cards during spring training, their pal Sy slipped them a renewal, which they gladly signed. All in all, from the players' standpoint, it seemed too good to be true.

From Marvin Miller's viewpoint, the process was highway robbery. Not long after Miller became the first executive director of the Major League Baseball Players Association in 1966, he discovered a stack of Topps contracts in his office. As he pored through the language, he could not believe how one-sided the deals were. While Topps made millions from the sale of baseball cards, the players did not get a percentage of sales. All they received was a paltry $125 apiece. What made it particularly insulting was that the players actually thought they were getting a great deal. Berger had better access to clubhouses than Miller, even though Miller was allowed in by virtue of the players' collective bargaining agreement.

Born in Brooklyn in 1916, Miller grew up a fan of the Brooklyn Dodgers. A series of labor-related jobs led to his hiring by the United Steelworkers of America in 1950. Within ten years he had become the union's chief economist and assistant to the president of the third largest union in America. In 1965, Jim Bunning of the Philadelphia Phillies and Harvey Kuehn of the San Francisco Giants approached him about taking over for the fledgling Players Association.

The players were a naive bunch. A proposal had been made to finance the PA with revenues from the annual All-Star game. Miller cringed: financing a union with management's money was illegal. The players also told Miller they had someone in mind to become his general counsel: former vice president Richard M. Nixon.

Six months later, after Miller suggested that Nixon perhaps was not the best choice for a high position in a labor union, Miller was hired as the first executive director of the Players Association.

When Miller started his job on July 1, 1966, the Association had $5,400 and an old filing cabinet in an office in the Biltmore Hotel in New York. The office belonged to Frank Scott, who had served as a commercial agent for some players, helping them obtain endorsements. Miller's first order of business was to raise money to operate the new union. In December, he established a new dues structure that required players to pay $344 a year. Unfortunately, that money would not come in until the 1967 season, and that was five months away. The Association needed funds immediately to pay for new office space and to meet the payroll of its four-person staff.

Few players had endorsement contracts and, except for a deal with Wheaties, there was no history of a group promotion other than with baseball cards. Of course, the players had never received royalties from Topps other than their $125 checks, and Joel Shorin, who had succeeded his uncle J.E. as president of Topps in 1959, had no intention of paying additional revenues to the new union. Miller decided that it was time for that to change.

In his first months in office, Miller met with Shorin and discussed a proposal to redraft Topps's contracts to give players a percentage of sales. In addition, Topps would no longer have exclusive rights to the players' pictures.

Shorin listened closely and shook his head. "There will be no changes," he said, "because, honestly, I don't see any muscle in your position. Topps has the players signed to contracts, and I don't see what you can do about it."

Miller told Shorin he would be in touch. It was true that he didn't have any "muscle." Not yet, anyway. The money to solve the PA's financial crisis would have to come from elsewhere.

Along with Dick Moss, the Association's general counsel, Miller drew up a group licensing program that would give the PA control over the use of player likenesses. Each player remained free to market the rights to his name, likeness, or signature when used individually, but only the MLBPA could contract for the players as a group. This way, star players such as Mickey Mantle did not have to worry about losing their individual deals because they were bound to the PA through group licensing.

In September of 1966, Miller visited each club and received authorizations for the group licensing plan. Miller and agent Scott then met with executives from Coca-Cola and negotiated a two-year deal for $60,000 a year that gave Coke the right to use the pictures of players on the underside of bottlecaps. Since Coke wanted to picture the players in uniform, it needed permission from the owners, who controlled the rights to team logos. Coke felt the owners' asking price was too high, and for a short time it looked as though the deal would fall through. Fortunately for the PA, Coke opted to print the bottlecaps with the team logos airbrushed out.

Thus, the PA's financial emergency was solved and the group licensing program began. As it turned out, much of the money from Coca-Cola was not needed. According to the authorizations the players had signed, any money not needed to meet the operating budget of the PA would be distributed to the players pro rata. Each player, manager, coach, and trainer who was in the majors for the entire 1967 season received a check for $100. Those who spent only a portion of the year in the majors received a proportionate amount.

Miller distributed the money during spring training in 1968, beginning an annual tradition. Since the average salary in 1967 was only $19,000, the extra $100 was much appreciated, so much so that although the licensing program had been conceived of as a stopgap measure, the players insisted on retaining it on a permanent basis. Each player happily signed up for the three-year group licensing agreement. By serving as the collective agent for player licensing, the PA hoped to prevent companies from negotiating individually with players to obtain a group of contracts as Topps had done. Of course, there was nothing to prevent Topps and manufacturers of bats and gloves from negotiating with minor leaguers, who were not members of the Players Association.

Miller's clubhouse visits became more popular than Berger's and his spring training checks became known as "Marvin Money." (In 1983, Ken Moffett succeeded Miller as executive director, but was fired after ten months on the job. Donald Fehr, who had succeeded Moss as the PA's general counsel, took over in November of 1983. Still, today's players—few of whom remain from the Miller era—refer to the checks as "Marvin Money.")

As Miller traveled from clubhouse to clubhouse obtaining authorizations for the group licensing agreements, he kept Topps in mind. He told the players how they were being stiffed by Topps and how Shorin had reacted when he tried to negotiate. "The only leverage you have is not to sign renewals," he said. "Eventually Topps will have contracts with no one."

Of course, the players would have to sacrifice their annual $125 checks. Some never would reap the benefits of a new system, since by the time the PA defeated Topps, they would be out of baseball. For players who had come to regard Berger as something of a doting uncle, the news that Topps was the enemy was particularly difficult to believe. But Miller was convincing, and during spring training before the 1968 season, players began refusing Topps renewals. Berger rushed to Florida to do damage control, but he arrived too late. By the time the 1968 season began, the players had boycotted Topps en masse. Midway through the season, Miller received a call from Shorin. "I see your muscle," he said. "Let's sit down and talk."

Negotiations were slow and at one point Miller, hoping to enhance his bargaining position, offered Fleer the opportunity to purchase similar exclusive publicity rights. For $600,000, the Association would give Fleer exclusive rights to market baseball cards sold with gum for 80 percent of the baseball players. But since the players' contracts that were signed before the Topps boycott would not run out for another four to five years, the deal could not begin until 1973. Under the proposal, Fleer would not have to pay a penny until 1973 and even then no funds were due unless Miller delivered 80 percent of the players' exclusive licenses. As an alternative, Miller asked Fleer if it would be interested in the immediate rights for all players' trading cards sold with a product other than gum. Fleer declined both offers, claiming it only wanted to produce cards with gum and that 1973 was too long to wait.

Miller turned his attention back to Topps and, after months of negotiations, a new deal was reached. On November 19, 1968, Topps agreed to double its payment from $125 to $250 per PA member. The company also would pay a royalty of eight percent on sales up to $4 million and 10 percent on sales thereafter. In the first year, the PA received $320,000 in royalties on sales of approximately $4 million.

Topps, however, received a huge concession from the PA, which agreed not to "interfere with the Topps contracts, its procurement of such contracts, or its policy during the existence of this Agreement." Topps would advise the Association as to whether Topps would release its rights under its contracts with the players to permit the Association to license any proposal which otherwise infringed Topps's rights.

In effect, the Association still had to go to Topps for approval of almost any product depicting players, even though the PA controlled the rights through the group licensing program. The difference was that it now received hundreds of thousands of dollars from Topps in return.

By a slim margin, the Players Association had won the first battle. But the card war was just beginning to heat up.

2

A High-Stakes Card Game

Not long after Fleer turned down Marvin Miller's proposal to manufacture baseball cards for 1973, Don Peck realized his company had made a mistake. Peck, who had joined Fleer as a personnel manager in 1952, had worked his way up the corporate ladder to executive vice president. He helped put the company's baseball card sets together from 1960 to 1963, and even after Fleer sold its player contracts to Topps in 1966, Peck still harbored dreams of producing baseball cards—a feeling that only intensified when he was named president of the company in 1971.

Unfortunately, the offer Miller had made to Fleer while he was negotiating with Topps in 1968 was no longer on the table as 1973 approached. Peck now wished Fleer had accepted Miller's proposal to produce cards in 1973, even if they could not include gum. But the Players Association and Topps had settled their differences and now had a deal running to 1981 that, in Peck's mind, made it impossible for Fleer to enter the baseball card business.

Under terms of the agreement between Topps and the Players Association, Topps had to release its rights under its contracts with the players before the PA could license a product that infringed upon Topps's rights. Beginning in 1969, each time Fleer approached Miller and the Players Association with a proposal to print cards, Topps claimed its exclusive contracts prohibited them from doing so.

From 1969 to 1973, the Players Association managed to get Topps to waive its exclusive rights for card sets produced by Milk Duds, ITT Continental Baking, and Sports Promotions. But these cards usually were one-time-only sets made up of fewer than 100 players. Clearly, Topps was not going to allow a competitor to enter the market with a full-length set, especially one packaged with gum.

Resigned to being shut out of the card market, Peck took a different approach. In September of 1974, he went to Miller to obtain a license from the PA to market five-by-seven-inch satin patches depicting active major league players. Each patch would cost 25 cents. Admittedly, the idea of producing satin patches was a little offbeat, but Fleer believed it was the only type of product resembling baseball cards that the Players Association might be willing to license.

Pictures five by seven or larger with a sale price of 25 cents or more were excluded from Topps's rights, except that Topps retained a right of first refusal and could market the product themselves. Fleer's offer to the PA included a $25,000 guarantee and a royalty of 15 percent on sales. Topps president Joel Shorin told Miller that Topps had no intention of marketing the product. "The pictures won't sell," he said. "There will be large returns of merchandise, and worse, it would impede trading card sales."

Miller had become accustomed to Shorin disapproving of Fleer's proposals, but nonetheless had to agree. Thus the Executive Board of the Players Association refused to license Fleer's proposal, citing a fear that Fleer's product would remain on the shelves and prompt store owners to cut back on Topps baseball cards until the satin patches were sold. That, of course, would jeopardize the income the PA received as its percentage of Topps's sales.

And no one wanted that to happen. Since 1951, when Topps had entered the baseball card market, it had become inextricably linked with the sport itself. The arrival of the new Topps cards each year signified that spring had arrived. A rumor that a store had received its shipment from Topps was enough to break up a sandlot game, as kids scrambled for change. Topps cards had become a form of currency, traded between collectors and gambled in "high-stakes" flipping contests. Young boys kept cards of their favorite players in their back pockets and used the stats on the back of the cards to argue the merits of a player during card trades. Collecting Topps cards was an American tradition, one that Topps officials argued could be sorely damaged if the market were open to competitors. The PA, with its newfound wealth from Topps, reluctantly concurred.

Fleer was not the only would-be card manufacturer shot down by the PA in 1974. Late in the year, Topps informed the Association that Michael Aronstein, a prospective card producer, had been soliciting players for baseball card rights. The PA wrote Aronstein a letter, which read in part: "It has come to [our] attention that you have been soliciting Major League players, coaches and managers to grant permission to have their pictures used in connection with a baseball card collector set. The Major League Baseball Players Association is the exclusive assignee of the players, coaches and managers with regard to their property rights in connection with group promotions and group commercial endeavors. A project such as yours cannot be undertaken without a license to do so from the Players Association. In any event, however, a license cannot be granted to you since Topps Chewing Gum, Inc., is by contract our exclusive licensee for baseball cards either sold alone or together with confectionary products. In addition, the individual players, managers and coaches have contracts with Topps granting that company the exclusive rights noted above. You are hereby instructed to cease and desist from all your activities in this regard. Should you fail to do so immediately, we will bring an appropriate action for damages and injunctive relief."

Topps grew increasingly defensive of its license in 1974, asking the Players Association to halt the production of baseball cards manufactured by the Kellogg Company, an official licensee of the PA. In 1970, Kellogg's had kicked off its baseball card line with a 75-player set of simulated, three-dimensional cards. Single cards were available in selected brands of Kellogg's cereals while a mail-in program offered complete sets. Kellogg's achieved a 3-D effect with the cards by placing a color player photo between a blurred stadium background scene and a layer of ribbed plastic. Kellogg's had produced sets annually since 1970, the rarest of which was the 1971 line, the only one not available on a mail-in basis. (By 1994, the set was valued at $1,000.)

Topps maintained that it had exclusive rights to market baseball cards alone or with gum. But the Federal Trade Commission, in its 1965 decision, had ruled that cards could be marketed with certain products—such as marbles—that would not infringe upon Topps's rights to sell baseball cards alone. If collectors had to pay a premium for a product that contained baseball cards, it undoubtedly would cost more to manufacture and thus be priced significantly higher than Topps baseball cards. Therefore, it would not be in competition with Topps.

Topps disagreed, dubbing these items "sham" products, arguing that collectors were not making the purchase for the marbles or other sham items, merely the cards. While Topps conceded that there were non-confectionary premium products that could be sold with cards, it never specified the minimum value the product must have in order to not interfere with its rights. In discussions with agents of the Players Association, Topps even cited marbles as an example of a sham product that *would* effectively infringe Topps's rights to sell cards alone— even though the FTC had ruled to the contrary.

In 1974, Kellogg's sold packages of 54 baseball cards for $1.50 plus a box top from one of Kellogg's cereals, which at the time sold for 60 cents. Topps balked, contending that Kellogg's four-year-old practice did not meet the minimum value of a non-confectionary premium product. Unlike its dealings with Fleer, the Players Association did not yield to Topps's pressure, but instead obtained a waiver from Topps to continue to license Kellogg's. Of course, the PA had proof that the Kellogg's card program could succeed. Unlike Fleer, Kellogg's already was providing the PA with licensing revenue.

For Fleer, 1974 would have been a bad year even without its rejection by the PA. The company lost $309,261, the second time since 1969 it had endured a losing year. Not that its profitable years were eye-popping either; of Fleer's three money-making campaigns during the period, 1973 was the best, with a net income of $382,354. The company's annual sales of $8–$12 million represented only one-fifth of Topps's figures.

For Peck, who now had spent the better part of his 22 years at Fleer trying to become a baseball card manufacturer, 1974 was particularly frustrating. Not only had Topps and the Players Association refused the satin patch proposal, but his colleagues at Fleer had grown impatient with his plan to sell baseball cards. Frank and Gilbert "Bud" Mustin, the owners of Fleer at the time, appreciated the work Peck had done trying to get Fleer into the marketplace, but wondered if the fight was really worth it. For all of Peck's visions of grandeur, they reminded him that these were, of course, just baseball cards. "Maybe we have to accept the fact that this is the way it's going to be," they would tell Peck.

Early in 1975, Peck met with the Mustin brothers one last time to discuss baseball cards. "It's time we make a serious attempt to get into the baseball card market," he said. "Not old-timer cards, because we've done those, but today's baseball cards. I'm interested and driven to getting into this market because selling Dubble Bubble gum by the pound isn't going to do it for us in the long run."

"So what's your plan?" Frank Mustin asked.

"I don't have one," Peck said. "But I'm going to find one because we're having our head handed to us by Topps."

Peck could read the skepticism on the faces of the two brothers. Finally, he convinced them to let him bring up the topic at the next board meeting. There, he pulled no punches. "We can keep on doing what we've been doing, but I don't think you put my staff together just to sell bubble gum. We want to expand our product line and making baseball cards is the best way for us to do it."

A vote was taken and, to Peck's surprise, the board authorized him to pursue a baseball card license by whatever means necessary. Still, it was not a wholehearted endorsement. "We support you on this," Bud Mustin said. "It's your baby and we're behind you all the way. But try to keep the involvement of the board as limited as possible."

Next, Peck met with Fred Ballard, Fleer's attorney, in Philadelphia. Together they drafted a letter detailing Fleer's legal right to be in the baseball card business. Not long after, in April of 1975, Peck took the letter to New York and met with Miller and Dick Moss, the PA's general counsel. Peck reiterated his feeling that the baseball card market was big enough for two companies. Miller did not necessarily disagree, but was not impressed with Fleer's proposals to date. Fleer's five-by-seven patch offer guaranteed only $25,000 in royalty payments but projected over $1 million in annual sales. The executive board of the Players Association, made up of player representatives, was skeptical of a marketing plan that offered little guaranteed payments with promises of huge royalties. And, as always, there was the question of whether Topps would approve.

As a last resort, Peck asked Miller if the Players Association would join with Fleer in a lawsuit against Topps. Miller declined.

"We may have to fight you on this," Peck told Miller. "We feel we need to be in the marketplace to round out our business. It's that simple."

On the train back to Philadelphia, Peck pondered his options. Fleer could take Topps and the PA to court, but that was not an attractive alternative. Even if Fleer ultimately won, it might be years before the company ever produced a card. And the legal fees would be staggering. There was one other possibility, albeit an unlikely one. Topps could waive its exclusive rights so that Fleer could pursue a license to sell stickers, stamps, and decals depicting active major league players. Peck called Shorin.

"Joel, we need to talk baseball cards."

"There's nothing to talk about," Shorin said.

Peck mentioned the letter and the vote of Fleer's board of directors. Reluctantly, Shorin agreed to meet Peck in New York for lunch on April 17, 1975. On the train ride up, Peck thought of a backup plan. If Shorin refused to waive Topps's rights, he would propose that Fleer become a sublicensee of Topps, much like O-Pee-Chee, a Canadian manufacturer that had produced cards identical to Topps, only in French. Peck wanted to produce cards so badly that he would work with or even for Topps if that's what it would take.

Peck met Shorin for lunch and handed him the letter from his attorney, Ballard. Shorin brushed his hand through the air, as if waving off a fly. "There's no point in reading it," he said.

"I really wish you would," Peck said.

Shorin read the first paragraph and stopped, shaking his head. Peck leaned forward. "Joel, we're going to have to take you to court on this."

"You do what you have to do."

Peck got up from the table and said good-bye, leaving a cold turkey sandwich behind. He had not even bothered proposing the idea of becoming a sublicensee.

Three months later, in July, Fleer filed an antitrust suit in U.S. District Court in Philadelphia, naming Topps and the Players Association as codefendants.

Fleer contended that Topps and the Association "have monopolized and unlawfully restrained trade in baseball cards in violation of Section 1 and Section 2 of the Sherman Antitrust Act." Topps's player contract practices, Fleer alleged, restricted entry into the baseball card industry, resulting in monopoly profits for Topps.

The card war had escalated. But it would be five years before the court issued a ruling.

■ ■ ■

After Fleer filed suit, Joel Shorin met with Topps's attorneys at the Bush Terminal in Brooklyn. "It looks like they're serious," Shorin said. "But this is no different than the FTC suit. We have exclusive rights and there's nothing they can do about it."

While Topps officials did not look forward to years of legal fees, they remained confident that they would prevail. The antitrust suit was mentioned only briefly in Topps's annual report in 1976. "In the opinion of the Company's management the ultimate resolution of this matter will not have a material effect on the accompanying financial statements." It was hard not to feel confident at Topps. After seeing profits drop 17.4 percent in fiscal 1975, it enjoyed its best year to date in 1976.

Ironically, while Topps argued that competition in the baseball card field would destroy the market, it welcomed other companies into the bubble gum business. In the same annual report, Topps said: "we believe that this competition will serve to expand the market by creating greater consumer consciousness for the bubble gum products we sell through our strongly established distribution channels."

Back in Philadelphia, Don Peck read the report and shook his head. *Expand the market. Greater consumer consciousness.* Those were the exact arguments he was making for Fleer's entry into the baseball card business.

Of course, Topps had no control over the number of bubble gum manufacturers that entered the market, and it was not difficult to see how increased competition in the gum industry had, indeed, improved business. For fiscal 1976, the year ending February 28, Topps had sales of $55.75 million, up 11.2 percent from 1975. Its net income of $2.3 million was up 37 percent from the previous year.

As the bubble gum business grew, so too did Topps. The company announced plans to build a 50,000 square foot plant in Ireland, its first manufacturing facility outside the United States, and purchased a second U.S. plant, in Scranton, Pennsylvania, to go with its first in Duryea, Pennsylvania. Hoping to jump-start its European presence, Topps entered into an agreement with Trebor Sharps Ltd., the largest sugar confectioner in Great Britain, to distribute Topps products in the United Kingdom and Ireland. Meanwhile, the company's presence at home was boosted during the 1975 World Series when the finals of the Joe Garagiola/ Bazooka Bubble Gum Blowing Championship were broadcast by NBC. (In a close contest officiated by National League umpire Dick Stello, Kurt Bevacqua of the Milwaukee Brewers outblew Philadelphia Phillies catcher Johnny Oates for the title.)

But while Bevacqua and Oates blew Bazooka, millions of American kids were discovering the taste of Bubble Yum, a new line of bubble gum marketed by Lifesavers, Inc. Unlike the hard pink slabs sold by Topps (Bazooka) and Fleer (Dubble Bubble), Bubble Yum was a soft gum that came in a variety of juicy flavors. Its release, in the fall of 1976, coincided with a strike by Topps workers at the plant in Duryea, Pennsylvania. The seven-week work stoppage ended with a three-year collective bargaining agreement, but Topps would suffer long-term effects. Sales for fiscal 1977 remained steady at $55 million, but net income was down 50 percent. By the end of the year, Topps had unveiled its own line of soft bubble gum called "Smooooth N' Juicy." But by then Bubble Yum had entrenched itself as the market leader.

In the summer of 1977, things began to improve for Topps. It produced cards in conjunction with the hit movies *Star Wars* and *Close Encounters of the Third Kind*, along with a set for ABC's popular television series *Charlie's Angels*. When the Food and Drug Administration announced that the artificial sweetener saccharin had been found to cause cancer in laboratory animals, Topps moved quickly, removing saccharin from its sugarless products. For fiscal 1978, Topps recorded a net income of $1.8 million on sales of $61.5 million. Fleer, behind the sales of Dubble Bubble and "Gatorgum"—a soft, Gatorade-flavored gum designed to quench thirst—had sales of $15.2 million.

In 1978, sales of Topps baseball cards reached a new high of $9.2 million. Of that, $847,000 went to the Players Association in royalties, more than three-quarters of the record $1.1 million in licensing revenue generated for the PA. As the antitrust suit continued through the pretrial stages, Topps maintained that it had the exclusive right to produce baseball cards and was providing record revenues to the Association. Why fool with a good thing?

Addressing the ongoing litigation with Fleer in its 1978 annual report, Topps said, "We believe it is ill-founded and that we will prevail again as we did before when this competitor's complaint caused us to defend our position with the FTC. The issues are essentially the same. We anticipate that a trial could take place this year and the results will parallel the complaint dismissal and vindication we received from the Federal Trade Commission in its decision of 1965."

Topps added to its profitable non-sports card line in 1978–79, producing cards for the movies *Superman*, *Grease*, *Jaws II*, and *Rocky II*, along with a set for *Mork and Mindy*, the television show starring Robin Williams. But while Topps's dominance of the card market continued, it was losing market share in the gum business to Bubble Yum. While Bubble Yum sales had reached $100 million a year and new flavors became immediate hits, Topps's research and development team scrambled to come up with a new gum that could compete with Bubble Yum. The result was "Super Bazooka Bubble Fudge," a chocolate flavored gum. Released in April of 1979 with a huge marketing campaign highlighted by a commercial featuring Cincinnati Reds catcher Johnny Bench, the gum was supposed to appeal to both chocolate lovers and gum chewers.

But chocolate lovers found the concept of chocolate gum offensive and gum chewers were appalled at the taste of Bubble Fudge. Topps, which had targeted much of its marketing resources to Bubble Fudge, found it to be an impossible sell. Sales of baseball cards, meanwhile, leveled off as collectors were not impressed with the drab design of the 1979 set. The only excitement came from a misprinted card of Texas Rangers second baseman Bump Wills, whose card was printed as if he were a member of the Toronto Blue Jays. The mistake marked the second time Topps had slighted the Wills family; Bump had followed his father, former Dodgers infielder Maury Wills, to the major leagues.

Late in 1979, Topps found itself struggling to meet its payroll. After experiencing revenue growth of more than 100 percent in the preceding 15 years and an uninterrupted run of 36 profitable years, Topps considered filing for bankruptcy as an option to get the company out of its financial woes brought on by the huge losses of Bubble Fudge.

Joel Shorin called an emergency meeting of the eight-man board of directors on February 29, 1980, one day before the end of Topps's fiscal year. "The business is in trouble," he said. "I've done everything I can. The only one who can save the company is Arthur."

The other board members looked at Arthur Shorin, who in 22 years at Topps had risen from marketing assistant to vice president. It was a long way from his years as a childhood music prodigy. After high school, he had attended the Oberlin Conservatory of Music for a year, before his father convinced him to return to New York, where he could study music at the renowned Juilliard School for music, dance, and drama and take marketing classes at New York University. J.E., whose wife Naomi had died, also hoped his son would keep him company. "I would really like to see you in our business," he said. "This just keeps your options open. Besides, I'm alone and I'd really like you to come back."

That was all Arthur needed to hear. While at Juilliard, he wrote hundreds of songs. Two of them—"You're Everything Wonderful" and "You Don't Know"— were recorded by entertainer Steve Lawrence. At one point, Arthur received a royalty check for $13,000. Still, J.E. hoped he would follow him to Topps. "You're in business already. There's no difference between selling gum and selling songs. And just think, you'll be the best musician in the gum business."

In November of 1958, at the age of 23, Arthur Shorin joined Topps. He still received royalty checks, but was surprised at how little he missed the music business. In a sense, he was still in the entertainment industry, only now he was in the business of entertaining children. His wry sense of humor was a perfect fit with the folks at the Bush Terminal, where Topps created such products as "Garbage Candy" and "Wacky Packages," parody stickers of popular consumer products.

Now, 22 years after his father talked him out of the music business, he was being asked to take over the company. Shorin looked at the other board members and saw the concern in their eyes.

"I'll give it a try," he said.

Thus, Topps Chewing Gum, Inc., took the unusual step of having its chairman/president and executive vice president switch roles. Arthur Shorin became chairman of the board and would oversee Topps's day-to-day operation, while Joel stayed on as president and chief operating officer.

Arthur Shorin had to hurry to save Topps. The business owed $7 million to each of two banks and needed an additional $7 million to operate. For fiscal 1980, Topps had suffered a loss of $8,850,000, or $4.98 a share. Shorin met with a consortium of banks and was granted operating capital for two weeks. When that period was over they met again, and Topps was given an additional two weeks. So it would go for the rest of 1980.

Shorin slashed payroll in half, eventually reducing Topps's workforce from 2,000 to 900. He changed the company's long-term strategy, scrapping the plan of making large investments in advertising and marketing. While Topps had set a goal in the late 1970s of becoming a $100–$150 million consumer products company that would take on the likes of the William Wrigley, Jr., Company and General Mills, Shorin put a plan in motion that would capitalize on Topps's strengths: Bazooka and trading cards. "We have to remember what we're good at," he later told the board. "We entertain kids and capitalize on pop culture."

Topps's subsidiary in Ireland was put on the block and Shorin cut back on office expenses and overhead. Stockholders only had to look at the annual report to see the money-saving measures in action. The mimeographed report for 1980 included no pictures and was "produced at minimum expense as part of the stringent cost control program instituted by the company."

For the first time, Topps acknowledged the toll that Fleer's antitrust action had taken. "General and administrative expenses in fiscal 1980 reflected higher legal fees related to a lawsuit by a competitor alleging violations of antitrust laws in connection with the company's exclusive license from baseball players for the use of their pictures."

By June, Shorin had restored the banks' trust in Topps and the emergency was over. Then, on June 30, a decision came out of U.S. District Court in Philadelphia that would change Topps and the baseball card business forever.

■ ■ ■

Perhaps it was appropriate that Fleer, which had played the role of outsider looking in on the baseball card business, received a sympathetic ear from a man named Newcomer.

U.S. District Court Judge Clarence Newcomer found that Topps and the Players Association had restrained trade in the baseball card market in violation of the Sherman Antitrust Act. Newcomer found no inherent legal rights that gave Topps the ability to act as the only manufacturer. He wrote that "Topps's rights are not protected by any patents or copyrights, nor were they at any time protected by patents or copyrights. There is no legal requirement that either Topps or an individual enter into an exclusive, as opposed to a non-exclusive, contract for the use of the player's picture. Topps did not have its market position thrust upon it."

Topps's contention that another company could compete for player contracts was dismissed. Newcomer found that the Topps contracts not only did not promote competition, but contained a number of restrictive clauses. During the term of a contract, a player could not assign to another card company the rights held by

Topps, even if they took effect after the contract expired. A player was bound to Topps for his first five major league seasons, whenever they occurred. If a player spent six years in the minors, he was bound to Topps—and only Topps—for 11 years.

Since Topps was an established force in the business, Newcomer wrote: "a competitor facing at least six years of uncertainty before it can market even an inferior trading card product is likely to take its capital and its energies elsewhere."

Newcomer found that Topps's only competition was, in effect, the Players Association, since only the PA could license another card manufacturer. But: "the Association refuses to grant licenses for the sale of baseball cards with low cost non-confectionary products, because, in its self-interest, it wishes to avoid conflict with Topps's rights. . . . The effect of this odd combination of interlocking rights and conduct has been to exclude completely any meaningful competition to Topps."

In its defense, Topps contended that it had exercised its contractual rights without attempting to expand them unlawfully, and that it was the PA that was responsible for foreclosing non-confectionary competition with Topps. "Topps's position," Newcomer wrote, "is like that of the boy who killed his parents, later to throw himself on the mercy of the court because he was an orphan. . . . the joint unlawful conduct in this situation can be summarized in one sentence. Topps and the Players Association have acted jointly in excluding Topps's competitors."

In effect, Newcomer concluded, Topps had financed the Players Association's "cautious approach to the licensing of baseball card products that would have competed with Topps's product."

Newcomer ordered Topps permanently enjoined from enforcing the exclusivity clause in its standard player contract and from including the clause in future player contracts. The company also was prohibited from expanding its rights under its current contract. Newcomer instructed the Players Association to award at least one new license to produce baseball cards before January 1, 1981. Fleer would have a right of first refusal, but only until it received a license or January 1, 1981, whichever came first.

In awarding damages to Fleer, Newcomer noted that the company had not had much success marketing trading cards, never having had a card product that reached $750,000 in sales. Since Fleer did not have Topps's brand name or distribution system, there was no guarantee that the company would have been successful. Newcomer awarded Fleer the princely sum of $1, trebled pursuant to Pennsylvania statutes to $3, along with attorney's fees.

During the next 14 years, the baseball card market grew from Topps's $9.2 million in sales into a $1 billion business ($2 billion counting football, basketball, and hockey cards). In hindsight, the decision worked out for everyone.

For the Players Association, Newcomer's decision was an enormous victory, although it did not realize it at the time. While Marvin Miller had staunchly disagreed with Joel Shorin about Topps's exclusive rights, he often had helped

Topps enforce them. Still, he wrote in his 1991 memoir, *A Whole Different Ballgame,* that he was shocked to be named a codefendant in the suit. "Ironically, we lost the case *and accomplished our main objective.* But imagine the stupidity of such a decision. The record, and plain common sense, showed that the Players Association could only benefit from breaking the Topps monopoly, and, in fact, it had struggled to do just that. Regardless, a federal court decided that the Association had joined with Topps to *prevent* competition. Go figure."

Miller was not so confident about an expanded market benefiting the PA at the time, however. In an October 4, 1980, column in *The Sporting News,* Miller told sportswriter Bill Madden that although the opening of the card market to competition would mean more revenue for the players, it did not necessarily figure to be more beneficial to them. "I'm not an expert here on all the testimony that was given," he said. "But my feeling was that splintering the market by having it non-exclusive might very likely result in something less than what we had when it was exclusive."

Topps also benefited from the decision. As is often the case when a monopoly is broken, competition improved the product and the market expanded. Joel Shorin died in 1987, but Arthur Shorin, in an interview for this book, maintained that nothing was stopping Fleer from entering the market so long as it did not sell baseball cards alone or with a confectionary product. So why did Topps spend five years and thousands in legal fees fighting Fleer?

"When they filed suit," Shorin said, "we could have gone to the judge and said they could make cards with something else. And the judge would have said 'They can!' and Fleer would have said 'We can!' And that would have been the end of the suit. And we would have given them Marketing 101. If they wanted to come in, then fine. But we weren't going to make the bed for them. We didn't use that as a defense. We used the economics of the market. We didn't believe there was room for anyone else."

Of course, Topps's economic view of the market was proven wrong. And Topps had given no indication that it would allow any non-confectionary card product to be produced without a fight. Topps never specified what product would have been acceptable to market cards with, labeling any suggestions as "sham products" and advising the Players Association that proposals such as Fleer's five-by-seven satin patches would destroy the market. While the Players Association, in hindsight, clearly would have benefited from increased competition, it had made no effort to license Fleer or another major card producer.

"It's easy to say that Topps would have acquiesced to us now," Peck recalled. "Whatever we would have tried, Topps would have come after us. We thought of everything we could possibly stick in there, all of which our attorneys thought was illegal. The point is, nobody had the vision of how large that market was. I didn't either, but I knew it was a hell of a lot larger than just Topps. The Players Association didn't think it was possible to grant us a license. If they really thought the market was bigger, how come *they* didn't take Topps to court?"

On a sticky summer day in Philadelphia, Topps and its attorneys left the courtroom and began preparation for an appeal. Newcomer's decision would be overruled a year later by the U.S. Court of Appeals, but it would be too late. After 25 years, the baseball card market was open for business.

■ ■ ■

While Topps and Fleer battled in Philadelphia, the executives of the Donruss Company hatched their own plan to enter the baseball card market.

The Memphis-based Donruss was formed in 1958, taking its name from its two owners, Don and Russ Wiener. Prior to that, it was known as the Thomas Wiener Candy Company. Though it never had manufactured baseball cards, Donruss rivaled Topps in the non-sports collecting world, issuing television and movie cards since the 1960s. Its projects included cards for television shows such as *The Green Hornet*, *The Six Million Dollar Man*, *Dallas*, and *The Dukes of Hazzard* and movies such as *Saturday Night Fever* and *The Dark Crystal*. Donruss also issued several cards of music stars, including Elvis Presley, Kiss, and The Osmond Family.

As the antitrust case went on in Philadelphia, Donruss president Stewart Lyman and vice president of marketing Paul Mullan prepared a proposal for the Players Association. If Fleer won, the market would open not just for Fleer, but for any company the Association wanted to license. Within weeks after the decision, card company executives arrived in Marvin Miller's office with a proposal. But they were not from Fleer, which had fought for six years to get into the business. They were from Donruss.

Topps's contract with the Players Association called for Topps to pay royalties of eight percent on sales up to $4 million and 10 percent of sales in excess of $4 million. Lyman and Mullan offered nine percent on sales up to $4 million and 11 percent for sales over $4 million. Miller, surprised that someone other than Fleer had shown up, accepted the terms and Donruss became the second baseball card manufacturer. When Peck arrived at the Players Association the following week, he was prepared to sign on for the same rate as Topps. Instead, Miller told him that Fleer would have to pay the nine and 11 percent rates, since Donruss had upped the ante. Peck reluctantly agreed; after years of fighting, he figured, why battle over a few percentage points?

Miller and Peck awkwardly shook hands and Peck headed back to Philadelphia. Nearly six years had passed since Fleer had filed suit against Topps and the Players Association. As Peck rode the train back to Philadelphia, he had no idea that he had helped create a sports card market that by 1991 would become a $2 billion dollar business.

CHAPTER

3

A Whole New Card Game

With the baseball card market now open to competition for 1981, collectors had an alternative to Topps baseball cards for the first time since 1956.

Judge Clarence Newcomer's decision gave Fleer and Donruss, who finalized their deals with the Major League Baseball Players Association in September, just five months to print and deliver cards to stores in time to compete with Topps in late January 1981. For companies that had never produced cards on a grand scale, five months meant their inaugural cards would be a rush job.

Not surprisingly, mistakes were made. Donruss listed Cardinals' outfielder Bobby Bonds as having hit 986 home runs, 231 more than Hank Aaron, the all-time leader. The company's card of Houston Astros pitcher Vern Ruhle pictured teammate Frank Lacorte. Cleveland Indians' infielder Duane Kuiper's cards were printed as "Dwayne" Kuiper.

Fleer also made gaffes. The cards of Kurt Bevacqua of the Pirates and Tim Flannery of the Padres were printed with reverse negatives, making the cards look like mirror images of the actual photo. Darrell Evans of the Giants was misspelled "Derrell" Evans. But the most glaring error Fleer made, at least from the perspective of star-crazy collectors, was the misspelling of Yankees' standout third baseman Graig Nettles as "Craig" Nettles.

Donruss and Fleer combined for more than fifty errors in 1981. In most instances, the companies publicly apologized for the mistakes and announced plans for corrected versions of the cards. But this only increased interest in the error cards. Collectors reasoned that either version of an error card would be produced in lesser quantities than a card printed consistently throughout the press run.

Values for both versions soared, with the Craig Nettles card—corrected early in the Fleer run—topping the price list at $20.

Fleer and Donruss were not the first companies to produce error cards. Topps had a long history of mistakes. In 1969, the photo of California Angels infielder Aurelio Rodriguez turned out to be that of an Angels batboy. Before the 1974 season, as rumors circulated of the San Diego Padres moving to Washington, D.C., Topps went to press with Padres players pictured above team nameplates that read "Washington, N.L." And of course Bump Wills of the Texas Rangers appeared on his 1979 card above a Blue Jays namebar. But Topps never made the number of errors that Donruss and Fleer did in 1981.

Not everyone was enamored with error cards. Bill Madden, in his collecting column in *The Sporting News*, wrote: "What makes this hype over error cards so ridiculous is that we are talking about cards that are available by the tens of thousands. A $1 price tag on these cards is an insult to cards of 10–15 years ago which are still available for $1 apiece in many cases."

Opinions on the quality of the 1981 sets varied. Only Fleer included a card of Fernando Valenzuela, the flamboyant Mexican pitcher who went on to win the National League Rookie of the Year award. Interestingly, the card read "Fernand" Valenzuela. Donruss was the only company to issue a card of Montreal Expos rookie Tim Raines. Topps, which with 726 cards had the largest set, was the lone manufacturer to include the likes of Dodgers outfielder Pedro Guerrero and Cleveland Indians pitcher John Denny.

Fleer was picked as "set of the year" by *Sports Collectors Digest* and *Baseball Hobby News*. Donruss was criticized for its thin card stock, while Topps was panned for its card design, which featured large team baseball caps in the lower left-hand corner. Not that Fleer's cards were extraordinary. A frequent refrain among collectors was that baseball cards were only Fleer's second most attractive product of 1981; the company also issued a sexy set of "Here's Bo" cards featuring actress Bo Derek from her film *Tarzan the Ape Man*.

■ ■ ■

Fleer and Donruss were not the only newcomers to the card market in 1981. The Players Association, freed from the constraints of Topps, licensed card products for Squirt Soda and Coca-Cola to go with veteran Kellogg's. A St. Louis company, Perma Graphics, released a set of plastic "credit" cards with player photos on the front and stats on the back. Even Topps got into the licensing game, issuing a 33-card set of "Big Hitters" for Drake's Bakery Products.

The Players Association reaped the benefits of its new licensees, earning more than $600,000 in additional income from Donruss and Fleer in 1981. While sales figures for neither privately-held company were released, the amount of royalty fees paid indicated that Fleer and Donruss combined for at least $8 million in sales. Stewart Lyman, president of Donruss, estimated that the baseball card market had expanded by 80 percent because of the two companies. Fleer president Don Peck agreed. "I think we shocked the hell out of a lot of people with the amount of revenue we generated from the baseball card market."

But Donruss and Fleer, together with their new ally the Players Association, had to figure out a way to stay in the market for 1982. On August 25, 1981, a three-judge court of the U.S. Court of Appeals overruled the decision of district judge Clarence Newcomer, upholding Topps's exclusive rights to market baseball cards alone or with gum. In a decision written by judge James Hunter III, the Court of Appeals ruled that a rival card manufacturer could compete with Topps by seeking licenses with minor league players.

Peck could not believe it. He and Fleer had spent the better part of the 1960s proving that it was impossible to compete with Topps in such a manner. "I don't think the court fully understood what it would take for us to try to compete under those circumstances," he told *The Sporting News* after the decision. "It would cost literally hundreds of thousands of dollars for us to sign up minor league players and then get into a bidding war with Topps over the availability of major league players.

"And there is no guarantee the minor league players are ever going to make it to the majors. When you combine that with the fact that Topps has staggered expiration dates on its contracts with the major league players, it would take years for us to have enough players to put out a competitive set of cards."

But unlike his previous battles with Topps, Peck now had Marvin Miller firmly on his side. Miller and the Players Association had been codefendants with Topps in the original suit and now, ironically, had beaten Fleer on appeal. But now that Miller had seen that the baseball card market could expand by two companies and yield the PA an additional $600,000, he did not want to give up the players' new revenue stream.

Fleer took its case to the Supreme Court, but its petition for a hearing was denied. Instead, Miller and the two new companies—both of which had included gum in their 1981 cards—decided to package cards in 1982 with something else. Fleer, the company that invented bubble gum, opted to include team logo stickers of the twenty-six baseball clubs. Donruss decided to package its cards with a perforated cardboard card that broke down into puzzle pieces.

Even though baseball players had angered their fans by going on strike for 50 days in the summer of 1981, collectors were forgiving. In the absence of baseball, they focused their attention on collecting three times as many cards as were available the previous year.

The market for new cards was growing. And just as some collectors were debating the merits of Topps, Fleer, and Donruss, others were discovering the untapped value of older cards.

■ ■ ■

To look at the glitzy, trade-show atmosphere of many of today's major baseball card shows, it's difficult to imagine that just two decades ago they began as backroom swap meets that looked more like flea markets than conventions. And unlike today's collector, who can find a card show in even the most remote sections of the country on any given weekend, early card collectors had to travel to major cities, where shows took place no more than twice a year.

Card shows had their origin in the early 1970s. Often, they were not baseball card conventions so much as part of larger antique shows that happened to include a section of tableholders who dealt in baseball cards. As baseball card collecting increased in popularity, antique dealers included shoeboxes and binders of baseball cards as part of their displays. Soon conventions dedicated solely to baseball cards began popping up across the country.

In 1975, two veteran collectors staged a show at Spring Garden College just outside of Philadelphia. Ted Taylor, the school's athletic director, and Bob Schmierer, a personnel manager of an engineering firm, had been friends in high school in the 1950s and had become reacquainted through their burgeoning card-collecting hobby. The two figured they could lure collectors to the Spring Garden gymnasium for a show that would benefit the school while bringing collectors together to buy, sell, and trade cards.

A week before their first show, an advertisement appeared in the Philadelphia newspapers. Irv Lerner, one of a dozen or so collector-dealers who traveled the country buying baseball card collections, was setting up at a Philadelphia hotel. Like most barnstorming buyers, Lerner put a simple want ad in the paper, with the date, time, and hotel where he would be available to purchase cards. People would come with dusty collections, finding it hard to believe that someone actually would pay for old baseball cards, and gladly sell them to Lerner and the other traveling buyers.

Lerner's hotel buy was scheduled for the same weekend as the Spring Garden show. What made the situation worse for Schmierer and Taylor was that Lerner was setting up shop not far from his home in northeast Philadelphia. Unlike the unknown buyers from out of town, Lerner had developed a reputation in Philadelphia for paying a premium for old cards in mint condition. Potential collectors for the Spring Garden show might instead go to Lerner's hotel room.

Schmierer and Taylor contacted Lerner, who invited them to his home to discuss the situation. There, the promoters asked him to cancel his hotel room and take a table at the Spring Garden show instead. Lerner agreed, and the show attracted a modest crowd of several thousand collectors. But over the next three years, as cards were pulled out of closets and attics, the show grew to 14,000 attendees, united by a collecting fervor that came to be known as "The Hobby." Collectors referred to "The Hobby" in reverential tones, as in "The Hobby has never seen a card sell for that much" or "He's a big player in The Hobby." Collectors became known as "hobbyists." Among the many publications that began printing in the late 1970s was a San Diego–based magazine called *Baseball Hobby News*. The sale of cards, particularly older cards, by dealers at shops and card shows, where they were marked up from their original retail price, became known as the "secondary market."

By 1977, the Philadelphia show ranked as the largest in the country, attracting dealers from 32 states. In 1978, the show had become so big that fire marshals threatened to close the event. Realizing that they had outgrown Spring Garden College, Taylor and Schmierer began searching for a larger facility for the 1979 show. Taylor, writing in *Sports Collectors Digest*, proudly announced that the show had moved to the "spacious, modern George Washington Motor Lodge," just northwest of Philadelphia along the Pennsylvania Turnpike in Willow Grove.

Across the country, in Los Angeles, three other collectors—Gavin Riley, Steve Brunner, and Mike Berkus—had staged an annual Labor Day card show since 1971 in conjunction with the Southern California Sports Collectors Club. It was, they believed, the oldest running show in the country. Like the Philadelphia convention, the Los Angeles show had grown steadily, and the promoters added a Memorial Day show in 1976. After the fifth annual Memorial Day Show, in 1980, Riley asked his partners if they would consider holding a "National Convention" in place of the Labor Day Show.

"A National Convention?" Berkus asked. "You must be kidding. Changing the name of our Labor Day show to the National Convention won't make a difference."

But Riley was convincing. The Hobby had grown to the point where it needed a national forum. While Southern California was hardly a central location, the tourist appeal of the area would draw vacationing collectors. It might also attract national media and draw attention to The Hobby.

Berkus and Brunner were not the only ones who doubted that a National Convention would work. "We already put on the greatest national convention in The Hobby," Taylor said to Schmierer. "We *are* the National Convention."

Riley, Brunner, and Berkus booked the Los Angeles Airport Marriott for August 28 through September 1, 1980. In a modest, mimeographed ad in the August edition of *The Trader Speaks*, a popular hobby newsletter, they promised seminars on collecting, workshops, auctions, exhibits, and a kickoff banquet all within the Marriott's 12,000-square-foot ballroom. "Come one, come all," it read.

Lew Lipset, a columnist for *The Trader Speaks*, implored collectors to attend. "Many collectors, whose names are well known, but have seldom ventured out of their home states, have indicated their intention to go. The 'names' that will be present and the sheer size promise to make this the biggest buying and selling convention ever, but its importance shouldn't be confined to that. . . . I hope many of you can take the opportunity to go to California and participate in what promises to be a happening."

For a West Coast show, the first "National" was a success, attracting 156 dealers and 5,700 collectors. (Ironically, the Major League Baseball Players Association would hold one of its pivotal strike meetings in the same ballroom 10 months later.) Joe Moeller, who had pitched for eight seasons with the Los Angeles Dodgers, spoke at the kickoff banquet. At the end of the event, Midwest show promoters Lloyd and Carol Toerpe made the only bid to host the second National the following July in Detroit.

Back in Philadelphia, Taylor and Schmierer read the reports from the National and smiled. Only 5,700 collectors. That wasn't even half what they averaged at Willow Grove. Said Taylor: "I don't think we have anything to worry about."

They didn't, at least not yet. That same year, the Philadelphia show launched the price explosion that would fuel The Hobby for years.

■ ■ ■

A few weeks before the Philadelphia Card and Sports Memorabilia Show in March of 1980, Taylor received a call from an Indianapolis promoter, who had just completed a show. "Business was terrible," he said. "If you're smart, you'll unload what you have and get out of The Hobby. The boom is over."

Schmierer and Taylor found that hard to believe. True, Taylor had publicly blasted the idea of a National Sports Collectors Convention, contending that The Hobby could not support the show in addition to the Philadelphia shows. But it hardly looked like the boom was over. "Let's see what happens," Taylor told Schmierer.

As usual, more than 11,000 collectors came to the George Washington Motor Lodge. As he did during previous shows, Taylor ran auctions on the Saturday of the two-day show. Standing at a podium along the wall, wearing a T-shirt that read "Happiness is a 1952 Mantle," Taylor conducted three auctions over the course of the day while the show continued. Normally, the sales proceeded quickly, without much discussion or delay.

Taylor felt this show might be different. The day before, three 1952 Topps Mickey Mantle cards had been consigned. Taylor planned to auction off one during each of the three sale periods: 11 A.M., 3 P.M., and 7 P.M.

The 1952 Mantle had taken on a magical quality. Although Bowman had produced a card of Mantle in 1951, collectors considered the Topps version the more valuable of the two. Not only was it the most popular card in the first full set Topps ever made, but it was considered one of the rarest of the post–World War II cards. It was part of the elusive fourth series of Topps cards, the last 96 cards Topps had issued in 1952. Until 1974, Topps had staggered the release dates of its cards in order to maintain interest throughout the baseball season. In 1952, Topps issued the first 80 cards in March, cards 81–250 in May and cards 251–310 in late July. Cards 311–407 were scheduled to hit stores late in the summer, but were delayed. By then it was football season, and collectors were looking for football cards.

Store owners who had leftover quantities of the first three series never ordered the fourth, and Topps was left with a huge quantity of series four in its warehouse. (It was a pattern repeated many times over the next 20 years, so high-series cards became worth more than low-series. Topps discontinued the practice in 1974, issuing the entire card run at once.)

In 1960, Topps vice president Sy Berger tried to get rid of the 1952 cards that were cluttering the warehouse. He tried unsuccessfully to sell them to carnivals— at the rate of ten cards for a penny—figuring they could be used as prizes. When that failed, he contracted with a disposal company to have them dropped in the ocean. Two garbage trucks loaded the cards at the Bush Terminal in Brooklyn and drove two blocks to the dock at Narrows Bay, where they were loaded onto a garbage scow. A tugboat, with Berger aboard, pulled the scow out into the Atlantic Ocean, opposite the Atlantic Highlands in New Jersey.

"How about right here?" the tugboat driver asked.

"Looks good to me," Berger said.

The driver pulled a lever, opening the bottom of the scow, and tons of 1952 Topps fourth-series baseball cards—including Mickey Mantle card No. 311— plunged to the bottom of the Atlantic.

Topps never revealed what percentage of the fourth series was dropped in the ocean, but as the card market grew, the story was often repeated. And when the first Mantle card came up for bid at the 11 A.M. auction at the Philadelphia show, Taylor recounted the tale once again.

The card typically sold for $700 at the time, but the bidding at the GW Motor Lodge quickly went to $800. Walter Hall, a veteran Massachusetts dealer, bumped the price up to $1,000. As a hush fell over the room, Taylor smiled. Whenever Hall got into the bidding, he knew, prices would soar. The bid went to $1,500, then to $2,000. Hall was up against Rob Barsky and Bob Cohen, two young card dealers who ran the R&B Trading Card Company in Montgomeryville, Pennsylvania. The bidding went to $2,500, and moments later Taylor announced the sale of a 1952 Topps Mickey Mantle to R&B Cards for the astonishing price of $3,100. (Taylor and Schmierer, as the promoters, received 15 percent of each sale as commission.)

Asked by a local newspaper reporter why he had paid such a price for the card, Cohen replied "Because I already have it sold for 34 [hundred]."

For the next four hours, the room buzzed with talk of the sale. Was the card really worth that much? And if so, what would it mean for the rest of the card market? Certainly it would have an effect on the entire price structure of The Hobby.

At 3 o'clock, Taylor took the podium again and announced that there was another '52 Topps Mantle on the block. Again, Hall entered the bidding and again R&B Cards purchased the card, this time for $3,000.

Now the room was really hopping. If just one card had sold for $3,000, it could have been dismissed as a fluke. But two? Of course, R&B had purchased both of them. Maybe they were trying to bump up the price of the 1952 Mantle. But if they really thought the card was worth $3,000, they were not alone in that opinion since others were involved in the bidding.

At 7 o'clock, Taylor stepped up to the podium for the third time and revealed that a third Mantle card was for sale. "Well folks," Taylor said. "Maybe this time someone else will win a Mantle."

No chance. The third Mantle, while not in the pristine condition of the other two, again sold for $3,000. And, once again, the winner was R&B Cards.

As the show ended, Barsky and Cohen received a mixed response. Some dealers offered congratulations while others wondered if they were crazy. Taylor and Schmierer knew one thing: The doom their colleague from Indianapolis had predicted evidently had not made its way east to Philadelphia.

During the following weeks, the two promoters and R&B Cards were deluged with interview requests. Articles on the sale appeared in the Philadelphia newspapers and were picked up by the wire services. "It completely changed the price structure," recalled Taylor later, while a public relations director for Fleer. "It transformed us from an ailing hobby—or at least one that people thought was ailing—into the beginnings of a big business driven by investment."

With so much publicity from the Philadelphia show, Mantle cards were discovered in droves. By September, the card had settled back in at $700. At the Philadelphia show September 27, Hall purchased a Mantle at auction for $760. Afterward, he told John Helyar of *The Wall Street Journal,* "Now's the time to buy."

Clearly, the market had softened. A 1954 Hank Aaron rookie card sold for $275 at the auction in March, but only $90 in September. A 1953 Willie Mays failed to draw a minimum bid of $80.

Still, the March Philadelphia auction had a lasting impact on the card market as former collectors searched for lost collections in the hopes of cashing in. The Hobby was hardly in trouble. In fact, the market for baseball cards was just beginning to grow.

But there was one problem with the massive number of cards coming out of attics and shoeboxes around the country.

Not all of them were real.

■ ■ ■

Jack Petruzzelli thought he had seen it all. As a detective in Fullerton, California, he had investigated robberies, rapes, murders, drug trafficking—the most hideous crimes human beings could commit upon one another. In his 10 years on the force, he had been shot at more times than he cared to remember and often wondered why he stayed in a profession whose members received an automatic spot on the endangered species list.

A longtime collector of baseball cards, Petruzzelli moonlighted as a card show promoter, organizing shows throughout Orange County, many with Gavin Riley, Steve Brunner, and Mike Berkus. It wasn't a lucrative business—at least, not yet— but Petruzzelli could see potential in the growing field. Already, hundreds of collectors flocked to his shows, all convinced that they could make a fortune off the baseball card boom. It was a curious phenomenon, this tendency of collectors to treat cards like penny stocks, but Petruzzelli had long since given up trying to understand people. Nothing surprised him anymore.

At least, that's what he thought when he was summoned by his superiors early in 1982 to investigate a new crime, one that hit close to home. Two men were suspected of masterminding a scheme to sell counterfeit baseball cards at a card show in February. As Petruzzelli received the details of the alleged crime, his heart started racing and his blood began to boil. The incident had taken place at the Holiday Inn in Fullerton, at a card show he had promoted!

The reprinted card was a Topps "1963 Rookie Stars" card that featured head shots of four players. Three of the four—infielders Pedro Gonzalez of the New York Yankees, Ken McMullen of the Los Angeles Dodgers, and Al Weis of the Chicago White Sox—never became stars. The fourth player was a young second baseman for the Cincinnati Reds named Pete Rose.

Rose, then 41, had entered the 1982 season with 3,697 hits and seemed poised to make a run at Ty Cobb's all-time hit record of 4,190. Collectors who had watched Mickey Mantle's 1952 rookie card soar to $3,000 looked at Rose's 1963 rookie card and saw immediate investment potential. Even at its going rate of $200 it seemed extremely undervalued—at least relative to the strange economics of the secondary market.

Using his contacts in the sports card business, Petruzzelli investigated the counterfeits and discovered that Sheldon Jaffe, 41, a businessman from Calabasas, California, had arranged for their production. Jaffe's associate in the deal, 29-year-old Michael Nathan of Woodland Hills, had organized the distribution of the cards through two 17-year-old collectors.

After a three-month investigation, Petruzzelli arrested the two and, much to his surprise, received immediate confessions. According to Jaffe's statement, the counterfeiting had started out as a lark. He went to a printer to make up some cards to pass out to friends, and when the cards looked so much like the originals he couldn't resist selling them as the real McCoys. The two juveniles had sold them to dealers for $100 apiece.

Jaffe and Nathan cooperated in the investigation, helping Petruzzelli track down the dealers who bought the cards and making full restitution. Nathan spent 30 days in jail. Jaffe was sentenced to two days in jail and fined $1,000.

During the course of the investigation, Petruzzelli confiscated 13,000 counterfeit Rose cards. When Jaffe and Nathan were convicted, the cards were marked for destruction and placed in the shredding room of the Fullerton Police Station. Not long thereafter, Petruzzelli received a call from Jaffe's lawyer wanting to know how they could get the counterfeits back.

"Sorry," Petruzzelli said. "Those cards have been shredded."

Unbeknownst to Petruzzelli, the shredder had broken down months earlier and the cards were still in the room, in a moving box under a stack of newspapers. Nathan's attorney filed a court order requiring the Fullerton Police department to stamp the cards "original counterfeit" and return them to the defendants.

Petruzzelli was livid. "No way am I stamping that shit," he told his superiors. "I went out and busted these guys and hell if I'm going to sit here and stamp 13,000 cards, give them back and say 'Here you go, fellas. Enjoy.'"

Despite Petruzzelli's protests, the cards were returned. Petruzzelli did not have to stamp the cards himself, but spent an afternoon supervising the operation. As he sat in the room and simmered, two police cadets stamped 13,000 cards. Later, they were returned to Jaffe.

Ironically, since the case was well publicized, the notorious counterfeit cards became instant collectors items. Soon the reprints were selling for $25.

"The whole thing still pisses me off," Petruzzelli recalled a decade later. "Jaffe went out and sold about 10,000 of the cards for $3 or $4 apiece for a profit of $30,000 to $40,000. So he gets fined $1,000, spends a few days in jail and makes out big time. I had dealers selling these cards at my shows by telling people that the reprints were rarer than the real ones.

"The biggest problem I had was that nobody understood what was really going on. The attitude was: 'Hey, these are just baseball cards and this is the first time we've really had anything like this. It's not that big a deal. It's just a one-time thing.'"

The Rose counterfeits, when placed alongside the real cards, were difficult to tell apart. But upon close glance, a white dot could be seen above Ken McMullen. And unlike the thick cardboard of Topps, the counterfeits were printed on a lighter cardstock, much like the Fleer and Donruss cards of the early 1980s. That so many dealers were fooled was due not so much to the skillful work of the printers but to the fact that counterfeiting was virtually unheard of; previous attempts that had come into The Hobby were obvious reproductions.

With the industry wised by the incident, Petruzzelli doubted that counterfeiting would happen again. In a 1983 interview with *Sports Collectors Digest*, Petruzzelli said: "I don't think you're going to see any more of that stuff. The phony thing is over. I don't think people want to risk making counterfeit cards now. If they start messing with that, they know they're going to get caught; there are just too many experts out there who can tell if a card is fake and then they'll nail the dealer. I don't think anyone wants to get stuck with a 'crook' label."

But that was a risk other counterfeiters were willing to take, and the Rose card incident was only the first sign of a problem that would fester in the years to come.

∎ ∎ ∎

Despite the gloom-and-doom predictions of former Topps president Joel Shorin, the opening of the baseball card market benefited Topps as much as the Major League Baseball Players Association, Donruss, and Fleer. For fiscal 1982, which included the 1981 baseball season, net income at Topps rose 41 percent from $3.51 million to $4.96 million on sales of $65 million. The following year, as Topps's common stock split, net income increased to $5.93 million. While Arthur Shorin's reorganization of the company was largely responsible for the turnaround, the increased interest in baseball cards also had an immediate impact. If nothing else, as the 1982 annual report stated: "There have been major reductions in legal expense in connection with the successful conclusion of costly anti-trust litigation, initiated by a competitor, in connection with baseball picture cards."

In 1984, just four years after Topps had considered filing for bankruptcy, management made a decision that would make Topps insiders very wealthy. Since its inception in 1938, Topps had prided itself on its ability to measure the pulse of American culture and capitalize with hip new products. As the Reagan Eighties unfolded, Topps officials spotted a new trend that would help the company more than any card or gum product. This one came from nearby Wall Street and was known as a leveraged buyout.

In an "LBO," an investment firm—in Topps's case Forstmann Little & Co.—works with company management. Together, they buy the company using money raised from banks and the public sale of securities. The debt is paid down with cash from the company's operations and augmented, in some instances, by selling off pieces of the business itself.

In 1984, Forstmann Little took Topps private for $98 million. During the next three years, business boomed for Topps. For the year ending February 28, 1987, Topps's revenues doubled from $73 million in sales to $147 million. Much of the increase came from Topps's introduction of "Garbage Pail Kids" sticker cards, a spoof on the popular Cabbage Patch Kid dolls. Instead of a cuddly, moonfaced Cabbage Patch Kid, Garbage Pail Kids were ghoulish cartoon delinquents often pictured armed with knives and other dangerous weapons. Introduced in 1985, Garbage Pail Kids was a rare card product that captured the attention of girls as well as boys. Parents were not amused by Garbage Pail Kids, however, and bombarded Topps's headquarters with letters protesting the product, which they felt promoted violence. But, as is often the case when parents protest, kids only wanted the product more. (For fiscal 1988, the Garbage Pail line brought in revenues of $48 million for Topps. Shortly thereafter, Cabbage Patch creator Xavier Roberts sued for violation of copyright and Topps retired the product.)

In May of 1987, Topps sold 12 percent of the company (1.7 million shares) to the public for $13 a share, raising $22 million. In its investment prospectus, Topps recognized the growing speculation in baseball cards. Topps said demand for its sports-related products almost doubled in fiscal 1987 "partially as a result of increased consumer interest in the investment and collectible value of baseball cards."

Topps and Forstmann Little officials, feeling Topps's stock was undervalued, re-leveraged the company in January of 1988, paying out a special $10 per share dividend to stockholders at a cost of $139 million.

For Topps insiders and Forstmann Little officials, the deal was a coup. They had bought the stock for 75 cents a share in 1984, then sold it for $13. An original investor could have earned 70 times his initial stake. *Financial World* magazine, in an April 1988 article on Topps, included an artist's rendering of a Topps card featuring chairman Arthur "IPO" (for initial public offering) Shorin. Forstmann general partner Brian Little later told *Fortune* magazine "this has been the single most successful deal we've ever done." Outsiders who bought the shares didn't do so badly either. With the $10 dividend to go with shares that rose from $13 to $17 immediately after the dividend was announced, investors had $27 worth of assets to show for their $13—doubling their money in under a year.

Of course, the dividend payment left Topps with $143 million in long-term debt. But Topps officials were confident they could pay it off quickly. The baseball card market, after all, was just heating up.

■ ■ ■

The 1952 Mickey Mantle cards sold at the George Washington Motor Lodge in 1980 created a snowball effect. Prices of older cards boomed, creating an environment for counterfeiters. But it was not until 1984 that the market for baseball cards turned sharply from a nostalgic hobby into a business fueled by investors driven to make a profit in the upstart market.

The notion of investing in rookie cards was a natural outgrowth from the sale of the Mantles. While the 1952 Topps Mantle was not his first card (the 1951 Bowman was), collectors recognized the Topps version as the true rookie. Investors reasoned that if a Mantle card could appreciate from a penny to $3,000 in 30 years, it stood to reason that the rookie cards of players in the 1980s might appreciate accordingly.

Such reasoning had several flaws. Collectors did not save cards in 1952 with the hope of a big payday in the future. Many cards were discarded by housecleaning mothers or damaged in card-flipping contests. Also, as demand for cards grew following the breakup of the Topps monopoly, more cards were produced than in the 1950s, with a greater percentage saved by collectors who now put a price tag on cards. And, of course, it was unlikely that Topps, Fleer, or Donruss was going to dump its excess cards in the Atlantic Ocean as Topps had with the Mantles and the rest of its leftover 1952 cards. (Topps, incidentally, contracted with a Phoenix card dealer named Michael Cramer in the 1970s. Cramer purchased Topps's "closeouts," unsold cards that had been returned to Topps. Cramer, in turn, sold them through the secondary market of dealers and card shop owners.)

Nonetheless, the 1952 Mantle card became the basis for the new economic structure of the market that became known as "Rookiemania." Investors likened baseball cards to the stock market, with the rookie cards akin to stocks offered in an initial public offering. Just as they invested in promising companies, they poured money into young stars with seemingly bright futures.

The phenomenon began in 1981 when the freshly minted rookie cards of Fernando Valenzuela and Tim Raines began selling for a dollar apiece at card shows. For veteran collectors, the news was disturbing. Paul Richman, a *Sports Collectors Digest* columnist, wrote:

At first it was just another aspect of our broad hobby; the goal—to collect the earliest card of every baseball star or star to be. Now it has become an obsession to some, a business to others, and an investment in the future for many more. The Rookiemania has swept The Hobby, and the scars are just beginning to form. . . . Interestingly, it is the young and/or beginning hobbyists who are setting this trend. It is disheartening to see a kid spend his money on recent star cards that most people in his neighborhood still have. . . . Where will the hobby lie after the rookie craze? Will there be 10,000 current rookie dealers competing for the collectors' money?

The answer was a resounding *yes*. Just as error cards dominated The Hobby in 1981, hoarding rookie cards became the focal point of the business by 1983. Investors stockpiled as many rookie cards as possible from a promising crop of young players that included Wade Boggs, Tony Gwynn, and Ryne Sandberg.

But while 1983 was a good year for the baseball card business, 1984 was even better. The person most responsible was a 23-year-old first baseman for the New York Yankees named Don Mattingly. In his first full season, Mattingly won the American League batting title with a .343 batting average, leading the AL with 207 hits and 44 doubles. He also hit 23 home runs, drove in 110 runs and led AL first basemen with a .996 fielding percentage. With good looks and a down-to-earth demeanor, Mattingly appeared to be the next royalty in the Yankees storied history, following the lineage of Babe Ruth, Lou Gehrig, Joe DiMaggio, and Mickey Mantle.

All three card companies produced a card of Mattingly for 1984, but the Donruss version was the most sought after. After two years of virtually the same card style, Donruss made dramatic improvements on its card design in 1984. More importantly, from an investor's standpoint, Donruss appeared to have reduced its press run in that year. Although Donruss did not release its production figures, it seemed like there were fewer Donruss cards—at least to the investors putting away as many Mattinglys as they could find.

Donruss also recognized the importance of the rookie card market, including 20 "Rated Rookie" cards as part of its 660-card set. The idea was the brainchild of Bill Madden, the columnist for the New York *Daily News* and *The Sporting News* who served as a consultant to Donruss, writing card backs and recommending players for the set. Among the Rated Rookies he chose for 1984 were Joe Carter, Sid Fernandez, and Ron Darling. (Most of the Rated Rookies, such as Brad Komminsk, Mike Brown, and Chris Smith, never prospered in the majors.) Mattingly, who had accumulated too many at-bats in 1983 to still be considered a rookie, was not included among the Rated Rookies.

By the end of the 1984 season, Mattingly's card had risen to $20, pushing the price of the set up to $80—an unheard of price for a set that came out before the season priced at $14.

Over the next three years, spurred on by young prospects such as Roger Clemens, Kirby Puckett, and Jose Canseco, the Mattingly incident was repeated. Rookiemania grew and the national media took notice. In the June 1986 issue of the financial magazine *Nation's Business*, a subhead read: "Baseball cards—coveted by youthful fans—are now being snatched up for investments by serious collectors." In April 1987, *Barron's* magazine chimed in with "Topp-Flight Investment: Why Baseball Cards are a Hit with Their Fans."

Then, in June 1988, *Money* magazine published a study by two Marquette University professors, David S. Krause and George Kunter. Their research found that, from 1980 to 1987, baseball cards had a compound average return of 42.5 percent, outperforming "all other comparable investments this decade," such as corporate bonds (14 percent), common stocks (12.7 percent) and treasury bills (7.2 percent). *Money* headlined the article "Baseball Cards Bat .425: An intriguing new academic analysis shows that rookie offerings have been the top investment of the 1980s, rising more than 40 percent a year." Two months later, *Advertising Age* proclaimed "National pastime—it's in the cards."

The *Money* magazine study relied heavily on the prices listed in the *Sport Americana Baseball Card Price Guide* and *Beckett Baseball Card Monthly*, both published by former card dealer James Beckett of Dallas. A veteran collector who traveled the country in the 1970s buying collections, Beckett had become something akin to the Federal Reserve Chairman of the baseball card industry; the values listed in his monthly price guides had become both an indicator and an influencer of the market. By 1988, a collector had to look no further than one of his price guides to see a business on the verge of an explosion.

4

Chairman of the Hobby

As a kid, the last thing Jim Beckett figured he'd grow up to be was the head of a publishing empire. But like so many of the men who have made their fortunes in the sports memorabilia industry, Beckett's rise to power was a calculated process.

As head of Beckett Publications, Dr. James Beckett III has been widely regarded as the most powerful person in the sports card industry. While he does not determine who gets to produce cards nor manufacture cards himself, his publications are the recognized authorities on what each card is worth. Every month, his magazines include fresh price guide information that is almost universally followed. In a speculative business, that means Beckett could play God. If the frequent analogy of the sports card business to the stock market is true, then Beckett's role in many ways would be like having control over the agate type that appears in newspapers each day from Wall Street. Not surprisingly, Beckett's magazines are often referred to as "the *Wall Street Journal*s of the sports card industry."

From a modest beginning in North Dallas in 1984, Beckett Publications grew to seven magazines. There are dozens of other sports card periodicals, most of which contain price guide information, but none are as widely read as Beckett's baseball, football, basketball, and hockey monthlies.

Just how much influence does Beckett have? Approach a sports card dealer at a card show or shop about the price of a card, and most often he'll refer to the latest issue of Beckett. Thousands of shop owners across the country sell Beckett magazines in their stores, and since the prices are determined through a national survey of their fellow dealers, most swear by the information. Since boys aged 7 to 11 represent a large block of collectors, Beckett Publications is one of the first things some of them learn to read.

In 1977, if you had asked a youngster if he would trade his Pete Rose card for an Andre Dawson, he would have laughed. Who would want a Dawson card? He had just reached the majors. Rose was an all-star third baseman. He had hit .323 the previous year with 10 home runs and 63 RBI. Back then, baseball card trades, much like baseball trades themselves, were determined by who put up the most impressive statistics. Grade-schoolers who barely knew long division could recite a litany of baseball statistics. Trade one of baseball's best players for an unproven rookie from the Montreal Expos? Are you joking?

Flash ahead to 1989. Ken Griffey, Jr., son of Ken Griffey of the Cincinnati Reds' Big Red Machine of the mid-1970s, is a rookie outfielder for the Seattle Mariners. At age 19, he earns a starting job in spring training. Upper Deck, the new card company on the block, debuts its first baseball set with Griffey, Jr., as the first card. Not long after the set hits the market in March, the card sells for between $5 and $10. Ask a kid if he would trade his 1989 Andre Dawson card for a Griffey, Jr. Again, the youth would have laughed. Who would be stupid enough to trade a 10-cent Dawson card for a $10 Griffey? Haven't you read Beckett?

This is not a reflection on Dawson; indeed, "The Hawk" had hit 299 home runs heading into the 1989 season and had been the National League's Most Valuable Player in 1987. Despite bad knees, he looked like a strong candidate for baseball's Hall of Fame.

The difference in these examples—only 12 years apart—speaks volumes about how the card business changed dramatically in such a short time. By 1989, the market had become so investor-driven that the rookie cards of promising prospects were selling for 100 times those of players like Dawson who had one foot in Cooperstown. Kids growing up in the 1950s, 1960s, and 1970s memorized the statistics on the backs of cards. The eighties kid pored over Beckett, quoting prices like little stockbrokers. Young boys no longer referred to sports cards as *trading* cards since there was very little trading taking place—just buying and selling. Jim Beckett may not have been responsible for the baseball card explosion, but he did throw gasoline on the fire.

With so much potential power in an industry fueled by rumor and innuendo, it's not surprising that Beckett has been accused of everything from printing misleading information to insider trading. The rumors have proven false, and it's a testament to his integrity that even as on-line price guides have sprung up with what computer networks claim is up-to-the-minute information, the industry has never wavered in its dedication to Beckett as the last word on pricing.

Beckett, a born-again Christian with a slight build and soft-spoken demeanor, downplays his role. "If I had all the power everyone thought I had, it would be pretty incredible. I probably have more than I think I do, and less than everyone else thinks I have."

■ ■ ■

Jim Beckett purchased his first baseball cards in 1956 when his father, a can company worker, gave him a penny for a pack of cards. The 7-year-old Beckett's first card was Spook Jacobs, a second baseman for the Kansas City A's. In 1994, according to *Beckett Baseball Card Monthly*, the card was worth $12.

James Beckett, Jr.'s job took the family around the country, from Pittsburgh to Chicago to Wheeling, West Virginia, and ultimately to Tyler, Texas, where Jim Beckett finished high school. When the family moved to California, Beckett stayed behind in Texas, where he enrolled at Southern Methodist University.

While at SMU, he answered a newspaper ad by Gervise Ford, who later would invest with Beckett and another collector named Wayne Grove in a Dallas card shop called First Base. When it appeared to Beckett that he and Grove might be the only serious collectors in all of Texas, he realized he would have to relocate to the Midwest to pursue his hobby in earnest. In 1975, Beckett, who had earned a Ph.D. in statistics, moved to Ohio to teach at Bowling Green University.

It was during the mid-1970s that Beckett, along with about a dozen other collectors-turned-dealers, began traveling the country in search of baseball cards. A week before each trip, Beckett would place a classified ad in the newspaper of the city he planned to visit: "Buying Baseball Cards. Saturday. Holiday Inn. 10–6." Beckett would check in on a Friday night, clear the bedroom furniture off to one side, and set up a table to do business.

Sometimes, nobody would show up. Other times, only a few collectors would come to the hotel. But more often than not, a steady stream of people arrived with shoeboxes of cards that had gathered dust in the attic for years. With no price guides, nobody knew for sure what the cards were worth. Only the traveling buyers, who understood the market from attending a growing number of sports card conventions and reading a newsletter called *The Trader Speaks*, knew that older cards were appreciating at a rapid rate. The general public knew nothing of the rising interest in baseball cards; most showed up at hotels hoping just for a few dollars. The traveling dealers called the transaction a "laydown." Someone appeared in their room, laid down the cards on the table, and asked: "How much will you give me?"

As more entrepreneurs got on the circuit, however, it became increasingly difficult to make a killing. Those collectors who did sell at hotels began to hear whispers about a lucrative market in baseball cards and wanted to make sure they did not get fleeced by the barnstorming card sharks.

During a stop in Springfield, Illinois, an aggressive young man approached Beckett in his hotel room. "He was very pushy," Beckett recalled. "He plopped his box of cards down and said 'Look, I want to sell my cards, but at my price. Don't try to talk me out of it. Don't even try to negotiate with me. We're going to do it my way, at my price, or we're not going to do it at all. Do you understand?'"

Beckett, not knowing what the box contained, didn't know what to say. But since the man was so adamant, he agreed. There would be no negotiating.

"I want ten cents a card," the man continued. "Not five cents or eight cents. Ten cents. Are we straight on that?"

Beckett nodded and began to shuffle through the cards, most of which were from the 1970s. But as he made his way to the back of the box, the cards started getting older. There were cards from the early 1960s and enough cards to complete the 407-card 1952 Topps set (valued at this time at $6,600). As Beckett's heart began pounding, the seller told him matter-of-factly that those cards had belonged to his older brother.

Beckett nodded while his mind raced. Even at 1975 prices, the cards were worth over $1,000. There were only a couple thousand cards. At ten cents apiece, that would be only a few hundred bucks!

"Are you sure you want to do this?" Beckett asked.

At that point, the man grew angry. "Look buddy, I've heard about you guys. I know you're working me over, and you're starting to piss me off. You have to buy these cards."

"Whatever you say," Beckett said.

Beckett bought the entire lot for less than $500. Now a multimillionaire as a result of his publishing business, Beckett smiles at the memory.

It was entirely different back then. You had the knowledge, but it was not your responsibility to educate the consumer. I wasn't robbing him. Heck, in that case he might have hurt me if I didn't buy the cards off him. You thought nothing of paying less than 50 cents on the dollar. Nowadays, with price guides, people know what cards are worth. But back then, nobody knew as much as this small group of guys.

We were like explorers. We'd make maps of where people had been and chart out what land was still left to be conquered. It was exciting, a great way to see the country. Sometimes nobody showed up, but when you're young and single, you're thinking "Hey, what's a weekend?"

Which isn't to say the life was without its problems. In 1977, Beckett's Oldsmobile Cutlass was stolen in Boston. When he notified the police, he did not mention that the trunk was full of baseball cards, figuring the cops would not understand that this represented a huge financial loss. Two days later, the police called, saying they had recovered the car. When Beckett went to retrieve it, everything in the glove compartment was gone. He approached the trunk convinced the cards were stolen, only to find them still there. The thieves had dumped the cards throughout the trunk, but had not taken a single card.

"You have to remember," Beckett said. "*Nobody* back then thought these things were worth anything. People thought we were crazy. It's like if you put an ad in the paper today saying you want to buy old grocery bags. People would think you were nuts, but they'd bring them in and be more than happy to sell them to you for cash. Sure, we bought a lot of stuff that went up in value, but we were taking a financial risk. But I sleep well at night. I mean, we used to tell some people who were hesitant that there's no hurry to sell."

The Boston incident made Beckett realize that life on the road was getting dangerous. By 1978, as the sports card hobby was gathering momentum, the notion of opening a hotel room to walk-ins had become a dangerous proposition.

Mike Berkus, who was part of the circuit, remembers when he came to that same realization. During a trip to Minneapolis, a man came to his hotel room with a laydown of cards from 1948 to 1955. The cards were in perfect condition, but all of the star players were missing. Berkus offered $500. "You'd have five or six grand if you had the stars," he told the seller. "What happened to the stars?"

"I don't have them," the man said firmly. "This is what I have."

Berkus paid out $500, and the man left. But for the rest of the afternoon, as customers came to the room, Berkus became more and more uncomfortable, as if someone were watching him. He told his buying partner that he was going to get something to drink. When he went outside to the vending machines, the man jumped out at him.

"I asked him if he forgot something," Berkus recalled. "He pulled his jacket back, and I could see a pistol. He told me 'I just wanted to see if you guys were going to laugh at me.'"

"Why would we laugh at you?" Berkus asked.

"The guys last week laughed at me. They made fun of me. They ripped me off. I wanted to see if you guys were going to laugh at me."

The next day, Berkus found out which dealers had gone to Minneapolis the previous weekend and bought the star cards. "I was still at the hotel and I called them up and said, 'I want to thank you guys. You almost got me killed. You want to stop making jokes about people selling cards?'"

Kit Young, who also traveled across the country looking for cards, once purchased a valuable collection of 1950s cards from a man in Hawaii. Later, he was approached outside the hotel by the seller, who was with a few friends. "Needless to say, they made a convincing argument that maybe I owed them some more money," Young said. "In truth, I probably did, but you didn't know what price to charge since there were no price guides."

Berkus learned in Minneapolis that there were no more unexplored lands and that the business was getting too crowded. By the end of 1978, the circuit was close to death. Men such as Beckett, Berkus, and Young, who were in the business long before it exploded in the mid-1980s, parlayed their incomes from their days as traveling buyers into small fortunes. By 1993, Young's San Diego sports-card mail order business did over $5 million in sales annually. In 1993, Beckett unveiled his sixth publication, a line of tribute magazines to aging stars such as Nolan Ryan and Joe Montana. In July of 1994, he issued a seventh magazine, dedicated to motor sports and collectibles. And Berkus, of course, has emerged as the industry's ultimate insider, earning handsome incomes from consulting work for companies such as Upper Deck and The Score Board, Inc.

Beckett, ironically, dealt the final blow to the buying tours in 1979 when he and Denny Eckes published the first edition of *The Sport Americana Baseball Card*

Price Guide. Prospective buyers now could educate themselves on current card prices and arm themselves for negotiations. Soon Beckett saw a need for more up-to-date pricing information and in November of 1984, he launched the first issue of *Beckett Baseball Card Monthly.* In the inaugural issue, he set a modest goal for the industry. Writing in the "Owner's Box" section, Beckett said: "The baseball card collecting hobby is not yet universally recognized as being the third most popular hobby behind coins and stamps—that is one of my personal goals."

By 1985, baseball card collecting had hurdled both coins and stamps. As the sports card hobby turned into an industry, the magazine grew from a 10,000 circulation in its first year to 850,000 in 1992. The football, basketball, and hockey card magazines followed, along with a fifth publication devoted to young stars from all four sports.

While *Beckett Baseball* began as a price guide, it expanded into a glossy magazine that included contributions from baseball writers across the country. Still, the focal point remained the price guide. To keep up with the business, Beckett assembled a staff of six price-guide analysts and formed panels of dealers nationwide to rate cards on a monthly basis.

The Beckett price guide illustrates how vast the field has grown. It requires just 11 pages to list the prices for cards produced from 1948 to 1980, since there were never more than two lines of cards made in any one year. By comparison, it takes 14 pages to list the 105 different card sets and subsets produced by the five licensed card manufacturers in 1993.

Even though the 100-dealer panel is listed in each issue, Beckett continually has had to fight off allegations of price fixing. Since he made a living as a dealer, rumors have persisted that he has used the guide to boost prices of cards he owned, then sold the cards at a profit. All have proven false. While Beckett did own a stake in the First Base card store with Grove and Ford, he phased himself out of the operation by 1985. Even Grove and Ford have split, each opening their own card stores.

While most of the industry agrees on the Beckett guide as the official pricing source, not everyone agrees on how it is to be used. For each card or sets of cards, two prices are listed: a high and a low. According to the Beckett guidelines, the prices represent a range that the cards have sold for during the previous month. In practice, however, card dealers tend to look only at the high column when pricing cards for sale.

Many collectors make the mistake of not reading the guidelines and assume the price listed is the price their cards are worth. In reality, card dealers buy cards at 50 percent of book value if the cards are in mint condition, and for a lesser percentage based on a sliding scale for cards with creases, nicks, and other imperfections. The sale still is dependent on whether a buyer can be found. For many cards of the post-1973 era, which have been both produced and saved in greater quantities, there is much less demand.

"You sound like a broken record sometimes, but our guide is just that—a guide," Beckett said. "Ultimately, a card is only worth what someone will pay for it."

In the card business, however, that's often an easy rule to forget. With cards marketed by both manufacturers and dealers as limited-edition, one-of-a-kind, can't-miss investments, many collectors overlook the Beckett guidelines, stockpiling cards in the belief that, at the very least, they can sell their cards for the prices listed in Beckett and other guides.

Beckett himself cautions collectors against such unbridled optimism. He points to his column from the first Beckett magazine, where he hoped baseball card collecting would surpass coins and stamps. Both the coin and stamp businesses crashed in the 1980s with all the overtones of tulipmania, so perhaps it's not surprising that the sports card market softened in 1992.

Beckett, who has seen the industry from every possible angle, said he struggles sometimes to find the middle ground between what dealers would like to think their cards are worth and what people are actually willing to pay for them. "Since you're dealing with so much fanaticism, things get out of whack at times. But we have to represent what's going on, even if that's not real. That's troubling to us because we have a real social conscience. It goes on in other places, but you can't have theoretical prices about what cards should be worth."

Theoretically, card companies should care little about what value Beckett places on their cards. The Beckett prices reflect only the value of cards on the secondary market, where card dealers bump up the price of individual cards and sets based on perceived supply and demand. Manufacturers' profits come only from the wholesale price of cards. So even if Beckett says a 1989 Upper Deck Ken Griffey, Jr., card is worth $10 just months after it was produced, Upper Deck sees only the wholesale price it received for cases of cards that included Griffey.

But if prices in Beckett demonstrate a pattern of short-term investment growth for the cards of a certain manufacturer, it generates excitement for that company's future products, effectively serving as free marketing and advertising. For companies whose cards are not included in Beckett, it's almost as if they don't exist, since there are no prices for dealers and collectors to use as a reference point. All of which, according to Beckett's critics, could place him in a position to set prices rather than report on them.

Beckett says he's been fair across the board, only including major card sets officially licensed by the four major sports leagues and their players' associations, and shying away from smaller sets, such as a line of baseball cards in Spanish by Pacific Trading Cards, and Canadian-based O-Pee-Chee's baseball cards printed in French. In an industry in which the working arrangements between league licensing officials, card manufacturers, dealers, and even certain trade publications often seem to border on the incestuous, Beckett has made it clear to his staff that they must avoid such entangling relationships. While staff members are encouraged to collect cards, stockpiling cards for investment purposes is strictly taboo. Even freebie and promotional cards sent for review purposes must be turned in for distribution to charity.

"We have to be fair to all parties," Beckett said. "You have to have integrity and I think we've done very well there. We have quarterly ethics seminars to discuss situations that come up. Is it all right if one of the companies wants to treat you to a round of golf? That's probably acceptable. But to fly you across country and wine and dine you? No way.

"We can't avoid criticism as long as there are cards that go down in value and there are cards that aren't included. People are going to be unhappy. But in our business, we have to draw the line on what sets we include and what gratuities we accept or send back. When we send things back, that gets people's attention."

Beckett's philosophy often comes across as holier-than-thou, and indeed there is a strong religious fervor in the offices of Beckett Publications. Beckett told *Dallas Life* magazine in October of 1991 that the company's "written corporate culture" is consistent with his "born-again" experience in 1980.

"Would it be sacrilegious to say that we want to be a source for wisdom?" Beckett asked. "We want to be representing some good ideals. We're not going to hit people over the head with the fact that me and a number of the leaders of the company . . . well, let's just say we have high moral standards. We don't promote people because they're Christians or anything. But they must have good ethics and moral character. It isn't what you say you are, but what you demonstrate."

In November of 1993, Beckett Publications held a grand opening celebration for its new headquarters in North Dallas. With 150 employees, Beckett had grown too big for the unmarked office building it occupied in a nearby shopping center. Ironically, nearly 20 years before, Beckett himself had left Texas for Ohio because that's where the collecting hobby was most developed. These days, with card manufacturers Pro Set and Pinnacle Brands (formerly Score) cranking out cards within 20 miles of Beckett headquarters, the most powerful city in the business is Dallas, which is also the home of the most powerful man.

Standing on the floor of the National Sports Collectors Convention in Chicago in July of 1993, Beckett paused. There were 1,000 dealer tables, along with more than 100 corporate booths. More than 60,000 collectors would come through the doors of McCormick Place. Many wielded one of Beckett's magazines.

"I was a big-time dealer and I miss that. But I can't buy and sell collections like I did in the seventies. I think I could do that now, but I choose not to because of the perception of a conflict of interest. This is America. You ought to be allowed to sell some cards. But if I sold a lot of cards, people would talk.

"Twenty years ago, it was just baseball cards. While none of us were purely collectors, none of us were into it solely with money-making motives. We all enjoyed the action. I mean, people didn't even want money for their cards back then. Often, they just wanted to trade. I miss those days."

Perhaps Beckett has had the last laugh. Even though it's not listed in any price guide, the first issue of *Beckett Baseball Card Monthly* sells regularly for over $100.

CHAPTER

5

A House of Cards: The Origins of Upper Deck

By 1988, The Hobby had become big business. No longer did collectors pursue cards purely for pleasure. Now everything had its price. Armed with Beckett price guides, collectors tried to predict which rookie baseball players would become the superstars of tomorrow and provide them with a payoff once their initial cards soared in value.

But while The Hobby was growing, the cards themselves had remained the same. Even though printing technologies had improved, the 1988 baseball cards varied little from the first Fleer and Donruss cards produced in 1981. Not surprisingly, the counterfeit problems that began in 1982 with the reproduction of Pete Rose's 1963 rookie cards had reached epidemic proportions by 1988. Anyone with access to a decent printing press, it seemed, could reproduce baseball cards that looked like the originals.

What The Hobby needed was a card that reflected the printing advances of the 1980s. Also, it needed a card that would deter counterfeiters.

What The Hobby needed, in short, was Upper Deck.

■ ■ ■

The young man said his name was Eric Davis, but Bill Hemrick knew it was only an alias. If you're going to go by an assumed name at a baseball card show, Hemrick thought, don't use the name of one of baseball's current young stars. How stupid can you be?

Standing behind his card display at the Anaheim Holiday Inn, Hemrick huddled with "Davis." It was shortly before Christmas, 1986, and the baseball card industry was booming, driven by a young New York Yankee first baseman named Don Mattingly, whose 1984 Donruss rookie card was the hottest on the market. In his first three full years in the majors, Mattingly had hit .343, .324, and .352. He was 25 years old and played for the New York Yankees, a team inextricably linked to baseball greatness. Many felt he was a sure bet for the Hall of Fame.

Mattingly's rookie card was worth $90 at the time—if you could find it—and Hemrick had none, a fact he was reminded of constantly by collectors looking for the card. Davis asked Hemrick if he would be interested in buying 100 Mattingly rookie cards. Hemrick looked at the dealers on each side of him. Suddenly it didn't matter if the guy said he was Eric Davis or Bette Davis. He had Mattingly rookies, and Hemrick didn't want anyone outbidding him for the cards. "Let's step out to the lobby for a minute," Hemrick said.

Davis wanted $4,000 for the cards—cash. Hemrick couldn't believe it. He could easily sell the cards for $9,000. He went back inside, returned with the money, and bought the cards. As he stood in the lobby and watched Davis leave the building, Hemrick's heart began to race. When he had become a baseball card dealer two months earlier, he never thought there would be this kind of cash involved. But for whatever reasons, people were willing to pay lots of money for baseball cards. It was like the stock market, only people weren't investing in businesses; they were investing in pieces of cardboard.

Hemrick had never collected baseball cards as a kid growing up in Ohio, but discovered them at a card show at Anaheim Stadium before a California Angels game in the summer of 1986. He bought a set of Topps cards and an unopened box of Donruss cards and immediately was hooked. When he got home, he sent his daughter out to buy another box of Donruss. Over the next four months, he bought tens of thousands of baseball cards. Finally, he told his wife, Linda, that he was going to open up a card shop. "Are you crazy?" she said. "You don't really think you can make a living doing that, do you?"

"Why not?" Hemrick asked her. The printing supply company he worked for was in the process of being sold, and he'd soon be out of a job. He was 47 years old, his two daughters were grown, and he had money in the bank. If it didn't work out, he'd find something else to do. He always had in the past. From the time he got home from Vietnam, he had been successful in a wide range of entrepreneurial endeavors. In 1973, he opened the first bicycle motocross track in the U.S. He had helped promote country music concerts. And what about the batting cage he bought in Riverside that cleaned up until they built a water theme park across the street?

"O.K.," Linda said. "But baseball cards?"

Now Hemrick was standing in a hotel lobby holding $9,000 worth of cardboard for which he had paid only $4,000. *This is too good to be true,* he thought.

As it turned out, it was. Hemrick had purchased $9,000 worth of counterfeit cards, the work of a local printer. But it was months before Hemrick found out the cards were fake. He sold some of the cards during the rest of the Anaheim show, and traded a couple dozen to a collector acquaintance named Jeff Marx, who dealt in Olympic pins from the 1984 Games in Los Angeles. Hemrick sold many of the Mattinglys at his Batters Up card shop near his home in the city of Orange. Other dealers had assured him that the cards were real.

A month after the Anaheim show, there were reports of fake Mattinglys surfacing across the country. In most cases the reprints were not as clear as the originals, but they so closely resembled the true cards that they often went unnoticed. It wasn't long before Hemrick, who had sold most of his 100 Mattinglys, was approached by angry customers. Hemrick promised a refund or an authentic Mattingly card to anyone who had purchased a counterfeit from him. This wasn't good enough for one man. A day after Hemrick replaced a fake Mattingly with a real one, he received a phone call. The man said the real Mattingly was scratched and asked if Hemrick would take it back for one in mint condition. Hemrick agreed, but when the man brought in the "real" Mattingly, Hemrick—by now an expert on counterfeits—spotted the fake instantly.

The man was adamant, calling Hemrick a crook. Hemrick called Jack Petruzzelli, who in the two years after the Rose incident had become *the* expert on baseball card counterfeiting, and the Fullerton police officer convinced the man that it would be wise to go away.

Hemrick estimates he lost more than $10,000 on the incident: the initial $4,000, plus the money he spent replacing the counterfeit cards. But it seemed no matter what he did, he was the guy who sold counterfeit cards. "Pretty soon, I was the guy who made the cards," Hemrick said. "That really soured me on collecting, and it made me realize what an amateurish profession I was in."

■ ■ ■

Still, Hemrick stayed in the business. In the summer of 1987, Hemrick and Marx—the Olympic pin collector—pooled their resources and opened a card shop four miles from Anaheim Stadium. Hemrick ran the business full-time while Marx, a planning supervisor for Ford Aerospace, helped out at nights and on weekends. Hemrick had amassed $50,000 in card inventory and Marx kicked in his collection of Olympic pins.

For the first few months, the store didn't have a name. Hemrick didn't want to use Batters Up again since many collectors linked it to the Mattingly counterfeit incident. They came up with dozens of ideas, but none seemed to fit. Marx sought suggestions from everyone, even his fellow plant workers. "How about On Deck?" he asked his colleagues at lunch.

"No, you want Upper Deck," said a worker from the Midwest. "When I used to live in Detroit, we used to all go sit in the upper deck at Tiger Stadium."

The Upper Deck, Marx thought. *Upper sounds like high end and deck sounds like a deck of cards.* He took the name to Hemrick. The Upper Deck it would be.

Located in a strip mall at the corner of La Palma Avenue and State College Boulevard, The Upper Deck had only 600 square feet of space, about the size of a dry cleaner's. Nestled between the Angelo Pizza Company and Reef's Tropical Fish and Pets, the store developed a strong base of customers. There was Jay McCracken, an avid collector who was the western region sales manager for Nestlé Foods. There was Randy Duvall, a termite inspector who popped in between house calls; and Tom Geideman, a teenager who seemed to know every man who ever played in the major leagues and each player in the minors with big league potential.

Even with Hemrick's inventory, the store struggled. Hemrick worked 20-hour days, often sleeping on a couch in the storeroom. Marx pumped in $100 or $200 a week to keep The Upper Deck going. Some weeks the store made only $400. But Bill and Linda Hemrick had a rule: They never touched their savings. They lived off their income. One night McCracken and Hemrick stopped at McDonald's and Hemrick didn't have any money. McCracken, assuming Hemrick just needed to drop by an ATM, bought him dinner. Later he realized Hemrick couldn't afford to eat unless he touched the savings, which he had vowed he would not do.

Each day, it seemed, was an educational experience for the owners of The Upper Deck. The two men—Marx, at 34, was 14 years younger than Hemrick—learned the business from their customers, most of whom were 10- to 13-year-old boys.

The kids had discovered a way to find the best players among unopened packs of cards, particularly the ones packaged in cellophane. By looking at the card visible on the top of the pack, the youngsters could determine what other cards were in the pack since the collating machines for Topps, Fleer, and Donruss placed baseball cards in consistent sequences at the time. Jose Canseco, for instance, might always follow Rafael Belliard. Darryl Strawberry would come three cards after Billy Ripken. Donruss packaged most of its cards in colored "wax" packaging, but the bottom card was usually visible through the wrapper. Some dealers, armed with the secret sequences, cherry picked through boxes of cards and took out the packs that contained the most desirable cards. Since they were not opening the other packs, they could sell the rest of the cards.

When Hemrick realized what was happening, he was furious. Not at the kids but at the manufacturers. Wasn't it bad enough that the Topps cards—which in 1986 had red backs with black writing—were difficult to sort without straining the eyes? How hard could it be to mix the cards randomly? "If I was a manufacturer, I'd do things differently," he would tell Marx. "I'd have random sequencing and I'd print them on white card stock with some big old black numbers with circles around them so guys like me who sort cards 20 hours a day won't go blind."

And, most of all, he would do something to prevent counterfeiting.

■ ■ ■

Like Bill Hemrick, Paul Sumner was also going through a "mid-life crisis" in the summer of 1987. At 41, he had risen to vice president of sales at Orbis Graphic Arts, an Anaheim company best known for enhancing film for *Architectural Digest* magazine. The company's expertise was in color separation, a process where it took photographic film, improved the color quality, and readied it for printing. Like any firm involved in the printing business, Orbis's success depended on a constant flow of contracts and on keeping its facility going around the clock. Sumner's job was to solicit new business and keep the company busy.

With an experienced staff, Orbis's work featured stunning designs and bold, crisp colors that their competitors could not match. That didn't mean customers were knocking down the door. Since much of Orbis's equipment had been financed when the interest rate was 19 percent, it had to keep its prices at a premium. Other graphic arts companies had cheaper rates, but Sumner brought a steady flow of clients to Orbis. Sumner promised companies that no one could do a better job than Orbis with their annual report, catalog, or sales presentation. "We might be a little more expensive," he would tell prospective customers. "But you cannot get a better quality color separation job anywhere."

"People will pay more for quality," Sumner was fond of saying. "They'll gripe and moan initially, but once they see our product, they'll forget about the cost."

He was very convincing. As a deacon for the United Church of Christ, Sumner had become a captivating speaker and brought the same passion he had for his faith to his sales. In the mid-1980s, Orbis did $4–5 million in printing annually, and Sumner was usually responsible for half of the revenue. "No one could sell print jobs like Paul," recalled Greg Green, who worked with Sumner at Orbis and later at Upper Deck. "He was a born salesman."

Trouble was, he wasn't born to sell. If Sumner were a man who had aspired to a career in sales and marketing, he would have considered himself a success. But he was Paul Sumner, scientist and inventor. As a graduate student at Cal State–Long Beach between 1972 and 75, he was part of a team of students that developed the white light projection hologram which would become the standard on credit cards a decade later, serving as an anti-counterfeiting device. Sumner's education included an associate's degree in aeronautical engineering and postgraduate work in laser sculpture. His bachelor's degree was in marketing, but that was only so he'd never have someone else making money off his ideas and taking most of the credit.

He wasn't just a salesman. At Orbis, he was the expert on camera operations, computerized make-up systems, and laser scanners. He did everything but own the company. He liked working for Boris Korbel, the Czechoslovak owner of Orbis. But by the summer of '87, he realized he had become what he most feared: a guy working for someone else who made money off his ideas and took most of the credit—at least financially.

Once a year, Sumner took inventory of his life to see what he could do differently. It was a practice he learned from his late father, Merton Donovan Sumner, who had once written a book entitled *HARP: Humanistic Alcoholic Recovery Program.* Paul Sumner would ask his wife, Cindy: "What can I do with this body of knowledge I have?"

Cindy had no idea, but thought opening a hobby store would be a good diversion. So Sumner spent his weekends driving all over Orange County looking at hobby stores. He went in shops that sold antiques, dolls, dollhouses, model trains, coins, and comic books. In August of 1987, he purchased $400 worth of comic books. As the owner of the comic book store rang up the sale, Sumner mentioned he was planning to open his own hobby shop. "You might want to think about selling baseball cards," he said.

"Baseball cards?" Sumner asked. "You're kidding."

The store owner then told Sumner how baseball card collecting had become big business. He mentioned the Mattingly card selling for $90.

After ten minutes, Sumner had heard enough. He went home and told Cindy: "This is it. We'll start with baseball cards and comic books, and then we'll bring in dollhouses, model railroads, and coins. A family will walk into the store and they'll have to buy something because we've got everyone covered."

Cindy pondered the proposal. She was used to Paul's wild ideas. It seemed he came up with a new one every week. This time, though, he seemed serious. But, like Linda Hemrick, she had her doubts.

"Baseball cards?" she asked.

■ ■ ■

Bill Hemrick was upset. The store had been open for two weeks and it was still a mess. There were cards stacked in piles all over the tiny shop waiting to be sorted. It looked like someone was getting ready to build a house of cards.

The customer wanted to know when Hemrick would have the store straightened out. "Give me a couple weeks," Hemrick said.

"Thanks," replied Paul Sumner, who drove home wondering if the comic book store owner hadn't exaggerated the growth of the baseball card market. There was no way that that disorganized, hole-in-the-wall store he had just visited was going to make any money. His three-year-old son's bedroom was tidier.

Two weeks later, shortly before Labor Day, 1987, Sumner returned to the store. By now, the cards were sorted and filed and the store even had a name: The Upper Deck. Sumner noticed three brands of cards on display: Topps, Fleer, and Donruss.

"Which one is the best?" he asked Hemrick.

"This year, it seems like Donruss did the best job."

"Can I see a couple?"

Hemrick had a counterfeit Mattingly framed on the wall. If nothing else, it was a conversation piece. He put the card on the counter in front of Sumner, alongside a real Mattingly.

Sumner pointed at the fake card. "Hey, that card's been rescreened."

Hemrick could not believe it. It had taken him months to figure out the cards were counterfeits. Even now, veteran dealers had to look at cards closely to tell the difference. "How'd you know that?"

"I've been in the printing business for 15 years and it's easy for me to tell when something's been rescreened. Does this happen a lot?"

Hemrick told Sumner about the Mattinglys he had purchased. Counterfeiting was going to become a big problem, he said, because cards were so easy to duplicate. "If I could find a way to do it," Hemrick said, "I'd like to start a company that can prevent this from happening."

Sumner stared at the Mattingly cards. *That's it!* he thought. That's what he could do with the sum of his knowledge. He knew printing and he knew how to prevent counterfeiting. Just stick a hologram on a baseball card, like a Mastercard or Visa. Had no one thought of that before? These cards were produced on cheap cardboard. The color separations weren't nearly as vivid as the stuff they did at Orbis. He could produce a better baseball card. They might cost more, but people would be willing to pay for quality. Certainly this Hemrick guy would pay for cards he knew weren't counterfeit.

Sumner explained his role at Orbis, and the company's work in color separation. If they could produce high-quality film for *Architectural Digest,* they could certainly produce baseball cards. "You could prevent counterfeiting by putting a hologram on the card," Sumner said.

Both men were excited. "We could start a new card company," Hemrick said. "I'd be willing to venture what I have."

"I'll ask my boss and let you know," said Sumner, who rushed home to tell Cindy.

Cindy shook her head. "I thought you just wanted to *sell* baseball cards?"

■ ■ ■

DeWayne Buice was hungry. Standing in front of the locked door of Sun's Chinese Restaurant, in a strip mall at the corner of State College Boulevard and La Palma Avenue, the relief pitcher for the California Angels surveyed his options. There was a Black Angus across the parking lot and an Angelo Pizza Company three doors down from Sun's. In between there was Reef's Tropical Fish and Pets and The Upper Deck baseball card shop.

"Pizza?" his roommate Larry asked.

"No, I'm in the mood for Chinese. Let's ask the people in here if there's another one around."

Buice (pronounced "Bice") and Larry went into The Upper Deck. It was shortly before Thanksgiving, 1987. The baseball season had been over for six weeks. "Hey buddy," Buice said to Jeff Marx. "You got any cards of me?"

"I don't know," Marx replied. "Who are you?"

Bill Hemrick was in the back of the store sorting cards when he noticed Buice. "Jeff, don't you know who this is? This is DeWayne Buice."

Marx apologized. He had season tickets to the California Angels and should have recognized Buice, who had finished the year with 17 saves—a team record for an Angels rookie. Of course, Buice wasn't your typical rookie, having spent 10 years in the minors before making it to the Angels at the age of 29. Still, big leaguers didn't walk into The Upper Deck every day. Seeing Buice standing there, Marx was struck by a sudden inspiration. Other card shops had hired players to sign autographs on Saturday afternoons. They usually broke even on the deal; they'd pay the player in cash up front and charge for autographs depending on the fee and who the player was. "You ever do any autograph signings?" Marx asked.

Larry bit his lip to keep from laughing. *Who would want DeWayne Buice's autograph?* But Marx was serious, and so was Buice. "Let me check with my agent," he said.

A few days later, Buice called Marx. His agent, Bob Cohen (a different Bob Cohen from the one who had bought the Mickey Mantle rookie cards at the Philadelphia show in 1980), said Buice could sign at Upper Deck for two hours on December 19. It would cost $400. "Fine," Marx said. "Have Bob call us and we'll set it up."

Marx hung up the phone and told Hemrick, who exploded. "That's the last Saturday before Christmas! People are going to be out Christmas shopping. Do you know anyone who wants a DeWayne Buice signed photo for Christmas? I sure as hell don't. And where are we going to get four hundred bucks?"

Over the next two weeks, the two owners argued. "This guy's had one good year in the majors," Hemrick said. "He's 30 years old. It's not like he's going to the Hall of Fame."

But Marx liked Buice. Unlike other players he had met, Buice seemed like a regular guy. Spending a decade in the minors, living in cheap motels and eating macaroni and cheese every night, probably gave the guy a healthy dose of perspective. Plus, Buice was hilarious. He could do impersonations of the Munchkins from *The Wizard of Oz* and a perfect Maxwell Smart. "He'd be great in the store, Bill. Kids will love him."

Jay McCracken, the western region sales manager for Nestlé who frequented The Upper Deck, was also an amateur photographer. He said he could print up 100 photos for 75 cents a print. "Look," Marx told Hemrick, "if no one shows up, we'll have DeWayne sign them all for us. We can sell them in the store for five bucks each."

Hemrick reluctantly agreed. Marx took out an ad in *The Orange County Register*. They would charge $2 for Buice's autograph. If 200 people showed up, they would break even.

On the day of the appearance, Buice was late. It was 12:10 and already there were 200 people wrapped around the outside of the store, past Reef's Tropical Fish and Pets and Sun's Chinese Restaurant. Hemrick was frantic. This, he was sure, would ruin him.

"Where the hell is he?" he asked Marx.

"Relax, he'll be here."

The two had barely scraped up the $400, and Buice assured them he would arrive from an overnight trip to Las Vegas in time for the signing. If they lost the $400, Hemrick and Marx knew, they would have to close The Upper Deck and Hemrick would have no money to start a card company with Sumner.

At 12:15, Buice arrived. As angry as Hemrick was, he couldn't yell at Buice in front of the crowd. McCracken escorted Buice inside, and sat with him for two hours, collecting autograph tickets and keeping the line moving. Buice signed over 300 items, including photos, balls, and baseball cards. Despite Hemrick's fears, the day was a success. The Upper Deck came out $200 ahead on the Buice signing, along with the additional sales generated by the increased traffic in the store.

Hemrick was stunned. Buice had become a folk hero to Angels fans. Maybe he could help them get their card company off the ground. Buice finished the last of the autographs and got up to leave. The two spoke briefly about the card manufacturing idea and agreed to talk again soon.

■ ■ ■

In January of 1988, Sumner, Hemrick, and Marx met at the Angelo Pizza Company adjacent to The Upper Deck. On a yellow legal pad, they wrote out the original plan for the card manufacturing company. Sumner would provide the equipment and supplies through Orbis Graphic Arts to print the cards. Hemrick, in turn, would help secure the financing as well as the license from the Major League Baseball Players Association to produce the cards. Sumner and Hemrick would each own 50 percent of the company.

Marx wanted to be part of the company, but reluctantly declined. He liked the idea, but it was too big a risk. He was putting his sons Jeff, Jr., 10, and Justin, 6, through Catholic school and it was a struggle to pay bills with income from The Upper Deck and his modest salary at Ford Aerospace. As a divorcee, he got to play mother and father, picking the boys up at Little League baseball practice after work, fixing dinner, then going to work at The Upper Deck with Hemrick.

It wasn't as rough as it had been. Before he was far enough ahead to invest in The Upper Deck, Marx would raise extra money by taking a couple boxes of Olympic pins and baseball cards and setting up at weekend card shows at malls. Jeff, Jr., and Justin would tag along, often taking naps under the table in sleeping bags. The $150 he averaged at mall shows often put the family ahead for the month. "We'd go out and buy a steak dinner instead of beans," Marx recalled. "It was a true hustle."

Although Marx now pumped hundreds of dollars into The Upper Deck each month, there was no way he could quit Ford Aerospace to join Hemrick and Sumner. Still, he wanted to help where he could.

"What are we going to call this company?" Sumner asked.

Marx took a sip from his beer. "Why not Upper Deck? Upper sounds like high end, deck like a deck of cards."

"I like it," Sumner said.

It was settled. They had just formed the Upper Deck Company, dedicated to producing the highest quality cards in the business. As Hemrick walked Sumner out to his car, Marx looked at the yellow legal pad and finished his beer. *Too bad I can't be involved in this,* he thought to himself.

Sumner and Hemrick were still talking outside. Marx sighed and picked up the check.

■ ■ ■

In January of 1988, Lauren Rich picked up the phone in the New York office of the Major League Baseball Players Association. A man named Bill Hemrick was on the line, insisting he could make revolutionary new baseball cards if only she would grant him a license to do so.

It was the type of call the assistant director of the Players Association received often. Everyone had a new way to reinvent the wheel and if only she'd give them a license, they could make millions for the PA. Rich always thought it was funny that the callers never mentioned the millions they could make for themselves.

With the card industry booming, Rich held the keys to the gold mine. Dozens of card companies and printing operations were lobbying her for "the next license." Her standard reply was that there would be no next license, at least not until 1991. The PA had just allowed a fourth company, Score, to produce cards for 1988. In just seven years, the number of card manufacturers had quadrupled. Licensing revenues were over $30 million annually, and baseball cards accounted for 90 percent of the windfall. But there was a danger of saturating the market. Revenues could decrease dramatically if collectors were turned off by a glut of cards.

Ultimately, licensing decisions belonged to her boss, Donald Fehr, who had succeeded Marvin Miller as executive director of the Players Association. Companies hoping to produce merchandise depicting the images of major league baseball players also had to be approved by a ten-player licensing committee. But both Fehr and the licensing committee usually went along with Rich's recommendations. It was her job to filter out the riffraff from the promising business proposals. Hemrick seemed to fit into the former category.

"I'm sorry, Mr. Hemrick," she said. "But there won't be any more licenses until 1991."

She was going to hang up, and Hemrick knew he would not get another chance to make his pitch. He told her about the Mattingly counterfeits and how baseball players were getting ripped off. So was the Players Association, which was not getting its true share of licensing revenues.

"I have the best baseball cards you can imagine right here," Hemrick said. "You may not think you need any more card companies, but you need something to stop this counterfeit problem."

Hemrick heard nothing but dead air. Was she still there, he wondered?

"Look, Mr. Hemrick," she said finally, "any prospective card manufacturer needs to give us a $1.5 million letter of credit up front."

This is great, Hemrick thought. *At least she's leaving open the possibility of licensing another company.*

"Fine," Hemrick said. "Should I make the check payable to the Major League Baseball Players Association?"

"No, no, no. We have an application process. We'll need to see a proposal, and ultimately some prototype cards. Let us know when you have those materials available."

Hemrick hung up the phone. *This might just work,* he thought. Of course, he had no idea where he would get $1.5 million dollars or even how to produce a prototype baseball card. Plus, he didn't get the impression from Rich that Upper Deck had a prayer of obtaining a license. He needed someone who could influence the Players Association. He called Buice and set up a meeting at Angelo's Pizza.

At Angelo's, Sumner and Hemrick promised Buice a 10 percent stake in Upper Deck if he helped them secure a license. They also needed him to pose for a prototype card. Most importantly, they wanted another player. They needed two prototype cards and one had to be of a star-caliber player. Buice was popular in Southern California, but they had to have someone with national appeal.

"Who'd you have in mind?" Buice asked.

"Wally Joyner," Hemrick said.

At 25, Joyner was the Angels' All-American boy. In 1986, he had finished second in the American League Rookie of the Year balloting to Jose Canseco after hitting .290 with 22 home runs and 100 RBI. He had improved in 1987, hitting 34 homers and driving in 117 runs. Born in Atlanta, Joyner was a devout Mormon who spoke with a slight Georgia drawl. He would be the perfect spokesman for Upper Deck.

Two days later, Buice called Hemrick. "Wally will do it for $300."

Three hundred bucks, Hemrick thought. *That's cheaper than Buice.*

■ ■ ■

The photo shoot for Buice was scheduled for President's Day, 1988, at Anaheim Stadium. Buice had received permission from the Angels to use the park and to be photographed in an Angels uniform, provided the prototype cards were only used for promotional purposes. Technically, the club was due a licensing fee, so the Angels charged Upper Deck the princely sum of one dollar.

Hemrick, Sumner, Marx, and McCracken—the Nestlé vice president who frequented The Upper Deck—met Buice at the stadium, but there was no sign that a baseball field had ever existed. Since it was February, and both the Angels and Los Angeles Rams were not playing, the stadium was the home of Mickey Thompson's off-road supercross. Instead of an athletic field, the stadium floor was covered by tons of dirt that had been molded into a track for motorcycles. The group had hoped to shoot Buice from the pitcher's mound against the backdrop of the stadium, but since the field was covered in mud, Buice's photo shoot had to take place in the bullpen. The photo ultimately chosen for the card was a close-up head shot.

Joyner was to be photographed at the stadium the next day, but the Upper Deck owners had him go to Cal State–Fullerton instead. Joyner pulled up in his Mercedes, changed into his uniform, and signed autographs for the four men. McCracken even had him pose with a box of Nestlé Crunch bars.

It looked more like a fantasy baseball camp than a photo shoot. The four took turns pitching to Joyner while the others shot the pictures. When it was over, Hemrick reached for his checkbook only to discover he had left it at The Upper Deck. Marx, who wasn't part of the venture, ran back to his van, where he had a personal check in the glove compartment. He wrote it out for $300 to Joyner, who held it next to his face and smiled. Someone took a picture.

As Joyner drove off, he wondered what Buice had gotten him into. He smiled to himself. *These guys think they can start a card company?*

6

Mac

While Paul Sumner, Bill Hemrick, and the regulars from The Upper Deck card shop tried to get their baseball card manufacturing idea off the ground, the rest of Upper Deck's future launch team was forming out of the offices of Orbis Graphic Arts. It was from this group that the central figure of Upper Deck would emerge: Richard "Mac" McWilliam.

Boris Korbel, the owner and president of Orbis, had a network of business associates to call upon to help organize what would become the Upper Deck Company. Many were more than just business associates; they were also his friends. Korbel, who had immigrated to the U.S. from Czechoslovakia in the mid-1970s, loved to entertain, both at home and at restaurants throughout Orange County. An elegant man with a wry, self-deprecating sense of humor to go with his thick accent and somewhat broken English, Korbel was immensely popular. Business acquaintances soon found themselves dining regularly with Korbel and attending parties he hosted, particularly his lavish Christmas and Super Bowl Sunday celebrations.

Among his group of business-related friends were three men who in 1971 had graduated together from Servite High School in Anaheim: Richard McWilliam, Andrew Prendiville, and Anthony Passante. Prendiville had met Korbel in August of 1980 at Tustin Community Hospital in Santa Ana after a car accident had left Korbel a quadriplegic. Prendiville, who had graduated from the University of California–San Diego law school, had just passed the California bar and begun practice as an accident litigator and personal injury attorney. A fellow Servite alum had called and told him about Korbel.

Prendiville negotiated a settlement for Korbel, who remained a quadriplegic for nearly a year. But he worked hard at his rehabilitation, walking first with braces, then crutches, and finally a cane. The two remained in touch and in 1981, when Korbel was looking for a corporate attorney to represent Orbis, Prendiville recommended another Servite alum, Passante. During that same year, Prendiville took Korbel to dinner and introduced him to an accountant friend of his, the third Servite alum, McWilliam.

That the Servite class of 1971 had remained close after ten years came as little surprise. For four years, the class had grown together, united by the Vietnam War, Woodstock, and the tumultuous 1960s. But even if the period of 1967–71 had not been a troubled one in U.S. history, the Servite atmosphere might have kept them together anyhow. Run by the Servites, a Catholic order of Jesuit brothers, the school in 1971 was an all-boys college prep academy of 600 students. Each day began with prayer, and masses were offered on holy days of obligation. Religion classes were included among the school's core curriculum of math, science, English, and foreign languages. Students learned why the church frowned on abortion, premarital sex, and masturbation—unpleasant news for Catholic boys just coming out of puberty who had not one, but three sister high schools of young Catholic girls in Orange County.

Nearly 100 percent of Servite graduates went on to college. And those underclassmen who did not take either their studies or Servite's strict discipline seriously found themselves transferring to public school. While Servite boys did not have to wear uniforms, collar shirts were required and jeans were strictly forbidden. Servite did not allow its boys to grow sideburns, and students were subjected to hair inspections to make sure they were not following the style of the day and growing their hair below the collar. It was a strict disciplinary code; in gym class, the boys were checked to make sure they were wearing athletic supporters. Violators were subjected to swats on the buttocks with a large wooden paddle. All in all, the lessons taught at Servite were a perfect fit for Orange County's ultraconservative political bent.

"We really became a close-knit bunch," said Chip Steeves, a Servite '71 class member who later joined Upper Deck as a security officer. "It seemed to breed a real us-versus-them mentality. It was as if we were all survivors together."

"Everyone in that school was someone you'd consider your friend," Passante said. "You had people from the very rich to the not so well off, but you were accepted because—whatever your financial status—you had the common ground of a strong Catholic upbringing."

Servite's social scene centered around its successful football team, which through the years has produced several professional players, most notably offensive lineman Blaine Nye (Servite class of 1964) and quarterback Steve Beuerlein (class of 1983). Sports played a major role at Servite, which taught that a healthy mind and body were dependent on one another. With only 600 students, there were team openings for anyone with modest talent and a willingness to play hard.

For McWilliam, an often sick boy who came from a modest financial background, playing sports was a luxury he could not afford.

■ ■ ■

Richard Patrick McWilliam was born October 20, 1953, the third of four children. His father had immigrated to the U.S. from Aberdeen, Scotland; his mother's ancestors were French.

In an interview for this book, McWilliam said that his father—now deceased—was defrauded out of a government loan and forced to bankrupt his business when Richard was 10. His mother went to work to support the family at Beckman Instruments near the McWilliams' home in Fullerton.

A year later, at the age of 11, Richard was the victim of food poisoning. Something had been mixed in with some mushrooms he had eaten, causing his heart to stop. He was rushed to a hospital and stabilized, so he quickly recovered. But over the next five years, he needed eleven follow-up surgeries, causing him to miss school for weeks at a time. He ran track as a freshman at Servite and played intramural sports through his sophomore year. But after certain procedures, the doctors would order him to stay away from physical activity for up to three weeks, which kept him from making a further commitment to Servite sports. (In a written response to queries for this book, McWilliam modified what he said in an earlier interview, saying he had "several surgeries" but denying that he had serious stomach problems. McWilliam said he has not had any physical difficulties since the age of 16.)

"My enduring memory of him in high school," one classmate recalled, "was seeing him at parties with a beer in one hand and a bottle of antacid in the other. I'd ask him why he was drinking if it bothered him so much. It wasn't so much that he wanted to drink but that he wanted to beat his stomach problems once and for all. It was like he was going to get over it by sheer force of will, as if he was going to drink beer even if he had to wash it down with a Maalox chaser."

The two childhood events, the bankruptcy of his father's business and his brush with death at 11, had a lasting effect on McWilliam. He worked tirelessly to make a better life for himself, going through a series of jobs and business ventures in high school and developing an interest in daredevil activities such as motorcycles, skiing, and surfing—high-adrenaline endeavors that do not attract the faint at heart.

"He was a risk taker, you knew it even then," said Frank Krogman, a friend from Servite. "He had cheated death once and was going to make the most of the rest of his life. We used to go skiing on sheets of ice. You'd go a half a mile down the mountain before you could stop. It was pretty dangerous, but Mac would go down balls out. He used to get pretty roughed up when he fell."

Mac, short for McWilliam. Someone stuck the name on him early at Servite. To family, he always was Richard, never Richie or Rich or Rick or Dick. But at school, he was Mac.

As a boy growing up in Fullerton, McWilliam never thought of his family as less fortunate than anyone else. But when he entered Servite in the fall of 1967, at the age of 13, he began to notice the wealthier areas of Orange County. The McWilliams could afford Servite's tuition of $650 a year, but Richard found that his family was on the low end of Servite's economic class structure. Many of his classmates, the children of doctors and lawyers from the upscale Irvine and Newport Beach communities, arrived at school in luxury automobiles.

"It was rough for us," McWilliam recalled. "But I didn't really think about the money part of it. If you don't have money, you don't know what it means. Now the surgeries I went through, *that* was rough."

When he began high school, McWilliam had built a modest, two-year-old lawn mowing business. In high school, while many of his classmates focused on sports, McWilliam worked after school. He took a job at Montgomery Ward's "Buffeteria," handling patrons as they went through the cafeteria-style service line. During the summers, he went to work for a cardboard manufacturer, laboring for 10-to-12 hour shifts. It was grueling duty, a lot of cutting, lifting, and stacking. McWilliam would come home with cuts on his hands and covered with glaze and glue that coated the cardboard boxes. But the company paid well— $3.70 an hour for starters—and McWilliam took as many hours as he could get.

Unlike his wealthier friends who worked after school for play money, McWilliam spent his money conservatively, saving and investing as much as possible. He constantly found ways to make money. He became a proficient auto and motorcycle mechanic, earning cash by fixing up old cars and bikes and selling them at a profit. He even, ironically, became one of the first in his class to drive to school— beating out many of his well-heeled classmates—driving a chocolate-colored van loaded with curtains and wood paneling. Not surprisingly, the young entrepreneur excelled in math. But with his work and other ventures, he had no time for the math club or much else in the way of extracurricular school activities. His entry in the senior yearbook lists his brief athletic experiences, along with Chess Club and something called the Junior Classical League.

"He had a phenomenal quest to not be as poor as his dad," said John Cvengros, a Servite classmate. "His dad worked long and hard but didn't seem to make as much money as he wanted to."

In the spring of 1971, the Servite seniors faced the prospect, albeit a remote one, of the draft and going to Vietnam. The draft had quieted down and the students did not worry about going to southeast Asia. Most had high draft numbers and, since all were planning to go to college, there were always deferments to fall back on. Certainly none of them *wanted* to go to Vietnam. Even in Orange County, the heart of Richard Nixon territory, support for the war had become nonexistent. Servite seniors were among the regulars at protest rallies in Fullerton.

After graduation, the first thing McWilliam did was grow a mustache and long hair. Whenever friends saw him, he was on a motorcycle, looking like someone out of the movie *Easy Rider.* Much of the Servite class of '71 stayed in southern

California for college and kept in touch through weekly poker games and by attending sporting events and concerts. McWilliam, who spent the first nine months after graduation working at the cardboard factory to earn enough money for college, usually was too busy. But if his favorite band, Jethro Tull, was playing, he would be the first to line up the tickets and plan the post-concert party.

McWilliam and fellow Servite alum Krogman started college together at Fullerton Junior College. The two, who had spent much of their high school years on skis and motorcycles, figured their love of the outdoors made them naturals for Fullerton's forestry and ecology program. They soon discovered otherwise, switching majors and earning associate degrees in business. McWilliam moved on to San Diego State University for a semester, then transferred to Cal State–Fullerton, where he received a degree in economics and accounting in 1976. "When he was 20 or 21, I remember him telling me, 'I'm going to be retired by the time I'm 40,'" Krogman said. "It was obvious he was talking about retiring as a millionaire. He was always very serious about that."

After graduation, McWilliam moved to Huntington Beach and went to work for the accounting firm of Main Hurdman. For much of his three years with Main Hurdman, he audited movie studios, commuting daily to Los Angeles and Culver City. In 1978, he borrowed money from his mother—his father died while he was in college—to buy his first home in Huntington Beach. "I was only making $12,000 a year," McWilliam recalled. "It wasn't what I expected. I mean, you go to school for five years like I did and you're only making $12,000 a year?"

In 1980, McWilliam, who had advanced to the position of audit supervisor, quit Main Hurdman and opened his own accounting practice, Richard P. McWilliam, C.P.A. The following year, Prendiville introduced him to Korbel and McWilliam began doing personal accounting work for Korbel as well as corporate work for his company, Orbis Graphic Arts. Through Prendiville and his younger brother, ophthalmologist Kevin Prendiville, McWilliam met another client, Dr. Kent Lehman, who ran Lehman Medical Clinics, Inc., in Orange County. Gradually, McWilliam built a lucrative business of loyal customers. Clients were pleased with the fast turnaround they received from McWilliam, a man who worked 18-hour days and never seemed to sleep.

After so many years of struggling financially, McWilliam now had discretionary income, which he poured into the booming southern California real estate market of the early 1980s. He purchased a second home in Corona del Mar and four triplexes in Orange County. Just as he had fixed up old cars and motorcycles in high school, he found he could purchase an undervalued building, make some improvements, and double his money.

By the time he turned 30, McWilliam had become a successful young entrepreneur and, according to people who knew him at the time, a millionaire. He opened his Huntington Beach home to parties, drawing from an extended network of friends and acquaintances from Servite and college for weekends of surfing, water skiing, and jet skiing. Guests were greeted by the familiar sounds of Jethro Tull, particularly "Bungle in the Jungle." But the lessons of McWilliam's youth left him extremely conservative with his money. Although he was a gracious host—friends knew they could call on Mac at any time of the night—he developed a reputation as a cheapskate.

"He was the type of guy who would invite you to a barbecue and tell you to bring your own chicken," John Cvengros said.

"One time a bunch of us went to a fancy restaurant," Andrew Prendiville recalled. "By now, he has a lot of money. The check comes and is placed by coincidence at Mac, who pulls out a calculator and tells everyone their share."

Afterward, Prendiville took McWilliam aside and ripped into him. "What's up with you? You should have picked up the tab and everyone would have sent you money later. If they didn't, then don't worry about it. You should just thank the Lord for what you have."

On September 28, 1986, McWilliam was married in Huntington Beach. Among the groomsmen were Prendiville and McWilliam's brother, George. As the wedding party set up for photos, George complained that Richard had made him pay for his own tuxedo.

Prendiville was stunned. "You're kidding? Your own brother wouldn't pay for your tux."

George laughed. "My brother! You mean, Fort Knox?"

After the reception, held at the Sea View Country Club in Huntington Beach, Prendiville was approached by a group of waitresses. "They told me, 'You folks were a lot of fun,'" Prendiville recalled. "'But you were our first cash bar ever.'"

According to Prendiville, the wedding guests spent over $2,000 on alcohol when for $400, the Sea View Country Club offered an unlimited open bar. Traditionally that would be the financial responsibility of the groom. (McWilliam, who had Passante draw up a prenuptial agreement, divorced in 1989.)

■ ■ ■

In the weeks leading up to his wedding, McWilliam sold his business and went to work for Lehman Medical Clinics. There he used his expertise in real estate to seek out, purchase, and develop sites for new clinics. Not long after McWilliam joined Lehman full-time, he met Mike Berkus, who was then working for a telemarketing firm that had been retained by Lehman to research customer awareness. Berkus had moonlighted as a traveling baseball card buyer in the 1970s and helped organize the first National Sports Collectors Convention in 1980. For Lehman, Berkus researched the medical field, interviewing doctors and nurses and trying to figure out how the profession could return to what it was originally intended to be—a service industry.

Berkus's pet peeve was that people did not want to wait for hours to see a doctor, especially when they were sick. Wasn't there any way patients could be pre-registered over the phone so that when they arrived at a clinic they would not have to go through a mountain of paperwork? He was amazed at the aloofness of doctors. "Do you realize how long these people wait to see you?" he asked. "No, you don't, do you? Lehman Medical is trying to turn this into a service industry and they can't do it without you. Nurses and receptionists can do everything right, but patients still have to wait for you in some little room."

Berkus's arguments made sense to McWilliam, but it was impossible to change the medical profession overnight. While their paths would not cross for three more years, Mike Berkus had made a lasting impression on Richard McWilliam.

■ ■ ■

Shortly before Christmas, 1987, the same weekend DeWayne Buice signed autographs at The Upper Deck card shop, Boris Korbel held a holiday party on a boat called the *Spirit of St. Louis,* which was docked behind the Rusty Pelican restaurant in Newport Beach. During the party, Andrew Prendiville went out for a smoke and ran into McWilliam. The two men, now 34, stood along one side of the boat, away from the others.

"You know, Mac," Prendiville said, half-sarcastically, "it sure is funny how you always end up with the best of everything."

McWilliam took a drag from his cigarette, and gazed out at the water. "Andy," he said, "I believe you reap what you sow."

Prendiville looked at McWilliam and chuckled. He had not heard such a platitude since their days at Servite. It seemed funny coming from McWilliam, a man not normally given to introspection. Still, it made sense in an odd sort of way. For as long as he had known him, McWilliam had worked 18-hour days, whether it was in his garage working on bikes, in his own business cranking out tax returns, or setting up medical clinics for Lehman. "My old man worked his ass off for me," McWilliam would tell him. "I'll outwork anyone."

Nobody worked harder than Mac, Prendiville thought, but it seemed like he possessed an inordinate amount of luck. The guy seemed to have a Midas touch.

McWilliam and Prendiville finished their cigarettes and rejoined the party. McWilliam's good fortune had only just begun.

■ ■ ■

By the beginning of 1988, McWilliam again was ready for a change. He had spent twelve years as an accountant and real estate entrepreneur and had grown tired of putting on a suit and tie every morning.

In late February, he received a call from Korbel, whom he had not spoken with since he sold his accounting firm and went to work for Lehman. Korbel said one of his employees, Paul Sumner, had come up with an idea for a revolutionary new baseball card. Two major league baseball players were involved, the California Angels' Wally Joyner and DeWayne Buice, and Sumner had gone so far as to take photos of them to use for prototype baseball cards.

McWilliam and Korbel met for lunch. Korbel said that while they were not yet looking for an investor, they probably would need one. If McWilliam were to become involved, Korbel said, he would need to sign a confidentiality agreement.

"No problem," McWilliam said.

The company was called Upper Deck, named after a local card shop Sumner had stumbled into when he got the idea to make a better baseball card. McWilliam's proposed role, Korbel said, would be to bring in capital for Upper Deck through his own holdings or from other investors. Korbel was not sure how much money they would need, but there was talk of letters of credit to Major League Baseball and its Players Association. Orbis could handle the initial color separations, but a print site would have to be acquired.

McWilliam nodded. Korbel said Anthony Passante, who was serving as the company's corporate counsel, would draw up the paperwork. An organizational meeting was scheduled for March 10, 1988.

"I'll be there," McWilliam said.

7

On Deck

On that tenth day of March, 1988, the first organizational meeting of the Upper Deck Company was held at 6:00 P.M. at Orbis Graphic Arts. Present were Paul Sumner, Boris Korbel, Richard McWilliam, Anthony Passante, DeWayne Buice, and Bill Hemrick.

Buice, who was two weeks into spring training, flew into Orange County Airport following the Angels' afternoon game with the Cleveland Indians in Tucson, Arizona. The Indians, helped by two Wally Joyner errors, won 6–2.

Sumner, as Upper Deck president, brought the meeting to order. "Gentlemen," he said, "we stand here this evening to begin a wondrous journey together. I would like to begin by reciting our corporate prayer. If you would all please bow your heads."

McWilliam and Passante looked at each other, both apparently thinking the same thing. *Corporate prayer?* It seemed to Passante like something they might do at Servite, where classes often began with prayer. But maybe Sumner had the right idea; they'd need a little help from above to launch Upper Deck.

"Dear God," Sumner began. "Here we are, the group of us, creating a new corporation. The Upper Deck Company—it's like having a little baby, so fresh and young and tender. Give us the wisdom and strength to guide ourselves through this place called Earth. Give us the knowledge to raise this entity with poise and confidence. Help us to lay our foundation on sound principles and to organize its power in such a form, as it will be, to most likely effect its safety and happiness. And for the support of this endeavor with a firm reliance on the protection of divine providence, we mutually pledge to each other our sacred honor—Amen."

"Amen," the other five men said in unison.

McWilliam and Korbel proposed that Passante be retained as Upper Deck's corporate counsel. There were no objections and Passante was officially hired. Next was the matter of stock distributions. The original agreement between Sumner, Hemrick, and Buice, composed on the yellow legal pad at Angelo's Pizza, was forgotten since Hemrick had not obtained a license from the Players Association nor generated the financing for the company.

Under the new plan, Sumner, as founder and president, would receive 430 of the 1,000 shares. Korbel would get 170 shares and hold the title of vice president of manufacturing, creating a strange business relationship between him and Sumner. As owner of Orbis, Korbel would provide the initial production facilities for Upper Deck. He also was Sumner's boss, even though he would report to Sumner as an Upper Deck vice president.

Hemrick was appointed vice president of marketing and given 170 shares— much less than the 50 percent he started with at Angelo's. Buice was awarded 120 shares on the condition that he help obtain the license to print from the Players Association. McWilliam would receive 110 shares if he provided Upper Deck with the initial start-up money and secured an investor who would back the launch.

The meeting was adjourned after two hours, and the company incorporated twelve days later. On April 7, Passante issued the stock certificates.

■ ■ ■

The brochure was entitled "The Corporation." Written by Sumner, it included pictures and capsule profiles of the seven men involved in Upper Deck: Sumner, Korbel, Hemrick, Buice, McWilliam, Passante, and Joyner. It was to be sent to the Major League Baseball Players Association, Major League Baseball Properties, and other groups Upper Deck would do business with, as an introduction to the company. Like much of Sumner's work, it was written with religious overtones. Readers got the impression Upper Deck was on a mission from God.

Buice and Joyner were listed as vice presidents for public relations. "Mr. Joyner, as a rookie first baseman for the California Angels," the pamphlet read, "was selected to the 1986 American League All-Star squad. His acceptance by Major League owners, players and fans is an outcome of placing God in heaven and his family first. His personal relationship with the universe and its order co-incides [sic] with an underlying theme of the Upper Deck Company of putting one's house in order."

According to the Buice biography, DeWayne "has a bubbling personality which has gained him popularity among teams and he developed into one of the top relievers in his rookie season. His stick-to-itiveness, stemming from a boy of six years old to college at Cal State University, Dominguez Hills, plus his personality and wit, give the Upper Deck Company a deeper dimension while dealing with a sometimes so hecktic [sic] world."

Under the heading of objectives, the brochure read: "We have created a powerful marketing tool and an exciting addition to the current baseball card offerings. We offer complete turnkey design, production and printing services within predetermined cost guidelines. The benefits the Upper Deck Company provides are: counterfeit-proof cards, a fresh new look to meeting baseball card needs that results in greater interest, increased acceptance and higher customer satisfaction, preset standards and costs to guarantee performance, satisfaction and quality, and a complete marketing program with product delivery dates to ensure rapid customer acceptance."

The brochure even recognized the investment element of baseball cards. "This program will satisfy the needs of the majority of the customers with an investment and collection potential and an opportunity, yet unheard of for America's favorite sport—baseball. Please call us!"

■ ■ ■

Bob Cohen tried not to laugh. His client, DeWayne Buice, sure could tell some stories, but this one was ridiculous.

"So these guys think they can just waltz into the Players Association, throw pictures of you and Joyner on the desk, and walk out with a license to make baseball cards? I don't think so."

As a sports agent/attorney, Cohen did not earn the bulk of his money representing players like Buice. Players such as Oakland A's slugger Mark McGwire, another client, commanded the big contracts and, therefore, the bigger commissions for their agents. But Buice could make Cohen laugh, even when he thought he was being serious.

Sitting in his Los Angeles office, Cohen listened to Buice over the phone. He was rambling on about holograms and counterfeit-proof cards. "Don't you know Lauren Rich of the Players Association?" Buice asked. "I thought you and her go way back. If you could arrange a meeting for us. Just one meeting's all we need. We'll go to New York. I mean, they'll go to New York, I'm playing—"

"All right, DeWayne," Cohen said. "I'll see what I can do."

Cohen knew Rich through his work as a player agent. *Surely Lauren received dozens of proposals from card companies,* Cohen thought. *But if it came from a group that included members of the Players Association, she might be more inclined to listen.*

Cohen called Rich, who agreed to meet with Upper Deck on May 23. She would need to see a complete marketing strategy, along with sales projections, a distribution system, and a plan to finance the operation. She also wanted to know how Orbis Graphic Arts intended to produce baseball cards when it was in the business of color separation.

McWilliam, being the one man with disposable income, was to finance the trip. If they were going to make a positive impression, he said, they had to look like an established company. Everyone would wear a suit and tie. They would stay in the finest hotel available in New York. McWilliam even arranged for limousine transportation from the hotel to the offices of the Players Association at 805 Third Avenue. Most importantly, they had to bring Cohen along since he lent credibility to Upper Deck. Even if he said nothing, his presence alone would help.

The traveling party would consist of Korbel, Sumner, McWilliam, Hemrick, and Passante. Cohen would arrive separately in New York on the evening of May 22.

McWilliam had been responsible for making the airline arrangements, but when the five men arrived at Los Angeles International Airport on the morning of May 21, they found that there was no record of the reservations. The United Airlines flight to New York's John F. Kennedy Airport was close to capacity, so the men split up and sat throughout the plane.

When they arrived at the Westbury Hotel, they found no record of their hotel reservations either. McWilliam instructed them to put their rooms on their own credit cards, and they would be reimbursed later. The four men were puzzled; McWilliam was supposed to be fronting the money for the trip for the company, and already they had purchased plane tickets and hotel rooms with their own plastic.

Cohen was a reluctant participant. He knew Upper Deck had very little chance of receiving a license, but went to New York out of consideration of Buice. When he arrived at the Westbury, he found Hemrick and Sumner working in the hotel manager's office.

"What are you doing?" Cohen asked.

"We're working on the business plan," Hemrick replied.

"Now? The meeting is tomorrow."

Korbel, McWilliam, and Passante soon returned, and the six worked on the business plan well into the night. Cohen could not believe what he had gotten himself into. Not only did his five traveling companions know nothing about the licensing process, he thought to himself, they also were a bizarre bunch. Sumner had a booming voice and dominated every conversation. He answered questions with fourteen-paragraph responses, usually digressing into something totally unrelated. His stories were usually humorous, and listeners usually forgot what they had asked him in the first place. But he came across as pompous and condescending, which would not go over well with the Players Association. Hemrick tended to speak in whispers, but lost his temper easily. Even though his title was vice president of marketing, he still looked at the business from the eyes of a baseball card dealer, worrying more about who was going to get how many baseball cards and when. Korbel seemed to know what he was talking about, but with his broken English, you never knew for sure. McWilliam was a shrewd financial guy, but if Upper Deck didn't have enough investment capital, would it even matter? All in all, the five were a perfect match for an eccentric like his client Buice.

James Buchanan "Buck" Duke, head of the American Tobacco Company, an early producer of baseball cards. (Courtesy of Duke University Archives)

The T206 Honus Wagner card, the "Holy Grail" of baseball cards. (Courtesy of Richard Wolffers Auctions)

The 1952 Topps Mickey Mantle. (Courtesy of Richard Wolffers Auctions)

Topps Chairman Arthur Shorin. (Courtesy of Arthur Shorin)

Dr. James Beckett (second from right), chairman of Beckett Publications, shown with Dallas Cowboys quarterback Troy Aikman at a 1993 charity event. (Beckett Publications publicity photo)

Bill Hemrick (left) and DeWayne Buice. (Author's collection)

Paul Sumner (middle) and Jeff Marx (left) pose as autograph seekers during the Buice photo shoot. (Author's collection)

Buice poses for Upper Deck prototype cards at Anaheim Stadium, 1988. (Author's collection)

Buice and Jay McCracken (right) promoting Upper Deck's new cards at a Memorial Day, 1988, show at the Disneyland Hotel. (Author's collection)

Wally Joyner, despite early involvement in Upper Deck, did not pursue ownership after the Major League Players Association ruled him ineligible to take stock from the company. (Author's collection)

Jay McCracken (right) presents the first Upper Deck cards to George Moore of Tulsa Baseball Cards, March 1, 1989. (Upper Deck publicity photo)

Ken Griffey Jr.

The 1989 Upper Deck Ken Griffey, Jr., "rookie" card, now worth $70. (Author's collection)

Ted Williams signed 2,500 cards for random insertion into 1992 Upper Deck baseball cards. (Upper Deck publicity photo)

From left: Hall of Famers Ferguson Jenkins, Harmon Killebrew, and Gaylord Perry have been among Upper Deck's stable of hired autograph signers. (Upper Deck publicity photo)

Mike Berkus, veteran sports card dealer, show promoter, and one-time Upper Deck consultant. (Author's collection)

Upper Deck hockey card spokesman Wayne Gretzky (left) and Robert Pelton, whose Pelton & Associates advertising and creative design agency developed many of Upper Deck's sports cards from 1989 to 1992. (Courtesy of Pelton & Associates)

Height: 5'11" Weight: 170 lbs. Bats: Right Throws: Right Born: 10-20-53 Alta Dena, California

YR	TEAM	AVG	G	AB	R	H	2B	3B	HR	RBI	BB	SO	SB
92	FIELD OF DREAMS	.333	1	3	0	1	0	0	0	0	0	0	2
1	TOTALS	.333	1	3	0	1	0	0	0	0	0	0	2

McWilliam impressed onlookers with his all-out style of play and desire to excel in whatever he does. His awesome display of speed drew immediate comparisons to all-time stolen base king, Rickey Henderson. Scouts were eager to sign McWilliam for the 1993 season, but it will reportedly take a record bonus to do so.

Upper Deck CEO Richard McWilliam, shown here at Upper Deck's "Field of Dreams" weekend in 1992. (Author's collection)

Upper Deck headquarters, Carlsbad, California. (Author's collection)

Later, as the men waited in front of their hotel for taxis to take them to the Players Association—the limousine also had fallen through—Cohen turned to Passante. "I don't know about this," he said. "These guys are totally clueless."

Fortunately for Upper Deck, PA executive director Donald Fehr, a no-nonsense man who likes to get right down to business, was not available for the meeting. Instead, the five Upper Deck executives were met by Lauren Rich and Mark Belanger, the former Baltimore Orioles shortstop who had become Fehr's special assistant.

Cohen introduced the members of the Upper Deck Company and announced the schedule of presentations. Korbel spoke first. He spoke of Orbis Graphic Arts' work in color separation, and how Upper Deck could produce an *Architectural Digest*-quality card. The company was in the process of purchasing additional equipment to print the baseball cards, but there was no doubt Orbis could handle the initial color separation and pre-press work. Upper Deck soon would open its own facility 12 miles from Orbis in Yorba Linda. It was there that Upper Deck would produce a baseball card far superior to any currently on the market.

The two PA representatives were impressed with Korbel. Even though the Czech was sometimes difficult to understand, he had developed a self-deprecating attitude about his accent. Korbel had found that since people had to make such an effort to understand him, they often listened to him more than to people who spoke perfect English. The accent, in cases such as these, often worked to his advantage.

Next up was Sumner, who was to talk about how holograms could be applied to baseball cards. A skilled raconteur, Sumner rarely had trouble communicating. Before the meeting, his Upper Deck colleagues had worried that Sumner might go on talking for hours. As chairman of the board of deacons at his church, Sumner had spoken in front of large groups many times. But this was different. The fate of the Upper Deck Company depended on this presentation. When Sumner got up to speak, he came down with stage fright.

"I'm Paul . . . Paul Sumner," he began. "I'm the, uh, president of the Upper Deck Company."

The others sensed his nervousness. As Sumner struggled to compose himself, Rich broke in, hoping to guide Sumner along. "Mr. Sumner, tell us how the hologram is to be applied to the cards."

The question put Sumner at ease. He talked about his experiences at Cal State–Long Beach, where he helped pioneer holographic research. He explained what a hologram was: a photographic image in three dimensions made without the use of a camera lens by a reflected laser beam of light on photographic film. He told the story of the Don Mattingly counterfeits and how he had met Hemrick. Upper Deck would prevent counterfeiting, he said, through a process called foil stamping. A nonremovable hologram would be applied to each baseball card, just like a credit card.

Sumner paused. He didn't know what to say next. The other seven people in the room tried not to stare at him. They looked at the ceiling, the table, or each other. The silence was embarrassing.

Finally Hemrick, who was sitting across from Belanger, said "Mark, what if a young boy purchases a card for 50 cents and it's not worth the paper it's printed on? If this counterfeit problem is not corrected, this hobby is going to be destroyed for kids. Only seven years have passed since it was just Topps. We've had Donruss, Fleer, and Score, and now there's the possibility that no one else will be licensed until 1991. Hopefully there will still be a hobby in '91. It could all crash just as quickly as it's grown if some measures aren't taken. With your permission, we could bring some legitimacy to The Hobby."

By now, Sumner had sat down and McWilliam had gotten up to give his financial report. Based on a projected production run of 60,000 cases at $400 a case, Upper Deck would do about $24 million in sales for 1989. The figure came through Hemrick from Jay McCracken, who based it on what he knew of candy sales from Nestlé. McWilliam wasn't sure Upper Deck could handle such a large print run, but $24 million seemed like a good starting point; it was probably less than what the PA wanted and more than Upper Deck could produce. But he knew if they forecast anything less than $24 million the PA might reject Upper Deck outright.

But $24 million was not the figure the Players Association wanted to hear. With a royalty rate of 11 percent, the PA would earn only $2.64 million off $24 million. It required a $1.5 million letter of credit from all licensees, and expected card companies to at least triple the amount. For the year ending February 27, 1988, Topps had made $127.2 million from the sale of collectible cards. True, Topps also produced football and hockey cards, as well as the popular Garbage Pail Kids, but baseball card sales accounted for more than half of the revenue. Rich knew Fehr would want to hear a larger projected sales figure, but she would bring that up later. For now, she wanted to know how Upper Deck planned to sell the cards. "Do you have a distribution system in place?"

"Yes, we do," Hemrick said. "We've decided to go with Consolidated Freightways as our distributor."

The Upper Deck representatives didn't know the difference between a shipping company and a distributor. When Rich had asked for a national distribution system, she wanted to know what candy wholesalers and major retail chains were going to carry Upper Deck baseball cards, not who was going to deliver them. Anyone can hire a company to ship something. She wanted to know how they intended to sell the product.

"What I meant was, whom do you intend to sell your product to?" Rich said.

"Oh," said Hemrick. "Well, we plan to sell a lot of it to The Hobby."

"The Hobby?"

"Yeah, card shops, dealers, people like that."

"Well, gentlemen," Rich said. "You've made a very impressive presentation here today. We'll be in touch."

The Upper Deck executives thanked the Players Association representatives and left the conference room, along with Belanger. Cohen stayed behind with Rich.

"Look, Lauren," Cohen said. "I know it doesn't look like much. But these guys do know printing. Maybe if you and Don came out to Anaheim and saw what they had—"

"Hey, I like the cards," Rich said. "They're better than anything that's on the market now. If they can come up with the financing and the national distribution system, we'd be very interested."

"You're kidding. After what you just saw in there?"

"Yeah, they're a little disorganized. But what start-up company isn't?"

Cohen relayed the news to the five executives. "If you guys can come up with the financing and find a few national distributors—not a shipping company—you might just get a license."

As the group erupted in high fives, Cohen turned to Passante. "You know, this just might work."

■ ■ ■

While the owners of Upper Deck were busy trying to obtain a license, Jeff Marx and the customers from The Upper Deck card store were conducting informal market research. Marx, along with McCracken, Tom Geideman, and Randy Duvall, took the prototype cards of DeWayne Buice and Wally Joyner to hobby stores in Orange and San Diego Counties and kept a file of business cards of store owners interested in buying Upper Deck cards. The idea was twofold: to show the Players Association that there was interest in a fifth card company and that Upper Deck had a commitment from dealers to buy large quantities of cards.

"I read in print once where someone was saying Upper Deck did this big demographic test," Marx recalled later on. "Yeah, right. That was our demographic test, going around to card shops and handing out prototypes."

The public debut of the Upper Deck prototypes was at a Memorial Day weekend card show at the Disneyland Hotel in Anaheim promoted by Fullerton police detective Jack Petruzzelli. Hemrick and McCracken rented a dealer table and handed out uncut sheets of prototypes that had five cards of both Buice and Joyner. The two players showed up the Saturday before Memorial Day and for three hours autographed the sheets for collectors anxious to obtain the first Upper Deck cards produced. Some collectors turned down the autograph opportunity, preferring to keep their cards in mint condition. The cards, after all, might be worth less later if they were "defaced" with an autograph.

Before Buice left for the Angels game with the Baltimore Orioles at Anaheim Stadium, he autographed a sheet for McCracken. It read, "Hey Jay, let's make millions."

■ ■ ■

The Angels began a four-game series with the Milwaukee Brewers in Milwaukee on June 2. For Buice and Joyner, it was their first chance to meet with Paul Molitor, a key member of the Players Association's licensing committee.

The committee was developed in the mid-1980s to deal with the increasing number of proposals the PA was receiving from companies wanting to produce merchandise depicting major league players. After Donruss and Fleer had received licenses to produce baseball cards for 1981, the PA got dozens of requests from groups wishing to capitalize on the growing card market. There were also businesses that wanted to manufacture other products such as T-shirts, plastic cups, posters, caps—anything depicting a player's name and picture. If a product was limited to one or two players, the company did not need permission from the PA, provided the players in question agreed to the deal. But if merchandise featured three or more players, it needed a group license from the PA.

It was a very successful operation for the players. For each product sold, the PA received 11 percent of the wholesale price. By 1986, the PA was receiving $25 million from its group licensing program, 90 percent of which came from baseball cards.

Licensing was also a large source of revenue for the owners of the 26 baseball teams. Since most products were to show players in uniform, companies also had to obtain a second license from Major League Baseball Properties, the marketing arm of the 26 teams. Like the PA, MLB Properties earned a similar percentage from the sale of licensed products. Both groups also required a guarantee of at least $1 million in licensing revenue for many products, which eliminated many start-up companies that were incapable of millions in sales.

Revenue from licenses obtained through MLB Properties was divided equally among the 26 team owners, even if New York Yankees caps, T-shirts, and jackets sold at a rate 10 times greater than those of, say, the San Diego Padres. Of course, the Yankees could sell their own items at Yankee Stadium and official team stores and reap the benefits of larger retail sales. But as far as MLB Properties was concerned, all 26 teams were created equal. Whether a licensed company sold a Yankees or Padres jacket, the licensing royalty was divided 26 ways—28 ways beginning in 1993, when the Florida Marlins and Colorado Rockies were added to the National League.

If a product only included team logos and not player images, such as clothing, mugs, or bed linens, a company had to deal only with Major League Baseball

Properties. But in the case of baseball cards, which used logos and player pictures, permission from Properties and the PA was needed. And since it made no sense for a baseball card company to acquire the rights to logos if it didn't have a license from the players, the Players Association was contacted first. If the PA approved of a card company, MLB Properties often did as well, since the PA already had researched the prospect of the product's success.

The Players Association office in New York investigated each company that submitted a proposal. The ones that looked promising were forwarded to a vote of the licensing committee, which meets once during the season and twice in the winter. The committee generally accepted the recommendation of PA officials, although it occasionally voted down an idea that is not in good taste, such as toilet paper decorated with player images.

At 31, Molitor was one of the most respected men in the game in 1988. Known for his all-out play and soft demeanor away from the field, "Molly" was revered by teammates and opponents alike. As a member of the ten-man licensing committee, which included the Mariners' Dave Valle, Tim Leary of the Los Angeles Dodgers, and Jim Gott of the Pittsburgh Pirates, Molitor's vote was no more important than any one of the other nine players. But Buice and Joyner knew Molly's support would go a long way toward a favorable decision by the group. Not only was Molitor active in the PA as the Brewers' player representative in 1988, he also was one of the game's top players. In 1987, he had hit .353 with 16 home runs, 75 RBI, and 45 stolen bases. He also led the American League in doubles and runs scored and had chased Joe DiMaggio's record 56-game hitting streak before being stopped at 39 games.

Molitor finished batting practice, and was walking toward the Brewers' dugout when Buice handed him the prototype cards.

"We're involved in this new card company, Molly," Joyner said. "These cards seem a lot better than any of the ones currently on the market."

Molitor put his bat down and examined the cards. He had never collected baseball cards, although he did collect baseballs autographed by Hall-of-Famers. Like a wide-eyed youngster, he ran his fingers along the white card stock and marveled at the glossy photos of Buice and Joyner. There were many other baseball cards; too many, in fact, thought Molitor. But these cards went far beyond the gray cardboard that had been sold for the last century.

"If you get a chance, would you talk to the licensing people in New York?" Buice asked. "It's a good product and we'd like you to help get it going."

This certainly is strange, Molitor thought. *The card business is getting so big that players are even getting involved.* Molitor picked up his bat. "I'll see what I can do."

■ ■ ■

Over 12,000 collectors attended the ninth annual National Sports Collectors Convention July 6–10, 1988, in Atlantic City, N.J. Paul Sumner and Bill Hemrick tried to speak to all of them.

The first "National" had attracted a modest 5,700 collectors to the Los Angeles Airport Marriott in 1980. The show had grown each year, and by 1985 was attracting most of the major dealers of cards and sports memorabilia in the country. For Upper Deck, which would initially have a difficult time selling to major retailers since there were four card lines already on the market, acceptance by dealers was essential. If dealers would buy 65,000 cases—the 60,000 figure had been raised following the meeting in New York with the PA—then Upper Deck would have no trouble selling to retailers in 1990. Of course, if dealers did not buy Upper Deck, nobody would.

Hemrick and Sumner flew to Atlantic City and set up a small booth at "the National." Upper Deck had printed a third version of the Buice and Joyner prototypes, with an oval hologram on the bottom of the card back, and sent most of the press run of 20,000 ahead to the Atlantic City Convention Center. Hemrick and Sumner gave each collector a Buice and a Joyner card and offered dealers a chance to buy cases, which would each contain roughly 10,000 cards. Each dealer received a navy-blue brochure that told of Upper Deck's new baseball cards, "the most exciting new product in baseball history." By solving the problems that other card companies had chosen to ignore, Sumner said, Upper Deck would be the champion of the collector. The cards, therefore, would be called the "Collector's Choice."

As a veteran dealer, Hemrick could relate to the shop owners and part-time card sellers who visited the booth. He stressed that Upper Deck's cards would be counterfeit-proof and come in a foil pack to prevent tampering. He promised the dealers that they would not have to wait to receive their cards, that Upper Deck would fill its small orders first. "When I ran my shop, I couldn't get any new product until the market was already saturated," he told the dealers. "But we'll see that everyone gets cards at once. We won't have wholesalers getting their cards a month before hobby dealers."

Like Marx, McCracken, and the regulars from The Upper Deck card shop, Hemrick and Sumner took business cards and wrote on the back the number of cases each dealer wanted. Since dealers were not required to fill out a purchase order or offer credit references, they verbally committed to hundreds of cases. People who made a few thousand dollars a year as weekend card dealers were committing to hundreds of thousands in Upper Deck baseball cards.

On the first day of the show, Don Bodow approached the Upper Deck booth and introduced himself to Sumner. Bodow, like most showgoers, was intrigued by the new, glossy cards. "Put me down for 1,000 cases," Bodow said.

"You got it," Sumner said.

Bodow had no idea how he would pay for 1,000 cases at $400 apiece. He operated a small baseball card mail-order business out of his home in Syracuse in addition to running the Don Bodow public relations and marketing firm. He certainly didn't have $400,000 to front for baseball cards. But, like the other dealers swarming around the Upper Deck booth, he felt he could pre-sell the cases for at least $500 apiece to dealers in upstate New York. By the time he received the cards, he planned to have the $400,000 to pay Upper Deck, along with $100,000 profit.

By the end of the show's first day, Sumner and Hemrick had commitments for the entire run of 65,000 cases. Sumner called Korbel. "Boris, we're entirely sold out. They absolutely love us!"

After the show, Sumner and Bodow were on the same flight from Atlantic City to Newark. The plane was half empty, and Bodow sat down across the aisle from Sumner, reintroduced himself, and asked about Upper Deck's marketing department. Sumner said Upper Deck didn't have a marketing department, only a vice president of marketing and an outside consulting firm, Pelton & Associates. They seemed more than capable of handling the job, which had just become easier with the sellout of the entire press run at the National.

Over the course of the 45-minute flight, Bodow mentioned his marketing firm and background as a collector. He also convinced Sumner to sell him an additional 4,000 cases. Bodow said it had been his experience that some card dealers exaggerated their finances to receive product, and Upper Deck probably would be stuck with a portion of the 65,000 cases.

The two deplaned in Newark and shook hands. Sumner said he would contact Bodow if they expanded their marketing department and would change Bodow's order from 1,000 to 5,000 cases.

Bodow did some quick math. He had just committed $2 million he didn't have to baseball cards that didn't exist.

■ ■ ■

The Upper Deck board of directors met July 12 at the offices of Orbis Graphic Arts. Sumner called the meeting to order at 6:15 P.M.

McWilliam, as vice president of finance, said Upper Deck needed $3 million in start-up capital. The company had to secure two letters of credit: a $1.5 million royalty guarantee to the Players Association and a $421,000 note to Noland Paper, which would supply the paper for the 1989 baseball cards. The remaining $1.079 million would be used to purchase equipment and cover payroll.

McWilliam suggested that, although it would be preferable to offer stock to an outside investor, he could obtain the necessary funding if Upper Deck agreed to repay a loan with 15 percent interest. The other board members—Korbel, Sumner, Hemrick, and Passante—rejected the idea of offering anyone a stake in the company, but agreed to a loan at 15 percent, to be repaid within six months. McWilliam said he would report back to the board about the availability of the funds by July

15. If he was unable to come up with the money, then he would surrender his 11 percent ownership in the company, since he was given the shares on the condition that he secure the necessary funding. McWilliam excused himself, saying he wanted to get to work immediately on the matter.

Hemrick, as vice president of marketing, made the next presentation. Since Upper Deck's entire first-year run had been sold at the National in Atlantic City, he said, there was no immediate need for a marketing strategy or sales force. Sumner disagreed, noting that he had hired his brother-in-law, Chip Fiandaca, to spearhead what he felt would be an aggressive sales and marketing campaign. He also remembered what Bodow had said. "How can you say we don't need any marketing, Bill?" Sumner asked. "Nobody even knows who we are. What if those dealers in New Jersey don't really have the money to buy the cards?"

Korbel and Passante looked at one other and sighed. Once again, Sumner and Hemrick were arguing. It was difficult to believe these two men had ever found enough common ground upon which to build a business relationship.

Hemrick was quickly realizing he was outnumbered. Since the first board meeting four months earlier, it was evident who was running the show. Korbel was Sumner's boss at Orbis, but since Sumner was president of Upper Deck, he had final say in everything. Upper Deck, in many ways, was Orbis. The company operated out of the Orbis offices, was run largely by Orbis people, and even included Sumner's relatives. McWilliam and Passante were not Orbis employees, but had known Korbel for years and done accounting and legal work, respectively, for Orbis.

"Fine, Paul," Hemrick said. "If that's the way you see it, then I must not know anything about marketing."

He turned to Korbel, who earlier in the meeting had been appointed chairman of the board. "Boris, I want to resign as vice president of marketing."

Korbel accepted the resignation, but stressed that Hemrick would remain a vice president of the corporation. But as the meeting adjourned, everyone, including Hemrick himself, knew his days with Upper Deck were drawing to a close.

■ ■ ■

Donald Fehr and Lauren Rich of the Players Association made their first trip to Upper Deck the following week. Unlike the meeting in New York two months earlier, their visit to Anaheim went well for Upper Deck. Cohen and Korbel gave a tour of Orbis Graphic Arts, and Fehr and Rich left impressed with the quality of Orbis's color separation work.

The Players Association representatives stopped short of awarding a license to Upper Deck; the company still did not have a national distribution system or the financing to ensure a $1.5 million letter of credit for the 1989 baseball card run.

If Upper Deck could present those two things, Fehr indicated, he would award a license.

Fehr and Rich were impressed with Korbel, so impressed that they later let it be known that there was a third condition Upper Deck had to meet in order to receive a license. If Korbel was the president of Orbis and chairman of the board of Upper Deck, he should also be the president of Upper Deck. Besides, he was much easier to deal with than Sumner, whose reputation had been sealed during the New York meeting. Sumner, of course, could remain in the company, but as a vice president. Cohen relayed the desire of the PA to the board.

Although the board never took a formal vote, by the end of July, Korbel had become the second president of the Upper Deck Company.

8

Shuffling the Deck

No one heard from McWilliam until the next board meeting on July 26. His terms had changed dramatically from their discussion two weeks earlier. He told the board he had obtained a commitment from City National Bank of California for $1.7 million. McWilliam would obtain the financing personally, but would require personal guarantees from each shareholder to secure the loan.

In order to obtain the money, McWilliam also wanted to be compensated. In addition to a cash payment of $140,000, he also demanded $10,000 a month so long as his personal guarantee to the bank was required; $10,000 for each $100,000 used by Upper Deck; total control of cash disbursements, and an increase in stock ownership from 11 to 16 percent.

"Don't we have any other proposals?" Hemrick asked.

"No, not right now, but I've been talking to other potential investors," McWilliam said.

McWilliam excused himself, leaving the rest of the group to ponder his proposal. The board was stunned; McWilliam had no right to demand additional shares. He was given 11 percent of the company in return for a promise to provide the financing. Now that he had done so, he couldn't ask for more.

"Either he's in or he's out," Korbel said. "He can't just make promises, then make us wait all this time only to jack up the terms."

The board unanimously rejected the plan and Korbel told Passante to inform McWilliam that he was being removed from the board and to return his 110 shares immediately.

Passante called McWilliam, who refused to return the stock certificates. "Richard, you're being unreasonable," Passante said. "If you want to stay in the company, lessen your demands. If not, you have to return the stock."

McWilliam hung up on Passante. Korbel knew Andrew Prendiville was closer to McWilliam, so he had Prendiville call McWilliam on July 28. Prendiville reached McWilliam in his car.

"Look, man, this is a gold mine here," Prendiville said. "I don't know what you're up to, but Boris is tired of you fucking with him. Either you're in this or you're not, but stop trying to dick everyone around."

"They're getting dicked around? What about me?" McWilliam asked. "I'm the only one putting up any money here and all I'm getting is 11 percent."

"Fine, Richard, if you don't like it, give up your stock and forget about it."

The phone call broke up as McWilliam drove out of range. Prendiville slammed the phone down. "I don't believe this guy."

While the owners of the Upper Deck Company tried to retrieve McWilliam's shares, there was a more pressing issue. Noland Paper had given Upper Deck a deadline of August 1 to purchase paper for the 1989 baseball cards. Since the paper Upper Deck wanted had to be ordered from northern Italy, Noland needed $100,000 to secure the shipment in time to meet Upper Deck's production run.

Korbel, Hemrick, Sumner, and Passante met July 29 at Orbis. Passante said Dr. Kevin Prendiville, an ophthalmologist and younger brother of Andrew Prendiville, would loan the company $100,000. Korbel verbally agreed to guarantee the loan, and the paper order was secured.

Two days later, McWilliam and Korbel met at Korbel's home. Afterward, Korbel called Prendiville. "I can't believe I didn't throw up," Korbel said. "His terms are so ridiculous. He's out."

But McWilliam refused to leave. The next week Korbel received a letter from McWilliam's lawyer, Ben Frydman. The letter said McWilliam would surrender the stock in return for the money he had advanced the company (approximately $70,000) along with an additional $150,000 for the time and effort he said he'd expended on Upper Deck.

For the first three weeks of August, no one could reach McWilliam, who was surfing in Hawaii. He would let his lawyer deal with Upper Deck. He knew Upper Deck had no potential investors and would have to negotiate with him if they wanted to survive.

There was one other possibility. Korbel and Passante flew to New York August 21 to meet with Dr. Jerome Zuckerman, a physiologist and collector who had taken a tour of Upper Deck in June. Zuckerman owned Sports Heroes, Inc., a small firm in Oradell, N.J., that sold sports memorabilia, and said he would be interested in investing in Upper Deck. Korbel told Zuckerman in June that it looked like they had the necessary capital, but would keep Sports Heroes in mind. Korbel was just being polite; he had no intention of bringing in another investor. But two months later, Zuckerman loomed as the only alternative to McWilliam.

Passante and Korbel met Zuckerman for dinner in New York. "We need three million," Korbel said.

"That's no problem," Zuckerman said. "But we want 51 percent ownership."

Korbel did not want to give up control of the company. "I'm afraid we can't offer you that."

"Then I'm afraid we don't have a deal."

Korbel and Passante thanked Zuckerman for his time. On the flight home, the two discussed other prospective investors, but could come up with no serious possibilities. "Looks like it's back to Richard," Korbel said.

When they returned, Sumner reached McWilliam in Hawaii and asked if he would be interested in meeting for lunch with him and Korbel. The three met in Newport Beach, and it was decided that a new investor agreement would be drafted. McWilliam would provide $2.4 million in cash or letters of credit to guarantee Upper Deck's obligations to the Players Association, Noland Paper, and Phoenix Corp., which was to lease printing presses to Upper Deck. In return, McWilliam would receive 27 percent ownership in the company.

For McWilliam, the deal was a coup. Without much budging from his July 26 proposal, he had increased his ownership position in Upper Deck from 11 to 27 percent. True, he would now have to personally guarantee the loans instead of having the entire board take the risk. But in the five weeks since he made his proposal, Upper Deck had become a far less risky investment. It had publicly announced that it had received a license from the Players Association—even though Upper Deck still had nothing in writing—and had secured the paper to print the cards. To date, he had put up just $70,000 cash while nearly tripling his investment position.

McWilliam's stock in Upper Deck was rising in more ways than one.

■ ■ ■

For nine months, Jay McCracken had struggled to decide his future. Unlike Hemrick or Sumner, he had much to lose by joining Upper Deck on a full-time basis. In 1988, he celebrated his tenth anniversary with Nestlé Foods, which meant he was fully vested in its 401(k) plan. He had three daughters, each four years apart, and he and his wife Jane were in the middle of a twelve-year run of college tuition bills. How could he give up his job security at Nestlé to join a bunch of guys who often seemed to have no idea what they were doing?

McCracken already felt like he was part of the company. He had frequented Hemrick's store long before Buice and Sumner had stumbled in. He had left work early to attend the Joyner photo shoot, and he felt his pictures of both Joyner and Buice were better than the ones Sumner had shot that ended up on the prototype cards. But since Sumner was president of Upper Deck at the time, his photos were chosen. Although McCracken was not part of the company, he helped out whenever he could. Along with Jeff Marx, Randy Duvall, and Tom Geideman, McCracken had taken the prototypes to card-shop owners throughout Orange and San Diego Counties to generate interest. Like everything else, McCracken did it on his own time.

Not part of the company? "Where would Bill Hemrick be without me?" he would ask Jane during one of their frequent discussions about whether to leave Nestlé. As a customer at The Upper Deck card shop, McCracken had taught Hemrick everything he knew about the baseball card business. Hemrick had become vice president of marketing and often relied on McCracken for insight not only into marketing, but also sales, distribution, and how the candy industry operated. How was Hemrick going to launch Upper Deck's first product when he didn't even know the difference between a manufacturer and a distributor? Hemrick had once asked McCracken if Nestlé could be Upper Deck's distributor.

"Bill, you just don't understand," McCracken said. "Nestlé is a manufacturer, not a distributor. If Nestlé made the cards, they would want to own the business. Nestlé doesn't work as a distributor. They have their own distributors."

McCracken knew he could do Hemrick's job. Indirectly, he was doing it already. McCracken felt there was no one who understood the business better than he did. He had 20 years' experience working in sales and distribution for the candy and food industries, first at Hunt Wesson Foods, then Nestlé. Plus he understood the sports card market. Unlike Topps, Fleer, Donruss, and Score, Upper Deck would have a hard time initially selling its cards to companies like Kmart and Southland Corp., owner of the 7-11 store chain—the backbone of the candy distribution network. The market was saturated, and there was no way the major retailers would accept a fifth brand of baseball cards when there were four established lines already available. Start with the hobby dealers, McCracken had suggested to Hemrick, and work your way into the major retail outlets. Once every baseball card shop owner in the country is raving about Upper Deck cards, then the 7-11s and Kmarts will follow.

"Only collectors understand how this crazy market works," he would tell Jane. "Those guys might be good businessmen, but the baseball card industry is not a conventional business. You get The Hobby excited about the cards and everyone else will jump on the bandwagon. If you try to beat Topps by becoming a better Topps, you'll get your butt kicked. You have to be a collector to understand how all this works. Those guys aren't collectors."

■ ■ ■

Born in Atlantic City, N.J., in 1940, McCracken grew up a Phillies fan and still could rattle off the starting lineup of the 1950 Whiz Kids easier than any of the current Phillies teams. He cringed whenever someone mentioned the 1964 Phillies, who led the National League by six and a half games with 12 to play but lost 10 straight and blew the pennant to the St. Louis Cardinals. His love of baseball had spawned an interest in baseball cards that continued into adulthood.

It was that love that made a move to Upper Deck so tempting. He could combine his expertise in sales and marketing with his passion for baseball and collecting. But would Upper Deck actually work? Would collectors support a fifth card company? McCracken remembered collecting in the early 1950s. Back then, kids usually collected Topps or Bowman, rarely both. It was like living in New York where you rooted for one baseball team and despised the others. McCracken had been a Bowman collector and hated Topps. Most collectors, however, bought Topps, which ultimately bought out Bowman and held a virtual monopoly on the card industry from 1956 until 1981.

But while there had been room for only one card company in the 1960s and 1970s, there was still space for an upscale card design in 1988. Still, McCracken didn't want to leave Nestlé until he was certain of two things: that he would not have to work with Hemrick and that Upper Deck had a license from the Players Association. In August, the company had announced it had obtained permission from the PA, but Hemrick had told him there was nothing in writing. In the same conversation, Hemrick had mentioned he had resigned as vice president of marketing and would become a distributor for Upper Deck, selling cards out of a new store. If he could be the first dealer with Upper Deck cards, he said, he could make a fortune.

That didn't sound like a wise move to McCracken. But if nothing else, Hemrick had figured out the difference between distribution and manufacturing.

Hemrick said he'd recommend McCracken to become his replacement and would set up a dinner meeting with Korbel. A few days before meeting Korbel, shortly after Labor Day, 1988, McCracken was in Dallas on business with Nestlé. As western regional manager, he had offices in Los Angeles and Dallas and often stayed at the Sheraton Hotel in Arlington, which was adjacent to Arlington Stadium, home of the Texas Rangers. Late in the afternoon, McCracken drove the 10 miles from his office to the Sheraton, where the California Angels were staying during a four-game series with the Rangers. He hoped to talk to Buice or Joyner to find out how close the Players Association was to awarding Upper Deck a license.

In the lobby, McCracken found Joyner, who was on his way to batting practice. Joyner didn't remember him until McCracken brought up the photo shoot.

"I'm trying to decide if I'm going to join Upper Deck," McCracken said. "Is the Players Association going to give them a license?"

"You're asking the wrong guy," Joyner replied.

"Aren't you still involved?"

"They're still using my name to market the stuff and that's all I'm going to say about it."

Joyner walked away. McCracken called up to Buice's room, but he had already left for the park. He called Jane and told her what Joyner said.

"If they're still using Wally's name, they must be close to getting a license," he said. "If Korbel makes me an offer next week, I'm going to accept."

McCracken hung up with Jane, walked over to the window, and stared out at Arlington Stadium. A line of fans had formed outside the gate, waiting for the park to open so they could watch batting practice. Somewhere inside, McCracken figured, Joyner and Buice were lobbying their fellow players on behalf of the Upper Deck Company.

McCracken changed his clothes, and went to watch his last baseball game as Nestlé's western regional sales manager.

■ ■ ■

Unbeknownst to McCracken, Buice and Joyner were no longer working on behalf of Upper Deck. Not long after their early June discussion with Molitor in Milwaukee, the Players Association had ruled that active players could not have an ownership position in a company licensed by the PA because there was the appearance of a conflict of interest. The PA decided that it would not license any company that had current players involved, since it would look as though the players had helped obtain the license.

Which, of course, is exactly what happened in the case of Upper Deck. Buice had brought in his agent, Cohen, who helped negotiate the license. By the time the PA made its ruling, Buice and Joyner already had contacted most of the licensing committee, lobbying them for support. On the surface, the PA's decision looked like a no-win situation for Buice and Joyner. They could resign their positions from Upper Deck and relinquish any claim to future profits or they could remain involved with Upper Deck. Of course, if they remained, Upper Deck would never get a license.

The PA's ruling stemmed from a conversation Joyner had had with Dave Valle, the Seattle Mariners catcher who was on the licensing committee. Valle loved the cards, but was reluctant to vote in favor of granting Upper Deck a license. "Everyone will say I voted for it not because of the card but because Wally Joyner was involved in it," Valle said. "And if I don't vote for it, what's going to happen the next time I see you on the field? I'm caught in the middle."

The PA reached a compromise with Buice and Joyner. They could hold an option on the stock until their careers ended. In the meantime, they could not work directly in the promotion or marketing of Upper Deck. The PA rejected Buice's proposal that his stock be placed in his parents' names.

At a July 5 Upper Deck board meeting, Buice had been removed from the board and replaced by Anthony Passante, Upper Deck's legal counsel. Buice was in Toronto with the Angels and missed the meeting, but agreed to resign from the board and have his 120 shares transferred into a stock option.

For Joyner, ownership in Upper Deck never was a serious issue. From the time he posed for the prototype cards at Cal State–Fullerton, he knew Upper Deck was a long shot. Unlike Buice, he had a long and lucrative career ahead of him. Why make waves with the Players Association over a company that might never produce a card? In the spring of 1988, Upper Deck had offered Joyner a 5 percent ownership position, but Joyner's agent, Barry Axelrod, felt Joyner should receive more. It was Joyner, after all, who was the marquee name behind Upper Deck. Buice was a journeyman minor leaguer and he had 12 percent of the company. His star client, meanwhile, was getting only 5 percent.

If Joyner could receive only 5 percent for helping to secure a license and promote the cards, Axelrod suggested that Joyner's appearances for Upper Deck be limited and that he fly first class whenever on corporate business. It seemed like a reasonable proposal, but at the time the only thing Upper Deck could offer was an ownership position. It had no money for first-class travel, only stock. Negotiations broke off, and by the time the Players Association made its ruling in late June, Joyner felt pursuing the stock wasn't worth the hassle. He just wanted to be compensated for the use of his likeness. He thought the $300 he had received in February was for the photo shoot only, not for unlimited use of his image. The Upper Deck board had decided during its July 12 meeting that Joyner would be paid $10,000 for the use of his image. But now that his face was plastered all over Upper Deck marketing and promotional material, that seemed like a paltry sum. So when McCracken approached him at the Sheraton in Arlington, asking what he thought about Upper Deck, Joyner didn't feel like giving a glowing endorsement.

Joyner, interviewed in July of 1993 about his involvement with Upper Deck, said, "I'm playing baseball for a living and I get paid well for doing it. The money I would have made with Upper Deck—I never would have had to use it. It would have been nice to have, but there are headaches that come with it. The money I'm making now I probably won't ever spend either, so why worry about it? I'm happy. My family's happy and we don't need anything. Logically speaking, it was a mistake. Finacially, it might have been a mistake. In terms of the livelihood of my family, it was probably a blessing. My only disappointment was that even after what I did for the company, they didn't pay me what I felt I was supposed to get. But I don't worry about it. It's not like I'm hurting."

Upper Deck meant much more to Buice, who was 31 and no longer the ace closer for the Angels that he had been the year before. He had spent 10 years in the minors trying to make it to the big leagues; and now that he had, there was no guarantee that he would be around much longer. If Upper Deck succeeded, he wouldn't have to worry about getting cut; he could live off Upper Deck dividend checks. But it was becoming increasingly clear that he would not be able to retain all 120 shares. The company needed money and the only way they could raise it was by offering stock to additional investors. Since he was not directly involved in Upper Deck, the other investors probably would ask him to surrender some of his shares.

Ironically, Buice knew plenty of guys with enough money to invest in Upper Deck. Problem was, they were all Major League baseball players.

■ ■ ■

When McCracken returned to Anaheim after his momentous post–Labor Day decision, he had dinner as planned with Korbel and agreed to start September 20 as Upper Deck's vice president of sales and marketing. Korbel agreed to match McCracken's salary at Nestlé and provide a company car.

Hemrick, meanwhile, already was negotiating the terms of his departure. Since returning from the National Sports Collectors Convention in Atlantic City in July, he had grown increasingly frustrated working with Sumner. The July 12 board meeting was the beginning of the end, and now Hemrick was being forced out. He had hoped he could stay on with limited duties, but even those had been taken away. Hemrick would arrange a meeting with a distributor only to have Sumner insist on attending the meeting by himself. Sumner had hired his brother-in-law, Chip Fiandaca, as national sales manager and retained Pelton & Associates to handle the product design and assist in the marketing. With McCracken now aboard, there was nothing left for Hemrick to do.

Hemrick wasn't worried about leaving. He'd become a distributor for Upper Deck. He'd get Upper Deck cards first, giving him an edge on other wholesale outlets. If dealers wanted product the moment it left the factory, they'd have to go to Hemrick. As a former dealer, he knew how quickly prices for new cards could soar, particularly when they trickle out of the factory while the glitches in a new operation are worked out. If he could acquire cases for $400 wholesale and sell them for $800, he'd make more than he ever could as a 17 percent owner. Or so he thought.

It would be another job switch for a man who had never been able to stay put. After graduating from Ravenna (Ohio) High in 1959, Hemrick spent eight years in the Army, then worked three years in the *Los Angeles Times* circulation department. Later, he opened a T-shirt shop and a bicycle motocross track called Western Sports-A-Rama in Orange. Before starting his baseball card business, he had worked for two printing companies as a sales representative. Now it was time to move on again.

Two days after McCracken started, Hemrick and Upper Deck reached an agreement that would cost Hemrick millions of dollars in future dividends. Hemrick agreed to sell 130 of his 170 shares back to Upper Deck in exchange for the right to purchase 3,900 cases (roughly 42 million cards) through 1993. Hemrick could purchase the cards at the discounted rate of $210 a case, half off the wholesale price, for a savings of $1.64 million. He would also receive 300 free cases of baseball cards, worth $126,000 wholesale, and still have 40 shares—4.2 percent of the company.

The agreement was signed September 22, 1988, although it had been agreed to in principle during the September 6 board meeting, when a stock redistribution plan was discussed. Under the plan, Korbel would receive 340 shares, Sumner 310, McWilliam 270, Hemrick 40, and Buice an option to purchase 40. (Buice's option did not count toward the number of outstanding shares, which totaled 960.)

Buice, like Hemrick, also sold much of his stake back to Upper Deck. Since he would have to give up some of his shares to a new investor anyway, he figured he would get some cards for it. On September 15, Buice signed an agreement surrendering his 120 shares in return for a four percent stock option and 700 free cases of cards, worth $294,000 wholesale.

Hemrick wanted to protect himself in case Upper Deck never launched the cards, which seemed increasingly likely given its haphazard organization. If Upper Deck failed, of course, he would never see any of the cards, but he would only be liable for 4 percent of the company's debt instead of 17 percent. It was hardly the 50 percent stake he started out with eight months earlier when he and Sumner had agreed over pizza at Angelo's to split the business equally. But now it didn't matter; he didn't want to work with these guys anyway. If the company succeeded, he'd still be far better off than he had been nine months earlier, when he was working 20 hours a day and wondering how he would come up with $400 to pay Buice to sign autographs.

Under the terms of the agreement, Hemrick was to remain employed by Upper Deck through the pre-production phase of the baseball cards, for which he would be paid $400 a week. Once that work was completed, his "obligation" to Upper Deck would cease. Since Hemrick's work already had effectively ended, the company decided to relieve Hemrick of his obligation immediately. That put McCracken in the awkward position of having to fire the man who had made the recommendation that got him his job.

"You can't fire me, Jay," Hemrick said. "I'm an owner. I'm not leaving. Period."

McCracken shrugged, and went back to work. For two weeks, Hemrick simmered in his office, spending his time sorting his personal collection of baseball cards. Whenever anyone asked him about Upper Deck business, he referred them to McCracken or Sumner. After two weeks of staring at the same cards, Hemrick got up and left.

On October 1, Buice and Hemrick decided to pool the cards they would receive through their settlement agreements and enter the distribution business. Their new company was called "Elite Cards."

Jeff Marx, who still was working at Ford Aerospace, could not believe the news of the Buice-Hemrick partnership. Only ten months had passed since he had to convince Hemrick to pay Buice $400 to sign at The Upper Deck. It was Hemrick who nearly blew up at Buice when he was 15 minutes late for the signing. Now the two were in business together.

Hemrick and Marx had sold The Upper Deck in July, but the tiny shop's legacy continued to grow.

9

All Decked Out

Richard McWilliam's $2.4 million went quickly. The financing that was to secure the $1.5 million letter of credit to the Players Association instead went to start-up costs. In a span of six weeks, from October 1 until November 15, McWilliam's money disappeared in chunks. There was a lease for a new facility in Yorba Linda, California, along with construction costs for the new plant. The printing press and equipment, leased from Phoenix Corporation, cost $1.2 million. Upper Deck paid back Dr. Kevin Prendiville his $100,000 loan for securing the paper deposit, with $10,000 interest. There was a modest monthly payroll of $20,000, along with office equipment and printing supplies.

Upper Deck, which thought it had sold its entire press run of 65,000 cases at the National Sports Collectors Convention, had little income. When Jay McCracken took over as vice president of sales and marketing on September 20, he found the company had purchase orders for just 1,000 cases. The sale of the other 64,000 cases would have brought in $27 million. But no one was buying. At least, not yet.

By November, McWilliam was facing financial disaster. To secure the financing for Upper Deck, he had put up his real estate holdings, and now the company was going to sink before it printed its first cards. He placed a desperate call to an old friend named Adrian Gluck, an investment banker who had helped McWilliam take Lehman Medical public. Gluck specialized in finding investors willing to roll the dice on high-risk start-up companies.

"Who do you know that can help us?" McWilliam asked.

Gluck (pronounced "Gluke") thought to himself. There were high-risk start-ups and then there were no-way-in-hell start-ups. Upper Deck seemed to fall in the latter category. A person willing to take a risk in Upper Deck, if there was such a person, could not look at the company from solely a business perspective; if they did, they'd be pretty stupid to sink their money into Upper Deck. And the people with the type of money Upper Deck needed—McWilliam was asking for $3 million—did not get their money by being stupid.

No, Gluck thought, the person who invests in Upper Deck would have to be able to overlook the pitfalls and see the romance in the product. Someone who made business decisions not just for financial reasons but because they absolutely loved the product. Millions of Americans collected baseball cards, a phenomenon Gluck—who lived in Romania until he was 16—had never experienced as a child. But in his travels, he had found the collecting mentality to be universal. Once someone got hooked on a collectible, it became an addiction, whether it was art, antiques, or baseball cards. And what was Upper Deck if not the ultimate baseball collectible: a company that would revolutionize the trading cards that four generations of American boys had grown up collecting? Surely, there was someone out there willing to throw money into Upper Deck.

Gluck contacted Detroit businessman Richard Kughn, whom he had worked with on several business ventures. At 59, Dick Kughn was still very much a little boy. The owner of a vast real estate and business empire, he was best known for his hobbies: collecting antique cars and model trains. He would be a perfect fit for Upper Deck. He had better be, Gluck thought; he couldn't think of anyone else daring and spontaneous enough to invest in the company.

■ ■ ■

Born in Detroit in 1929 and raised in Cleveland, Kughn began his career as a laborer, and then became a foreman and a field engineer. He returned to Detroit in 1953 to join The Taubman Company, a chain of department stores, eventually becoming the firm's No. 2 man, riding the shopping mall boom of the 1970s into a tidy personal fortune. When he retired as vice chairman of Taubman in 1983, he turned his attention to his hobbies, often investing in companies related to his two favorites: cars and trains.

At the age of seven, Kughn acquired his first Lionel train by salvaging a set he found in his neighbor's trash can. Two years later, he received a new train set for Christmas and continued to add trains and accessories to his collection all his life. At 17, he and a friend built a 1923 Model T touring sedan from scratch, using parts out of a junkyard. They drove it their senior year of high school, the beginning of a life-long love affair with cars. When he returned to Detroit, he began amassing a car collection that by the late 1980s rated among the finest in the country.

His first passion, however, was toy trains. Kughn often remarked that there was nothing he enjoyed more than spending a day with his model trains. After his retirement from Taubman, his friends joked that since he was devoting so much time to his Lionel trains, he ought to buy the company.

The Lionel Manufacturing Company began in 1900 and in 1902 issued its first catalog of electric trains, capitalizing on Americans' fascination with the railroad. The company grew, and by the 1920s had produced more than one million train sets. But production was halted during World War II, and after the war the company struggled to regain its previous popularity as young boys turned to airplanes and other toys. Lionel changed ownership several times, and was eventually purchased by Kenner-Parker Toys, which moved the company from Mount Clemens, Michigan, to Tijuana, Mexico.

There the company experienced quality and production problems, and when Kenner-Parker let it be known in 1986 that Lionel was for sale, Kughn's friends called him the same morning and the joke turned into a serious business proposal. After his advisors looked into the company and came back with a positive report, Kughn purchased Lionel for a reported $25 million and moved it back to Mt. Clemens. Since Lionel had been in Mexico only a few years, much of the old staff rejoined the company. Kughn bought a factory next door to the original facility, expanded the production capacity, and almost immediately the company returned to its glory days of the 1920s. Annual sales climbed 150 percent to $50 million for both 1987 and 1988. The new Lionel rekindled interest in older Lionel models, which soared in value as new collectors entered the hobby.

■ ■ ■

It was a pattern Gluck could see happening with Upper Deck. For seven years, since Topps' virtual monopoly was broken in 1981, interest in vintage baseball cards was on the upswing and the market for new cards was soaring. But unlike Lionel trains, which had made technological improvements to its classic models, the current baseball cards varied little from those of the Fifties. If Upper Deck could reinvigorate the sports card hobby the way Lionel had revamped the model train business, Gluck told Kughn, the profits could be substantial.

Shortly after Thanksgiving, 1988, Kughn and his wife Linda met with Boris Korbel, McWilliam, Gluck, and McCracken in Los Angeles. Like Dr. Jerome Zuckerman, Kughn said it was his normal policy to obtain majority ownership in companies in which he was investing. But since McWilliam and Korbel had put everything they owned into the company, that seemed like an unreasonable request. Kughn would settle for a stake no less than that of the largest shareholder in return for a $3 million investment. He would give the company half of the money up front for the letter of credit to the Players Association. The other half was contingent on Upper Deck reaching its sales projections in time for a January meeting in either Detroit or Cleveland.

Korbel and McWilliam left the meeting ecstatic. Kughn's money would put them over the top. Of course, someone was going to have to take a massive cut in ownership. It wouldn't be DeWayne Buice or Bill Hemrick, who already had been dropped to 40 shares apiece. Korbel would have to give up some of his shares, but wasn't willing to surrender too many. He had taken Orbis Graphic Arts to the brink of extinction by devoting most of its assets and time to Upper Deck. He deserved as much as Kughn.

Korbel called Sumner, who reluctantly agreed to take a cut. Sumner still felt 310 shares was the appropriate compensation for what he had brought to the company, but since he had not put up a penny in financing, he knew he would have to give up some stock. If he resisted, the other board members would outvote him; he didn't want to end up like Hemrick.

At the December 12 board meeting, Kughn's investment was approved and the stock was redistributed. Kughn, Korbel, and McWilliam would receive 260 shares apiece; Sumner 140, Hemrick 40, and Buice an option to purchase 40. Gluck, who would later replace Hemrick on the board of directors, received $300,000 for bringing the deal together.

It was not quite a year to the day since Buice had signed cards in Hemrick's Upper Deck card shop, but the makeup of the Upper Deck Company had changed dramatically. Hemrick and Sumner, the founders who once owned 100 percent of Upper Deck by virtue of a contract written on a yellow legal pad at Angelo's Pizza, now possessed a combined 18 percent of the company. With Kughn aboard, Upper Deck's ownership was complete.

■ ■ ■

As difficult as it was to obtain the financing for Upper Deck, it was easy compared to the challenge of producing the first cards.

Various companies had produced baseball cards for over a century when Upper Deck was formed in 1988, but from a design standpoint Upper Deck was starting from scratch. The idea was not to become a better Topps or an improved Fleer, but to reinvent the wheel, to create a card unlike any produced in the past. So to avoid repeating the mistakes of other card manufacturers, Upper Deck refrained from hiring plant managers and press operators away from other companies, people who might be resistant to change. It would be easier, Sumner felt, to teach baseball card production to quality printers than to teach quality printing to baseball card producers.

Not surprisingly, Upper Deck's initial production team was made up of men from Sumner's network in the printing industry. Shortly after Kughn put up the financing, Bob Ruggieri, who had worked with Sumner years earlier, was hired as plant manager. Like many men in the printing business, Ruggieri had ink in his veins. Both his father and stepfather had been commercial printers. As a kid, Ruggieri was fascinated by the notion of bringing colors to life. By the age of 35 in 1988, he had spent his entire professional life perfecting the color separation process. His customers marveled at the lithographs, signs, and brochures he produced. The colors seemed to jump off the paper.

Ruggieri had received awards for his work and considered himself as much an artist as a printer. When Sumner asked him to leave the commercial print industry to join Upper Deck, he laughed. He thought of his stepfather, who used to run the presses that attached the red carbon sheet to the back of airline tickets. Producing baseball cards, at least the ones he had seen, seemed almost as challenging. But after listening to Sumner talk about *Architectural Digest*–quality cards, foil stamping, and holograms, Ruggieri knew these were no ordinary baseball cards. As plant manager, he would oversee the entire operation.

There are three steps in baseball card production: pre-press, printing, and finishing. Pre-press begins with the selection of the photos and the color separation. For Upper Deck, the color separation process would be a strength, since Orbis Graphic Arts had been on the cutting edge of that technology through its work for *Architectural Digest*. There was nothing drastically wrong with the color quality of Topps, Fleer, Donruss, and Score baseball cards, but Sumner and Ruggieri knew that the colors could be much improved. Why have a card that looks like the back of a cereal box when you could have a photo that resembles a magazine cover?

Color separation is a simple process, but a difficult one to do well. The challenge is to take a negative, separate its colors onto four transparencies, and transfer the image onto paper. It begins once the photo is selected and a negative is placed in a machine called a scanner, which displays the shot on a computer screen. At this point, card companies transpose words onto the photo, such as the player's name, team, and position, much the same way a magazine or newspaper would superimpose headlines onto color photos. The final image is produced on the same transparent film used to make presentations on an overhead projector.

The transparencies are of four colors: black, yellow, cyan, and magenta. When separated, the photo image is indecipherable; the colors look like blobs of ink. But when stacked together, they form a bright, crisp image of the photo. The transparency is converted into a plate, which is used to print the cards. It sounds easy, but the problems come in production. Pete Rose's Cincinnati Reds' hat might look fire-engine red on a transparency, but come out looking brick red, or even orange. Ruggieri's expertise was in making sure colors were separated properly in pre-press, and balancing the water and chemicals during production to prevent the colors from washing out.

Upper Deck's 700-card set was divided into seven forms for printing. Each form had 100 cards divided into rows of 10. Each form was two-sided, with four aluminum plates of 25 cards positioned together to make up each side. A 700-card set required 56 plates. It is a common perception that companies use one set of plates to produce sports cards. Often a manufacturer will even issue a photo of one of its executives demolishing the plates, with an accompanying press release saying that, with the plates destroyed, it would be impossible for additional cards to be produced. This, however, is a misperception. With several billion cards being made off some press runs, it would be impossible for a plate to go the distance without wearing out or breaking. So multiple plates are made; the publicity photos usually are taken from the destruction of the final plates. This does not mean additional cards could not be produced. So long as the original negatives were available, new plates could be made. But it would be a time-consuming process.

In 1988, cards produced by Topps, Fleer, Donruss, and Score came off the presses and went straight to the finishing department, where they were cut, packaged, boxed, and shipped. Upper Deck added an additional step to its printing process. After its cards were printed, they were stamped with a hologram to prevent counterfeiting.

It was a simple, productive process, at least in theory. Sumner had projected that Upper Deck would be producing 500 cases (5.4 million cards) a day by November 15. But it would be well into 1989 before anyone actually opened a pack of Upper Deck baseball cards.

■ ■ ■

Upper Deck and Tom Geideman were a perfect match. Geideman, who had been one of Bill Hemrick's customers at The Upper Deck, became one of the company's first employees in the fall of 1988. During his first month on the job, Geideman made a decision that would go a long way toward making Upper Deck baseball cards the hot commodity in the 1989 baseball card market.

Hemrick and Paul Sumner originally were in charge of selecting the players for the 1989 card set, but the task eventually fell to Geideman, who had an impeccable knowledge of baseball players both past and present. Most importantly, from Upper Deck's standpoint, Geideman followed the minor leagues, and could rattle off the top prospects of any team in baseball. Anyone could look at a list of major league baseball rosters and pick 700 players for a card set. The challenge was to pick the top rookies, whose cards would attract speculators to the product and boost sales. With the market driven by rookie card investment, the success of a card line hinged on which future superstars were put in the set. If one company overlooked a rookie whom its competitors included, and the player then went on to have a spectacular season, collectors would ignore the cards without the rookie.

When Topps released its cards before the 1986 season, it did not have a card of Oakland Athletics rookie Jose Canseco. Fleer and Donruss included Canseco, and when it became apparent early in the year that Canseco was the favorite to win the American League's Rookie of the Year award, collectors bought up Fleer and Donruss cards. By the time the season was over, Canseco's Donruss card had soared to $60 on the secondary market. Largely because of Canseco, who hit 33 home runs and drove in 117 runs, dealers were selling the Donruss and Fleer sets for more than $100. Topps put Canseco in its 132-card "update" set, but by the time it was released late in the baseball season, it was too late; collectors already recognized Fleer and Donruss cards as the true Canseco rookies.

The companies learned a lesson from Topps's mistake in 1986 and stepped up their scouting efforts of minor league players. Since the cards had to be chosen by Thanksgiving, it was difficult to get a read on which rookies would make Major League rosters out of spring training. Each team had at least a half dozen prospects capable of making the big league roster. Since it was impossible to include them all, the card manufacturers had to make an educated guess. That guess, in the case of Upper Deck, belonged to Geideman.

Geideman was an avid follower of the Seattle Mariners. The team had struggled in the standings since its first game in 1977 and usually had a pick at or near the top of baseball's annual amateur draft, when teams select the nation's best high school and college players. With the first pick in the 1987 draft, the Mariners took Ken Griffey, Jr., who at 17 had just graduated from Cincinnati's Moeller High School. The son of Ken Griffey, the right fielder of the Cincinnati Reds' "Big Red Machine" of the 1970s, Griffey, Jr., was seen as a can't-miss prospect. The only question was how long the young outfielder would have to spend in the minor leagues before joining the Mariners. Griffey, Jr.—Junior to his teammates— began the 1988 season with the Mariners' Class A farm team in San Bernardino, California, eventually working his way up to Class AA Vermont. Despite missing most of the year with a back injury, Junior hit 13 home runs and drove in 52 runs, looking, as expected, like a rising superstar.

When the season ended, Junior seemed likely to begin the 1989 season with the Mariners' top farm team in Calgary. The Mariners felt that Junior, still two months shy of his nineteenth birthday, probably needed another year of preparation in the minors. Like any other top prospect, he would get a chance to make the parent club during spring training, but most likely he would begin the year in Calgary.

Geideman didn't see it that way. The Mariners had finished in last place in the American League West in 1988. Their Opening Day starting lineup had included a lackluster outfield of Mike Kingery, Mickey Brantley, and Glenn Wilson. In 12 years, the team had employed seven managers and never had a winning record. What did they have to lose, Geideman figured, by starting the year with Junior on the major league roster? And what did Upper Deck have to lose by including Junior in its 1989 set? If he made the Mariners, Upper Deck might scoop the other companies by having the only card of Griffey. If he didn't, Upper Deck still would have the first card of a player who undoubtedly would make the majors in 1990. Even if he spent '89 in the minors, collectors still would want to hoard Griffey cards as an investment for the future.

The first 26 cards of Upper Deck's set would be rookies. In 1984, Donruss had included a 20-card subset of "Rated Rookie" cards numbered 27–46. The practice was a hit with collectors and dealers, who liked the idea of having the investment-quality cards at the front of the set. Donruss continued the Rated Rookie series in subsequent years, and Geideman decided that Upper Deck would do the same for 1989.

Shortly after the World Series ended, Geideman finalized the lineup for the 1989 cards. The 26 rookies included future stars Gary Sheffield, John Smoltz, and Randy Johnson as well as players such as Dante Bichette, Felix Jose, Mark Lemke, and Sandy Alomar, Jr., who would go on to have productive careers. (Also included were such forgettable players as Rolando Roomes, Luis Medina, Dave Otto, and Van Snider.)

The honor of appearing on card No. 1 went to Griffey, Jr. But since Griffey had played in the minors the year before, Upper Deck had no photos of him in a Mariners' uniform. Instead, Geideman took a snapshot of Griffey in a San Bernardino uniform and cap and had it computer enhanced to make it look as if Griffey were in uniform for the Mariners. Using a computer graphics process called Scitex—the modern equivalent of the airbrush—Geideman "promoted" Griffey, Jr., to the Mariners in November of 1988.

The selection of Griffey, Jr., for the first card was not the only instance where Geideman injected his personal biases into the numbering process. He had a particular disdain for the Los Angeles Dodgers, and decided that card number 666 (the legendary number of the Devil) would go to a Dodger. Since Kirk Gibson had won Game One of the 1988 World Series for the eventual World Champion Dodgers with a dramatic, pinch-hit home run off Oakland's Dennis Eckersley, he would be saddled with No. 666 for 1989. (Geideman continued the practice in later years, using 666 for Dodgers' rookie Jose Gonzalez in 1990, outfielder Mickey Hatcher in 1991, pitcher Bob Ojeda in 1992, and reliever Jim Gott in 1993.)

With Upper Deck struggling to get its first cards out the door, Geideman's choice of Griffey, Jr., as the leadoff card went virtually unnoticed until spring training, when Junior hit .359 and was named the Mariners' starting center fielder for Opening Day.

■ ■ ■

For nine months in 1988, Anthony Passante had served as counsel for Upper Deck. Along with his partner, Andrew Prendiville, he felt he had played a vital role. He had filed the articles of incorporation, made two trips to New York on behalf of Upper Deck, and served as corporate secretary during board meetings. Although the work was done in his official capacity as counsel, he felt he was part of a special endeavor made up of longtime friends and associates. He had known McWilliam for 20 years, and had socialized with Korbel for nearly a decade. When McWilliam had left the company during the summer and Upper Deck needed $100,000 to secure the paper order from Noland Paper, Passante had put together a loan from Prendiville's brother, Kevin. It was all one big extended family. Or so he thought.

Passante was under the impression that he was not only counsel to Upper

Deck, but also an owner. During the August 2, 1988, board meeting, when McWilliam's departure from the company had been discussed, Passante believed the 110 shares McWilliam owned had been divvied up; Korbel was to get 80 and Passante 30. Although there had been no stock certificates placed in Passante's name, he thought he had a verbal commitment from Korbel to hold his (Passante's) shares as part of his own.

When Passante arrived at Orbis Graphic Arts for the December 12 meeting, he was handed a fax from Dan Lybarger, who at the time was serving as controller for both Orbis and Upper Deck. The fax was a new shareholder agreement, revised to include Kughn's investment. The agreement was written by Ben Frydman, the lawyer McWilliam had hired in August to write the letter demanding the return of the money McWilliam had advanced the company, along with the additional $150,000.

As Passante read the fax, it became clear that the Newport Beach law firm of Stradling, Yocca, Carlson & Rauth would be handling Upper Deck's affairs and that the small firm of Passante and Prendiville was fired.

Passante, still looking at the fax, began to walk toward the conference room. McWilliam, noticing what he was reading, stopped him in the hall. "Oh, yeah. I forgot to tell you. You're out."

"I figured that," Passante said. "But was somebody going to let me know?"

Passante turned and went to Korbel's office, holding the fax in front of him. "I'm sorry," Korbel said. "I didn't get a chance to tell you."

Passante shook his head and left. He remained Korbel's personal attorney for nearly a year. But his business with the Upper Deck Company was over. The next time the young attorney would come in contact with Upper Deck, it would be from the other side of the courtroom.

■ ■ ■

McWilliam and McCracken flew to Cleveland January 16, 1989, to meet with Kughn. The second half of the financing was contingent on sales projections, and the figures to date were not good. Upper Deck had purchase orders for 23,140 cases—not even half of the 65,000 case press run.

Kughn was not pleased. They had promised that at least half of the run would be sold by the meeting. McCracken tried to put a positive spin on the shortfall. The 23,140 cases represented $8.8 million in revenue. Besides, only 8,063 cases had been sold to candy, tobacco, and magazine wholesalers, half of what McCracken felt they would sell. Upper Deck would have no problem signing up additional accounts at the winter convention of the National Candy Wholesalers Association in Phoenix. "The estimate of double our current business is very conservative," he told Kughn.

McCracken said 30,095 cases would be sold to national accounts, although only 5,184 cases had been sold so far. He presented Kughn with a list of 40 accounts, including every major drugstore chain and wholesale club in the country. The name of an Upper Deck representative who was pursuing the sale was listed alongside each account. Many of the key accounts were being handled by Bob Bove (pronounced "Bo-vee"), who had worked with McCracken at Nestlé. Now Upper Deck's national account manager, Bove worked out of St. Louis—partly because he had lived there his whole life and wanted to stay and partly because from there he could more easily handle sales in the Midwest.

Kughn read the list, unimpressed. "So why aren't we selling?"

"Look, Dick," McWilliam said, "we've had some minor production problems, but they've been cleared up. People are waiting to see the cards come out. Once we get one case out, the rest of them will follow quickly and they'll be beating down our door. I have no doubt we'll have the entire run sold by March."

March! McCracken thought to himself. He doubted that there would be a case of cards out of the plant by March. To hear McWilliam tell it, the cards were being produced as they spoke. It was a good thing Kughn was 2,500 miles from the facility, where Sumner, Ruggieri, and the boys were doubtless still trying to figure out how to get their new press running.

Kughn looked at the national account list again. "Are you sure about this?" he asked McCracken.

"We'll sell 30,000 cases to the national accounts," McCracken said, making sure he was not agreeing with McWilliam.

"Then you've got yourself a deal," Kughn said.

After they had thanked Kughn and left, McWilliam turned to McCracken. "They'll be out by March, right?"

McCracken sighed. "I hope so, Richard."

■ ■ ■

Upper Deck could not stay in Anaheim for long. The auxiliary building the company used at 1174 North Grove Street next to Orbis Graphic Arts was not big enough to hold the growing company's office staff. And, of course, there was no room to print cards. Orbis had a small press, which had been used to produce the prototype cards of DeWayne Buice and Wally Joyner. But it was in the business of color separation. It did not have printing capabilities to do an entire run of baseball cards.

In December, Bob Henry received a phone call from McWilliam. Henry, a building contractor based in Westminster, just south of Los Angeles, had supervised several projects for Lehman Medical when McWilliam was its controller. Now McWilliam wanted to know if Henry would oversee the interior construction of a new facility in Yorba Linda, just 12 miles from Orbis, that would produce baseball cards. McWilliam had shown Henry the prototype cards in June, wanting to know of he or anyone else he knew would be interested in investing. Henry's response was typical. "I don't know, Richard," he had said. "Baseball cards?"

But when McWilliam called shortly before Christmas with a construction job and the news that the financing had come through, Henry joined Upper Deck as an all-purpose contractor. The company seemed to have moved forward quickly since June. But when Henry arrived at the plant on January 18, his 42nd birthday, he found it hard to believe the place was expected to crank out cards in a matter of weeks. The building was practically deserted, which he expected. He had, after all, been hired to do a buildout of the facility. There were a few dozen plant workers struggling to figure out how to operate Upper Deck's new six-color press. A few others were setting up the foil stamper, which would apply the holograms. There wasn't much to the physical plant. A previous contractor had installed bathrooms. But other than that, the building was a shell.

Henry had no doubt he could finish the buildout in a matter of months. But as he drove away from the new Upper Deck headquarters at 23705 Via Del Rio, he wondered how they ever expected to produce cards. Weren't they supposed to have been out by November?

■ ■ ■

The initial success of Upper Deck, ironically, came not from its revolutionary new baseball cards but from its inability to get the cards off the printing press and out the door.

When McCracken joined Upper Deck September 20, the plan was to ship the 1989 baseball cards beginning November 15. The strategy behind the early release date was twofold: Upper Deck would get a jump on the other card companies, while positioning itself to become the first manufacturer to launch a summer "update" set of cards which would include top rookies and players who were traded or signed as free agents after the regular edition had come out.

The launch date had been pushed back until the end of January, then to the spring, which made sales more difficult since no one had actually seen the cards. Each day Upper Deck failed to release cards, it seemed, phone calls to Upper Deck increased. Everyone wanted to know if the company was still in business. Don Bodow, the former Syracuse mail order dealer who by now had joined Upper Deck as vice president of marketing, began answering his phone by saying "We're still in business. Don Bodow, speaking."

Upper Deck's distribution network was divided into three categories: The Hobby, which consisted of baseball card–shop owners and their distributors; candy, tobacco, and magazine wholesalers, which sold cards to newsstands and smaller convenience stores; and national accounts, chains such as Kmart, Wal-Mart, and Toys "R" Us.

Response from the latter two groups, as expected, had been slow. McCracken knew the success of Upper Deck depended on acceptance by The Hobby, the network of card-shop owners and distributors that generated interest in the card business. If the word in The Hobby was that Upper Deck was the hottest product on the market, the national accounts would follow. McCracken had no doubt Upper Deck would sell the 65,000 cases for 1989. The trick was to generate interest for 1990, when the company could jack up production and increase sales. The easiest way to get The Hobby excited was to have dealers so thrilled about Upper Deck that their customers would forget about the other card manufacturers. And the only way to do that, McCracken knew, was to make the cards accessible to hobby dealers.

Unlike Topps, Fleer, Donruss, and Score, which sold nearly all of their cards through retail outlets and networks of candy distributors, Upper Deck offered its cards to any hobby dealer who could produce a business card and license, a seller's permit, a tax resale card, and a photo of his store. For dealers accustomed to having difficulty in obtaining cards, Upper Deck was a godsend. That, combined with the quality of the new product, allowed Upper Deck to fulfill its self-fulfilling prophecy; it became the Collector's Choice even before the first cards hit the street. The dealers who had purchased Upper Deck hyped the cards to their customers, who waited anxiously for the cards. The production delays, while unfortunate, actually served to increase the hype.

Since the National Convention in Atlantic City, word in The Hobby was that Upper Deck's product would be extremely scarce. Even though card companies did not release their production figures, the 65,000 case figure sounded minuscule to most collectors. In its sales literature, Upper Deck estimated that there were "1.5 million collectors (maybe more). Our limited production of 60,000–70,000 cases means that only about a million of each card will be manufactured. Obviously every collector won't be able to own a set of Upper Deck's premier edition."

Still, sales were slow. Even in the speculative hobby market, only 821 dealers opened accounts with Upper Deck. The fear was that Upper Deck would never get off the ground. If Upper Deck never came through with the cards, the dealers would have to try to get their money back from a nonexistent company. Unlike the candy wholesalers and national accounts, who paid for the cards based on sales, hobby dealers had to put up their money before they received the cards. A failed $2,000 investment in five cases of cards could put a small store out of business.

When Upper Deck did not launch the cards November 15, the company received a few phone calls from concerned dealers. It was not unusual for card manufacturers to miss their scheduled launch date, and McCracken apologized for the delay.

But as November became December and then January, and the callers went from concerned to belligerent, McCracken pressed Sumner. Each time, Sumner would point to a wall in his office, where he had the production schedule mapped out down to the hour. "Jay," he would say cheerfully. "We'll be printing cards in two weeks."

McCracken had his doubts. He would go next door to Orbis and ask the plant workers if it were possible to get their first cards printed in two weeks. The workers were in the color separation business, but from what they knew about printing and dealing with Sumner's bold forecasts, they had to laugh. There was just no way the cards would be ready in two weeks.

At Yorba Linda, the plant workers were still trying to figure out the press. Had they been making cards like Topps, Fleer, Donruss, or Score, things would have gone smoothly. But these were new cards and new technologies. No one had ever made cards with aqueous coating *and* holograms. The founders of Upper Deck, when scheduling the release date, failed to realize that there would be a learning curve involved. But even if the plant employees had caught on quickly, they were not prepared to deal with the problems of the press's roll coater, which applied the aqueous coating that gave the cards a glossy finish. On the rare occasions when the workers could get the roll coater to work, the sheets of cards would stick together. Sheets trickled out. A few would come through perfectly, then a series would come through stuck together. It was a painstakingly slow process. Valentine's Day arrived, and Upper Deck still had not released a single case of baseball cards.

■ ■ ■

For weeks, McCracken and Bove had told customers that the cards were finally going to be released on March 1. But since they had changed the date so many times before, few dealers and distributors expected the cards to really go out the door. Even McCracken and Bove had their doubts. Sumner and Ruggieri insisted they would make the date, but it didn't take a printing expert to look at the machinery and know that it was an unrealistic prospect. The operation looked like it was held together with Band-Aids and baling wire.

The entire process seemed like a rocket launch countdown. Just when they thought they had all the kinks out of the press, something would go awry and the system would shut down, pushing the release date back.

But this time, Sumner assured them, the cards would be ready. It was decided that McCracken would hand-deliver the first case off the press to whomever had made the first order. Bove would fly in from his office in St. Louis. A photo opportunity would be scheduled, along with local media coverage. "Do we really want the press there?" McCracken asked. "What happens if the cards don't come out? We'll look like idiots."

"You'll have the cards in time," Sumner said.

McCracken made plans to deliver the first two cases to George Moore of Tulsa Baseball Cards. Moore had been the first card store owner to send in a check following the National Sports Collectors Convention in Atlantic City. He had made a down payment of $2,000 on 10 cases in July, then sent in the balance of $2,000 in December. Like everyone else, Moore was wondering if he was ever was going to see the cards. Unlike Topps, Fleer, and Donruss, which had begun as candy manufacturers, Upper Deck was not an established company. There were constant rumors of bankruptcy. Moore was pleased when Upper Deck had called in January about scheduling a photo shoot, but told his employees: "I'll believe it when they get here."

On February 27, McCracken reluctantly made plane reservations and called Moore. He also called the *Tulsa World* newspaper and hired a photographer to be on hand when he and Bove arrived.

With less than 48 hours left in February, the countdown was on again. When McCracken left his office on the 28th, the cards still were not ready. After dinner, he called Sumner, who told him the cards would be ready after midnight. When McCracken arrived, the cards were printed and cut, but not packaged.

McCracken looked at his watch. It was 12:30. His flight left Ontario Airport in Orange County in just six hours. He went home and tried to sleep for five hours. As he drove back to Upper Deck, he said a prayer. "Please God, let the cards be ready."

This time, the cards were packaged and waiting. McCracken loaded the cards, and went directly to the airport. Even though the cases were too big to be considered carry-on items, McCracken took the cards onto his Delta flight. He had to change planes in Dallas and wasn't about to risk losing the cards. Who knew when the next ones would come out or even if there would be more cards?

Bove met McCracken at the Tulsa airport, and together they drove to Moore's store and delivered the first two cases of Upper Deck baseball cards. Even though it was a Wednesday morning, Moore's store was full of customers anxious to finally see the new Upper Deck baseball cards. Bove and McCracken felt like Santa Claus as they each carried a case into the shop. The photographer took a picture of McCracken and Moore. The following day, the *Tulsa World* ran a story, copies of which were sent out by Upper Deck to dealers and media to prove that the company had actually produced cards.

Bove and McCracken were still smiling as they drove back to the airport. After nearly four months of dealing with angry phone calls from card dealers, they could now say the cards were being shipped. If nothing else, the first two cases were sold, paid for, and delivered.

The next several million would be much easier.

10

Rookie of the Year

As Upper Deck struggled to get its first cards to stores, Fleer inadvertently became the hot product of 1989. The company that had captured the attention of collectors in 1981 when its first card set included a number of misspellings and misprintings had again created an uproar with an "error" card.

As collectors opened Fleer's cards in January of 1989, they discovered that the cards of Baltimore Orioles second baseman Billy Ripken included a colorful greeting. Ripken posed for his photo holding a bat over his right shoulder. On the knob of the bat, just below Ripken's left hand, the words "Fuck Face" were written in black magic marker. Ripken later said he was unaware of any writing on the bat, and that he never would have posed with the bat had he known about the writing.

Vincent Murray, who had succeeded Don Peck as president of Fleer, learned of the obscenity January 17 and ordered the presses stopped and the offending words blotted out. But it was too late; a significant quantity of the "obscenity card" hit the market. The card attracted national attention and investors, armed with the news that only a limited number of the obscenity card existed, rushed to acquire it. The price for the card soared, peaking at $125. Packs of 45-cent Fleer cards sold at card shows in January of 1989 for $6 apiece.

Murray announced that Fleer would gladly give collectors who did not want the X-rated card in their collection the opportunity to exchange it for a corrected version. The offer, not surprisingly, elicited little response.

Fleer, through no fault of its own, had taken the early lead in the 1989 baseball card market. But it soon would give way to the new company from Yorba Linda, California.

■ ■ ■

Just because Bob Bove and Jay McCracken had delivered the first two Upper Deck cases to George Moore of Tulsa Baseball Cards on March 1 did not mean that Upper Deck was cranking out baseball cards. For the next few weeks, cases trickled out of the plant at the rate of seven to ten per day. With customers waiting for 65,000 cases, Bove and McCracken were left to continue playing damage control on the phone.

As plant manager, Bob Ruggieri had been doing essentially the work of two people, directing color separation as well as printing. At the end of March, Ruggieri, whose expertise was in color separation more than printing, was named the assistant plant manager in charge of pre-press and color separation and a new plant manager was hired.

The new man, Harold "Buzz" Rasmussen, Jr., had 20 years of experience in commercial lithography. Rasmussen found that the production of baseball cards, even Upper Deck baseball cards, was not that much different from printing lithographs. Many of the problems Upper Deck had encountered were typical frustrations in lithography. The ink had to be balanced properly, the press needed constant adjustment, etc. Instead of trying to teach factory workers how to produce baseball cards, Rasmussen trained the workers as commercial lithographers. What were baseball cards, he figured, but tiny lithographs?

The press staff caught on quickly, and by the middle of April, Upper Deck was producing 200 cases a day. Even the troublesome roll coater had been conquered. By the end of the month, the daily output had increased to 400 cases. By early May, Paul Sumner's forecast of 500 cases a day had been exceeded. But while production had kicked in, Bove and McCracken still took dozens of phone calls each day from anxious customers. The cases, which sold for between $370 and $420 wholesale depending on when they were purchased, were going for $800 on the secondary market. Dealers who received Upper Deck product were doubling their money instantly. But since all 65,000 cases could not be printed and shipped at once, some dealers were left waiting, wondering if the market would still be there once they received their cases.

By Memorial Day, the 65,000 cases had been shipped. For Rasmussen and the production staff, the end of the first press run was a proud moment—even if they had made mistakes along the way.

■ ■ ■

Just as Fleer and Donruss had made errors in their haste to produce their first baseball cards in 1981, Upper Deck also made several gaffes in its inaugural set in 1989. None of the mistakes were as colorful as Fleer's Ripken, but they nonetheless helped make Upper Deck the card industry's rookie of the year.

The card of the Tigers' Pat Sheridan was printed without him labeled as an outfielder. But the most noticeable mistake was in the card of Dale Murphy, the star outfielder for the Atlanta Braves. The photo, an upper body shot of Murphy holding a bat over his right shoulder, had been printed with the negative reversed, making it appear as if Murphy had posed with the bat over his left shoulder. McCracken said later that the card had been checked by ten proofreaders. But none of them noticed the reverse negative. At first glance, it's an easy error to miss. The word "Braves" went across Murphy's chest with the familiar tomahawk logo underneath it. But the insignia was obstructed by Murphy, whose arms crossed his chest in the photo.

With only a small portion of its press run out the door, Upper Deck officials realized the Murphy error. Like other card companies, Upper Deck came under fire from collectors and dealers who charged that the errors were done on purpose to generate interest in the product. That wasn't the case with Upper Deck. They were too busy trying to launch their cards to concoct that kind of scheme. Plus, it cost time and money to stop the presses.

Sometimes it wasn't worth the trouble. Not long after Upper Deck's first baseball cards were shipped, McCracken received a call from a collector who was wondering when Upper Deck was going to correct the Jose Uribe card.

"What's wrong with the Jose Uribe card?" McCracken asked.

The caller, undoubtedly inspired by the Ripken incident, pointed out that there was an obscenity on the back of the Uribe card. McCracken pulled out a Uribe card, looked at the back, and saw nothing. There was Uribe, in action at shortstop for the San Francisco Giants.

"Exactly," said the caller. "Now look at the outfield fence behind him. There's an advertising sign on the outfield wall that says 'world's largest title insurer.' Uribe's body is blocking out the last two letters in the word title, so it looks like 'world's largest tit insurer.'"

McCracken hung up the phone. This was getting ridiculous. "Now if we dignify that call by fixing the Uribe card, we have another Ripken situation on our hands," he told his colleagues. "We don't need that kind of publicity."

But the Murphy card, it was decided, was worth the cost of correcting. Since Murphy was one of baseball's best and most popular players, it would not look good for Upper Deck to screw up his card in its premier edition. The company fixed the error, and the reverse negative card shot up in value. McCracken told The Hobby press that only 20,000 Murphy cards had been printed. By July, the error card was listed at $75 in *Beckett Baseball Card Monthly*.

■ ■ ■

The manufacture of baseball cards was not the only production going on at Upper Deck's new Yorba Linda headquarters. Bob Henry, the contractor Richard McWilliam had hired in January, was busy overseeing the buildout of the new facility.

It was a gradual process. As Henry's construction crew completed work on parts of the two-story building, employees moved from Anaheim to Yorba Linda. The press room, where the cards were produced, was completed first, although one wall was enclosed by a temporary barrier to allow for additional equipment to be brought in. Next came the color department, where the color separation work was done, and the cafeteria.

The administrative offices were located upstairs, and since their completion was not necessary to produce the cards, Henry's crew scheduled them for last. So while the cards were produced in Yorba Linda, much of Upper Deck's management team remained 12 miles away in Anaheim.

It was not a productive means of conducting business and in early April, McWilliam issued a challenge to Henry. A board meeting was scheduled for April 12, and if Henry had the new conference room finished in time, he would receive a case of baseball cards as a bonus. Henry's crew worked frantically, laying the carpet in the room the day before the meeting.

The meeting took place at Yorba Linda, and Henry received his case of cards. In May, Upper Deck acquired an additional press. By the end of June, the company's new 35,000 square-foot facility was complete.

But it would not hold the growing business for long.

■ ■ ■

In the Connecticut offices of SportsNet, they had never seen anything like the 1989 Upper Deck baseball cards. Created in 1982 as a communications tool for coin and jewelry dealers, the on-line computer network became an electronic marketplace for sports card and memorabilia dealers when its original area of business, the coin market, softened in the mid-1980s. As the sports card business grew, many of the original SportsNet coin dealers became baseball card dealers, and SportsNet became a means for dealers to buy, sell, and trade baseball cards.

In 1989, SportsNet had more than 200 sports card and memorabilia dealers subscribing to the service. Instead of individual cards or sets, whose prices were chronicled in the pages of *Beckett Baseball Card Monthly*, vending cases were the commodity of choice among SportsNet traders.

A dealer could buy or sell cards on SportsNet by placing an ad on-line. If there was heavy trading in a particular card or case, the price went up accordingly.

Much like Beckett Publications, SportsNet had a major influence on the price of sports cards.

By the summer of 1989, cases of Upper Deck's new baseball cards had risen to $1,200 a case. Nobody it seemed, could get enough Upper Deck. Company officials had worried that the suggested retail price of Upper Deck baseball cards (89 cents) would frighten away collectors. After all, packs of Topps, Fleer, Donruss, and Score sold between 40 and 50 cents. Now 89 cents looked like a bargain as packs sold on the secondary market for between $2 and $3.

For dealers who had committed to Upper Deck between September and December of 1988, when it looked as though the company might never produce cards, the success of the '89 baseball cards provided a huge payday.

Kit Young, a San Diego card dealer with 20 years experience in The Hobby, said Upper Deck's 1989 baseball cards were the ultimate symbol of the speculative fervor surrounding the baseball card business from 1985 to 1992. Young, who specializes in pre-1970 baseball cards, received a call in late 1988 from Don Bodow, Upper Deck's vice president of marketing. A longtime collector himself, Bodow knew of Young's reputation as a major player in the industry, and offered him a chance to buy Upper Deck's premier product.

"The ironic thing was that they offered me credit, but I wouldn't have given them credit," Young recalled. "Once the '89 baseball [product] hit, it sold like hotcakes. We'd get more and more calls on it each day. We'd throw out a higher price each day and people were willing to buy. The market went nuts over it. If you had the right product—and this wasn't just true of '89 Upper Deck— you could make $10,000 off of 20 cases without even trying.

"People became self-proclaimed geniuses. I've often felt that back then I could have picked somebody up off any street corner, given them some start-up money, and they could have made $50,000–$75,000 a year easily."

Those who turned down Upper Deck lost out. Bove, the company's national sales manager, met with a senior buyer for a major retail chain in April of 1989, not long after the first two cases had been delivered to Tulsa Baseball Cards. The buyer looked at the suggested retail price of 89 cents a pack and asked if there was a mistake.

"No, that's our price," Bove said. "We have a higher quality product."

"You've got to be kidding me," the buyer replied. "Don't you know that trading cards are a 45-cent item?"

"Yes, but we're here to change that."

"Well, you guys seem to know what you're doing, but I just don't think this is going to work."

In July of 1989, Bove attended the National Convention of Candy Wholesalers in Washington, D.C., and ran into the same buyer.

"Go ahead," the man said. "Call me the biggest idiot in the world. I don't suppose you have any product left?"

It was a question Bove heard often. The answer, of course, was no. But even after the company had shipped its entire production run, it still received phone calls from card dealers and entrepreneurs begging for the opportunity to buy cards. One day, Bove took a call from one man who was particularly adamant. "I'm sorry," Bove said. "But we just don't have any more."

"But I have a check for $25,000 that I'd like to invest in your company. And then I'd like to buy some product."

Bove hung up the phone. Where, he wondered, were these people six months before when they were struggling to sell enough cards to secure Richard Kughn's investment?

McCracken and Bove, who now controlled the dispersal of the hottest cards in The Hobby, became mini-celebrities. McCracken, who was a California Angels season ticket holder, used to arrive at his seats and find them covered with the team logo hologram stickers that Upper Deck included in each pack. (Even eight years after Topps's virtual monopoly had been broken, companies still had to include a product with the cards so as to not violate Topps's exclusive right to market cards alone or with gum.)

When McCracken joined Upper Deck in September of 1988, he received a Ford Aerostar as a company car. His daughter, observing how much her father enjoyed his new job, ordered him vanity tags that read "UPPRDCK." McCracken drove the car proudly through Orange County, waving to fellow drivers who recognized him by his license plates.

But in the summer of 1989, as Upper Deck cards soared to $1,200 a case, McCracken had the plates removed. Just months after the first two cases of cards had been delivered to George Moore of Tulsa Baseball Cards, Upper Deck cards had become so hot that McCracken worried that someone would mistake the Astrostar for a delivery vehicle and he would become a carjacking victim.

■ ■ ■

In July of 1989, Boris Korbel stepped down as president of Upper Deck. The task of running a growing company that operated in organized chaos had become too much for a man who only eight years earlier had been a quadriplegic and still walked with a cane and occasionally used a motorized wheelchair. Now that Upper Deck had moved into its own headquarters, away from that of Orbis Graphic Arts, its business affairs were no longer intertwined. Plus, assistant plant manager Ruggieri had established a new pre-press and color separation room at Upper Deck, which meant he no longer had to use Orbis's facilities.

The new president, the board decided, would be McWilliam. For the previous eight months, McWilliam gradually had severed his ties with Lehman Medical and now was operating as an Upper Deck vice president on a full-time basis.

The move was both appropriate and ironic. McWilliam, who had used his background in real estate and development to organize the buildout of Upper Deck's Yorba Linda facility, now would employ his financial skills to take Upper Deck to the next level. Plus, with Upper Deck rapidly expanding, there soon would be a need for a new facility to be purchased and built. Here too McWilliam's expertise would be important.

But it was only a year since McWilliam's original financing proposal had been rejected and the board had moved to dismiss him from the company. Now he was in charge. Of the six men who had made the trip to New York to meet with the Players Association in May 1988, only McWilliam and Sumner were still involved in Upper Deck on a day-to-day basis. Hemrick had left to become a distributor and Passante had been fired. Bob Cohen, who negotiated Upper Deck's license with the PA, was not active in company affairs, although he did receive the right to buy Upper Deck product in consideration for his services. (Cohen also received one-half of one percent of gross sales of baseball cards, along with a $1,000 monthly retainer.)

Now Korbel, whose Orbis Graphic Arts had provided not only the startup materials but many of Upper Deck's employees, was stepping down. Kughn, who had joined the company in December 1988 when he became a 27 percent stockholder, lived in Detroit and concentrated on his other two companies, Lionel Trains and Carail.

That left McWilliam, who at 35 had endured a tumultuous ride to become president of the hottest company in the trading card business.

■ ■ ■

In the summer of 1989, Upper Deck contacted the PTS telemarketing firm to conduct research on the sports card industry. Bodow, Upper Deck's vice president of marketing, set up an appointment to meet with PTS at UDC headquarters in Yorba Linda.

On his way out the door, the PTS marketing representative who took the call stopped at the office of Mike Berkus, who was working for PTS at the time. "You collect cards, ever hear of Upper Deck?" he said.

Berkus explained his background in the sports card industry, how he had traveled the country buying cards in the 1970s and helped organize the first National Sports Collectors Convention in 1980. "I tell you what," he said. "I'll go meet with this Bodow guy. You can keep the commission, but since I know the language of the industry, it might be best if I went."

Upon arriving at Upper Deck, Berkus ran into McCracken, who he knew from attending card shows in Orange County. As Berkus walked down the hall to see Bodow, he noticed a nameplate on the door of an office. It read Richard McWilliam.

"Excuse me," he said to a secretary. "Is that Richard McWilliam who used to be with Lehman Medical?"

The secretary said she didn't know, but offered to get Mr. McWilliam. "No, that's O.K.," Berkus said. "I'm late for my meeting with Don Bodow."

Berkus stepped into Bodow's office and introduced himself. He explained his background in marketing and promoting trade shows, particularly hobby card shows. He mentioned how he had traveled the country buying collections and helped organize the first National.

Bodow was not impressed. "Well, I had a big mail-order business in Syracuse for years and I've never heard of you."

Berkus couldn't believe the arrogance of the guy. "Excuse me?"

"I said, I've been in this business a long time and I've never heard your name."

Berkus fired right back. "I wouldn't use the term 'big mail-order dealer' in this room right now," he said. "But there's only the two of us here so you can call yourself whatever you want."

Just then, McCracken walked by. Bodow asked him if he knew who Berkus was. "Yeah," McCracken said. "He started the National. He traveled all over the country buying cards."

When McCracken left, Bodow turned to Berkus. "I'm sorry, Mr. Berkus, but I don't think we can use you."

"Why not?"

"Because we can't trust you."

Berkus had heard enough. "Now you listen to me, Mr. Big-Time mail-order dealer. You cannot use me because you don't like my attitude or because you're not impressed with me or that there are better candidates, but don't tell me you can't trust me. You don't even know me. So let's not throw the insults around too much, O.K.? For one thing, you will not find another telemarketing firm that knows squat about this industry. You're going to be speaking Latin to these people and they're not going to have a clue what you're talking about. Your telemarketing program will be mediocre at best."

Berkus got up to leave. "By the way, I noticed the name Richard McWilliam over there. Was he with Lehman Medical?"

Bodow nodded. "I tell you what," Berkus said. "Let's go say hello."

As Berkus barged into McWilliam's office, he remembered that he hadn't seen McWilliam in three years. He hoped McWilliam remembered him. "What are you doing making baseball cards?" Berkus asked. "You don't know a baseball card from a playing card. What happened to you and Lehman Medical?"

McWilliam smiled. "That's a long story. What brings you to Upper Deck?"

Berkus explained how Bodow had called PTS for telemarketing help but, after chatting with him, didn't want to hire the company.

"That's ridiculous," McWilliam said. "When can you start?"

■ ■ ■

It took McWilliam a while to learn about sports. Having spent most of his child-hood and all of his adult life concentrating on work, he never developed the pas-sion that he saw in other members of the company who had watched sports since childhood. "It wasn't that I didn't have the interest," he recalled in an interview for this book. "It's just that I was always too busy working."

McWilliam had never collected cards like vice presidents Bodow and McCracken, nor had he followed sports to the point where he could rattle off the starting lineups of teams from the 1960s. But as his involvement with Upper Deck grew, McWilliam immersed himself in the American culture of sports. He read sports magazines, along with baseball hobby card magazines, and began at-tending more sporting events. His education was a gradual process, but he soon became well versed in all four major sports, able to talk knowledgeably about players and teams. But it took a while.

During the first month of the 1988 baseball season, McWilliam, Sumner, Korbel, and Upper Deck corporate counsel Anthony Passante received tickets to an Angels game courtesy of DeWayne Buice and Wally Joyner. As the group en-tered Anaheim Stadium, McWilliam turned to Passante. "So this is a baseball game," he said. "Tell me, how long do they usually last?"

Passante was stunned. Ever since high school, Mac had been a workaholic, but was this really the first game he had ever attended? (According to McWilliam, it was not. "My father used to take us to baseball games from time to time and in fact he was an avid fan of Frank Howard. He used to say he was a frustrated player and would boast as to the power of a home run hitter. In addition, my favorite player during my formative years was Sandy Koufax. I became less of a sports fan as I entered the professional business world because of time commitments.")

McWilliam worked hard to cultivate his image as an athlete and sports fan. He told several newspaper reporters that he had played baseball in high school and college. Inevitably, he was described in print as a "former high school and college baseball player." McWilliam was telling the truth; he did indeed play baseball casually during his educational years. But there is no record at any of the schools he attended of him playing varsity baseball.

In 1988, when the Major League Baseball Players Association ruled that Joyner and Buice could not take an active role in Upper Deck, the company began a search for another player spokesman. McWilliam called Andrew Prendiville for advice.

"Andy," he said. "Have you ever heard of a guy named Tony Gwine?"

"Who?"

"Tony Gwine, he plays for the Padres."

Prendiville chuckled to himself. "You mean Tony Gwynn. It rhymes with 'win.'"

"Yeah, right," McWilliam said. "Tony Gwynn."

Gwynn, the star right fielder for the San Diego Padres, never became a spokes-man for Upper Deck. Two years later, in an executive meeting in 1991, Upper Deck planned its promotion for its first set of basketball cards. McWilliam spoke up. "Have any of you heard of a former basketball player named Jerry West?"

The executives looked at one another. Was McWilliam not familiar with Jerry West, the Hall of Fame guard for the Los Angeles Lakers who was now the team's general manager?

"Yeah, why?" McCracken asked.

"We've been in contact with him about doing a promotion for basketball."

"Sounds like a good idea," McCracken said.

"Yeah, I thought it might be."

Upper Deck included a 10-card subset of "Jerry West Heroes" cards in its 1991–92 basketball cards. West also autographed 2,500 cards, which were randomly inserted in packs.

McWilliam's sports knowledge was improving, and he eventually became an avid sports fan. Still, he was not exactly a sports encyclopedia. (In an interview for this book, held in McWilliam's office June 25, 1993, the day after the San Diego Padres shocked the baseball world by trading Gary Sheffield to the Florida Mar-lins for three prospects, McWilliam greeted the author by holding up the sports section of *The San Diego Union-Tribune* and saying: "Can you believe the Padres traded Tony Gwynn?")

In many ways, though, McWilliam's relative lack of fan experience helped him maintain a professional distance from the legendary sports figures who did busi-ness with Upper Deck. "He's very much the businessman," said Bruce McNall, who while owner of the Los Angeles Kings in 1992 combined with Upper Deck to form a new company, Upper Deck Authenticated, to market autographed sports memorabilia. "Maybe the fact that he hasn't gotten addicted to sports like the rest of us is a strength of his."

Certainly it helped one afternoon in the summer of 1989 when Reggie Jackson showed up at the offices of Upper Deck looking to buy cases of baseball cards. After the receptionist informed McWilliam that a Mr. Reggie Jackson wished to see him, McWilliam called Bodow.

"Reggie Jackson," McWilliam said. "He's the baseball player who hit all the home runs in the World Series, right?"

"Yeah," Bodow said. "Why do you ask?"

"No reason," McWilliam replied and hung up the phone. Bodow was an avid autograph collector who might have annoyed Jackson by asking for an autograph. McWilliam met Jackson at the reception desk and took him back to his office. The two hit it off immediately, and by the end of the day, McWilliam finally had found a spokesman for Upper Deck baseball cards.

Meanwhile, Bodow went back to work, wondering what Reggie Jackson had to do with Upper Deck.

■ ■ ■

Shortly before Christmas, 1989, a holiday party was held at Upper Deck's corporate headquarters in Yorba Linda. For the employees of the Upper Deck Company, there was much to celebrate.

A year earlier, Upper Deck had neither a print site nor enough capital to launch its first baseball cards. As recently as March, it looked as though the cards would never come out. Now, nine months later, Upper Deck was on top of the card-collecting world. Its glossy new baseball cards had become the hit of the industry and plans were underway to obtain licenses to produce football, basketball, and hockey cards. Its 1989 set was worth $60, according to the December issue of *Beckett Baseball Card Monthly*. The price did not include the Dale Murphy "error" card, valued alone at $125, according to Beckett.

Part of the success, of course, was luck. Upper Deck's inability to produce baseball cards in a timely fashion had only served to increase demand as cases trickled out of the factory. Part of it, also, was due to Tom Geideman, the employee who picked the first crop of rookies for Upper Deck, being not only an astute judge of baseball talent but also an avid follower of the Seattle Mariners and Ken Griffey, Jr. And part of it, ironically, was due to ten Upper Deck proofreaders failing to recognize that the Murphy card had been printed backwards.

But Upper Deck owed much of its success to Sumner's idea that he could make a better baseball card using his experience in color separation and holography. His idea had made him and the other four owners of Upper Deck very wealthy.

Since Upper Deck was incorporated in 1988 as a sub-chapter "S" corporation for federal income tax purposes, it was able to distribute directly to its shareholders its earnings prior to any federal income tax. For 1989, Sumner, McWilliam, Korbel, Kughn, and Hemrick split $4 million in dividends from sales of $46 million. McWilliam, Korbel, and Kughn, as 27.08 percent owners of the company, each received $1,083,200. Sumner, who held 14.6 percent of the stock, got $583,333 while Hemrick (4.2 percent) received $166,666.

Cohen, for his role in negotiating the contract with the Players Association, received $50,000. The one-half of one percent commission on gross sales was capped at $50,000 for 1989. Early in 1990, Cohen received an additional $50,000 after Upper Deck had had the license for six months.

All told, according to company sources, Upper Deck produced 125,000 cases of baseball cards in 1989. In addition to the 65,000 cases of low-series baseball cards produced in cases, Upper Deck issued a high series of cards in August numbered 700–800 as well as cards already sorted into sets and singles.

As the employees of the Upper Deck Company toasted their success, Bob Henry stood in the back of the party room and surveyed the scene. Although he was only a contractor, he felt part of the Upper Deck family. The building the partygoers stood in was a result of the construction project he had supervised. From this site, the most popular cards in the world were produced.

But the building he had completed in the early summer was already too small for the growing company. The sales, marketing, and finance departments were crammed into areas meant for a staff a third the size.

Upper Deck had boomed from 20 employees to 360, all of whom tried to operate in 35,000 square feet of office and plant space. Upper Deck had acquired two nearby buildings to handle the growing company, boosting its overall square footage to 80,000. Upper Deck had become so big so quickly that receptionists struggled to handle all of the incoming phone calls. Employees joked that the official name of the company was now "Upper Deck: Please Hold."

As Henry sipped a glass of punch, Sumner walked up and put his arm around him. "Looks like you're going to build another project for us, Bob."

"You're kidding," Henry said.

"Nope. We're looking at 15 acres in Carlsbad. It has a beautiful ocean view. It's going to be great."

Henry found McWilliam, who confirmed the plan. Sumner's site was just one of several they were looking at in San Diego County to build a new Upper Deck headquarters.

Things had moved so quickly, Henry thought to himself. "Tell me Richard," he said. "Did you think we would reach this point so fast?"

McWilliam put his glass of punch down and smiled. "No doubt in my mind, Bob."

Henry reflected on the irony of it all. Through a combination of a good idea, hard work, and dumb luck, Upper Deck had emerged as the top card set in the business. *Baseball Hobby News* magazine had named it the card set of the year. True, Upper Deck was not yet in the same league as Topps, which for the year ending February 25, 1989, would record sales of $142.5 million from sports cards, primarily baseball. (Just two years earlier, Topps's sports card sales were $59.2 million.)

But the market was growing. And while Topps was still tops, it had a new competitor in the upper deck.

11

Bugs Bunny, Willy Wonka, and the Mexican Mafia

By 1990, security had become a major problem at Upper Deck. With Upper Deck cards soaring in value the moment they were shipped from the plant, workers realized that they could make money on the side by smuggling cards out of the plant and selling them to local card shops.

The Upper Deck workforce came from Orange and Los Angeles Counties and worked in three eight-hour shifts. For the most part, they were industrious workers. Buzz Rasmussen, Upper Deck's plant manager from March of 1989 until November of 1991, marveled at how quickly they learned the business and how effectively they worked as printers and packers.

But with Upper Deck cards selling for a premium at card shows and hobby stores, the company began to attract a new breed of worker: gang members. Upper Deck cards could be turned into cash quickly, with the proceeds going to support the drug trade or other gang activities.

"I had just left a printing job in south-central L.A., where you have hamburger stand shootings every night," Rasmussen recalled. "My first night at Upper Deck, we had a security meeting to discuss all the gang-bangers we had in there. I'm thinking 'Wait a minute, I just left south-central for beautiful Yorba Linda and I have to worry about gang-bangers?'"

The gang members came up with creative ways to sneak cards out of Upper Deck. An elaborate network was set up to get cards from various points in the plant into the parking lot. The network of workers who trafficked in cards became known as the "Mexican Mafia," since many of the participants were

Hispanic. The company fired dozens of Mafia "members," but it seemed it could not break up the organization.

Ira Gosdin, a former photographer who joined Upper Deck as its director of security in January of 1989, said: "There were a lot of really good people working there, but you had five percent that gave everyone else a bad name. They were stationed at different points in the plant and came up with elaborate hand signals to inform each other when it was safe and when security was around. If someone brushed their hair back with their right hand, it meant security was on the way.

"The easiest way cards would disappear was through the women who sorted the cards. They'd have a sweater or purse at their feet and appear to accidentally drop some cards. Later they'd pick up the sweater or purse and go to the bathroom, where they'd transfer the cards."

Gosdin said that on several occasions, he discovered cards being sold to card shops near Upper Deck headquarters. "Our workers would come in with a stack of cards wrapped in a cellophane sweet-roll wrapper—the same sweet rolls we sold at Upper Deck."

"It was a dangerous situation," recalled Tony Loiacono, who upon joining Upper Deck in January of 1991 oversaw security in addition to his work as vice president of marketing. "There would be gang members working inside running cards to gang members waiting outside in the parking lot. These were hard-core gang members. It was scary."

Ironically, Upper Deck plant workers could buy cards through legitimate channels. In 1989, the company held an employee sale, where each plant worker could purchase one case of cards at the wholesale price of $400. Many plant workers could not afford to buy a case, but were recruited by some of their entrepreneurial colleagues to buy cases, for which they were paid $500 on the spot. One industrious worker stockpiled 200 cases, which at the time were selling at card shows for $1,200 apiece.

In October of 1991, Upper Deck completed its move south to Carlsbad. Nestled in a canyon in the northern San Diego suburbs, the new headquarters were 25 miles north of San Diego and 50 miles south of Yorba Linda, far from any organized gang activity. While many plant workers moved south with the company, the gang members stayed behind. Part of the reason was because of the location of the new building. But the new plant, with a state-of-the-art security system that featured video cameras and motion detectors, was a major deterrent to card theft.

Whatever the reason, the Mexican Mafia was left behind in Yorba Linda.

■ ■ ■

The first company to react to Upper Deck's upscale line of 1989 baseball cards was Donruss. In 1990, Donruss issued a 528-card set of baseball cards called Leaf, the candy company that in 1983 had purchased Donruss from General Mills.

Like the 1989 Upper Deck, the 1990 Leaf set was produced on a glossy, white cardstock. Like '89, when Upper Deck had the foresight to predict Ken Griffey, Jr., as a rising star, Leaf benefited by being among the first companies to print a card of Frank Thomas, the rookie first baseman for the Chicago White Sox.

The White Sox had selected Thomas in the first round (seventh pick) of the 1989 amateur draft. After 71 games at the Class A level in 1989, Thomas was promoted to Class AA Birmingham to begin the 1990 season. There, he hit .323 with 18 home runs and 71 runs batted in before the White Sox summoned him to Chicago, where, in just 191 at-bats, he hit seven home runs and drove in 31 runs. At 6 foot 5 and 257 pounds, Thomas had the rare combination of ferocious power and a keen batting eye. He walked often, hit for a high average, and, for a big man, struck out infrequently. He was also only 22 years old.

Score and Topps also had rookie cards of Thomas for 1990, but because of the popularity of the Leaf set, Thomas's Leaf card became the most sought after. (By 1994, the card was worth $50–$75, according to *Beckett Baseball Card Monthly*. But unlike Upper Deck, Leaf was not counterfeit-proof. By the end of 1991, a rash of Thomas counterfeits had appeared in The Hobby.)

Upper Deck, meanwhile, had overlooked Thomas, both in its low regular series and its summer high series.

Slowly, the other card manufacturers were catching up.

■ ■ ■

Officially, Paul Sumner retired from Upper Deck on August 1, 1990, and Sumner himself describes his departure as voluntary. But it appears it was anything but a voluntary retirement.

When Richard McWilliam succeeded Boris Korbel as president in July of 1989, the balance of power at Upper Deck immediately shifted. Sumner, the original Upper Deck president who had been Korbel's top salesman at Orbis Graphic Arts, no longer had an ally in the president's office. As the head of the creative and design department, Sumner had gotten to do exactly what he wanted to do when he founded Upper Deck with Bill Hemrick: create better baseball cards. He worked in tandem with his friend, Robert Pelton, whose Pelton & Associates advertising and design agency had worked for Orbis. Pelton had helped design Upper Deck's first baseball cards and drew up the company's first marketing strategy out of his offices in Redondo Beach, California. Since then, Pelton had provided much of the marketing, creative, and advertising ideas for Upper Deck. For Sumner, whose background was in sales, Pelton's help was a godsend.

Korbel had acted as a buffer between McWilliam and Sumner. The two men, while both committed to the goal of making Upper Deck the leader in the sports-card business, were polar opposites in terms of personality and professional background. Sumner, who had spent much of his career as a salesman, now got to use his creative ideas at Upper Deck. He surrounded himself with associates from his former jobs in the printing industry, creating in Upper Deck something of a Paul Sumner network.

"He would show us his dividend checks," recalled Greg Green, who worked with Sumner at two previous companies, and then again at Upper Deck. "We had all worked together at various jobs and to see one of your own break free and make all this money, it was great to see."

McWilliam, with his background in accounting and finance, focused on the bottom line. He grew impatient with Sumner and his eccentricities and became frustrated when there were delays brought about by the creative department. When McWilliam became president, Sumner's duties gradually diminished. Members of his department began feeling pressure to report directly to McWilliam.

In July of 1990, Sumner took a vacation to Tahiti. He had fought with McWilliam for a year and needed a break from the company he had started nearly three years earlier when he walked into Hemrick's Upper Deck card shop.

While Sumner was in Tahiti, he received a telegram from Upper Deck. McWilliam was asking him to leave the company. Upper Deck would issue a release saying he had resigned.

Bob Henry, Upper Deck's all-purpose contractor, recalled a discussion he had with McWilliam while the two were driving from Yorba Linda to Carlsbad to inspect the site for the new headquarters in July of 1990.

"Richard wanted Paul out of there," he said. "He said that he was moving up in the company, there would be a struggle, and Paul would be out of the company."

Pelton wrote Sumner's letter of resignation. "Always make sure you're referred to as the founder of Upper Deck," Pelton told him. "Richard is so paranoid that people will think that he wasn't the one who founded Upper Deck, that he wasn't the man. You were the founder and no one can take that away from you."

In November of 1990, Sumner started Donovan Publishing, a book manufacturing business in Newport Beach, California. Named after Sumner's father, Merton Donovan Sumner, Donovan would manufacture, according to company literature, "journals, workbooks, guidebooks, collectibles, artwork and more." Pelton came aboard as a 10 percent investor. Sumner remained a 14.6 percent owner of Upper Deck, as well as a member of its board of directors. (Sumner, asked about his departure in an interview for this book, said he "retired.")

With Sumner gone, the power struggle was over. McWilliam had emerged the winner. On August 1, 1990, McWilliam issued a memo. The memo stated that Sumner had retired as Upper Deck's executive vice president and would serve as a consultant in the future and that his presence at Upper Deck would be missed.

■ ■ ■

On August 24, 1990, Pelton presented Upper Deck's 1991 marketing strategy in a meeting of Upper Deck executives at Yorba Linda.

According to research commissioned by Pelton, there were 5.2 million baseball card collectors in the U.S. Of those surveyed, 77 percent listed "good investment" as a reason they collected and 61 percent had become collectors since 1985, reflecting the increased interest in cards as an investment. The respondents, on average, planned to spend $430 on baseball cards in 1990.

In 1985, according to Pelton's research, the baseball card market accounted for just $46 million in sales. But it had grown to $81 million in 1986, $145 million in 1987, $212 million in 1988 and $325 million in 1989. For 1990, Pelton estimated the market to be $573 million. If the market continued to grow at an average rate of 66 percent a year, the 1991 baseball card market could reach the billion dollar mark.

Upper Deck, Pelton said, represented 20 percent of the baseball card market in 1990. This despite the fact that Upper Deck ranked last among the five card companies in brand recognition and despite a distribution network skewed heavily toward hobby stores and distributors that serviced candy and tobacco wholesalers. As Upper Deck made further inroads into the retail sector, its brand recognition would increase.

Survey respondents ranked Upper Deck first in quality, card design, picture variety, and investment potential. But Upper Deck was ranked last among hobby dealers in service, including shipping, allocations, fulfilling orders, and overall customer service.

The marketing strategy for 1991, Pelton said, must continue to revolve around Upper Deck's higher-priced card. Upper Deck cards typically cost twice as much as those of its competitors. This had to be continued because Upper Deck's "higher quality and manufacturing costs require a higher price" and because Upper Deck's gross profit margin of 39.57 percent was lower than that of Topps (47.02 percent) and Fleer (43.88 percent).

But card production itself had to be increased, Pelton said. Upper Deck had effectively marketed its cards as hard-to-get, limited edition, investment-grade collectibles. But the restricted availability, Pelton said, could have an effect on the company's future performance.

"Kids have a particularly hard time finding Upper Deck cards," he said. "Investors apparently overbuy and hoard Upper Deck cards, further restricting availability. This overemphasis on appeasing investors creates the potential for excessive backlash if Upper Deck resale values deflate."

For 1991, Pelton presented two scenarios: a most likely and a best case. Under the most likely scenario, Upper Deck would produce $189 million in baseball cards for 1991 and $249 million in 1992. In a best case scenario, Upper Deck would produce $261 million for 1991 and $457 million for 1992. This did not take into account the production of hockey cards, which Upper Deck expected to begin by the end of the year, or the possible acquisition of licenses to make football and basketball cards in 1991.

Pelton went on to describe Upper Deck's advertising strategy for 1991, but the executives just nodded. Their eyes were still fixed on pages 48 and 49 of their 1991 "Upper Deck Marketing Plans" binders. Pelton's most likely scenario represented a 58 percent increase in sales. The best case projected a 117 percent increase. And that was just for 1991.

The Upper Deck Company was growing. The only question was how big it would get.

■ ■ ■

Upper Deck and Reggie Jackson seemed destined to meet. Jackson was looking for a gig—and some product—when he showed up unannounced at company headquarters in the summer of 1989. Upper Deck was in need of a celebrity spokesman for its baseball cards.

During his 21-year career in major league baseball, spent with the Kansas City/ Oakland Athletics, Baltimore Orioles, New York Yankees, and California Angels, Jackson emerged as a larger-than-life figure. His prodigious home runs reminded baseball fans of another man who spent his best years in Yankee Stadium, Babe Ruth. Wherever Jackson went, his teams won, capturing five World Series titles.

But as talented as Jackson was on the field, he was just as well-known for his flamboyant personality. He feuded with teammates, managers, and team owners. He reveled in the media fishbowl of New York, where he played from 1977 to 1981, and made no apologies for his "hot dog" playing style.

Away from the field, he was just as visible. He once accepted an invitation to a charity luncheon by saying: "Of course, I'm coming. What the hell would it be if Reggie Jackson wasn't there?" He maintained an extensive collection of antique cars and once made a guest appearance on the CBS sitcom *All in the Family*. When his career ended, he took a job as a World Series television reporter and made a memorable movie appearance—playing himself—in the slapstick movie *The Naked Gun*.

After joining the Yankees before the 1977 season, Jackson was quoted as saying he would be "the straw that stirs the drink." Jackson claimed he was misquoted, but his behavior and performance over the next five years more than lived up to the statement.

Although Jackson struck out 2,597 times and was a defensive liability as an outfielder, he arguably was baseball's biggest star in the 1970s. *Sports Illustrated* put him on the cover of its June 17, 1974, issue with the headline "Superduperstar." On his first day with the New York Yankees, he announced: "I didn't come here to become a star. I brought my star with me."

During Jackson's career, there were players who hit for higher average, such as George Brett and Rod Carew; men who hit more home runs, such as Hank Aaron and Willie Mays; and hundreds of outfielders who played better defense. But no one performed better under the spotlight than Jackson, who played so well in the playoffs and World Series that he earned the nickname "Mr. October." During Game Six of the 1977 World Series, he hit three consecutive home runs on three pitches from three different Los Angeles Dodgers pitchers, clinching the championship for the Yankees. The feat is now the standard by which other postseason heroics are measured.

In 1978, Standard Brands honored Jackson by producing a gooey candy called the Reggie! bar. The chocolate and peanut concoction had been made for years in Fort Wayne, Indiana, and called the Wayne Bun. Ross Johnson, the head of Standard Brands, had merely renamed it after his baseball star friend. Sales of the Reggie! bar were slow, however, and the product was discontinued in 1980. The candy prompted pitcher Jim "Catfish" Hunter, a teammate of Jackson's in Oakland and New York, to remark: "When you unwrap a Reggie! bar, it tells you how good it is."

Although the Reggie! bar flopped, Johnson kept Jackson on as a paid consultant to Standard Brands, and later Nabisco Brands. For his services, Jackson received a company apartment, a company car, and a personal services contract worth $400,000 a year. It was a great deal for Jackson, requiring just a few appearances at corporate functions and golf outings. But it ended about the time Jackson retired in 1987, and at that point Mr. October began looking for a new business arrangement to replace his relationship with Johnson.

After his retirement, Jackson became a regular on the baseball card show circuit, boasting that no one could sign as many autographs in one sitting as he could. While attending shows in southern California, Jackson befriended a memorabilia dealer and bodybuilder named Walt Harris, who had served as a personal trainer for Jackson and his Oakland A's teammates Jose Canseco, Mark McGwire, and Walt Weiss, in 1987.

From 1987 to 1989, Harris appeared at card shows throughout southern California with a massive display of balls, bats, and photos signed by his friends from the Oakland A's. In the summer of 1989, when he needed more Upper Deck baseball cards, he asked Jackson to approach the company.

In Richard McWilliam, Jackson found another Ross Johnson. Despite McWilliam's limited background in sports, he immediately hit it off with Jackson. McWilliam found that Jackson's contacts in the sports world could greatly benefit Upper Deck, as could Jackson's ever-present star quality. (By 1993, Jackson had a personal services contract with Upper Deck for $500,000 a year, a $1 million deal to sign autographs for the company, an executive office at company headquarters, a seat on the company's board of directors, and the title "assistant to the president.")

But in 1990, he was still just Reggie Jackson, baseball card spokesman for Upper Deck. It was during that year that Don Bodow, Upper Deck's vice president for marketing, was inspired to combine Jackson with another candy bar concept.

But while the Reggie! bar flopped, Bodow's idea would define the sports card market in the years to come.

■ ■ ■

Bodow's young son, Michael, loved the movie *Willy Wonka and the Chocolate Factory*. Together they had watched the film—how many times, Bodow wondered? It was a good thing he had purchased the videocassette. Otherwise, he certainly would have paid more than $100 in rental fees.

The movie, based on the book *Charlie and the Chocolate Factory* by Roald Dahl, told the tale of young Charlie Bucket. Charlie, an impoverished youth, lived in a town that housed Willy Wonka's chocolate factory, which produced "the world's most wonderful candy."

No one from Charlie's town had ever been inside the heavily guarded Wonka Chocolate Factory. Nor had anyone met the mysterious Willy Wonka, who did not need to worry about workers stealing his candy formulas. Instead of humans, the plant was run by "Oompa-Loompas," tiny, troll-like creatures who lived in the factory.

One day, Wonka, played in the movie by Gene Wilder, announced that he would be opening his headquarters to five lucky children who discovered "golden tickets" inserted in Wonka chocolate bars. A mad rush ensued, with people buying dozens of bars at a time and ripping them open on the spot. One millionaire, who owned a business that shelled peanuts for roasting and salting, bought thousands of Wonka bars and ordered his workers to stop shelling and start unwrapping candy. His spoiled brat daughter, one Veruca Salt, just had to have a golden ticket.

It was just a children's fantasy, Bodow thought to himself as he watched the movie over and over. But the more he viewed it, the more it reminded him of the baseball card business and its collectors, who bought pack after pack of cards hoping to find a valuable card of a rookie or superstar.

What if Upper Deck could create the baseball card equivalent of the golden ticket, Bodow wondered? What if Upper Deck inserted a special card into a few random packs that collectors would frantically try to obtain?

Unlike Willy Wonka, Upper Deck could not just open its plant to five kids. The Yorba Linda facility had become too crowded and too chaotic for that. Besides, it was one thing to look at Wonka's river of chocolate and listen to the singing of the Oompa-Loompas. Kids would be bored silly watching presses run.

No, Bodow thought, the special "insert" cards themselves had to be the prize. If Upper Deck could create a small number of a particular card, a figure that would be announced to the public, it would set off a mad scramble by collectors to purchase Upper Deck cards. Sales would soar as collectors, and certainly investors, would buy large quantities in hopes of finding the insert card.

What if, Bodow wondered, Upper Deck created a special 10-card subset featuring its new baseball card spokesman—Reggie Jackson? The cards would be randomly inserted into packs of the company's "high series" set, the 100-card "update" set dominated by rookies. Furthermore, what if Jackson personally signed and numbered 2,500 cards? It would be as if Upper Deck created its own signed, limited edition artwork. Imagine a collector's delight when he or she opened a pack and found a card already autographed, by Mr. October no less. The cards would be worth hundreds of dollars on the secondary market. Each 89 cents spent on a pack of Upper Deck cards represented a 200-fold potential investment return.

The publicity Upper Deck would receive could be enormous, Bodow thought. He envisioned newspaper articles around the country reporting on local youths discovering a Jackson autographed card in their local convenience store with accompanying pictures of wide-eyed young boys holding Upper Deck cards.

They would call the concept "random insert cards," Bodow decided. The set itself would be called the Reggie Jackson "Heroes" line, the first of a series of limited edition subsets and autographed inserts featuring all-time baseball greats.

The idea was immediately implemented. Jackson signed 2,500 cards, which plant workers dropped into packs of high series baseball cards. (Jackson liked the concept so much that he began stockpiling his 1969 Topps rookie card. He wanted to acquire and autograph 563 of them—one for each of his home runs—and market them in 1993, when he was expected to be enshrined in the baseball Hall of Fame. After putting aside several hundred cards, he scrapped the project after the cards and his Bay Area home were destroyed by fires that swept through Oakland.)

Shortly after Labor Day, Bodow watched as the first shipments of the high series baseball cards left Yorba Linda. Somewhere, randomly inserted under the cardboard and foil packaging, there were 2,500 cards personally autographed by Jackson.

Willy Wonka would have been proud.

■ ■ ■

In the spring of 1990, Upper Deck obtained a license to produce hockey cards. While the news was cause for celebration at Upper Deck headquarters, company officials knew that selling hockey cards would present a far greater challenge than baseball cards had in 1989, even if the production facility was now running smoothly.

For most of its 73-year-existence, the National Hockey League was the unloved and unappreciated stepsister to professional baseball, football, and, at times, basketball. The league was dominated by Canadians and had struggled to build a strong fan base in the United States. Plus, it had an image problem. Many would-be fans, particularly those with young children, were turned off by a sport that allowed fighting as part of the natural flow of the game.

By 1990, league officials were trying to clean up their sport. They hoped to transform the NHL into family entertainment, capitalizing on the grace of its athletes as the NBA had with basketball players in the 1980s. That meant curtailing fighting, but more importantly, it meant a strong marketing campaign, which naturally began with a move to strengthen the position of hockey cards in the sports card market.

Since 1964, the only companies that had produced hockey cards were Topps and O-Pee-Chee, the Canadian manufacturer that made its baseball cards through a sublicensing agreement with Topps. The cards, like the NHL, experienced only modest success relative to baseball. But because of the popularity of hockey in Canada, the NHL's one-two punch of Topps and O-Pee-Chee put the league on equal footing cardwise with the NFL and NBA, which for much of the 1980s had no more than two licensed card companies apiece.

For 1990, the NHL gave permission to three additional companies to produce hockey cards: Upper Deck, Pro Set, Inc., of Dallas, and The Score Group of Grand Prairie, Texas. In addition, it allowed Topps to produce an additional card line under the name Bowman. (Topps, which had purchased Bowman in 1956, resurrected the brand name in 1989 when it released a set of Bowman baseball cards.)

Unlike 1989, when Upper Deck was the only new baseball card manufacturer, it would have to compete in a market that had grown from two to five licensees. Not only would Upper Deck have to produce the best hockey cards, but it would have to conduct a massive advertising and marketing campaign.

Robert Pelton and his staff decided that the best way to market hockey cards was by making Upper Deck a part of the game. Companies from other industries already had their names plastered on the dasherboards that surrounded hockey rinks. Each time players crashed into the boards, fans in the stadiums and those watching at home got an eyeful of advertising. News highlights of the game tended to focus on the goals. Thus, those companies whose ads were placed behind the net received even more advertising value for their dollar.

In November, Upper Deck began shipping its first hockey cards. By the end of the 1990–91 hockey season, Upper Deck had acquired board space in arenas in Chicago, Detroit, Edmonton, Los Angeles, and New York. The deals cost Upper Deck, on average, $100,000 a season. The Upper Deck name and its diamond logo were difficult to miss, even by Topps photographers. When Topps's hockey cards came out the following year, two of its cards had Upper Deck logos in the background.

The photo of Los Angeles Kings goalie Daniel Berthiaume was taken with Berthiaume in front of an Upper Deck board at the Los Angeles Forum. A Topps retouch artist tried to camouflage the logo, turning one of the "Ps" in Upper into a "B." But collectors could still see the familiar diamond logo peering out from behind the net. Part of an Upper Deck billboard also appeared on a Topps card of Vancouver Canucks defenseman Adrien Plavsic.

For Upper Deck, the plan worked perfectly. Not only was the Upper Deck logo appearing on sports highlights each night, but it had become so much a part of hockey that it was showing up on the cards of its competitors.

■ ■ ■

Now that Upper Deck had bought its way into hockey games, it looked for a means to get into baseball. The idea was to become part of the game itself. Since Upper Deck did not manufacture sports equipment, it had to take an unconventional route. In the case of hockey, it chose the dasherboards. For baseball, it chose a group of retired players to take the Upper Deck logo into ballparks throughout the country.

In 1990, the Equitable Life Assurance Society of the U.S. had sponsored a series of "Old-Timers" baseball games. The company paid players to appear at the games, flew them into the host cities, and promoted a full slate of activities that culminated in an exhibition held before a major league contest. For each game, Equitable made a donation to the Baseball Assistance Team (BAT), a charitable organization set up to provide financial aid to former big leaguers who had fallen on hard times.

The series had started out well, but gradually deteriorated. The same players tended to appear at every game, even if they had no connection to the city hosting the event. The players themselves were put off by the banquet that accompanied each game, where they ended up signing hundreds of autographs for invited guests and VIPs.

After the 1990 season, Equitable bowed out of the "Equitable Old-Timers Series" and Upper Deck signed on as the title sponsor. The first thing the company did was rename the games the "Upper Deck Heroes of Baseball." Not only was it consistent with the Upper Deck Heroes card concept that began with the Reggie Jackson insert cards, but it was a more dignified title for players than "Old-Timers."

The objectives of the Heroes program, according to company documents, included "to generate national/local publicity and goodwill for Upper Deck via a high profile sponsorship program that has enough meaning and authenticity to gain wide acceptance among media, public and players" and to "reposition series as more positive and respectful of former players and reinforce Upper Deck's image and position as inseparable from the fabric of the baseball family."

A secondary goal was to "maximize promotional use of Upper Deck products in on-site activities and consumer/retail promotions. . . . Fully explore merchandising/licensing opportunities with Series."

In 1991, Upper Deck hosted Heroes games in every ballpark except the Kingdome in Seattle and Chicago's Comiskey Park. For each game, Upper Deck assembled two rosters dominated by players who had played for the host team. Some of the bigger names became Upper Deck regulars, appearing at up to ten different games, including Paul Blair, Vida Blue, Bobby Bonds, Lou Brock, Orlando Cepeda, Tommy Davis, Rollie Fingers, Steve Garvey, Bob Gibson, Ferguson Jenkins, Harmon Killebrew, Al Oliver, Gaylord Perry, Boog Powell, Billy Williams, and, of course, Reggie Jackson.

The highlight of the tour came on May 11, when a Heroes game in Boston reunited Ted Williams and Joe DiMaggio at Fenway Park for the fiftieth anniversary of the 1941 season, when Williams batted .406 and DiMaggio hit in 56 consecutive games.

Williams, 72, and the 76-year-old DiMaggio did not play in the Heroes game. Instead, they entered the park from center field on golf carts. A picture of the two was taken during pregame introductions and picked up on the Associated Press newswire.

Like the hockey board advertising, the impact of the Heroes games could not be directly measured. But Upper Deck had achieved its goal of becoming "one with baseball." For each Heroes game, Upper Deck donated $10,000 to the Baseball Assistance Team. At the end of the year, BAT named Richard McWilliam its "BAT Man of the Year."

■ ■ ■

The idea, Upper Deck officials knew, was a little loony. Late in 1990, the company negotiated a contract with Warner Brothers to manufacture cards that would feature Looney Tunes card characters juxtaposed with major league baseball players.

In December, Upper Deck released an 18-card set to the media and hobby dealers. Entitled "Out by a Hare," the cards—when placed in numerical sequence—told the story of the Bugs Bunny All-Stars defeating the Daffy Duck All-Stars, 101–100, in a wacky game of baseball. A 297-card set called Comic Ball, which featured only cartoon characters, was released to the public later in the month.

(In July of 1991, Upper Deck unveiled "Comic Ball II," which featured Nolan Ryan and Reggie Jackson included in the story line. In scenes that called for dialogue, Jackson and Ryan were shown talking with the likes of Daffy Duck and Sylvester the Cat.)

But unlike Upper Deck's wildly successful baseball card product, Comic Ball never caught on among collectors since there were no rookie cards to collect. (By 1993, Upper Deck had absorbed a $15 million loss on Comic Ball.)

The idea, as it turned out, was loony in more ways than one.

■ ■ ■

On December 14, 1990, Anthony Passante filed a lawsuit against Upper Deck in Orange County Superior Court. Passante, McWilliam's former Servite High School classmate, had served as Upper Deck's original corporate counsel for nine months before being fired in December of 1988.

During his nine months at Upper Deck, Passante arranged a loan between the company and Dr. Kevin Prendiville, the brother of his law partner, and fellow Servite alum, Andrew Prendiville. The $100,000 loan, which Upper Deck later repaid with interest, had been paid as a deposit to Noland Paper, which was providing the paper for Upper Deck's first baseball cards.

In his suit, Passante alleged that Upper Deck's board of directors had promised him 3 percent stock ownership in the company in return for arranging the loan. Upper Deck disagreed, prompting the suit, which named as defendants the company, McWilliam, Boris Korbel, and Richard Kughn. Andrew Prendiville, whom Passante had promised half of his three percent interest, was listed as a co-plaintiff.

The twentieth reunion of the Servite Class of 1971 was rapidly approaching. But at least three members of the class were no longer on speaking terms.

■ ■ ■

According to Upper Deck production records obtained for this book, the company shipped 270,054 cases of baseball cards in 1990. Of that total, 160,728 cases (1.74 billion cards) were packaged in foil cases; 62,266 cases (747.2 million cards) were sold in complete sets; 24,726 cases (213.6 million cards) were sold in special grocery store display units and 15,313 cases (147 million cards) were sold as singles. Upper Deck also sold 7,021 cases of its baseball "update" or high-series set. All told, Upper Deck shipped nearly three billion baseball cards for 1990, resulting in sales revenue of over $100 million.

Upper Deck began shipping its first hockey cards in November. In the final two months of 1990, the company shipped 45,925 cases (476.2 million cards) of hockey cards. In December, Upper Deck began shipping its new Comic Ball cards, sending out 15,996 cases (82.9 million cards). Together, the two products accounted for over $20 million in sales.

Along with its Comic Ball card line, Upper Deck produced 61,298 wristwatches featuring either a Bugs Bunny fiftieth anniversary logo, a baseball team logo, or a Looney Tunes design. The watches did not sell as well as expected and, according to company sources, Upper Deck lost $3 million on the project.

Still, in just one year, Upper Deck had gone from $46 million in sales to $120 million. For 1990, the company issued $35 million in distributions to its shareholders. McWilliam, Korbel, and Kughn, as 27.08 percent shareholders, each received $9,478,000. Sumner, who had a 14.6 percent stake, received $5,104,167 while Hemrick, who held the remaining 4.2 percent, got $1,458,333.

But as profitable a year as 1990 had been for the Upper Deck Company, 1991, as Pelton had projected, would be even better.

12

A National Extravaganza

By January of 1991, the executive board of Upper Deck was in place. After two hectic years, the company had settled in at Yorba Linda. And while the three buildings that made up corporate headquarters already had become too small for the growing business, Upper Deck had established a strong management team to deal with the chaos.

With Sumner gone, McWilliam was the only member of the board of directors who dealt with the company on a day-to-day basis. After McWilliam, Upper Deck's office hierarchy consisted of roughly a dozen executives.

Jay McCracken, the longest tenured of the executives, and Don Bodrow were vice presidents of sales and marketing respectively. Dennis Sienicki, who had worked as a controller for Xerox and Pitney Bowes, had succeeded Dan Lybarger as Upper Deck's chief financial officer.

The creative and design team was headed by Brad Maier, who had joined Upper Deck in October of 1990 as art director. Maier had worked for a T-shirt production company called "Crazy Shirts" in Hawaii. It was there, in the mid-1980s, that he met McWilliam. The two became quick friends and McWilliam did some accounting work for Maier. The two socialized, and later Maier introduced McWilliam to a woman who, in 1990, became McWilliam's fiancee.

When Maier arrived at Upper Deck, Greg Green figured his days were numbered. As the manager of creative services, he performed many of the duties that were part of Maier's new job, such as card design and photo selection. Green had worked with Sumner at Orbis Graphic Arts and previously at another print company. When Sumner was dismissed in August of 1990, Green figured he would soon follow.

But Maier found Green to be very helpful in teaching him his new job, and made it a point to tell McWilliam. Green, much to his surprise, remained at Upper Deck, performing the same tasks he always had. The only difference was that now he had someone to help him organize the growing creative department. One of their top employees was a young man named Michael Merhab, a former restaurant maître d' who met McWilliam through a family connection. Like Tom Geideman, Merhab had an impeccable knowledge of sports.

Upper Deck's creative and marketing staffs were augmented by Pelton & Associates, the advertising, marketing, and design company located in Redondo Beach, California. The company was headed by Robert Pelton, who had worked with Sumner and Orbis Graphic Arts and had assisted Upper Deck since 1988, when it designed the prototype cards of DeWayne Buice and Wally Joyner. Since then, it had served as an all-purpose consulting company for Upper Deck, providing everything from card design, advertising, and marketing schemes to placing newspaper and television advertising.

Buzz Rasmussen, who had helped get Upper Deck's press working in 1989, remained plant manager while Bob Ruggieri handled the pre-press and color separation departments.

Overseeing it all was Brian Burr, who held the rather ambiguous title of assistant to the president. It was his job to oversee Upper Deck's operations, particularly the plant. Burr supervised the security of the plant and also the production process itself. He also issued companywide memos and generally served as something of a sergeant-at-arms, which was perhaps appropriate given his military training at West Point. Prior to coming to Upper Deck in 1990, Burr had worked for four years in various managerial capacities for Pepsi-Cola.

It was an effective managerial team, but in McWilliam's eyes it still was one person short. By the end of 1990, McWilliam saw a need to boost Upper Deck's marketing department. Bodow's job had evolved more into a hybrid public relations–creative development role. What Upper Deck needed was someone to take Upper Deck's name recognition to the next level, to make the company a household name like Nike, the Beaverton, Oregon, shoe company that had come to prominence amid the fitness craze of the 1970s. McWilliam felt that Upper Deck, by capitalizing on the investment fervor of collectibles in the 1980s, could experience similar success.

In November of 1990, McWilliam received a call from Tony Loiacono. At 35, Loiacono had 12 years of sports marketing experience. At the time, he was an executive vice president for Foote, Cone & Belding/IMPACT, a Los Angeles promotions firm. In addition, Loiacono owned the rights to "Celebrity All-Star Hockey," a series of charity hockey games featuring actors and entertainers, most notably actor Michael J. Fox of the NBC television series *Family Ties*.

Loiacono wanted to know if Upper Deck would be interested in sponsoring Celebrity Hockey. McWilliam asked Loiacono to meet with him at his office in Yorba Linda.

The two hit it off immediately. McWilliam was impressed not only with Celebrity Hockey, but also Loiacono's background in marketing. "Tony," he said, "you're the kind of guy I'm looking for to head up my marketing and advertising."

Loiacono smiled, wondering to himself if he was being offered a job. Upper Deck had produced some beautiful baseball cards for the last two years, but you would never have known that this was a company that would distribute dividends of $35 million to its shareholders on sales of $120 million for 1990. The entire building seemed ready to burst. Employees were packed into tiny cubicles. Even McWilliam, the president of the company, had an office that was only 100 square feet. But the facility aside, the company seemed to operate in total chaos.

"What exactly are your objectives marketing-wise?" Loiacono asked.

"I want to get off the pages of hobby magazines and become a well-known brand in the marketplace," McWilliam said.

Loiacono smiled again. "Richard, I don't think you can afford me."

McWilliam leaned forward, looking Loiacono straight in the eye. "You'd be surprised."

Still, Loiacono was not offered the job on the spot, but invited to apply for the position of vice president of marketing. In January of 1991, Loiacono interviewed at Upper Deck along with six other candidates. One by one, they were brought into a conference room to meet with McCracken, Rasmussen, Sienicki, Maier, and Ruggieri. The three strongest candidates, the panel felt, were Loiacono, Steve Mitgang, and Bruce Regis. Mitgang and Regis were young marketing executives in their late twenties from Reebok and Hunt Wesson Foods, respectively.

The job went to Loiacono, although Mitgang and Regis also were hired shortly thereafter. Mitgang joined the marketing department, while Regis became assistant to the president.

Upper Deck's executive management was now complete.

■ ■ ■

On the morning of January 29, 1991, Upper Deck executives gathered in a canyon located off Sea Otter Place in Carlsbad for the official groundbreaking of Upper Deck's new corporate headquarters.

About thirty people assembled in the dirt lot, including officials from the city of Carlsbad. They had come to watch the beginning of construction on the new 260,000-square-foot building, which would replace the three-building, 80,000-square-foot facility in Yorba Linda.

The marriage of Carlsbad and Upper Deck seemed perfect. The sleepy suburb in northern San Diego County was home to some of the city's more affluent residents, but seemed to reflect their desire to maintain a low profile. The city was perhaps best known for the La Costa Resort and Spa, a five-star vacation spot whose two championship golf courses made it a regular stop on the PGA and

Senior PGA tours. But its most recognizable landmark was a 100-foot windmill perched atop the Best Western Inn and Pea Soup Restaurant along the #5 Freeway, right next to the Palomar Airport Road exit.

Like the residents of Carlsbad, officials of the privately held Upper Deck wanted to remain low-key. The site for the new facility was nestled on a cul-de-sac two miles from Carlsbad Airport along Palomar Airport Road. On a clear day, as Paul Sumner had told Bob Henry 13 months earlier at the Upper Deck Christmas party, Upper Deck employees would be able to see the ocean from the second floor of the building.

As the ceremonial shovels of dirt were dug, Sumner held court with reporters. Though he had been dismissed from the company six months earlier, he still held a seat on the board of directors and owned 14.6 percent of Upper Deck, which more than entitled him to appear at events such as these.

Sumner retold the story of how he wandered into Bill Hemrick's card shop, saw the counterfeit Don Mattingly baseball cards and was inspired to create the "Cadillac of all cards."

"From the kid on the street to the Wall Street market, we became the new collectible on the market," Sumner told *The San Diego Tribune*. "We've made quite an impact on the industry. There never was a company like Upper Deck to compete against."

McWilliam, not normally given to hyperbole, said: "We intend to put Carlsbad on the map as the Card Collector Capital of the World."

■ ■ ■

In January of 1991, Upper Deck received a license from NFL Properties and the NFL Players Association to produce football cards. Just as the company had turned to Bob Cohen for help in obtaining a license from the Major League Players Association in 1988, it had again looked to the Los Angeles attorney for help in getting permission to produce football cards.

Cohen, in turn, had enlisted the help of Marvin Demoff, a sports attorney whose clients included Miami Dolphins quarterback Dan Marino. In return for procuring the license, Cohen and Demoff were to receive two percent of the first $20 million of annual net sales of football cards and one percent of the annual net sales in excess of $20 million. They also received the right to purchase 1,050 cases of football cards at the lowest wholesale price.

Unlike Major League Baseball and its Players Association, which after licensing Upper Deck had put a cap on the number of companies that could produce baseball cards, the National Football League had been much more liberal in granting permission to companies wishing to manufacture football cards.

In 1988, Topps was the only company that had produced football cards. But as the market for baseball cards both old and new grew, so too did the demand for cards from other sports. The NFL, which always had been a distant second to Major League Baseball in the card market, suddenly found that it had an untapped source of revenue in football card licensing royalties.

The league quickly went to work making up for all the years football cards had been ignored by collectors. In 1989, the NFL licensed two companies to produce football cards: Score, which had begun making baseball cards in 1988, and Pro Set, Inc., a Dallas-based company. In 1990, the NFL added two more licensees: Fleer and Action Packed, a new card manufacturer located in the suburbs of Chicago. For 1991, Upper Deck would be joined by yet two more companies: Pacific Trading Cards of Lynnwood, Washington, and Cincinnati-based Wild Card.

In just three years, the number of football card manufacturers had grown from one to eight. The football card market, like the rest of the sports card business, was experiencing unbridled growth.

The only question was when—or if—it would ever stop.

■ ■ ■

The scene was Sotheby's auction house in New York City, in a large banquet-sized room that, on the morning of March 22, 1991, housed examples of many of the most valuable cards in the baseball card industry. The cards, mainly early twentieth-century tobacco issues, had come from veteran collector James C. Copeland, who had consigned 873 pieces of baseball memorabilia to Sotheby's for a sale that would take two days.

This was no ordinary auction and the bidders present were not ordinary collectors. With the card market continuing to grow, and with no apparent ceiling in sight, the wealthiest collectors in the country had gathered at Sotheby's to spend thousands of dollars for cardboard that once came free in packs of cigarettes. Those collectors who could not attend sent representatives or made arrangements to bid by phone.

The sale was expected to bring in a total of $5–7 million. On the morning of March 22—a Friday—800 well-heeled collectors packed the room. Over the next three hours, they bid furiously for 195 lots, together spending more than $1 million. A 1952 Topps Mickey Mantle card sold for $49,500, more than tripling the pre-auction estimate of $12,000–$15,000. Lot number 195, a set of the treasured T206 tobacco cards—minus the three most valuable—sold for $99,000.

Then came lot number 196, the item that had drawn many of the bidders, as well as a row of television cameras and dozens of reporters. Shortly after noon, auctioneer Robert Woolley stepped to the podium to announce lot 196. A hush fell over the crowd as the bidders flipped through their Sotheby's auction catalogs. The item needed no introduction; everyone knew it simply as the most valuable card in the industry.

Wooller paused, reveling in the moment. Then, sounding like a cross between a carnival barker and a boxing ring announcer, he proclaimed, "And now, The Holy Grail."

It was overstatement, but for baseball card collectors, not by much. The T206 Honus Wagner card carried a pre-auction estimate of $125,000 to $150,000. If it sold in that range, it would become the highest-priced card ever. Most in the room thought it would, since the Wagner—one of only 50–80 estimated to exist—was in pristine condition. Its corners were sharp and the card had faded little in the 80 years since it had been printed.

Everyone knew the story, or stories, behind the T206 Wagner. Shortly after Buck Duke's American Tobacco Company went into production of the T206 set in 1909, Honus Wagner, the Pittsburgh Pirates star regarded by many fans as the greatest shortstop in baseball history, strongly objected to having his card included. The popular reason was that Wagner, a nonsmoker known as "The Flying Dutchman," did not want his name and likeness being used to promote tobacco products. The colorful anecdote generally was accepted by collectors, even though Wagner appeared in other tobacco sets, as well as in tobacco advertisements. He even chewed tobacco; a 1948 card of Wagner as a Pirates coach showed him dipping into a pouch.

A notoriously tough negotiator, Wagner announced his retirement before the 1908 season, supposedly for health reasons, before accepting a raise to return. But given Wagner's acceptance of other tobacco sets, it's likely that his objection was more one of his compensation from American Tobacco than of any strong opposition to cigarettes. Whatever the reason, American Tobacco pulled the Wagner card, but not before a quantity had been printed and shipped out in cigarette packs.

The card went largely unnoticed until 1939, when longtime collector Jefferson Burdick published *The American Card Catalog*, which chronicled the history of baseball cards. Burdick had a difficult time locating a Wagner to photograph for the book, which started the rumors of its rarity. Even though other cards were considered more scarce, the controversy surrounding the T206 Wagner, along with the popularity of the T206 set and Wagner's Hall of Fame status, made the acquisition of a T206 Wagner the ultimate goal of baseball card collectors. In 1960, it was valued at $50. By 1975, it had risen to $1,500. In 1981, the year after Topps's monopoly was broken and the market for older cards expanded, the Wagner was valued at $15,000. In 1989, it became the first card to sell for $100,000.

Now, two years later, that record price seemed destined to fall. The only question was by how much. The room buzzed with anticipation as Woolley called for an opening bid. When he received one of $228,000—twice the pre-sale estimate—the room filled with gasps of astonishment. As the bidding continued in increments of $10,000—between two bidders, one in the room and one on the phone—the stunned crowd grew quiet. When Woolley announced a bid of $300,000, it broke out in applause, then again became silent as the bidding continued to soar.

In the room, Mark Friedland kept raising his paddle. A collectibles dealer from Aspen, Colorado, Friedland had set a limit for himself of $330,000. As he quickly and calmly responded to each bid by the collector on the phone, Bill Mastro, a veteran dealer hired by Sotheby's as a consultant for the auction, continued to listen on the phone and bid accordingly. Friedland and the crowd wondered who the mysterious bidder could be. Only Mastro and the Sotheby's officials knew the identity of the man, a novice collector and professional hockey player named Wayne Gretzky.

Friedland ignored his personal limit and continued to push the bidding. He and Gretzky went back and forth quickly as the crowd listened silently in disbelief. When Gretzky hit the $400,000 mark, the crowd again erupted in applause.

Friedland immediately countered with a bid of $405,000. Gretzky responded in seconds, raising the card to $410,000. Friedland, who had matched each Gretzky bid without hesitation, signaled that it was over. Woolley hammered down the gavel at $410,000 "to the bidder on the phone."

Sotheby's 10 percent buyer's premium added $41,000 to the card, bringing the final selling price to a staggering $451,000. Baseball cards had risen to the status of rare art, a fact not lost on the crowd at Sotheby's, which had built its business on the sale of treasured paintings and sculpture.

Afterward, Friedland told the assembled press that he dropped out of the bidding when it became apparent the phone bidder was willing to pay whatever price necessary for the Wagner card. "I gave it my best shot. But when he passed the $400,000 mark, I knew he was prepared to go all the way to a half-million if that's what it took to get the card. At that point, I decided to drop out."

Still, the press wanted to know, who was the phone bidder? Sotheby's declined to reveal the source until it received permission to do so. A few hours later, it was announced that the card had been purchased by Gretzky and Bruce McNall, the owner of Gretzky's hockey team, the Los Angeles Kings.

For McNall, an investor in a wide range of fields including rare coins, racehorses, and movie studios, the deal was the latest in a series of eye-catching purchases. Typically, his critics scoffed at the outrageous prices McNall paid, only to shake their heads later as he reaped a huge profit.

The man had a Midas touch and constantly was on the prowl for a new game in which to roll his dice. With the Wagner purchase, McNall found a welcome audience in the baseball card and collectibles industry. And it was only a matter of time before he found his way to the offices of the Upper Deck Company.

■ ■ ■

In 1991, Richard McWilliam began to tighten the reins at Upper Deck. Employees began receiving memos on everything from corporate travel to office furniture to an official policy on sports fantasy leagues played in the office.

Memos typically ended with a threat: Any employee in violation of said memorandum could or would be summarily terminated. For instance, on April 22, 1991, McWilliam issued a memorandum stating that any employees soliciting favors or tickets from teams or organizations which Upper Deck dealt with would be terminated.

Terminated. The word evoked memories of *The Terminator*, the science fiction thriller starring Arnold Schwarzenegger. Employees joked that a leather-clad, gun-toting Schwarzenegger would appear in their office and announce "You have been targeted for termination." After each McWilliam memo, distributed officewide but usually aimed at a specific department, friends of the offenders would walk into their office and, affecting Schwarzenegger's Austrian accent, intone: "You have been targeted for termination."

■ ■ ■

It had taken Topps two years to catch up with Upper Deck. When Upper Deck issued its upscale, glossy line of baseball cards in the spring of 1989, the company had an innovative new card line on the back burner. The success of Upper Deck, however, transformed it into a top priority.

On April 25, 1991, Topps unveiled a new line of baseball cards called "Stadium Club." The cards were printed on thicker cardstock than regular cards and were treated with a special ultraviolet coating to give them a glossy finish. The photos were particularly crisp, the result of an imaging process Topps employed through an exclusive agreement with Kodak. On the back of each card was a small reproduction of the player's rookie card. But the most unique feature was the "full-bleed" photo images used for the cards.

Prior to 1991, most baseball cards were designed with some sort of border outline. As a result, the card photos looked as if they were framed. The Stadium Club cards came with a borderless design that made the photo image 25 percent larger than other cards. The suggested retail price for Topps Stadium Club was $1.25 per 12-card pack. But like the 1989 Upper Deck, the price for Stadium Club quickly soared on the secondary market. Collectors found it difficult to find Stadium Club packs for under $4.

The first series of Stadium Club (300 cards) was a smash hit. Within a month of its release, it was selling for $100 a set. It seemed no one could get enough of Topps Stadium Club.

Even Topps's annual report, issued in the spring of 1991, became a sought-after collector's item.

Each one came with samples of the new Topps Stadium Club cards.

■ ■ ■

Brian Burr, who ran the operations end of Upper Deck with the same military efficiency he had learned at West Point, had taken over much of the memo writing for McWilliam. Burr became something of an enforcer for the president. When executive meetings would deteriorate into heated arguments between vice presidents, McWilliam often had trouble bringing the session back to order. (In truth, McWilliam liked to see his vice presidents at each other's throats. It fostered competition, which in turn yielded better products and a more effective company.)

But Burr didn't see it that way. No one would ever ignore a general's command, and here were these subordinates paying no attention to McWilliam. "Excuse me," Burr would loudly announce. Then, pointing at McWilliam, "This is the president."

It became a running joke. Sometimes the vice presidents would stop the meetings themselves and point at McWilliam, saying: "He's the president, right Brian?"

In April, Upper Deck hired San Francisco 49ers quarterback Joe Montana to be the spokesman for its new football cards. Burr issued a memo, and employees again started looking for Schwarzenegger.

The memo announced Montana's upcoming visit, and Burr wanted to make it "ABSOLUTELY clear" that no employee could ask Montana for an autograph, picture, or any other kind of favor. Anyone engaging in such unprofessional behavior would be subject to "disciplinary action to include termination."

■ ■ ■

For those involved in the sports card industry, 1991 would go down as the most successful year in history. Interest reached an all-time high, card companies made their greatest profits, and the business of manufacturing and selling sports cards showed no sign of abating.

Never was that more apparent than at the National Sports Collectors Convention, held July 4–7 at the Anaheim Convention Center, just blocks from Disneyland.

The two men in charge of the event were familiar names in The Hobby: Jack Petruzzelli and Mike Berkus. Berkus, along with Gavin Riley and Steve Brunner, had organized the first National in 1980, which attracted 5,700 collectors to the Airport Marriott in Los Angeles. Over the next four years, the show traveled from Detroit to St. Louis to Chicago to Parsippany, New Jersey, before the original promoters brought it back to southern California for 1985, this time to Anaheim. The three founders enlisted the help of three other men as promoters, including Petruzzelli, the Fullerton police detective who had been involved in the investigation into the counterfeit Pete Rose cards in 1982.

The 1985 National had attracted 15,000 and subsequent shows drew between 12,000 and 30,000 collectors each year, rotating from Arlington, Texas, to San Francisco, Atlantic City, New Jersey, Chicago, and back to Arlington, Texas. Petruzzelli, along with his wife Patti, bid for and won the rights to promote the 1991 show.

By this time, the promotion of the National had become a full-time job, and when the Petruzzellis learned in 1990 that they would be hosting the event for 1991, Jack quit his job as a detective. After 19 years investigating murders, robberies, and the drug trade, he figured promoting the National would be less stressful. And certainly more profitable.

Late in 1990, Petruzzelli hired Berkus as the business manager of the show. Berkus set out to transform the National from a large hobby show into a corporate extravaganza. For the first time, the National would consist not only of card and memorabilia dealers, but also the card manufacturers themselves.

With a map of the 350,000-square-foot Anaheim Convention Center as his guide, Berkus drew a "corporate island" consisting of 144 booths. He solicited the major card companies, along with hobby magazines and other companies that manufactured sports-related collectibles. In addition to the fee for the booth, each corporate display would be required to produce a commemorative item for exclusive distribution at the National. The event, Berkus promised the companies, would offer them a chance to promote their products before thousands of diehard collectors.

The first corporation to sign up was Upper Deck, which had employed Berkus's PTS marketing firm in 1989. Next came Pro Set, the Dallas-based football card manufacturer. Other companies soon followed, and by February, the entire corporate island was sold out.

In April, Berkus took a tour of the facility and was horrified when he discovered how big 350,000 square feet actually was. The Anaheim Convention Center consisted of three halls, which could be separated by sliding walls. He and Petruzzelli had booked all three. Now, with the walls drawn back, Berkus looked at the empty space and found it difficult to see from one end of the "room" to the other. It was going to take tens of thousands of people to make the show look busy.

For the next three months, Berkus and the Petruzzellis conducted a massive advertising campaign, touting the National as "The Hobby's Premier Event." They took out ads in hobby publications and booked airtime on southern California radio stations. They even rented billboards around Disneyland and the Convention Center. The goal was to make sure everyone within a 30-mile radius of Anaheim knew about the National.

On July 3, the night before the show began, Berkus toured the facility with police and fire marshals and predicted a crowd of 50,000. The officials said they were prepared for 70,000.

But more than 100,000 collectors showed up for the four-day event, not counting the 30,000 turned away by fire marshals. Local radio stations urged collectors and motorists to avoid the mass confusion and traffic tie-ups and stay away from the convention. One station reported that it would take two and a half hours to navigate the two-block stretch from the #5 Freeway to the Convention Center. Once there, the lines didn't stop; many of those who got through the turnstiles had waited in line for up to five hours.

Depending on how the convention was viewed, it was either a mob scene or a roaring success. And the party most responsible was Upper Deck.

■ ■ ■

For its National Sports Collectors Convention promotion, Upper Deck produced a four-card prototype set of Comic Ball II cards featuring Nolan Ryan and Reggie Jackson. The two athletes would appear juxtaposed with Looney Tunes characters in the upcoming Comic Ball II line, and Upper Deck created the prototype cards to kick off the set. Collectors who came to Upper Deck's booth on July 4 and 6 would receive Ryan cards; Jackson cards would be handed out on July 5 and 7.

Upper Deck, of course, was not the only card manufacturer to produce cards for the National. When Berkus had made it a requirement for corporate boothholders to distribute special promotional items, he did it as a means of attracting collectors to the show. If they could get special cards that were not available elsewhere, he figured, it would be an added incentive to attend. And if the cards were only available at the National, collectors naturally would presume they were produced on a limited basis—even if the companies did not disclose the size of their production runs.

What Berkus did not anticipate was the corporate island and the "promo" card distribution becoming the focal point of the show itself. The first day of the show, July 4, was open only to dealers and table holders, at least in theory. Others hoping to enter the show needed a business license proving that they were legitimate dealers or business people in the sports collecting hobby.

By the end of the first day, a line of hundreds of people extended outside the entrance of the Convention Center. Several enterprising young men were doing a brisk business selling "business licenses." For $20, collectors could purchase a photocopy of a California business license that would allow them entrance to the show.

As a result, an unexpectedly large crowd showed up on the first evening. But rather than heading for the 800 tables belonging to dealers who had traveled from around the country, most of the collectors headed straight toward the corporate island. As collectors entered the Convention Center, they could turn right and go to the dealer area, or go left to reach the corporate area.

The line that extended out the door was for those collectors hoping to get to the corporate area. Many in line did not realize that they could enter from the right and go immediately to the dealer area.

But many who were in line *did* want to get to the corporate island, where they could load up on valuable promo cards. As they entered the area, the first booth they saw was Upper Deck, which had earned the position when it became the first manufacturer to commit to the National.

The Upper Deck booth was 20 by 20 feet. Decorated with blow-up baseball cards and vibrating from music blaring from four speakers, the Upper Deck booth would have been difficult to miss under normal circumstances. But on July 4, Upper Deck had four Los Angeles Rams cheerleaders at the booth distributing Nolan Ryan cards. Also on hand was McCracken, along with his assistant Pat Lissy, and Randy Duvall, the former termite inspector and customer of The Upper Deck card shop who now worked for Upper Deck under McCracken.

As collectors rushed into the show, the Upper Deck booth became a feeding frenzy. Standing behind a display case, the seven people manning the booth saw only a sea of hands, all reaching out for a Ryan promo card. No matter how quickly the workers gave the cards out, it seemed, the crowd only grew bigger.

It was as if Upper Deck were handing out free $20 bills. In a sense, they were. Next to the corporate island at the food court, dealers had set up shop with briefcases and calculators, offering $20 for each Ryan card.

The show had opened at noon, and by 4:30 P.M. the Convention Center was packed. Not only had Berkus's fears of not drawing enough attendees been alleviated, but so many dealers—or collectors armed with fake business licenses—had shown up that the fire marshals ordered everyone who was not a table holder or corporate sponsor to leave the building. At 6:30, when order had been restored, the show reopened.

But while the corporate island turned into a mob scene, the day's biggest trouble erupted in the dealer section. There, thieves walked off with display cases containing nearly $500,000 worth of vintage baseball cards. As dealers continued to set up their display tables on the night before the show officially opened to the public, the culprits loaded display cases onto dollies and wheeled them out of the show. Since there was so much unloading going on anyway, no one realized that a theft had taken place. (The victims, Joe Bosley and Dan McKee, owners of The Old Ball Game card store in Reisterstown, Maryland, and Larry Levine, owner of a card business called Memory Lane in Redondo Beach, California, later filed suit against the Convention Center and the National promoters. The suit was settled out of court in 1994 on terms that were not disclosed.)

While Berkus scrambled to appease the fire marshals, he called a meeting of the corporate sponsors. "We've got to do something about these promo cards," he said. "If we go on like this when the show opens to the general public, someone could get hurt."

It was decided that the promo cards of all the companies would be given to the promoters, who would put them in plastic bags. Instead of going from booth to booth like trick-or-treaters, collectors entering the show would receive a bag that contained every promotional item.

When the show reopened at 6:30 P.M. on July 4, collectors raced back to the corporate island. McCracken and Duvall put the cards for the remaining three days on a dolly, which Duvall was to roll into a back room where the promo bag stuffing was taking place. Fearing that he might be mobbed along the way, Duvall enlisted the help of two security guards, who provided him with a police escort. From 6 P.M. until 4 A.M. July 5, Berkus, the Petruzzellis, and 50 show staffers stuffed 6,000 promo bags.

■ ■ ■

For three more days, the promo hysteria continued, only now collectors got their promo cards all at once. That did not alleviate the lines, however. Petruzzelli and Berkus had done such a thorough promotion job that the fire marshals constantly warned them that they would have to close the show. As a result, no collectors could enter until others had left.

When the dust settled, more than 100,000 collectors had attended the 12th National Sports Collectors Convention. The promoters figured another 30,000 had tried to get in but had grown tired of standing in line and gone home. No previous National had drawn more than 30,000 attendees.

As the show came to a close, Petruzzelli surveyed the convention floor and marveled at how The Hobby had grown. A brisk business was still taking place at the food court, where dealers were now offering $125 for the complete, four-card set of Jackson and Ryan.

Petruzzelli had spent 19 years as a police officer and now here he was again, investigating a robbery and organizing crowd control. Is this what The Hobby had become, he thought? Didn't anyone care about collecting anymore?

When Petruzzelli had investigated the Pete Rose counterfeit cards nearly a decade before, he never could have envisioned that The Hobby would explode like this. The Rose counterfeits had inspired the Mattingly counterfeits, which in turn had influenced the founders of Upper Deck, which had stolen the show here in Anaheim.

When the National ended and the money was counted, the event grossed more than $1 million. Petruzzelli and Berkus each received six-figure paydays for their efforts.

The Hobby, according to research commissioned by Action Packed Sports Cards and its parent company, LBC Sports, Inc., accounted for $1.4 billion in wholesale sales of new products for the year ending June, 1991. That figure, of course, did not include the millions collectors spent on cards on the secondary market, nor the money spent on autographs, memorabilia, and other sports collectibles.

As Petruzzelli watched the last of the 100,000 showgoers depart the Anaheim Convention Center, he thought of that phrase: The Hobby. It no longer seemed accurate, not with 144 corporate booths and tens of thousands of collectors acquiring and selling promo cards like penny stocks.

Clearly, this no longer was just a hobby.

13

Top of the Deck

In July of 1991, Richard McWilliam addressed the issue of office fantasy sports leagues. Fantasy or "Rotisserie" baseball had been popularized by a 1984 book and grown into a national phenomenon.

The game was simple: A group of fans drafted teams of actual baseball players and, based on their players' actual performance in eight to ten statistical categories over the course of a season, a winner was determined. Fantasy players found themselves glued to the boxscores in the sports sections of their morning newspapers and called fellow team "owners" with trade offers. Owners boasted of their team's performance, admiring their skill in assembling a team and proclaiming that they could do a better job running a baseball franchise than the people who actually did.

While fantasy owners hoped to win the league and thus prove themselves to be the most knowledgeable baseball mind, they had another incentive: money. Typically, league owners contributed an entry fee at the beginning of the season, along with "transaction fees" over the course of the year for trades and roster moves. The top three to five teams, depending on the size of the league, split the winnings.

Although fantasy baseball, which has inspired similar games for football, basketball, and hockey, involves an element of gambling, money is not the chief motivation. In a league of 12 owners, only five owners win money. Of those five, usually no more than three earn more than they spend. While all team owners hope to "make it into the money," most consider their entry fee the price for playing; winning is merely a bonus.

McWilliam, who by now knew who Tony Gwine/Gwynn was and had met dozens of sports figures himself, had no intention of playing in a fantasy sports league. He frequently noticed the employees in the creative department discussing their leagues, proposing trades, and comparing statistics. It seemed, all in all, a huge waste of time. But while worker productivity was a concern, the gambling issue was a bigger one.

On July 5, 1991, noting that a number of Upper Deck licensors had banned fantasy baseball within their own organizations, McWilliam issued a memorandum to Upper Deck executives announcing that Rotisserie baseball would henceforth be forbidden during office hours, and that "any employee caught . . . will be terminated."

Michael Merhab, the ringleader of the creative department's fantasy baseball league, asked McWilliam to make an exception. By playing in a fantasy baseball league, he said, the members of the creative department became familiar with every player in the major leagues. That made them more effective at choosing and presenting players for the card set which, in turn, made them more valuable Upper Deck employees.

Merhab, who unlike many of his fellow executives had the ability to successfully reason with McWilliam, was convincing. Thus, the creative department's fantasy sports league, along with the employees who played it, would not be targeted for termination.

The same day Rotisserie baseball was outlawed, McWilliam banned employees from approaching celebrity visitors to Upper Deck for autographs.

In a memorandum to all Upper Deck employees, McWilliam set out a policy that required his approval for any employee to seek an autograph at any Upper Deck event for his or her personal use. Employees would have to make written requests for autographed items to the managers responsible for the events. Anyone who violated the policy would be subject to termination.

■ ■ ■

In the summer of 1991, Upper Deck began taking orders for its first football cards. Hobby dealers could purchase between two and 24 cases of cards.

After the success of the 1989 baseball cards, dealers committed to 24 cases. Each order Upper Deck received requested 24 cases. Since there was no way the company could fulfill every order based on its production schedule, Upper Deck filled orders through a lottery. The orders that were received for 24 cases via overnight mail the day after dealers were solicited received their cards first. The others had to get by with two cases apiece until Upper Deck's production caught up.

All told, Upper Deck produced 94,332 cases of football cards between August and December, representing $38 million in sales.

■ ■ ■

"If you build it, he will come."

Everyone remembers the line from the 1989 movie *Field of Dreams*, the block-buster movie starring Kevin Costner. The film, based on the book *Shoeless Joe* by W. P. Kinsella, told the story of Ray Kinsella, an Iowa farmer who hears a voice in his cornfield telling him that "if you build it, they will come."

Kinsella plows over a portion of his crop and constructs a baseball diamond. Months later, dozens of dead baseball greats, including "Shoeless" Joe Jackson, walk out of Kinsella's cornfield and play baseball as Kinsella and his family watch in astonishment from bleachers in front of their home.

At the end of the movie, a long line of cars is seen driving to the field, full of baseball fans who will pay to see the players, thus saving Kinsella's farm from bankruptcy. The movie was a smash hit and built Costner's reputation as one of Hollywood's most bankable leading men.

For the 3,700 residents of Dyersville, Iowa, the site of the film, the novelty of *Field of Dreams* quickly wore off. Talk of a sequel soon faded, and although fans of the movie made pilgrimages to the little farm community to take a free tour of the set, the residents of Dyersville realized their 15 minutes of fame were over.

Or were they? In the fall of 1990, Dan MacClean had an idea. As the attorney for Don Lansing, one of the two owners of the famous field, MacClean felt the movie could be used for charity fundraising. An Old-Timers' exhibition or a base-ball clinic, MacClean believed, would attract thousands of paying customers to the field. MacClean wrote letters to all twenty-six major league teams, asking for support. Among his responses was one from the San Diego Padres, who recom-mended that he call the Upper Deck Company.

In January, not long after Tony Loiacono started work as Upper Deck's vice president of marketing, he received a call from MacClean. As the lawyer explained his idea, Loiacono's mind raced. This would be the perfect tie-in to Upper Deck's marketing campaign. They could draw upon their stable of former baseball greats who appeared in the "Heroes of Baseball" games. Loiacono could even call upon some of his celebrity friends from his celebrity all-star hockey exhibitions. They would jump at the chance to play.

The possibilities were endless. As a born-again Christian, Loiacono loved MacClean's idea of a charity tie-in. The movie, which had recently come out on video, was still fresh in the minds of baseball fans. Maybe they could even get Costner to show up. Loiacono called Andy Abramson into his office.

As Upper Deck's manager of sports marketing and promotions, Abramson would be in charge of organizing the Dyersville event. At 31, Abramson had worked with Loiacono at Foote, Cone & Belding/IMPACT. When Loiacono was hired by Upper Deck in January, he brought Abramson along.

Loiacono told Abramson about Dyersville. "This is great," Loiacono said. "If we market it, they will come!"

Seven months later, Upper Deck had put together an impressive schedule of events for Labor Day weekend. The Thursday before the holiday, Upper Deck put the media through a workout conducted by former Chicago Cubs catcher Randy Hundley. During the weekend, fans who paid $2,395 participated in a three-day fantasy baseball camp with Hundley, Reggie Jackson, and Bob Gibson. A cocktail party was held, along with autograph signings, a baseball card show, a youth baseball clinic, a golf tournament, and even a drama workshop.

Upper Deck's green diamond logo, it seemed, was everywhere. The players on hand for the weekend wore Upper Deck knit shirts. When they took the field, they wore uniforms that read "Upper Deck Heroes of Baseball."

On Labor Day, Jackson led a group of ex-players against a lineup of entertainment personalities, most of whom were regulars at Loiacono's celebrity all-star hockey games. As 2,000 fans gathered around the diamond, there was rustling in the corn beyond center field. Out stepped Jackson, along with Gibson, Lou Brock, Ferguson Jenkins, and Jay Johnstone. Their opponents, the "Hollywood Hitmen," included Kelsey Grammer from *Cheers*, Richard Dean Anderson (*MacGyver*), and Jason Priestly of *Beverly Hills 90210*. Costner did not attend.

For two hours under the Iowa sun, the Upper Deck Heroes of Baseball and the Hollywood Hitmen played on the Field of Dreams. The crowd sat in lawn chairs and on picnic blankets around the field. With no barriers to block their access, they chatted with the players and asked for autographs. Even Jackson, who was initially startled at how easily fans could approach him, signed for everyone.

It was a good weekend for Jackson, the biggest star on the Field of Dreams. The only public relations gaffe came on the bus ride from the hotel to the field, when Jackson was approached by a middle-aged man for an autograph.

"Yeah, sure," Jackson said. "That will be $20."

Al Ameskamp, whose farm included part of left field, was not sure if Jackson was serious. Nor were the other bus riders, including Upper Deck officials. An awkward moment of silence followed before Ameskamp, standing in the aisle, said "But I own the field."

Jackson smiled, took Ameskamp's baseball, and signed it. A potential PR disaster was avoided.

The weekend, from Upper Deck's standpoint, had gone perfectly. Loiacono observed the game proudly, thinking of an exchange in *Field of Dreams* between Kinsella and Shoeless Joe Jackson.

"Ray, is this heaven?" asked Shoeless Jackson, played by Ray Liotta.

"No," said Kinsella/Costner. "It's Iowa."

Loiacono watched the end of the *Field of Dreams* weekend, which raised $40,000 for the Easter Seals of Iowa, the Dyersville Little League, and the Baseball Assistance Team (BAT). This wasn't quite heaven either, he thought to himself.

But for Upper Deck's marketing department, it was close enough.

■ ■ ■

Ken Goldin sat in Richard McWilliam's office and couldn't believe what he was hearing. McWilliam and Steve Poludniak, Upper Deck's director of business and legal affairs, were making him a job offer.

Goldin already had a job, a pretty good one, he thought. Just 26, Goldin was the executive vice president of The Score Board, Inc., the first publicly traded firm that specialized in sports collectibles and memorabilia. For fiscal 1991, the Cherry Hill, New Jersey–based Score Board had recorded $32 million in sales.

It had been a rapid success story for Goldin. As a teenager in the 1970s, he collected baseball cards with his father, Paul, a majority owner of a company that manufactured heart monitors. Together, they advertised to buy collections and by 1980 they had spent close to $200,000 amassing an inventory of five million cards. In the next several years, they sold cards at weekend shows and through mail-order catalogs. As the baseball card market grew, the Goldins discovered that collectors were willing to pay a premium for the most valuable cards, particularly large quantities of promising rookies.

In 1985, when Ken was majoring in marketing and finance at Drexel University in Philadelphia, the two decided to turn their hobby into a full-time occupation. The first step was raising money for Score Board, which Paul accomplished by persuading a brokerage firm to underwrite a public offering. In September 1986, Score Board appeared as a risky penny stock offering on the NASDAQ stock exchange.

In 1987, the Goldins began buying huge volumes of cards from Topps, sorting out the star and rookie cards and selling them at premium prices in blocks of 50 to 1,000. While Topps sold its cards in complete sets, Score Board became the largest seller of "single" cards. Investors wanting to buy hundreds of one rookie card turned to Score Board. After the rookie and star cards were sold, the leftover cards, with little market value to collectors, were repackaged and sold as starter kits to retail chains.

In 1989, Score Board bought a modest 3,000 cases of Upper Deck baseball cards, but the following year the company became one of Upper Deck's top hobby buyers. During this period, Score Board branched out into the memorabilia market, signing athletes such as Reggie Jackson, Wayne Gretzky, Mickey Mantle, Ted Williams, and Joe Montana to exclusive contracts to provide autographs for Score Board. The players signed their names to thousands of balls, uniforms, plaques, and photos—anything the Goldins thought would sell. They then sold the memorabilia through department stores and their own mail-order catalogs.

Score Board paid astonishing sums for exclusive and semi-exclusive rights to athletes. Mantle signed a deal with Score Board for $750,000 a year that left him free to earn additional money signing at card shows, which he did for up to $30,000 a day. Joe DiMaggio, who had grown tired of the hassles of card shows, signed an exclusive deal with Score Board in 1991. The two-year deal paid DiMaggio a whopping $3.5 million a year. The Yankee Clipper could still sign for people who approached him in public or for charity, but otherwise he was exclusive to Score Board. The salary was remarkable for a 77-year-old who hadn't played in 40 years, but the Goldins were ecstatic over the deal. Paul Goldin estimated the contract would result in revenue of at least $10 million.

The Goldins became the first in the industry to peddle their merchandise on home shopping networks. They put Williams on the Home Shopping Network as a guest pitchman and even scheduled Pete Rose for an appearance on the "Sporting Collections Show" on the Minneapolis-based Cable Value Network. The show was slated for the evening of August 23, 1989, which turned out to be the day Rose was banished from baseball. Rose appeared anyway, hawking autographed balls for $39, bats for $229, and jerseys for $399.

As the market for single cards soured in 1990, the Goldins went out and bought their own card company, Classic Games, an Atlanta firm that manufactured a trivia game featuring baseball question cards licensed by Major League Baseball. When the Goldins were unable to receive licenses from any of the four major sports leagues to produce sports cards, they went into the "draft pick" card business, manufacturing cards of players who had just turned pro in their college uniforms. They marketed the cards as the "true" rookie cards since the Classic cards often came out before the rookie cards of players in their pro uniforms. Since minor league baseball players were not members of the Players Association, Score Board signed the top prospects to individual contracts and issued a set of minor league baseball cards, as well.

As Ken Goldin secured the card rights to young players in all four sports, he developed a huge network of agents and sports marketing representatives. In 1991, when Upper Deck included a number of top minor leaguers in its update set, it enlisted the help of Goldin to obtain the permissions. Goldin gladly agreed, figuring his help would ensure that Score Board remained tops on Upper Deck's distribution list.

Goldin was living every boy's fantasy. A multimillionaire at 26, he spent his days negotiating contracts with many of the top names in sports. He received more tickets to sporting events than he could ever use and got to work with his dad in a field they once toyed around in during their spare time.

Now, in October of 1991, Upper Deck officials were developing their own line of autographed sports memorabilia and wanted to know if Goldin would be interested in working for them. Goldin watched in astonishment as McWilliam presented him with a portfolio of million-dollar homes in the northern part of San Diego County. When Goldin had flown out from New Jersey, he thought Upper Deck wanted to discuss a card deal, or perhaps needed some more minor league card contracts.

"We're looking at going into the memorabilia business," McWilliam said. "We were looking at buying your company, but your stock is too high right now. We wouldn't know what to do with Classic, but we want the memorabilia business. So why don't you come out here and work for us?"

Goldin could not believe his ears. "Excuse me?" he said.

"We'll guarantee you a $400,000 salary, and get you a place to live," McWilliam continued. "Plus, you'll be able to share in what you do."

Share in what I do, Goldin thought to himself. *I already share in what I do. I'm the executive vice president and a major shareholder in a business my father and I started. These guys must not realize who I am. Then again, why should they? For all they know, I'm just a young guy who has risen quickly to executive vice president. But if you're going to offer someone a job, you should at least research his background.*

"That's a very nice offer, Richard," he said. "But Score Board is a public company and I have an employment contract, right?"

McWilliam and Poludniak nodded.

"You know what our stock is selling for, right?"

Again, the two men nodded.

Score Board stock was a hot commodity in the fall of 1991. It sold for $15 a share in September, but by November it had risen to $40.

"Do you know how many shares of stock I own?"

They shook their heads.

"Do you know who Score Board's chairman of the board is?"

Again, they shook their heads.

"Well, Paul Goldin is the chairman of the board. He's also my father. Between us, we own a million shares of Score Board stock. With that in mind, I really don't think I'd be interested in leaving the company."

Goldin politely excused himself. "If you gentlemen would like to talk further about selling some of Score Board's autographed memorabilia, let us know."

Goldin laughed all the way to the airport.

■ ■ ■

By the end of October, Upper Deck had moved into its new headquarters at 5909 Sea Otter Place in Carlsbad. For the first time since the company began, employees felt like they had enough room to breathe.

With 260,000 square feet, there was indeed enough space for everyone. The plant itself, which Rasmussen had designed, was located on the first floor of the two-story building. The executive offices were located on the second floor, all in a row, with a secretary seated outside each office at a work station. Unlike Yorba Linda, where only the top executives merited an office the size of a broom closet, Upper Deck executives now had 300 square feet all to themselves.

Visitors to the complex entered in an oval-shaped reception area with a floor covered in rose-colored marble. In the center of the area was a marble inlay in the shape of an Upper Deck logo. Behind the reception desk, a staircase covered in red carpeting rose to the second floor. A three-piece hanging that formed an American flag design decorated the wall behind it. All and all, it seemed more like an entrance to a bank or luxury hotel.

Upper Deck, employees noted, had finally arrived.

McWilliam took care that employees would not get carried away by the company's success. On October 28, 1991, he wrote a memo to Upper Deck's executives and middle managers that prohibited the use of a limousine service by any employee without his written personal approval. Two days later, he wrote a memo to all Upper Deck employees, forbidding them to move any furniture, telephones, or other equipment away from their work areas, in order to put a stop to employees' "trading" such things around the office. Both memos ended with the warning that any violator would be subject to discipline "and/or termination."

■ ■ ■

Brian Burr and Buzz Rasmussen never saw eye-to-eye. While Burr liked to run the operations side of Upper Deck with the same military efficiency he had learned at West Point, Rasmussen preferred a more personal approach.

When Rasmussen took over as plant manager in March of 1989, he made friends with the people who worked beneath him. It was, he felt, the best way to earn respect and foster an atmosphere of good morale. He made it a point to have lunch with the plant workers. He even organized the company softball team.

Rasmussen's managerial philosophy did not sit well with Burr, whose military training had taught him not to pal around with people ranked beneath him. "You shouldn't fraternize with these people," Burr would say.

"That's ridiculous," Rasmussen would reply.

After all, Rasmussen thought, he played racquetball regularly with McWilliam. When the company was still in Yorba Linda, Rasmussen often drove McWilliam to work since the two lived close together. By Burr's logic, wasn't McWilliam guilty of fraternizing with the "enlisted men"?

In October of 1991, Rasmussen was among the Upper Deck executives invited to Burr's wedding, but he did not attend. On the following Monday, Rasmussen ran into McWilliam in the hallway.

"I didn't see you at Brian's wedding," McWilliam said.

"Yeah, I had a prior commitment," Rasmussen said.

McWilliam shook his head. "Bad political move."

On the Wednesday before Thanksgiving, Burr fired Rasmussen.

Rasmussen stormed out of Burr's office and called McWilliam, who was spending the holiday at his cabin in Big Bear, a resort community 80 miles east of Los Angeles.

"Burr did *what?*" McWilliam asked.

"C'mon Richard, you know what's going on."

"All right," McWilliam said. "Give me a call on Monday and we'll talk."

Although Rasmussen and McWilliam met the following Monday, Rasmussen's tenure at Upper Deck was over.

It was not a happy holiday at the home of Harold "Buzz" Rasmussen, Jr.

■ ■ ■

In a memo dated November 12, 1992, McWilliam noted that recently "we" had named the new Carlsbad facility Upper Deck's "World Headquarters," but that "in the short term, I believe" that it is not an appropriate name. McWilliam said the new building would be designated on their new business cards—more humbly—as the "Corporate Headquarters."

Employees chuckled at this one. At the groundbreaking of the new headquarters, it had been McWilliam who promised to make Carlsbad the "Card Collector Capital of the *World*."

■ ■ ■

Even after Ken Goldin's visit to Upper Deck, McWilliam and Poludniak still hoped to bring Score Board on as a partner to help market Upper Deck's new line of sports memorabilia.

On December 5, 1991, Poludniak wrote to Ken Goldin as if Score Board and Upper Deck were planning a joint program to market autographed sports memorabilia. Poludniak asked for a list of the sports figures Score Board had under contract and for him to indicate whether the contracts were exclusive, which products any exclusive contracts covered, and "how long we can count on him/her being available to us."

Goldin read Poludniak's letter and laughed. Did Upper Deck really think he was going to divulge such sensitive company information?

■ ■ ■

In December of 1991, Upper Deck shipped its first basketball cards. Five months earlier, the company had received permission from NBA Properties—the licensing arm of the NBA—to produce basketball cards. McWilliam referred to that day as the happiest of his Upper Deck tenure.

Once again, Upper Deck had enlisted the help of Bob Cohen to obtain a card license. This time, in return for his assistance, Cohen—along with a colleague named Larry Rosen—received one-third of one percent of annual net sales and a nonrefundable advance of $100,000.

It was not difficult to understand why McWilliam was so pleased. The NBA had rapidly emerged as the most popular league in sports. Just a decade before, drug use plagued the NBA, and several franchises were on the verge of folding. But over the next decade, the league had flourished behind larger-than-life performers such as Magic Johnson of the Los Angeles Lakers, Larry Bird of the Boston Celtics, and Michael Jordan of the Chicago Bulls. In 1992, the NBA would provide the wildly successful "Dream Team" of its top stars to compete for the U.S. in the summer Olympics in Barcelona.

Upper Deck had approached the NBA as far back as 1989 for a license to produce basketball cards. But the NBA, unlike the NFL, took a wait-and-see approach to the sports card market. Rather than issue seven licenses in two years like the NFL, the NBA expanded the market gradually, not wanting to flood the business with too many card companies.

In 1989, the NBA issued its own line of cards under the name "NBA Hoops," which joined Fleer as the only two basketball card products. For 1990, the NBA licensed SkyBox, the Durham, North Carolina, card company that had produced NBA Hoops on behalf of the NBA. Upper Deck would be the only new card company for 1991.

In December 1991, Upper Deck shipped 39,135 cases of basketball cards, which accounted for $16 million in sales.

■ ■ ■

Relations between Upper Deck and Score Board were rapidly deteriorating. In September, Ken Goldin announced that he had signed Brien Taylor, the top draft pick in baseball's amateur draft, to an exclusive baseball card contract.

Under terms of the deal, Taylor could only appear on cards produced by Classic Games, the card-producing subsidiary of Score Board, until January 1, 1992. Since the first baseball cards by Topps, Fleer, Donruss, Score, and Upper Deck were scheduled for a December release, the companies would have to omit Taylor.

Only Topps and Upper Deck had plans to include Taylor, a 19-year-old, hard-throwing left-handed pitcher from Beaufort, North Carolina, whom the New York Yankees had selected. Both companies protested to the Major League Baseball Players Association, but since Taylor was a minor league player and thus not a member of the PA, there was nothing the PA could do.

Score Board/Classic thus had exclusive rights to produce the first rookie cards of Taylor, which it had acquired for a reported $300,000, until the end of 1991. Goldin also signed up several other top draft picks, including No. 2 pick Mike Kelly of the Atlanta Braves and No. 4 pick Dmitri Young of the St. Louis Cardinals.

Upper Deck planned to include Taylor and Young and had even released a checklist of its 1992 baseball card set that included both players. When Goldin protested, Upper Deck replaced the cards with other players.

For Goldin, who had been unable to obtain a license to produce baseball cards from the Players Association, the deals were a coup. He would have the first rookie cards of three of the top players from the June draft, although he would not be able to picture them in professional baseball uniforms. Still, he felt, collectors would embrace the cards as the true rookie cards.

For the last three months of 1991, Classic was the only company to produce cards of Taylor, Kelly, and Young. In January, after Taylor's contract with Classic expired, he signed an exclusive deal with Topps.

The Taylor contract was one of Goldin's finest moments. A year later, he would top the deal with a contract that gave Classic the exclusive card rights through December 31, 1992, to the top pick in the 1992 NBA draft.

Perhaps you've heard of him. His name is Shaquille O'Neal.

■ ■ ■

The sales figures for Upper Deck in 1991 were phenomenal. The company had net sales of $263.2 million, of which $67.5 million was profit. Of the $67.5 million, $66.6 million was distributed to Upper Deck's shareholders. Richard McWilliam, Richard Kughn, and Boris Korbel, who each held 260 of the 960 outstanding shares, each received $17,872,800. Paul Sumner, with 140 shares, received $9,625,000 while Bill Hemrick (40 shares) got $2,750,000. Bob Cohen, under his contracts for negotiating licensing agreements for Upper Deck, received over $500,000.

Of the $263.2 million in sales, $148 million came from the sale of 370,457 cases of baseball cards. Between the company's various packagings, Upper Deck sold 4 billion baseball cards in 1991. The rest of the sales figures came from hockey ($45 million; 109,117 cases), football ($38 million; 94,332 cases), basketball ($16 million; 39,135 cases), and comic ball ($16 million; 103,476 cases).

Upper Deck had grown so big that it even eclipsed Topps. With the success of Stadium Club, Topps recorded an all-time high mark of $202.1 million in sports card sales for the fiscal year ending February 29, 1992. But that figure was 23 percent lower than that of Upper Deck. With its candy and gum sales, as well as sales of entertainment cards, Topps did $303.2 million in total sales for the year. In that sense, it remained a larger company than Upper Deck.

Topps recorded $54.5 million in net income for the year, much less than Upper Deck's $67.5 million. But Topps, unlike Upper Deck, was not organized as a sub-chapter "S" corporation for federal income tax purposes and therefore had to pay taxes as a corporation. Its income before taxes for the year was $89.3 million.

Nonetheless, just two years after Upper Deck produced its first baseball card, it had leapfrogged Topps into the top position in the sports card business.

14

Dale Murphy and French Hockey

My personal philosophy in life is that positive things come from positive acts. If we have a hobby which is positive, the people in The Hobby are positive, they're going to be instrumental in making this hobby grow, and they're going to be instrumental in keeping The Hobby positive. When you have negative feelings in The Hobby, you're going to have a negative hobby. I believe that we've gone through a lot of our growing pains. A lot of people jumped into this hobby not really understanding what it was. A lot of people jumped in and said, "Hey, I can make a quick buck and be a happy guy." But I think a lot of those people have left and there are a lot of good people still involved in The Hobby. If we can get this positiveness going so when you walk into a card shop, you're having fun again, it will have a lot to do with making it positive. But I think in the long run, the people that are here now, are the people that are going to stay and help make it positive.

—Richard McWilliam
Sports Cards magazine, April 1994

With Upper Deck making so much money, it would be difficult to imagine board members and company executives engaging in any practices to make even more cash that might be perceived as unethical. Why risk damaging the company's sterling reputation? In addition to the river of cash flowing in, millions of collectors believed Upper Deck created the finest sports cards. By 1991, Upper Deck dominated the business; the cards were selling themselves. Consumer confidence was at utopian levels.

But according to formerUpper Deck executives, the company engaged in the ultimate no-no in the trading card business: the reprinting of baseball cards.According to these sources, Upper Deck president Richard McWilliam, on several occasions, ordered the managers of Upper Deck's production facility to reprint certain cards that had soared in value on the secondary market. The reprinting would take place months after the initial press runs had stopped, when collectors and dealers had assumed production was over. The cards chosen for reprinting were ones that were selling for a high value at card shops and sports memorabilia shows. Upper Deck, according to these sources, would reprint these valuable cards—which looked identical to the originals—and distribute them to board members and executives, who in turn would sell them directly to a privileged network of dealers, mostly in southern California. These dealers would sell them either to other dealers or directly to collectors.

Allegations of a reprint operation were heard in the sports memorabilia industry, but did not come to light publicly until Bill Hemrick filed a $10 million lawsuit against Upper Deck on September 7, 1993. Hemrick, the former owner of The Upper Deck card shop that was the site of the beginning of the company, remained a 4.2 percent owner of the company after selling back much of his stock in September of 1988. Hemrick's suit was filed in Superior Court for the state of California against Upper Deck, McWilliam, Boris Korbel, Richard Kughn, and Paul Sumner.

Hemrick's suit made several allegations. First, it alleged that the defendants engaged in "the secret manufacture and distribution to themselves of various sports trading cards," including "a reprinting of a famous error card which featured a reverse negative of Dale Murphy, a famous baseball player, which was originally printed in 1989, and which included the reprinting of approximately 13,500 such error cards which were then delivered to defendants."

Hemrick further claimed that "defendants have sold a portion of said reprinted error cards for their own account and have misappropriated and kept certain other cards for their own future speculation."

Also, Hemrick alleged that McWilliam, Korbel, Kughn, and Sumner "have taken possession of additional trading cards for their own benefit," including "an unknown number of French hockey cards which disappeared from any company inventory," along with reprinted prototype hockey cards featuring Wayne Gretzky and Patrick Roy and 15,000 cards of Joe Montana.

Hemrick's suit contended that Upper Deck's actions had damaged the company in a sum in excess of $10 million.

On September 22, 1993, Hemrick dismissed his suit and was quoted in an Upper Deck press release stating that his suit was based on erroneous information. The press release, issued by Upper Deck's director of communications, Camron Bussard, quoted Hemrick as saying "after disclosure of the investigation proved no wrongdoing on the part of the directors of the Upper Deck Company, I instructed my attorney to dismiss the suit. It turns out that the basis for my claims came from biased information from a disgruntled ex–Upper Deck employee. The information that is now available to me confirms that the commitment of the Upper Deck Board of Directors to maintaining the integrity of the Upper Deck Company is bearing fruit. I continue to support the efforts of Messrs. (Richard) McWilliam and (Paul) Sumner to preserve Upper Deck's position as the leading trading card manufacturer in the nation."

The suit was unusual. Hemrick was suing a company that he held 4.2 percent ownership in, making claims that potentially could have damaged his own financial stake. Then, almost as suddenly as he filed the suit, he dropped it.

Hemrick's suit came in response to a lawsuit Upper Deck filed against him for unresolved contractual issues stemming from Hemrick's settlement agreement. In the same press release, Steve Poludniak, Upper Deck's vice president of business and legal affairs, said Hemrick "filed his action in response to ours, which we looked at as slanderous at worst and a nuisance at best. The investigation and Hemrick's dismissal of his action proves beyond a doubt that we have managed our company on a high professional level, and in a manner consistent with the highest standards of business ethics and with the highest product integrity."

In an interview following Hemrick's dismissal of the case, McWilliam stated, "There was no basis for [Hemrick's lawsuit] at all."

According to sources interviewed for this book, Hemrick dismissed his suit in return for a $300,000 settlement. As part of the deal, according to the sources, Hemrick issued a statement denying the allegations he had made in his suit. Hemrick would not comment on the settlement.

But the story does not end there. A year-long investigation of Upper Deck has revealed that Hemrick's allegations were not off base and that, indeed, Upper Deck engaged in the ultimate trading-card taboo: the reprinting of sports cards.

■ ■ ■

The idea was simple enough. Until late 1992, when the sports card business softened, each time Upper Deck products came out, collectors scurried to stockpile cards for investment. That drove up the price of cards that were produced just days earlier.

Upper Deck, however, enjoyed none of these profits, receiving only the wholesale price. This, according to former company executives, drove McWilliam crazy. "He would yell and scream," a former executive recalled. "He'd say, 'That's my fucking money!'"

According to former company executives, Upper Deck's reprint operation began with its first card line, the 1989 baseball series. The reprinted cards, which were exactly like the cards printed earlier, were sold by McWilliam and certain board members through intermediaries to dealers for premium prices. If a certain card, for instance, was selling for $50 on the secondary market, McWilliam would order that an additional quantity be printed. He could sell 1,000 cards for $25,000 to a dealer, who could turn them around for $50,000.

"It was like we had the power to print money," said Bob Ruggieri, who worked in various production capacities for Upper Deck, including assistant plant manager, from 1989 until he was fired in October of 1992. "We knew exactly what was going on in the secondary market. The perception is that I, as a collector, have something that's so rare, worth x number of dollars according to Beckett [Publications]. You track it month to month. All of a sudden you see twice the number of product out there. I'll give you an example. You had a box of cards that was $100 now worth $50. You're thinking, 'What's up, what happened here?' You piss off a lot of people. You start to create an atmosphere of distrust about what's really happening with product. You put doubts in dealers and collectors' minds. It's just a matter of time before people find out and we'll wake up one day and find out that Upper Deck's credibility has gone right out the window."

Buzz Rasmussen, who was Upper Deck's plant manager from March of 1989 until November of 1991, said, "It's like insider trading. It's no different than when you know that a stock is going to go up, and you take action accordingly. The value [of the cards] went up because of the perception of limited production. What we were made to do was ethically and morally wrong. Totally wrong."

It should be noted at this point that there is nothing illegal about reprinting sports cards. Upper Deck has never engaged in counterfeiting cards, which is against the law in California and leaves counterfeiters open to copyright suits in states without such laws. But Upper Deck has maintained an unofficial policy since its beginning—according to several former executives interviewed for this book— of reprinting high-value cards. (The company never responded to written questions submitted by the author regarding its alleged practice of reprinting cards.)

In 1989, as the company struggled to get its first baseball cards printed, it made several errors, the most noticeable of which was the Dale Murphy card. A reverse negative accidentally was used for Murphy, then a star outfielder for the Atlanta Braves. Jay McCracken, then the vice president of sales, was quoted in several hobby publications at the time saying that only about 20,000 of the error card were released before it was corrected.

The card had been checked by ten proofreaders, but none of them noticed that the photo was reversed. At first glance, it's an easy error to miss. The word "Braves" went across Murphy's chest with the familiar tomahawk logo underneath it. But the insignia was obstructed by Murphy's arms, which were holding a bat over his right shoulder in the photo. When the card came out, the bat was over his left shoulder.

Errors occur frequently in the baseball card business, mostly by accident but often because of a player trying to fool a photographer; a left-handed player wearing a mitt on his left hand, an older-looking batboy at a photo shoot dressed as the player who was supposed to show up, etc. If the error is not corrected by stopping the presses and fixing the photo, the error card is worth no more than any other card. But often the error card is corrected, driving up the price of both versions, since both are produced in lesser quantities than the other cards.

The Murphy error captured the attention of collectors. Murphy, an outfielder for the Atlanta Braves, was one of baseball's best and most popular players at the time. Upper Deck fixed the error, and the reverse negative card shot up in value. The June 1989 issue of *Beckett Baseball Card Monthly* listed the card at $45. In the July magazine, it shot up to $75 and moved to $100 in the September issue.

Of course, Upper Deck saw none of that money. The Murphy cards, like those of any other player, were inserted in packs and sent out with the rest of the cards, which sold for roughly $420 for a vending case of 20 boxes, which contained 10,800 cards.

But Upper Deck, according to former company employees, made money off the Murphy error. In late summer of 1989, according to former plant officials, Rasmussen received an order from McWilliam to reprint the Murphy error cards. Rasmussen says that not knowing what was going on, he approached McWilliam, who told him he was reprinting the cards for "our archives 20 years down the road."

Rasmussen did not find the notion of a one-year-old company saving things for its archives that unusual. Actually, it seemed like a pretty good idea. Topps, with the help of Guernsey's Auctions, had just held an "Archives Sale" in Manhattan on August 19. Topps cleaned out its Brooklyn offices, auctioning items that had been gathering dust for as long as 35 years. Among the highest bids were those for the original artwork from the 1953 Topps Mickey Mantle and Willie Mays baseball cards, which were both purchased by The Marriott Corporation for $110,000 and $80,000 respectively. All told, the sale generated more than $1.5 million for Topps.

The 1989 Upper Deck baseball cards were printed on seven sheets. Cards numbered 1–100 appeared on sheet No. 1, cards 101–200 on sheet No. 2, etc. Since the Murphy card was No. 357, sheet No. 4 was placed back on the presses, and Rasmussen, along with two other employees from the plant, proceeded to reprint 13,500 Murphy error cards over the course of a weekend. The printed sheets were positioned on a guillotine cutter used for putting together 800-count boxes of one card. According to Rasmussen and Ruggieri, the cards were then cut, placed in the boxes, and given to McWilliam. McWilliam didn't respond to written questions about whether Murphy error cards were reprinted and how any reprints were distributed.

There is a popular perception among card collectors that there is only one set of plates used to print baseball cards, and once a production run has stopped, the plates are destroyed. But in fact, a plate usually will wear out long before the press run is over, usually after 500,000 sheets as the color separation deteriorates. The colors become less crisp and the ink does not transfer as cleanly. For larger card runs, four to six sets of plates are needed. Said McCracken: "We took publicity pictures of me and Richard at the end of [the '89 press run] destroying the plates. Anybody who knows anything about the printing business will tell you that's bullshit. You can make new sheets very easily."

The Murphy episode, according to former employees, was the first of many incidents of reprinting. In most cases, only a couple thousand of each card were printed. In 1990, Upper Deck erred on twenty-seven baseball cards—most notably the card of Baltimore Orioles rookie pitcher Ben McDonald—corrected seven of them, including McDonald; and according to Rasmussen and Ruggieri, reprinted all seven error versions after the prices for the error cards had soared on the secondary market.

"Richard would ask for quantities of all of them 'for the archives,'" Rasmussen said. "He would always say they were for the archives or for sometime down the road. He would have us make five or six thousand of every error card."

Interestingly, the Murphy card has plummeted in value. The card peaked at $125 in the December 1989 issue of *Beckett Baseball Card Monthly*.

By late 1994, the card was worth between $20 and $30, according to the September issue of *Beckett Baseball Card Monthly*. Part of the depreciation was natural, as most error cards peak not long after the mistake is discovered. But unlike past error cards of lesser players, Murphy was a superstar. Investors hoarded his cards when they were produced correctly; the error made the Upper Deck card all the more valuable. When the cards were released in March of 1989, Murphy was 32 years old, already had 334 career home runs, and looked like a lock for the Hall of Fame.

But Murphy's bat speed decreased noticeably during the 1990 season, and he was traded to the Philadelphia Phillies, where he spent two injury-plagued seasons. After latching on with the expansion Colorado Rockies in 1993, a bum knee forced him into premature retirement one month into the season. A youthful 37 at the time, he left the game with 398 homers and two Most Valuable Player awards—borderline Hall of Fame credentials, and certainly not the eye-popping numbers he was expected to compile.

Still, why would the cards go down in value so quickly and so drastically?

"Partly because of lesser interest and partly due to an early retirement," said one former Upper Deck executive. "But that can't explain all of it."

■ ■ ■

In the spring of 1991, Upper Deck's reprint operation turned into a gold mine.

A year earlier, the National Hockey League and its Players Association licensed Upper Deck—along with Pro Set, Inc., of Dallas and the Score Group of Grand Prairie, Texas—to produce hockey cards. They joined veterans Topps and O-Pee-Chee, a Canadian manufacturer that operates under Topps's license, producing baseball and hockey cards in French. In July of 1990, Upper Deck introduced its first hockey prototype cards at the National Sports Collectors Convention in Arlington, Texas. The cards were warmly received by investment-minded collectors, who gobbled them up amid the ever-present rumor of a limited production run.

The two cards, of Los Angeles Kings superstar Wayne Gretzky and Montreal Canadiens goalie Patrick Roy, still sell for $40 and $25 respectively, even though, according to Rasmussen and Ruggieri, the cards were reprinted months after their distribution at The National.

While Upper Deck employees gave out prototypes at the National, a meeting was held back at Yorba Linda to determine the marketing strategy for hockey cards. Since hockey would be Upper Deck's first non-baseball product, it had to generate the same excitement among collectors that the 1989 baseball did. That wouldn't be easy. Even though it would be Upper Deck's first hockey product, it would be close to impossible to duplicate the unbridled expectations of '89 baseball. That year, Upper Deck was the only new baseball product. This time, it would have to compete with hockey newcomers Pro Set and Score. A market that had been a virtual monopoly in 1989–90 with Topps and O-Pee-Chee— its Canadian affiliate—was now a five-company race to take advantage of the growing popularity of hockey in the U.S.

Robert Pelton, whose Pelton & Associates agency handled much of Upper Deck's creative design and marketing until the fall of 1992, had an idea. The U.S. was important, he felt, but so too was the Canadian collecting market. With the 1989 opening of SkyDome, the $500 million sports complex with a retractable roof that housed the Toronto Blue Jays, baseball had grown in popularity in Canada. So too had collecting. Pelton suggested that the company could expand the hockey market by issuing a version of the cards in French for distribution in Canada. A native Canadian, Pelton argued convincingly that while Upper Deck baseball cards printed in English were selling strongly in English-speaking areas of Canada, particularly Toronto, the French segment of the population remained untapped. True, O-Pee-Chee had produced hockey cards since 1968, but it lacked Upper Deck's quality and distribution system. O-Pee-Chee, as an affiliate of Topps, produced bland, gray cardboard cards very similar to those of Topps. Create a better hockey card in French, Pelton argued, and Upper Deck would reap the same rewards in Canada that it had in the U.S. in 1989 with baseball.

McCracken and Bob Bove, Upper Deck's national sales manager, disagreed. "Look," McCracken said, "for hundreds of years, the French have hated the English and the English have hated the French. We only have one distributor in Canada and he's in Toronto. He sells tons of English product, but nobody's going to buy the French stuff. Certainly the English won't. The French aren't collectors and don't have the collecting mentality. It won't sell."

McWilliam knew little about the hockey card market, but his ancestors on his mother's side came from France, and he didn't like McCracken implying that the French were somehow too snobby to become collectors. Plus, Pelton's arguments about an expanded market were convincing.

Upper Deck's 1990–91 hockey cards product consisted of 550 cards, divided into two series: a 400-card low-number series and a 150-card high-number series. The low series was shipped in November, with a French and English version going to Canada. As Bove and McCracken predicted, the French version did not sell well. While Canadians scooped up the English version, the French product sat on the shelves. But Pelton might also have been right. His plan to capture the French Canadian market hinged on a wide distribution system throughout the country. Upper Deck's network expanded little beyond the one Toronto wholesaler, and few cards ever reached the French-speaking areas of the country.

■ ■ ■

By Thanksgiving, McCracken and Bove were receiving sales reports indicating the French hockey was a dud. McCracken suggested that Upper Deck forget about a French version for the high series and release the entire run in English. "It's cost prohibitive to crank out a quantity in French if it's not going to sell," he said.

Pelton disagreed, contending that his fellow Canadians—even the French-Canadians—could become die-hard collectors.

A compromise was reached. A small quantity of French hockey—600 vending cases—was to be produced. Since the low series of cards consisted of 400 cards and the high series contained only 150, Upper Deck decided that the high series packs in both French and English would consist of eight low-series cards and four high-series cards. This, of course, was not popular with collectors, who by now had completed their low-series sets and did not want to purchase packs dominated by cards they already had.

A vending case of Upper Deck hockey contained 24 boxes, each of which contained 36 packs of 12 cards for a total of 10,368 cards per case. Since two-thirds of the cards were from the low series, each case had 3,456 high-numbered cards. With a production run of only 600 cases, that meant only 2,073,600 high-numbered French hockey cards.

To put this in perspective, Upper Deck produced 162,876 cases of its low-series baseball cards in 1990: 1.76 billion cards. The figure does not include cards distributed in factory sets (63,019 cases), grocery displays (24,716 cases), singles (15,668 cases), or update sets (7,500 cases). Upper Deck's entire press run for 1990 baseball was over three billion cards.

So the quantity of high-number French hockey cards, relatively speaking, was minuscule. But what if nobody cared? What if the original run of 620 cases—production runs tend to vary by 10 percent either way; the French hockey high went over by 20 cases—sat on the shelves in Canada like the low series?

Upper Deck, wanting to salvage something from the French hockey debacle, realized huge interest could be generated in the product if word got out that only 620 cases of the French hockey high series were produced. If nothing else, it would sell the 620 cases. Perhaps the industry would like the product, generating support for French hockey cards in 1991–92. Ideally it would set off a mad rush for the 620 cases, strengthening Upper Deck's position as the hottest name in the industry.

During the next few weeks, it was leaked that Upper Deck would be producing very limited quantities of high-series hockey cards—only 600 cases.

And with that leak, the race to acquire French hockey was on.

The 620 cases were produced and stamped with the production date of March 28 and March 29. By April 1, they were on their way to Canada. That date proved only appropriate for a product that became the cardboard equivalent of Fool's Gold.

■ ■ ■

In the Connecticut offices of SportsNet, they had never seen anything like French hockey. Even the 1989 Upper Deck baseball cards had not generated interest like this.

Created in 1982 as a computer trading network for coin and jewelry dealers, SportsNet became an electronic marketplace for sports memorabilia dealers when the coin market softened in the mid-1980s. As the sports card business grew, many of the original SportsNet coin dealers became baseball card dealers, and SportsNet became a means for dealers to buy, sell, and trade baseball cards.

In 1988, SportsNet had 150 sports memorabilia dealers subscribing to the service. By 1991, it had over 2,000 dealers on-line and vending cases had replaced individual cards and sets as the trading commodity of choice.

There are an estimated 10,000 dealers and distributors of baseball cards in the U.S. They range from the traditional mom-and-pop card shops that sprang up in strip malls across the country in the mid-1980s to mega-distributors that account for millions in sales annually.

Card distribution takes two forms: hobby and retail. For years, Topps's distribution network was almost exclusively retail. It sold most of its cards to supermarkets and convenience stores, since those were the outlets that were purchasing its gum and confectionary products. Since 1951, when Topps began producing baseball cards, kids had assembled their baseball card sets through countless trips to the neighborhood supermarket, candy store, or convenience store. Like Topps, Fleer and Leaf/Donruss started as candy producers. When they finally were able to produce cards in 1981, they had a distribution network already in place.

In the early 1980s, as more collectors realized they could make a full-time living selling baseball cards, Topps, Fleer, and Leaf/Donruss began receiving an increasing number of letters from dealers wishing to buy product directly. Most of the card dealers could not sell an entire case of 20–24 boxes, so the companies—

when they did sell to the "hobby market"—restricted their sales to major distributors and wholesalers.

This created a free-for-all whenever a new product was released. Hobby dealers would stake out supermarkets, toy stores, and 7–11s, snatching up unopened cards as soon as they hit the shelves. Some didn't wait that long and paid off stock clerks in order to receive the cards before they were put out for sale. It got so bad at Fleer's Philadelphia production plant that cars lined up outside the facility and trailed the company's delivery trucks to the retail stores. In 1990, a group of SportsNet dealers, frustrated by Fleer's distribution policies, organized the National Association of Sportscard Dealers and Manufacturers (NASDAM) in an attempt to open the lines of communication between the two groups.

When Upper Deck formed in 1988 as the fifth baseball card manufacturer and fourth since 1981, it had a difficult time initially selling to major retailers, who felt they already had enough card products in their stores. Instead, Upper Deck sold much of its product directly to hobby dealers, who could call Upper Deck directly with problems. They could even speak to McCracken, the vice president of sales. As a result, Upper Deck earned fierce loyalty from the dealers, who recommended the cards to their customers. The dealers took out full-page ads in hobby magazines touting Upper Deck product they had for sale. For Upper Deck, it was free advertising.

But with 10,000 dealers, not everyone can buy directly from Upper Deck. Even those that can, do not get as much as they want, so they turn to SportsNet. As soon as a product is released, SportsNet becomes a mini–stock exchange. Much like a stock's initial public offering, the price of a case of cards jumps initially, experiences heavy trading for a short period of time, then settles in at a price range where it remains relatively stable. By this time, the SportsNet traders have moved on to the next new product. Most of the people who made big money off the sports card industry during the industry's heyday of 1986–91 were not the shopowners but the big-volume brokers who bought and sold thousands of cases through SportsNet. Upper Deck's 1989 baseball product, for instance, wholesaled for roughly $420 a case, but quickly shot up to $1,200 on SportsNet.

The release of a card product is not exactly like an initial public offering. Dealers have access to the cards days before collectors do, and some dealers and distributors receive their product before others. Topps and Fleer cards tend to be available on the East Coast first, since both companies have production facilities in Pennsylvania. Upper Deck cards usually hit the market first in southern California, near corporate headquarters in Carlsbad—or, as was the case until October of 1991, in Yorba Linda.

With so many card products available, each has only a short window of opportunity for dealers to turn a quick profit. Because of this, many dealers pay extra to have their cards sent overnight delivery in order to keep up with their counterparts on the other side of the country. Others negotiate sweetheart deals with the companies to obtain the cards first.

5932 Sea Otter Place, the site of the repackaging of the 1990–91 French hockey high series cards and currently the home of Upper Deck Authenticated. (Author's collection)

Participants in Upper Deck's 1992 "Field of Dreams" baseball weekend. From left: Michael Merhab, Bob Gibson, Richard McWilliam, Reggie Jackson, Joe Hoerner, Jay Johnstone, Jay McCracken, Gene Oliver, and Vida Blue. (Photo by Ross Forman)

517

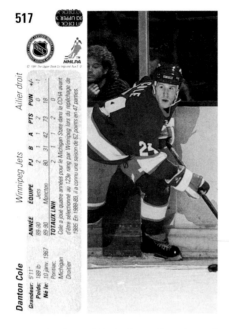

The back of one of the high-numbered French hockey cards. (Author's collection)

Upper Deck board member Reggie Jackson. (Photo by Ross Forman)

The hologram and packaging used for the Upper Deck Authenticated line of autographed sports memorabilia. (Upper Deck Authenticated publicity photo)

Upper Deck's "Comic Ball" line combined baseball players and cartoon characters. (Author's collection)

Upper Deck Christmas card, 1992. (Courtesy of Upper Deck)

Ken Goldin (left) and the late Paul Goldin, founders of The Score Board, Inc. (Courtesy of Score Board)

From left: Veteran sports card dealer Kit Young, Reggie Jackson, and Richard McWilliam at Young's 1993 hobby trade show in Hawaii. (Courtesy of Kit Young)

JAY & JANE McCRACKEN

Former Upper Deck vice president of sales Jay McCracken and his wife, Jane, now operate McCracken's Sportscards. (Author's collection)

TONY & LORI LOIACONO

Former Upper Deck vice president of marketing Tony Loiacono and his wife, Lori. (Author's collection)

MICHAEL & KAREN MERHAB

Former Upper Deck vice president of creative sports Michael Merhab and his wife, Karen. (Author's collection)

Richard McWilliam (left) and Reggie Jackson met former president George Bush at the White House, January 1993. (Upper Deck publicity photo)

Bob Ruggieri, Upper Deck's assistant plant manager from 1989 to 1992, reveals his former life on his license plates. (Author's collection)

Upper Deck basketball card spokesman Michael Jordan at the 1993 All-Star Game in Baltimore. (Author's collection)

Actor Bill Murray at the 1993 All-Star Game. (Author's collection)

Mr. October at the 1993 All-Star Game. (Author's collection)

The Ted Williams Card Company. From left: Former counsel Albie Cullen, Brian Interland, Ted Williams, John Henry Williams, and Tony Loiacono. (Ted Williams Card Company publicity photo)

Bruce McNall, former owner of the Los Angeles Kings and co-founder of Upper Deck Authenticated. (Courtesy of Los Angeles Kings)

Not long after word leaked out that high-series French hockey was limited to 600 cases, the cards began appearing on SportsNet. Many of the 620 cases were sold by a flamboyant dealer named Robert Amato. A former car salesman, "Big Bob" Amato, who has weighed over 400 pounds, operated a $20 million mail-order operation out of Milford, Connecticut. In the late 1980s, Amato licensed four "Big Bob's" franchises before his company went out of business.

Amato had purchased his French hockey through a middleman, who in turn had bought it from a Canadian distributor and brought it back to the U.S. There, it hit SportsNet, or "The Net" as its subscribers call it, at $2,000 a case, moving quickly to $4,000, then $7,000. By the end of April, 1991, it was being traded at $10,000 a case, with reports that it had sold for as much as $14,000. The cases that were opened and sold by the boxes were going for $500 apiece. Packs sold for $20 each. The French version of the rookie card of Detroit Red Wings rookie Sergei Fedorov alone was selling for $180.

Upper Deck's plan had worked beyond the most optimistic hopes of McWilliam and McCracken, who was deluged with phone calls. "I had guys begging me for product," McCracken recalled. "But there wasn't any more."

At least, there wasn't any more of the original stuff.

■ ■ ■

On May 3, 1991, with the high series of French hockey selling for over $10,000 a case on the secondary market and on SportsNet, Rasmussen received a handwritten note signed by Brian Burr, who held the title of assistant to the president. The note, which was acquired by the author for this book, ordered the plant to produce 1,000 additional cases of high-series French hockey. (Burr, who became Upper Deck's senior vice president of operations in 1992 and president of operations in August of 1994, initially agreed but later declined to be interviewed for this book.)

Burr did not sign his full name to the note, but instead put his first initial. The note read simply:

> Buzz,
>
> Richard has decided to go forward with the additional French hockey high series for sure.
>
> 1000 cases.
>
> B.

Later it was decided that the 1,000 cases were to include six high-numbered cards, unlike the original 620 cases, which contained only four high-numbered cards per pack.

Ever since the Murphy incident, Upper Deck had stamped each case with the date of production. That way, the company as well as the purchasers of the product would know which cases contained error cards and which held corrected versions. McCracken and Bove, who had worked for Nestlé Foods, knew from the food industry that when a product was contaminated, they could point to a certain date to determine which shipment was harmful.

The initial Upper Deck French hockey was stamped March 28 and 29, 1991, the two days of production. When reprinting commenced in May, plant workers initially stamped the cases accordingly. According to former Upper Deck officials, the first 100 of the reprinted cases were purchased by McWilliam and consigned to Walt Harris, the southern California sports memorabilia dealer and associate of Reggie Jackson. When the first cases hit the market stamped with May production dates, McWilliam and McCracken received angry calls from dealers accusing the company of reprinting cards.

According to Rasmussen, McWilliam was furious with him for stamping the cases with the correct date. "He called me into his office and said 'What the hell did you put *that* date on them for?'"

Upper Deck did not move into its new headquarters in Carlsbad until October 28, 1991. While the new building was being built during hockey card production in Yorba Linda, a team of employees led by Burr and Bob Henry, Upper Deck's all-purpose contractor, opened a packaging operation in Carlsbad in a building adjacent to the construction site. According to Rasmussen, Ruggieri, and two other employees, after the initial 100 cases and McWilliam's explosion, the rest of the packaging was done in Carlsbad.

McWilliam and McCracken, meanwhile, had to explain why some product was stamped with a May date and why it contained six high-series cards instead of four.

"I asked Richard what to do," McCracken said. "I was getting calls from people who wanted to know why this stuff was dated in May when we supposedly had made it and sent it in March. He told me to say, 'We've been getting product back and we had to re-case it.' So that's what I told them. When people asked me why the later cases had six high cards and not four, I told them that at the end of the print run, our machines were out of balance and were putting in six cards instead of four. Now, of course, there's no way we could have our machines do that in the middle of a run, but I was playing the role of PR guy/company spokesman and that sounded good. They bought it."

According to Rasmussen and Ruggieri, a total of 960 cases of cards were produced in the second printing, bringing the total number of cases to 1,580—more than doubling the initial press run of 620 cases. Those 960 "new" cases, in June of 1991, had a street value of $10,000 a case, or $9.6 million.

■ ■ ■

In May 1991, Upper Deck's production facility at Yorba Linda was taxed to the limit. With baseball and hockey card production taking place, along with plans to launch the first football cards in August, the press room operated around the clock. The company would move into its new 260,000-square-foot headquarters in Carlsbad in October, but until then it had to make do with the three-building facility in Yorba Linda.

Upper Deck had rented a building adjacent to the site where its new head-quarters were being constructed. Located at 5932 Sea Otter Place, the building became the headquarters for Upper Deck Authenticated in 1992.

According to Henry, who served as the do-everything contractor for Upper Deck from 1989 until he was fired on November 17, 1993, McWilliam met with him and Burr to decide what to do about the discrepancy in the packaging of the French hockey. According to Henry, it was decided that the 960 reprinted cases—minus the approximately 100 that were shipped out with the May date—would be trucked to 5932 Sea Otter Place, repackaged, and stamped with a March 28 production date. (Upper Deck did not respond to written questions about the alleged repackaging and back-dating of the "reprinted" French hockey cards.)

On a Sunday in late May 1991, Henry, Burr, Chip Steeves, and a fourth Upper Deck employee repackaged the cases of French hockey in Carlsbad. Steeves, a former Servite High School classmate of McWilliam's, worked in Upper Deck's security department until November 1993, when he was fired the same day as Henry.

The 800 or so cases had been trucked from Yorba Linda to Carlsbad and placed in steel storage bins inside 5932 Sea Otter Place. Henry hired a neighbor who worked as a truck driver to drive the cards to Carlsbad. Since the truck was loaded at night, Henry did not want to drive it to Carlsbad until the next morning. Rather than leave the vehicle at Upper Deck, Henry had it parked in front of his house in Westminster, California. Henry did not sleep well that night. He stayed awake worrying that the truck might be stolen. After all, it contained nearly $10 million in hockey cards.

The next morning, the cards were delivered safely to 5932 Sea Otter Place and placed in the steel bins. According to Henry and Steeves, the cards were removed from the bins, repackaged in new cases, and stamped with a March 28 date. Henry said he even hired four Mexican workers off the streets of San Diego to assist with the repackaging operation. "We paid them $25 apiece, cash," Henry said.

By 4:00 that afternoon, according to Henry and Steeves, the Upper Deck offi-cials and Mexican workers had repackaged 400 cases. The cases were placed on pallets, to be delivered to Upper Deck board members and executives. The re-maining cases—approximately 400, along with some loose boxes and packs of cards—were placed back in the steel bins without being repackaged. According to Steeves and Henry, those 400 cases still were in storage at Upper Deck when they were fired in November 1993. (Upper Deck Authenticated had moved into the building where the repackaging took place. The cards were moved into storage next door at Upper Deck.)

The 400 cases, the ones that were repackaged in late May of 1991, could certainly account for the large quantities of French hockey cards that made their way out into The Hobby. The company wouldn't answer a written question about whether reprinted French hockey cards were sold to The Hobby.

■ ■ ■

McWilliam and the rest of the Upper Deck board must have realized that it would be difficult to keep the second printing of French hockey quiet, since so many at the company were aware of the situation through Rasmussen and Ruggieri. In order to make everyone happy, several executives were allowed to purchase up to 14 cases of the product at the wholesale price of $407 a case. But there was a catch; the cards, as with any product purchased by Upper Deck executives, could only be purchased on the condition that they not be sold within the next year. Of course, this could not be rigidly enforced, and there was only a small window of opportunity to sell the product before it sunk in value.

Tony Loiacono, who had been with Upper Deck for only five months as the new vice president of marketing, said a meeting was held to resolve the situation. "We went in a room where nobody would know we were having a meeting and said, 'What are we going to do about this problem?' Seven of us were given an opportunity to buy 14 cases apiece; board members received 50 cases apiece."

Later, three additional executives were given the chance to buy 14 cases of French hockey. Loiacono kept his allotment stored at Upper Deck, and had not sold them when he was fired from the company in September 1992. A few days later, he called Burr to have his cards shipped to his ranch in Bonsall, California. When they arrived, the packs contained four high-series cards per pack, not six.

Loiacono immediately called Burr again. "I said, 'Come on Brian, send me the stuff I actually purchased,'" Loiacono recalled. A truck arrived shortly thereafter, with 14 cases of the second printing of French hockey. Loiacono, now a part owner of the Ted Williams Card Company, still has the 14 cases. In December of 1993, he took the author to a public storage building near his home and opened his personal unit. There, stacked amid personal possessions of the Loiacono family, were 14 cases of French hockey, stamped with a March 28 production date. Loiacono allowed the author to open a case and examine packs inside. They each contained six high-numbered cards.

Dennis Sienicki, the company's chief financial officer from 1989 to 1992, said he still has his 14 cases sitting in his garage. "When I first got them and they were selling for $10,000 a case, my wife went nuts when I told her that I couldn't sell them for a year," Sienicki said. "Now that it isn't worth anything, and it's still sitting in my garage, she's *really* going nuts."

Don Bodow, who in 1991 was a senior vice president of Upper Deck, says he also still has his 14-case allotment. "I look at it this way," he said. "It's still worth what we paid for it—barely."

The executives devised a way of rationalizing the reprinting to themselves.

"We knew what was going on and we knew it was wrong," said Ruggieri, the assistant plant manager. "And, yes, it was frustrating. Richard's way of dealing with it was when an executive knew about it or was concerned about it, he'd say 'Yeah, I'll cut you in. I'll give you some product or whatever.' That was his way of shutting you up. It was all a matter of greed. There was so much greed there it would make you sick. I rationalized getting some because I just wanted to have something to put away for my kids."

Asked why no one spoke out against the reprinting operation, Ruggieri responded: "A lot of people at Upper Deck just shut up and look the other way because they've seen what's happened to all the top management there," Ruggieri said. "You cross Richard and you're gone. There are a lot of people there afraid of losing their jobs. A lot of people. I'm talking about management down to guys on the finishing line. They're thinking, 'This sucks,' but they don't want to lose their jobs. They're making decent money. They won't rock the boat. They'll do whatever the company wants because they don't want to lose their jobs. It's a sad situation, but you have to think about feeding your family, given the economy of California, and that overwhelms your sense of priorities. Yes, you know it's wrong, and if it happened years ago at any other print shop, you would have had people saying 'Fuck off, Richard.' But these days, people are afraid to lose their jobs. I mean, look what happened to us."

Pelton, who came up with the French hockey idea, says he received five cases of French hockey to distribute to children during a trip to Africa in the summer of 1991. When he returned, having distributed only three cases, he said he sold the two remaining cases to a card dealer for $10,000 apiece.

"He asked me over the phone how many high-numbered cards were in each case," Pelton recalled. "I told him six and he told me to come over. I show up and he gives me cash. I thought 'Wow, this is a license to print money.'"

(Pelton, incidentally, sued Upper Deck after his agency was fired in 1992, contending that Upper Deck owed his agency for past bills. Upper Deck filed a countersuit, arguing that Pelton had not paid media outlets with whom the agency had placed advertising on behalf of Upper Deck. The two sides reached an undisclosed settlement in the summer of 1994.)

Asked why he would sell the French hockey, Pelton responded:

"It was wrong, but it reflected the way Upper Deck changed," Pelton said. "Making sports cards is something of a sacred trust. There's no lawbook, no rules, but people expect certain things. It's not something to take lightly by breaking the rules. Upper Deck breaks the rules by their sales distribution [giving certain dealers the earliest shipments of new cards] and by reprinting error cards. You would think there would be people who might say 'Wait, this is wrong. You can't reprint error cards and take them back into the marketplace.' But there's no law against that. Still, it's wrong. You don't do that.

"If you reprint sports cards and give them away to the owners of your company, there's no law against that. If they sell them to the owners, there's no law against that. But Upper Deck has stepped over the line. They've used cards as a form of currency by using it as compensation. By allowing people to buy product they've enriched themselves by allowing them to turn it into cash for themselves. They manipulated the market for their own advantage. In other fields, they call that insider trading."

■ ■ ■

From 1989–93, Upper Deck's board members had the right to purchase quantities of every product made at wholesale cost. In addition to cases, they also could purchase quantities of individual cards. Many of these cards were valuable "insert" cards that had achieved a premium price on the secondary "hobby" market of card dealers.

In addition to board members, other individuals had the right to purchase cards through these special channels. This group included Hemrick, the owner of The Upper Deck card shop who was not a board member but owned a 4.2 percent stake in the Upper Deck Company. Hemrick received product under terms of his September 1988 agreement when he sold back much of his stock. Bob Cohen, the lawyer who negotiated Upper Deck's original contract with the Major League Baseball Players Association in 1988, also received product, in addition to an annual payment of one-half of one percent on all baseball card sales.

Collectively, the group purchased a large quantity of cards. For instance, a company document dated August 8, 1992, obtained for this book outlined how much each board member/Upper Deck "associate" owed the company at that time. (The document did not indicate whether the amounts pertained to purchases of regular cases, insert cards, or both.)

Richard McWilliam owed Upper Deck $119,019. Board members Adrian Gluck, Boris Korbel, and Paul Sumner owed $128,791.80, $24,270, and $21,177.50 respectively. Richard Kughn was not listed.

Hemrick, who had begun a card distribution business called The Sporting Way, owed $55,248.60. DeCinces Sports Productions, the joint venture between Mike Berkus and Doug DeCinces to do consulting work for Upper Deck and provide cards and memorabilia to home shopping networks, had an outstanding balance of $247,524.

There was a seventh entry on the document. A total of $47,040 was due Upper

Deck from a company called Baseballs and More. The company, located in Costa Mesa, California, was a warehouse distributor operated by Walt Harris.

Harris was not a board member. Nor did he have a particular reason for receiving product from Upper Deck similar to Cohen, Hemrick, or DeCinces Sports Productions.

Harris had cultivated his deal with Upper Deck through Reggie Jackson.

■ ■ ■

In the late 1980s, Walt Harris began appearing at baseball card shows throughout California. As a bodybuilder and personal trainer, he stood out among baseball card dealers, a profession that seems to include among its ranks a disproportionate share of overweight, middle-aged men.

Harris, however, was different. In his late 20s, with blond hair and a deep tan, he set up at shows wearing shorts and T-shirts, which he rolled up at the sleeves to reveal his bulging biceps.

Harris's specialty was autographed sports memorabilia. His display booth, which he set up at shows in northern and southern California, was the envy of other dealers. It included large quantities of photos, baseballs, and bats signed by members of the great Oakland A's teams of the late 1980s, such as Jose Canseco, Mark McGwire, and Walt Weiss. Harris had served as a personal trainer for all three, and it was through them that he met Jackson, who finished his career with the A's in 1987.

Harris not only became Jackson's personal trainer, but also something of a business partner. Harris sold Jackson's autographed memorabilia at his booth, and even had Jackson on hand signing at his table on several occasions.

As Jackson became more involved in Upper Deck in 1990–91, he helped Harris become a hobby dealer for Upper Deck. But Harris, according to former executives, became much more than a regular hobby dealer for the company. Some reprinted cards and large quantities of individual cards that had risen to a premium value on the secondary market arrived there through Harris.

Harris sold the cards to a network of California dealers, most notably Al Carreon of AC Sales, who owned a card distribution business. Carreon appeared at shows in southern California with large quantities of Upper Deck insert cards. In July of 1994, in a phone interview for this book, Carreon said that the insert cards came from opening up cases that he had bought through Harris.

In August of 1994, however, Carreon told *Sports Collectors Digest*: "I wasn't really involved in cases, but I would get insert cards because there was a little more money involved in inserts. I got a nice portion. Let's say I got a significant amount and I bought what was available to me.

"It wasn't cheap, but it was cheap enough that I could sell it for half of market, so that whoever bought it from me could sell it at market price. If something booked at $10, maybe I could pay $3 so I could sell it for $6. I'd say it was 30–40 percent, and if it was a really hot commodity, sometimes even 50–60 percent. There was a lot of product I did lose money on. It wasn't always a winning proposition for me."

According to southern California dealers interviewed for this book, it was Harris who became a major source for Upper Deck's reprinted cards and large quantities of valuable insert cards. (Harris could not be reached to comment. Upper Deck's director of communications, Camron Bussard, declined requests for Reggie Jackson to be interviewed. Richard McWilliam, when asked what relationship Upper Deck had with Harris, did not comment.)

During a show at the Long Beach Convention Center in June of 1991, two pallets—each containing about 35 cases of French hockey—were brought into the show and set up at booths. One belonged to Carreon, the other to another dealer who also obtained product through Harris. According to dealers present at the show, the French hockey on the pallets contained six high number cards, which would have meant they were from the second printing.

The cases contained 24 boxes and were priced at $400 a box. The two dealers experienced a brisk business.

Given that people in The Hobby had been told that there were only 600 cases of French hockey produced, the sight of 70 cases stacked up like a supermarket beer display was a little unsettling.

Two veteran dealers looked at Carreon's display and shook their heads. "Can you believe this," one said to the other. "They printed 600 cases and sent them all to Canada and now, just out of the blue, a lot of them have made their way back into this room. Doesn't quite seem possible, does it?"

All of a sudden, there seemed to be enough French hockey for everyone. The next week, after the Long Beach show had ended, the price of French hockey went into free fall.

■ ■ ■

Not long after the French hockey hit the market in March 1991, *Beckett Hockey Card Monthly* valued the French hockey high-series cards at eight times greater than their English counterparts. But they dropped steadily in value. By 1993, they were listing for one and a quarter to two times the price of the English cards in the same magazine. The Sergei Federov card, which once sold for $180, had fallen to a price range of $4 to $10 in the September 1994 issue of *Beckett Hockey*. Of course, Federov did not become a superstar as quickly as hockey analysts expected, but such a dramatic slip in value suggests something more: supply unexpectedly outweighed demand.

James Beckett, whose Beckett price guides are the most followed source of sports card values, says the rapid decline in value for the French hockey was due to a feeling in The Hobby that there was much more out there than initially believed. Beginning in May of 1991, Beckett's team of price guide analysts, who travel to card shows across the country, began seeing large quantities of French hockey—both in unopened cases and stacks of star and rookie cards—at card shows in southern California.

"In the case of French hockey, we were trying to report the market," Beckett said. "It was fantastic when it first came out. To me, having been a collector and dealer, there was no precedent in The Hobby over the first 100 years to look at one set in relation to an almost identical set—in this case the French versus English version—and have a 1,000 percent premium. It's never happened. I can't remember anything starting out at 10 times greater than a nearly identical set.

"So just based on that, that multiplier was bound to come down to a degree. But it came down so quickly and we saw so much of the product in the hands of a few people that it was incredible. Some fallback in the French hockey would not have been a surprise. But the market crashed in that product. The perception was that there was a lot more out there—a whole lot more—than the original 600 cases.

"I don't have any evidence that they were doing anything wrong. It's their prerogative to print as much as they want. But I think it's unethical to print cards a year, six months, or even a few months after the press run has ended. It may not violate any licensing agreements, but it's definitely a situation where there's a betrayal of the public trust."

■ ■ ■

According to Ted Saskin, as director of licensing for the National Hockey League Players Association, Upper Deck's hockey card production for 1990–91 was properly accounted for.

"We've made some investigation," he said. "In my mind, I don't have all the answers. I know that, with the passage of time, things do seem to be going nowhere. I've heard the same rumors that they went back on press. If it did happen—and we have no definitive proof that it did—we would have a problem with a director of a company buying a case for $400, paying a royalty on $400, and then selling it for $12,000.

"But it also would raise a larger moral and ethical issue. People are buying this stuff on a hunch that it's valuable. It's an unregulated form of security trading and a lot of people get burned."

Judy Heeter, as director of licensing for the Major League Baseball Players Association, said she also had heard reports of Upper Deck's reprinting operation, but had discovered no evidence to support the claims.

"They have to pay us royalties on the net sales price," she said. "Normally, of course, that's the wholesale price. But if they did reprint cards that had achieved a different value on the secondary market, we would want our cut of what they received for that. Of course, the larger problem—if it indeed has occurred—is that they've destroyed the credibility of their company and hurt the image of the players.

"There's a problem when they're paying board members in cards. I'm not aware that they're selling cards like that on the secondary market. I've heard that. We've investigated that, but we could never find evidence to support that."

■ ■ ■

It bears repeating that what Upper Deck did was perfectly legal. A card manufacturer does not have to release its production figures, and is not bound to produce a specific quantity. Although word of the 600-case number leaked out, no official announcement of the size of the print run ever came out of Upper Deck.

One might wonder how these reprinted cards appeared in Upper Deck's accounting records. According to Dennis Sienicki, Upper Deck's chief financial officer until July of 1992, the sale of the French hockey cards was properly accounted for. The ten executives purchased their 14-case allotment with checks, and board members, who were provided with 50 cases apiece, always paid for the product they recieved, according to Camron Bussard, Upper Deck's director of communications. Once French hockey or reprinted error cards were sold to board members and executives, they were effectively on the secondary market.

The National Hockey League could certainly have a beef with Upper Deck, since Upper Deck board members and executives—rather than the company itself—benefited by selling product themselves on the secondary market. But Ilene Kent, as the NHL's director of licensing for collectibles, said in an October 1993 interview for this book that, like Saskin, she had investigated the allegations of French hockey being reprinted and found no proof that it had occurred. "We found no wrongdoing," she said.

Although it's true that collectors purchase sports cards not knowing how many cards are actually produced, they trust the manufacturers to produce the entire allotment at one time. And although the quantity of a card line is never known, it's assumed that it's limited to the amount originally produced.

"Think about it," said Rasmussen, the former plant manager. "Those poor bastards who bought French hockey at $10,000 a case are sucking wind. If we really had produced 600 cases, the economy being what it is, it still would have gone down in value. Then they wouldn't be sucking nearly as much wind."

■ ■ ■

Don Bodow's Willy Wonka-esque "insert card" idea was a huge success. The 2,500 autographed "Reggie Jackson Heroes" cards had captured the attention of collectors in 1990. Unlike the Dale Murphy error cards or the French hockey, however, the autographed cards maintained their value. In the September 1994 issue of *Beckett Baseball Card Monthly*, the autographed cards were worth between $250 and $350 apiece.

In 1991, Upper Deck had five players sign autographed Hero insert cards: Hank Aaron, Harmon Killebrew, Gaylord Perry, Ferguson Jenkins, and Nolan Ryan. Killebrew, Jenkins, and Perry each signed 3,000 while Aaron and Ryan autographed 2,500 apiece. In September of 1994, according to Beckett, the Ryan cards were worth between $400 and $600. The Aaron cards were valued at $200–$300, while the cards of the other three players were priced between $50 and $100. In 1992, Upper Deck continued the Heroes series with autographed insert cards of Johnny Bench, Joe Morgan, and Ted Williams.

The Heroes line was not the only insert card product. In 1991, Upper Deck inserted a ten-card "Silver Sluggers" set at the rate of one card per "jumbo" pack. The set included Jose Canseco, Barry Bonds, and Ryne Sandberg. In 1992, the company included a 25-card set of young stars called "Scouting Report."

Other companies followed the insert craze. In 1991, Score included cards autographed by Mickey Mantle. By 1993, the insert phenomenon had become so commonplace that it was hard to tell the regular cards from the inserts. For 1993, Beckett Publications lists 105 insert sets for the five major baseball card manufacturers. By that time, youngsters could be seen opening packs at card shows and expressing disappointment when all they received was a handful of regular cards. "I've often wondered why card companies don't just now wrap the insert cards with toilet paper and sell them that way," said longtime card dealer Mike Berkus. "Collectors don't want the standard cards anymore."

According to former Upper Deck employees, certain members of Upper Deck's board of directors kept quantities of insert cards for themselves. Once the cards began selling for a premium on the secondary market, these board members apparently sold them through their network of sports card dealers.

There were other cards Upper Deck produced that were particularly valuable. In 1990, four years before he decided to play baseball full-time, basketball star Michael Jordan took batting practice at Old Comiskey Park before a Chicago White Sox game. Upper Deck obtained a photo from the event, signed a contract with Jordan, and produced a Jordan "baseball" card that was inserted in packs of 1991 Upper Deck cards.

The card, released in January of 1991, immediately began selling for $35. Upper Deck announced that there were five to six Jordan cards in each case of 10,800 cards.

Although the card was supposedly produced on a limited basis, it suddenly began appearing in large quantities. On January 18, 1991, John Leptich reported in the *Chicago Tribune* that dealers had been given the opportunity to buy "lots of between 50–500 cards."

The Jordan card, according to former plant workers, was reprinted, with thousands of cards being distributed to select dealers. By the end of January, the card had fallen to $8. (There was rekindled interest in the card in 1994, when Jordan became a minor league baseball player. The September 1994 issue of *Beckett Baseball Card Monthly* priced the card at $11 to $18.)

The cards that had obtained a premium value—such as the French hockey, the Jordan baseball cards, the autographed Heroes cards, or any of the insert "subsets"—were kept in a special part of Upper Deck headquarters that could only be accessed by McWilliam, Burr, and certain security personnel. At Upper Deck's Carlsbad facility, the area was located on the first floor of the building adjacent to the UV department, where ultraviolet coating was applied to the cards. Employees dubbed the area "the black hole," since cards went in there and were never seen again.

At one time, the black hole was so big that vans could drive in for loading purposes. According to Steeves, certain dealers were allowed to pull their vans into the black hole and fill them with cards. "I was told to look the other way," Steeves recalled.

Steeves, who has known McWilliam since their days together at Servite High School, was asked why McWilliam might engage in such activities when he makes such an extraordinary amount of money in salary, dividends, and bonuses, as an officer, director, and shareholder of Upper Deck.

"I've never understood why he does what he does," Steeves said. "I think it's because he loves the power. Why does he do it? Because he can."

"Richard is in love with money," Robert Pelton said. "If I sent Richard an invoice and it was two dollars in his favor, that made his day. He fucked me out of two dollars. If I called him and said, 'Can I have my two dollars back?' he'd never give it back—ever. There's something in Richard's background that's made him so possessive of other people's money. It's bizarre."

■ ■ ■

On May 27, 1994, Upper Deck announced a new distribution policy. In a press release issued by Camron Bussard, the company announced: "In response to industry trends and as part of its long-term and ongoing efforts to control its product allocation, the Upper Deck Company released information today confirming new guidelines governing its product distribution policies.

"At the December [1993] board meeting, the Board of Directors limited the amount of product they may purchase from the company as part of their compensation. Board members may purchase up to three cases at wholesale pricing for their personal collections and charities. The members cannot purchase special products outside of these minimal allocations."

This action, the release stated, was in response to changes in the trading card business.

"Because the trading card industry has changed, things that were standard industry-wide practices three years ago are no longer healthy for the industry," said Richard McWilliam, President and CEO of The Upper Deck Company. "As before, we are confident that the small amount of product the board receives will have no impact on the trading card market, and we will continue to monitor this situation.

"In addition, the Upper Deck Company distributes its product through third-party contracts and other arrangements, the largest such obligation being to Robert Cohen—against whom The Upper Deck Company is currently seeking arbitration to resolve product-related contract disputes."

In addition, in a follow-up article written by former UPI sportswriter Bob Brill for *Sports Collectors Digest,* Upper Deck acknowledged that board members had purchased thousands of cases and sold them to local wholesalers. Much of the product, the article reported, was sold through Harris, who in turn sold it to dealers such as Carreon.

Bussard, Upper Deck's director of communications, was quoted in the article saying: "It is all legal, it's the board's company, we are privately held and they can do whatever they want. What made it seem like it was worse than it was is that all the product was sold in one small geographic area. The amount of product in the big scheme is relatively insignificant but since they sold it all in Orange County it made it seem like there was a ton of stuff out there."

The article did not address the allegations of reprinting, nor did Upper Deck address the issue in its press release.

On August 16, 1994, the author sent a list of questions regarding the alleged reprinting operation to McWilliam, who after his initial interview with the author in June of 1993 declined to be interviewed in person for this book. McWilliam did not respond to any of the questions. Instead, the author received a letter from Steve Mitgang, who along with Brian Burr succeeded McWilliam as co-presidents of the company the day before the questions were received. (McWilliam remained Upper Deck's chief executive officer.)

Mitgang did not address any of the questions. He wrote: "We believe that with the amount of information covering The Upper Deck Company already in the public domain, along with your own empirical research, you already possess all the information we can provide to you."

McWilliam's contention that the practice of board members being allowed to purchase significant quantities of product for their personal use was "standard industry-wide practice" was met with disbelief from officials of the other four major baseball card manufacturers interviewed for this book.

"We can't buy anything unless we go out to the store like everyone else," said Sy Berger, Topps's longtime vice president.

"Executives at Fleer do not receive any product other than samples to distribute to Fleer accounts and the media," said Paul Mullan, chairman of Fleer. "Anything else? No way."

Score, which changed its name in 1993 to Pinnacle Brands, created a committee to approve the release of products through non-sales channels, such as for charity auctions and promotional distribution.

"I'm not sure what industry [McWilliam] is talking about it being standard industrywide practice," said Michael Cleary, vice president of Pinnacle Brands. "But the idea of board members and card executives receiving product as some sort of compensation doesn't seem to be practiced beyond California."

Vince Nauss, vice president for Leaf and its Donruss subsidiary, said: "It's certainly not true here."

■ ■ ■

Although Upper Deck settled its suit with Bill Hemrick in September of 1993, the reprint issue did not go away. On August 3, 1994, Bob Cohen filed suit against Upper Deck in California Superior Court for the county of Los Angeles. Named as defendants were the Upper Deck Company, Richard McWilliam, Reggie Jackson, Boris Korbel, Richard Kughn, and Paul Sumner.

In 1988, Cohen, then the agent of California Angels' pitcher DeWayne Buice, had helped Upper Deck obtain a license to produce baseball cards through the Major League Baseball Players Association. In return, Upper Deck and Cohen entered into a contract that was to provide Cohen with: a retainer of $1,000 per month and one half of one percent of Upper Deck's annual gross sales of baseball cards, with a cap of $50,000 in 1989, $100,000 in 1990, and $150,000 thereafter. The contract was to survive so long as the company was not sold and any license to produce baseball cards was maintained by Upper Deck. Cohen later helped negotiate contracts for Upper Deck with the National Football League, its Players Association, and the National Basketball Association. For his services, Cohen received a percentage of sales for as long as Upper Deck was licensed by the NFL and NBA to produce cards.

Cohen's contracts with Upper Deck also gave him the right, like Hemrick, to purchase cards at the lowest wholesale price. In addition, Cohen would be among the first purchasers of Upper Deck cards to receive his shipments. In an industry where there is only a small window of opportunity to capture collector interest, this was particularly important.

In 1993, according to Cohen's suit, Upper Deck entered into negotiations with Cohen to buy out his contracts because, in McWilliam's opinion, if Upper Deck were to go public or be sold, its obligation to Cohen would be deemed a liability. Negotiations broke off and, according to the suit, Upper Deck breached its contract with Cohen.

Among the claims in Cohen's suit: "Upper Deck and its directors and/or officers, including defendants, warehoused numerous cases of cards to manipulate the market for their own advantage and the detriment of Cohen." The defendants "did not pay for these warehoused cases, but rather waited until the market supply dwindled, creating a scarcity, and then sold the cases at higher prices all for their own personal benefit and without the knowledge of Upper Deck's shareholders, customers or distributors. Once the availability of the cases became known, however, these principals would drop the prices, thereby causing investors and retail shop owners, and distributors such as Cohen who had purchased the cases at the high prices, to lose considerable sums of money."

"Defendants McWilliam and Jackson have created sham transactions whereby, for their own personal gain, they have provided discounts in the form of credits to certain distributors they either control or are affiliated with ostensibly because the goods were either damaged or returned when, in fact, they were neither. Such transactions result in defendants selling of merchandise at costs that unfairly compete with other distributors, such as Cohen."

The officers and directors of Upper Deck "deliberately sought to hurt the sales of Cohen's cards by, among other things, competing unfairly with Cohen and other wholesalers by receiving those cases that were most profitable first, before any other distributor, and by receiving products such as sets and/or single cards that no other distributor had access to."

The suit also addressed the reprint issue. Upper Deck's officers and directors, "reproduced for their own benefit cases of cards that were believed by the industry to be out of print and therefore highly profitable. After additional cases had been reproduced, the value of these cases dropped precipitously, thereby injuring Cohen and other wholesalers. Defendants also unfairly competed by taking huge quantities of product without payment and without the knowledge of anyone except defendants. These activities caused the value of Cohen's cases of cards to drop in value."

Cohen also alleged that Upper Deck "repeatedly failed to pay royalties to the sports organizations for which cards were licensed, surreptitiously raiding the manufacturing facilities on weekends and after hours of product, and hiding the sales of these raided products by demanding payments only in cash."

Upper Deck would not grant the author further interviews to ask about the Cohen suit. In an interview for "The Brill Report," a sports card industry newsletter published by former UPI sportswriter Bob Brill, Upper Deck general counsel David Cornwell addressed the issue of Cohen's contract.

"Our position is that Bob Cohen's agreements have outlived his ability to perform under those agreements," Cornwell said. "The issue of what happened years ago has no bearing on his present obligation or ability to perform under the agreements. It is his present ability to perform that is at issue."

■ ■ ■

In April of 1989, Bob Henry received a case of 1989 Upper Deck baseball cards for completing enough of Upper Deck's new headquarters in Yorba Linda in time for the board of directors to hold a meeting.

Henry said that in the summer of 1991, McWilliam promised him 20 cases of the reprinted French hockey if the production part of the company's new facility in Carlsbad was ready by September.

By September, according to *Beckett Hockey Card Monthly*, the French hockey had dropped significantly in value. The magazine listed the French version of the 1990–91 high-series hockey cards at five times greater than its English counterpart.

Still, even in September, 20 cases of French hockey would have been worth nearly $40,000 on the open hobby market.

In November, 1993, Henry was fired from his job as contractor of Upper Deck. Henry had never received his 20 cases, even though the production part of Upper Deck's Carlsbad headquarters was completed by September of 1991. Early in 1994, Henry negotiated a severance package from the company.

But it did not include 20 cases of French hockey. That was fine, Henry thought.

After all, who would have bought them from him now?

CHAPTER

15

Crisis

Having issued $66.6 million in dividends on sales of $263.2 million in 1991, McWilliam and Dennis Sienicki, Upper Deck's chief financial officer, began work on their financial forecasts for 1992.

Most companies, both public and private, issue dividends on a quarterly or yearly basis. While shareholders enter the year optimistic about possible dividends, they know that any distributions depend on the success of the company.

Upper Deck took a different approach, dispensing its dividends monthly and issuing a schedule of distributions to its shareholders at the beginning of the year. Since Upper Deck's initial success in 1989, McWilliam had sat down in the fall of each year and put together a financial forecast for the following year. In late 1990, based on Upper Deck's sales, profit margins, and dividends ($35 million), he projected that Upper Deck would earn and distribute around $60 million in dividends in 1991. He was pretty close.

With the success of the card industry in 1991, along with the fact that Upper Deck could produce basketball cards for the entire year in 1992—with no appreciable increase in fixed costs—McWilliam and Sienicki estimated that the company's profit distributions could actually double. The NBA was thriving, and the excitement surrounding the U.S. Olympic "Dream Team" had made basketball cards the hottest niche in the market. Since Upper Deck already had the printing capabilities and support team in place, the additional costs of another product would be modest.

With that in mind, McWilliam and Sienicki put together a monthly plan of profit distributions to Upper Deck owners McWilliam, Richard Kughn, Paul Sumner, Boris Korbel, and Bill Hemrick.

It was forecast that the owners would divide $100 million for calendar year 1992.

As far back as 1990, Sienicki had cautioned against scheduling dividends before the money came in. By committing money to stockholders, he felt, Upper Deck ran the risk of not being able to deliver should the market go sour. The shareholders, who with the exception of Hemrick were also board members, might commit their scheduled dividends to their respective businesses. What would happen, Sienicki wondered, if Upper Deck did not do well enough to meet the forecasts?

Of course, it was difficult to imagine the card business going bad, especially after 1991. Late in the year, Sienicki and McWilliam forecast $350 million in sales for 1992. With a profit margin of 25–30 percent, that meant dividends of around $100 million. McWilliam, Kughn, and Korbel alone were scheduled to receive monthly checks that would total in the neighborhood of $27 million apiece for 1992.

By doling out money on a monthly basis, Sienicki felt, it made it very difficult to conduct the company's day-to-day affairs since any excess cash was immediately distributed. At times, the company ran the risk of violating its credit agreements and covenants with banks and leasing companies.

Shortly after New Year's, 1992, Sienicki sent a memo to McWilliam outlining his concerns.

The memo, dated January 6, 1992, noted that Sienicki had previously expressed concern to McWilliam and the Upper Deck board of directors that the company was being "overly enthusiastic" in its distribution of dividends to shareholders. Sienicki warned that the practice was impairing the company's ability to secure immediately needed funds at reasonable interest rates (the financial results for December 1991 would show that Upper Deck had not complied with the financial convenants in its existing leases and bank credit agreements, and the company's practice of keeping its equity low made its prospective debt-to-equity ration less attractive to lenders). Sienicki urged that instead of sticking to a schedule set at the beginning of the year based on annual projections, Upper Deck should revise projected dividend distributions periodically during the year in light of the company's actual sales and production costs and the constraints imposed by its financial covenants.

It was probably hard for McWilliam to feel overly concerned. The day he received Sienicki's memo, *The Sporting News* released its annual ranking of the "100 Most Powerful People in Sports." At the top of the list was NBA commissioner David Stern who was praised, among other things, for the creation of NBA Properties, the licensing, marketing, and entertainment production arm of the NBA.

The Olympics in Barcelona were six months away and already the U.S. Olympic basketball Dream Team had become a marketing juggernaut. Basketball card sales were soaring, not just at Upper Deck, but at Topps, Fleer, and SkyBox. Stern's marketing efforts had transformed the NBA from a financially ailing league in the early 1980s into the premier sports organization of 1992. The boom could even be seen in the card market, where basketball cards had cut into baseball's dominance.

In 1987, only one card company—Fleer—produced basketball cards. But the market had grown since, and the NBA granted licenses to Upper Deck and SkyBox, a Durham, North Carolina, company that produced cards under its own name as well as that of "NBA Hoops." Topps, which had given up on basketball cards in 1982, was now one of a dozen companies applying for the next NBA license.

After Stern, the power list was composed of sports owners, television executives, agents, labor leaders, and athletes. At No.77, the name of the Upper Deck president appeared. The three-line blurb on McWilliam read "new, slicker style of card blew away competition, forcing Topps to answer by upgrading its product."

McWilliam, who three years earlier had to confirm Reggie Jackson's identity with Don Bodow when Mr. October arrived on his doorstep, now held a place among the power brokers of sports. It was a gradual process, however; like many news clippings, *The Sporting News* article referred to the Upper Deck president as Richard *McWilliams*.

■ ■ ■

For nearly three years, DeWayne Buice and Upper Deck had been locked in legal battles. The former relief pitcher for the California Angels who helped Upper Deck get its license to produce baseball cards now was far removed from the company.

Buice filed suit June 28, 1989, claiming Upper Deck had violated his September 1988 agreement to repurchase his stock. Over the next two years, Buice filed a series of amendments and additional claims, alleging fraud, unlawful corporate distributions, and intentional infliction of emotional distress.

On January 24, 1992, Buice and Upper Deck finalized a settlement. Buice agreed to liquidate his right to acquire 40 shares of Upper Deck stock in return for $17 million. Under the agreement, Buice would receive $4.25 million a year for four years, with annual payments issued each year on January 10 through 1995.

Of the $17 million, $6 million was paid in exchange for the "termination and extinguishment" of all Upper Deck's obligation to Buice, $5 million for the settlement and cancellation of all settlement payments that would have been due Buice under his stock option agreement, and $6 million for emotional distress and other personal injuries alleged to have been suffered by Buice.

For Buice, who had spent 10 years in the minor leagues living in cheap motels and eating macaroni and cheese, the settlement meant he never had to worry about money again. Buice had never been able to duplicate his success of 1987, when he saved 17 games for the Angels as a 29-year-old rookie. The following season, he went 2–4 with a 5.93 ERA and three saves.

In September of 1988, he and Bill Hemrick had pooled the resources from their initial settlement agreements and gone into the card distribution business together. That didn't last long (Buice and Hemrick, as Jeff Marx had predicted, never got along) nor did Buice's baseball career, which ended after a brief fling with the Toronto Blue Jays in 1989. Still, Buice made a comfortable living from the cards he received from Upper Deck in his initial agreement with the company, and he maintained hope that he would receive a later settlement from Upper Deck. With all that in mind, he lost his motivation to play baseball, and friends joked that he was the only man to ever give up one of the most coveted, lucrative professions in the world because he stood to make more money elsewhere.

Now that he had received his deal, Buice marveled at the irony. If Sun's Chinese Restaurant had not been closed on that evening in the fall of 1987, he never would have stumbled into Hemrick's Upper Deck card shop. Now he had a four-year deal worth $17 million, far more than he ever could have expected to earn in baseball. Wally Joyner, his former Angels teammate, had just signed a three-year deal with the Kansas City Royals that, along with his 1992 salary, would earn him similar money. But Joyner was a star; Buice figured he would not have lasted long in the majors even if he had not found Upper Deck. Besides, Joyner had to work for his salary; Buice could do whatever he wanted. He spent his days fishing and boating near his home in Incline Village, Nevada, with his wife and two sons.

"Once I got the money from Upper Deck, the hunger to play baseball wasn't there anymore," Buice recalled. "Baseball is a lot of fun, but it's a grueling eight months."

In an interview for this book, Paul Molitor, whom Buice and Joyner had approached in 1988 on behalf of Upper Deck before Molitor had left the Milwaukee Brewers for the Toronto Blue Jays, was informed of the terms of Buice's settlement. Molitor, a soft-spoken man not easily impressed, could not believe it.

"That's amazing," he said. "It gives you a good idea of the spectrum of the card business and memorabilia. I mean, this is one player involved with one company that made that much money. That makes your jaw drop."

Standing in the visitors' dugout at New Comiskey Park in Chicago, Molitor poured himself a cup of Gatorade and laughed at the irony of Buice's career. "And to think," he said, "we thought he just had a good forkball."

■ ■ ■

Even after Upper Deck became the largest manufacturer of sports cards in 1991, it worked to maintain its perceived position as the underdog to Topps. Like other card companies, Upper Deck did not release its production figures. But unlike publicly held Topps and Fleer, Upper Deck did not have to reveal its finances, which could be used to determine the size of production runs. Since Upper Deck's production figures and finances were kept private, it was easy for the company to maintain its image as a manufacturer of limited edition collectibles, even if its print runs were comparable to Topps.

Since its inception, Upper Deck had marketed itself as "the collector's choice." Upper Deck earned the trust, and the wallets, of collectors by making cards on the cutting edge of technology—unlike Topps, which until it unveiled Stadium Club in 1991 had cranked out the same bland, gray cardboard product for 40 years.

By positioning itself as a customer-service oriented champion of the collector, Upper Deck fostered an image of itself as the tiny David going up against Goliath Topps, the corporate gorilla that had tried to keep the business all to itself. It was easier to promote that image if collectors and dealers believed that Upper Deck was the little guy struggling to make it against big bully Topps. Although McWilliam would not reveal his finances, he encouraged the view of Upper Deck as the underdog, consistently stressing that "we're not as big as Topps."

"A lot of the industry is perception, what The Hobby believes," said Bob Bove, Upper Deck's national sales manager from 1989 to 1992. "We had to maintain the public view that our product was hard to get. It actually was in more markets but dispersed in such a manner that it didn't seem that way."

Even companies that were working with Upper Deck did not always get a look at the books. In the months after Score Board vice president Ken Goldin was offered a position with Upper Deck, the two companies continued talks about the possibility of marketing autographed sports memorabilia. Goldin wanted to know Upper Deck's financial position before he considered a partnership between the two companies. "I asked [McWilliam] how much business he did in a year within $20 million and he wouldn't say," Goldin recalled. "I asked him if he did more than $100 million or less than $100 million and he said, 'Sorry.' He was paranoid about it."

In early 1992, columnists and analysts of the business speculated that Upper Deck had surpassed Topps in sales and market share. In a March 1, 1992, column, Tom Blair of *The San Diego Union-Tribune* wrote that "in four years, Richard McWilliams' [sic] Carlsbad-based Upper Deck has become the highest-grossing sports card trading company in the world, topping even Topps."

Steve Poludniak, Upper Deck's vice president of business and legal affairs, called Blair to contest the story, prompting *The Union-Tribune* to run a correction: "Upper Deck, the sports card trading company, is privately held. And so VP Steve Poludniak won't say where its gross sales rank among trading card companies. But he will say my calling it No. 1 was wrong. Topps is still tops, he says."

Poludniak was correct, but Blair's statement also was true. In 1991, Upper Deck recorded $263.2 million in sales, although the figure did not become public until a 1993 court case. For the year ending February 29, 1992, Topps reported $303.2 million in sales, topping Upper Deck by $40 million.

But Topps, unlike Upper Deck, had $100 million in sales from Bazooka bubble gum, candy products, and entertainment cards. Its sports cards accounted for $202.1 million—$61 million less than Upper Deck. So while Topps clearly was the bigger company, Upper Deck had outdistanced its nearest competitor in the card market by 23 percent.

Topps was still tops, but as far as the sports card market was concerned, Upper Deck was alone in the upper deck.

■ ■ ■

Don Bodow had spent three years at Upper Deck. Now, he realized, it was time to leave. As the company blossomed in 1991, his role had decreased. He had spent his last year mostly on the phone talking to the media, serving as the unofficial spokesman for Upper Deck.

It was a perfect role for Bodow, a tall, thin man with impeccable manners and a wry sense of humor. With his thick mane of gray-white hair, which he combed straight back, and his $1,500 suits, he was the perfect representative for Upper Deck, traveling the country to trade shows and licensing meetings, reveling in the role of senior executive.

It was a part of his job that he took perhaps too seriously. When McWilliam issued the memo in 1991 outlawing unnecessary use of limousines, company executives dubbed it the "Bodow Rule." His suave style and impeccable grooming gave him a reputation as a stuffed shirt. "You'd walk past his office and he'd be in there doing his nails while talking on the phone to the press," a former colleague recalled. "We used to refer to him as Bon Dodow. People would say, 'Don Bodow: nice guy—great hair.'"

Still, Bodow's contributions to Upper Deck had been significant. He had developed the idea of the insert or "chase" card, which rapidly was becoming the norm in the industry. He had built the company's relationships with the licensing departments of the four major sports leagues. And his accessibility to the press had generated hundreds of positive press clips for Upper Deck.

As senior vice president of marketing, Bodow was, technically, second in command to McWilliam. But the position had become little more than a title. Bodow once had input into the development of the cards, but Brad Maier now directed the creative department. Tony Loiacono, who had come in a year earlier, had taken over the marketing department. It seemed to Bodow that the two were brought in to replace him.

On March 9, Bodow, citing a desire to pursue entrepreneurial endeavors, submitted his resignation. He met briefly with McWilliam and Steve Poludniak, then left for his home in the northwestern San Diego County suburb of Poway.

Later that day, a light above Bodow's office burned out, leaving his former secretary to finish the day in darkness. Employees who walked down executive row wondered if it was coincidence, or had the bulb been symbolically removed?

Whatever the reason, they didn't have Bon Dodow to kick around anymore.

∎ ∎ ∎

While Bodow walked out the door, his successor as vice president of marketing, Tony Loiacono, was finalizing a deal he hoped would make Upper Deck a household name. In early March, Loiacono assigned $5.5 million in advertising business to the high-profile Chiat/Day/Mojo ad agency of Los Angeles.

Chiat/Day had done work for Apple and Nike, two upstart companies that Loiacono thought were perfect models for Upper Deck. One of Chiat/Day's most famous campaigns for Nike was its 1983 "I Love L.A." television commercials, which featured Nike athletes in sites around Los Angeles, each proclaiming "I Love L.A."

The Nike influence at Upper Deck was not a coincidence. Given Upper Deck's early success, McWilliam and Loiacono believed there was no reason Upper Deck could not become the next Nike. McWilliam, a longtime admirer of Nike chairman Phil Knight, once visited Knight at Nike headquarters in Beaverton, Oregon. As McWilliam walked along the Nike "campus," past buildings named for Nike athletes such as Michael Jordan, Bo Jackson, and John McEnroe, he was struck by how effectively Nike had interwoven itself into what Knight often referred to as "the American culture of sport." When sports fans thought of Jordan or Jackson, they thought of Nike and its commercials. Entire teams, such as the Georgetown University basketball squad, were thought of as Nike affiliates because their coaches had endorsement deals with Nike.

Upper Deck, McWilliam and Loiacono believed, also had positioned itself as part of the American culture of sport. Through its sponsorship of Heroes of Baseball games, its advertising in baseball stadiums and on the boards of hockey rinks, and its recognizable cards, Upper Deck had become an inseparable part of the American sports scene in just three years. If the company were going to increase its visibility on that scene, it needed to take its marketing beyond the resources available through its first ad agency, Pelton & Associates. With the hiring of Chiat/Day/Mojo, McWilliam and Loiacono decided, Upper Deck gradually would phase out Pelton.

For starters, Chiat/Day received Upper Deck's basketball card account and its $3 million budget along with a new product called "Wall Stars," a line of basketball player photos with an adhesive backing. The photos were cutouts of NBA players, mostly members of the Olympic Dream Team, that could be placed on a child's bedroom walls and easily removed. Upper Deck earmarked $2.5 million to Chiat/Day for the Wall Stars promotion.

Pelton retained Upper Deck's $3.5 million account for baseball, football, and hockey cards.

At least for the time being.

■ ■ ■

While DeWayne Buice was severing his ties with Upper Deck, another former California Angel was just becoming involved in the company.

Doug DeCinces was born in 1950 and raised in southern California, the son of a real estate developer. He was drafted by the Baltimore Orioles in 1970 and spent the next five years in the minor leagues, during which time he may have saved the life of a young boy who would grow up and take his baseball job. The incident happened in 1972, when DeCinces was playing at Asheville, North Carolina, the Orioles' Class AA affiliate managed by Cal Ripken, Sr. Before one Sunday afternoon game, DeCinces was warming up in front of the first base dugout alongside Ripken's 11-year-old son, Cal Ripken, Jr., when suddenly shots rang out. DeCinces grabbed Ripken, Jr., and dove for cover. As it turned out, the gunman was a juvenile delinquent firing for fun from the porch of a house across from the ballpark.

DeCinces made it to the Orioles in 1975 and eventually took over third base from future Hall-of-Famer Brooks Robinson. From 1976 to 1981, DeCinces provided the team with a solid bat and steady defense but, as Orioles fans often pointed out, he was not the equal of Robinson in either area.

In 1981, Ripken, Jr., then 21 and one of the top prospects in baseball, arrived in Baltimore at the end of the season as a third baseman. DeCinces, who was now expendable, was traded to the California Angels and responded by having his best season, hitting .301 with 30 home runs and 97 runs batted in during 1982.

DeCinces was an active member in the Major League Baseball Players Association, serving for several years as the player representative of the American League. In 1984, as the baseball card market grew and licensing revenues for the Players Association soared, DeCinces organized the Player Licensing Committee. Each time a licensing proposal came to the Association, either directly to Lauren Rich or through its official licensing agent, Mike Schechter and Associates of Tampa, the 10-player committee decided whether to approve the product.

Licensing money, whether from baseball cards or other products, DeCinces felt, was a huge untapped source of revenue. There were dozens—perhaps hundreds—of companies out there looking to manufacture products depicting player images and team logos. The baseball team owners, who controlled the rights to team logos, clearly understood the significance. They had hired Peter Ueberroth as MLB commissioner in 1984 in large part because he had mastered the booming business of sports marketing. As the head of the Olympic Committee for the 1984 Games in Los Angeles, Ueberroth transformed the event into a corporate extravaganza, turning a $222 million profit on revenues of $718 million. The owners hoped he could do the same for baseball.

Not long after Ueberroth took office, he met with DeCinces to discuss labor issues. During the conversation, the topic of licensing and the marketing of baseball came up. "The Players Association and Major League Baseball need to capitalize on this," DeCinces said. "The potential dollars involved could be enormous."

Ueberroth agreed. "Our in-house survey says that baseball hasn't even scratched 10 percent of its licensing potential."

Not even 10 percent, DeCinces thought. Even he did not have that kind of vision. But as the licensing business, particularly the baseball card market, continued to soar from 1984 to 1987, DeCinces realized that Ueberroth's figures were accurate. In 1987, his last year in the majors, DeCinces addressed the executive board of player representatives and Donald Fehr, the Association's executive director.

"Guys, what you're seeing today in licensing money is a small part of it," he said. "You guys could be making $50,000 a man from this."

The players could not believe it. They had grown accustomed to receiving "Marvin Money" checks in spring training of $10,000 to $20,000. But $50,000?

"I'm not sure that's a realistic figure," Fehr said. "If you're talking about potential years down the line then . . ."

"No Don, I'm talking about in the next few years, if we market this correctly. I believe we haven't even touched the tip of licensing potential yet."

DeCinces' prophecy came true, and then some. In 1991, each player's licensing share came to $80,000. As the card market grew, revenues to the PA soared. Each time Topps, Fleer, Donruss, Score, or Upper Deck sold a case of cards, the Players Association received 13.2 cents on the dollar. For 1991, Upper Deck alone paid the Players Association over $19 million in licensing fees.

During years of collective bargaining between the players and owners, much of the licensing revenue was not distributed, but was kept as a strike fund, to be given out in the event the players walked off the job. In 1992, as the players prepared for labor talks, more than $60 million was held back for the strike fund. The irony was amazing: Each time a baseball fan bought a pack of baseball cards, 13.2 percent of the wholesale price went to the Players Association, to be used as leverage against the owners in the event of a strike. During the baseball strike in the summer of 1981, many players had to go out and get jobs. Salaries had ballooned since, but even if they had not, the players could have fallen back on the strike fund, thanks to the booming business of baseball cards. So each time fans bought a pack of cards, a portion of their money was going, potentially, to provide a safety net for a shutdown of the game that inspired them to collect cards in the first place.

DeCinces, who retired in 1988 after playing a year in Japan, saw none of that money. But he remained involved in the baseball card industry. While he was with the Angels, DeCinces met a friend of his teammate Rod Carew named Mike Berkus.

Berkus had gone to school in Minnesota with Carew's wife, Marilyn. In 1979, Berkus, who had moved to southern California nine years earlier, spent a day house hunting in Villa Park, California. After failing to find one he liked, he asked the real estate agent if there were any others on the market. The agent pulled his car up to one final house. "This house could be available," he said, "but it's very private and belongs to a celebrity."

"Really," Berkus asked. "Who?"

"I'm really not supposed to say, but it's Rod Carew, the baseball player for the California Angels."

Berkus got out of the car and started for the front door. The agent, thinking Berkus was going to bother Carew for an autograph, tried to stop him. But before he could, Berkus knocked on the door and Marilyn answered. The two hugged and by the end of the day, Berkus had bought the home from the Carews.

The home came with an added bonus; Carew lived next door to Nolan Ryan. Shortly after Berkus and his family moved in, Ryan signed as a free agent with the Houston Astros and moved away. But through Marilyn, Berkus became good friends with Carew. The two played gin rummy together and over the years Berkus came to know Carew's teammates Bob Boone, Bert Blyleven, and DeCinces.

After his retirement from baseball in 1988, DeCinces followed his father into the real estate development business. (He even bid unsuccessfully on the contract to build Upper Deck's new headquarters in Carlsbad.) He stayed active in baseball through player alumni events and had even served as a consultant for the 1992 film *Mr. Baseball* starring Tom Selleck. Having played in Japan in 1988, DeCinces not only helped Selleck with his hitting, but provided insight on what it was like for an American to play in the Far East.

During the 1991 National Sports Collectors Convention in Anaheim, Berkus enlisted the help of DeCinces to line up players to sign autographs at the show. It was easy work; DeCinces found players were more than willing to spend a few hours signing autographs for cash.

After the 1991 National, Berkus was at a crossroads in his career. He had helped build the National from a backroom swap meet to a corporate extravaganza that attracted 100,000 people. Through 20 years of involvement in the industry, he had developed an enormous network of contacts in the field. Among them was Upper Deck, which he had done telemarketing and research for in 1989 and whose employees he had gotten to know—for better or for worse—through the 1991 National.

What Berkus really wanted was to get involved with Upper Deck. But in what capacity? After the National, he had started a relationship with the Home Shopping Network, providing sports cards for a new line of shows that featured sports memorabilia. Home Shopping, it seemed, could sell anything at any price. With its high-pressure hosts and guest appearances by name athletes, the network sold sports memorabilia that dealers in The Hobby could not give away. In his first deal with Home Shopping, Berkus purchased 10,000 sets of 1988 Topps baseball cards from dealers he knew in The Hobby for $11 apiece. He sold them for $16 each to Home Shopping, which turned around and hawked them on the air for $24.95. Berkus could not believe it. Nobody in The Hobby wanted 1988 Topps sets, but Home Shopping had no trouble unloading them for more than twice the going rate.

Home Shopping valued Berkus's expertise in the industry. Rather than try to purchase cards from The Hobby or directly from the manufacturers—most of whom had no interest in dealing with Home Shopping—the network found it could get product quickly from Berkus. But Berkus needed help, both financially and in procuring the product. So he turned to DeCinces.

Berkus figured that a profitable arrangement could be made between Home Shopping and a card company, if one was willing to work with the Clearwater, Florida, network. There had to be a company that would pay him not only for his connections with Home Shopping, but also for his background in The Hobby and expertise in marketing. He thought of McWilliam, who had built Upper Deck despite little previous background in sports, let alone The Hobby. Certainly he would be interested in the services of Berkus and DeCinces.

Shortly after New Year's, 1992, Berkus approached McWilliam. "The single biggest disadvantage you have is that this has all got to sound like Greek to you, because you didn't grow up a collector," he said. "You can see what the card looks like. You can hear the drums in the jungle, but you can't understand why the collectors are following the beat. You need someone who can explain the hobby end of the market to you."

Berkus and DeCinces formed DeCinces Sports Productions, whose sole purpose was to serve as a consultant to Upper Deck. On April 23, DSP signed an agreement to provide Upper Deck with a monthly analysis of the baseball card hobby market. DSP would provide 2,000 hours of telemarketing research and establish a full-time office in Irvine, California, to conduct business on behalf of Upper Deck. DSP also would promote baseball card shows to be run in conjunction with the Heroes of Baseball games and set up kiosks in southern California malls to sell Upper Deck product. In return, DSP would receive an annual consulting fee of $675,000.

Nearly six years had passed since Berkus met McWilliam at Lehman Medical. But the relationship was just getting started.

■ ■ ■

In the months after Ken Goldin rejected Richard McWilliam's job offer, Upper Deck continued plans for a new line of autographed sports memorabilia. Since Score Board held the rights to many of the top names, Upper Deck attempted to convince athletes to jump ship.

May 22, 1992
Mr. Richard McWilliam
Chief Executive Officer
THE UPPER DECK COMPANY
5909 Sea Otter Place
Carlsbad, CA 92008

Dear Richard:

It has been brought to our attention that Upper Deck has approached certain current and former baseball players with whom Score Board currently has memorabilia and/or licensing agreements. In particular, it is our understanding that Upper Deck has made overtures to Stan Musial, Mickey Mantle and Hank Aaron. Each of these individuals is a party to a contract granting Score Board certain exclusive rights to sell memorabilia incorporating their respective likenesses and/or signatures. In all cases, the rights granted to us include the exclusive rights to sell memorabilia through television retail channels, catalogs, and retail outlets. Each of these agreements shall remain in full force and effect for a substantial period of time.

Based on these Agreements, Score Board has invested large sums of time and money to develop and market memorabilia and collectibles incorporating the likeness and/or autograph of Aaron, Musial or Mantle. The amount of product we have developed is extensive and will grow as these players continue to render their services required of them pursuant to our agreements. The extensive commitments of time and money we have undertaken ensure that Score Board will be marketing Aaron, Musial and Mantle memorabilia for a long time to come. We certainly expect that Upper Deck will not involve itself in any discussions, or conduct its business affairs in any manner that could be construed as tortious interference with our contractual relationships, or which might otherwise unlawfully diminish the value of our agreements.

Should you have any questions on the above, please do not hesitate to call me.

Sincerely,

Ken Goldin, Executive Vice President

■ ■ ■

Finally, Robert Pelton had gotten away from it all. Since Upper Deck allotted $5.5 million of its advertising budget to Chiat/Day/Mojo, his Pelton & Associates firm had received less and less communication from Sea Otter Place. It was as if they were just being ignored, even though they still had a $3.5 million account.

When he had had enough of the silent treatment, Pelton took a vacation to Borneo. For Pelton, vacations were not times of peaceful relaxation, but opportunities for adventure. He took African safaris and led expeditions, like this one, into the jungles of Borneo.

As he awoke at dawn on the morning of June 2, he was about as far away from Upper Deck as possible. But Upper Deck found him. As Pelton walked down a path from his hotel to board a helicopter that would take him into the jungle, a hotel employee ran after him, frantically waving a fax.

Pelton told the pilot to wait. The three-page document was a termination letter from Upper Deck. *How the hell did they find me here?* Pelton wondered.

The letter, written by Tony Loiacono, read in part: "our reasons for making this change in how we handle our advertising did not come easily nor [sic] quickly. Since our awarding of the basketball and new products work to Chiat/Day/Mojo in March we have attempted to make strides in synergy between the creative platforms, marketing strategies and media buying between both agencies. These attempts have not worked and in order for us to move forward as a marketing driven company this decision was necessary."

The firing, ironically, was not the low point of Pelton's "vacation." A plane he had chartered for 20 people was forced to crash land in the jungle. No one was seriously hurt, but the group had to find its way back to town. Along the way, they were arrested for trespassing.

Pelton eventually made it out of the jungles of Borneo. Getting out of Upper Deck would be much more difficult.

■ ■ ■

From the Sundial restaurant atop the Westin Peachtree Plaza hotel, the city of Atlanta fans out in every direction. During the course of a meal at the revolving restaurant, diners can take in the city's entire skyline.

As the sports card and collectibles industry gathered in Atlanta on July 8, 1992, for the 13th annual National Sports Collectors Convention, Topps officials met at the Sundial. It was an appropriate site for Topps. For the better part of 40 years, the sports card business revolved around the Brooklyn company. Now Topps executives were looking out into the card universe, just one of many companies in the market wondering when the boom, like the Sundial, was going to stop and what the new industry picture would look like.

It was Topps's first appearance at the National and its presence spoke volumes about both the event and the industry. During its monopoly on sports cards from 1956 to 1981, Topps conducted relatively little marketing and publicity for its cards. When Arthur Shorin replaced Joel Shorin as chairman of the board in 1980, one of the first budget cuts made to keep the company from going bankrupt came from Topps's modest advertising and marketing budget.

Topps, of course, had prospered since. But the legacy of taking a frugal approach to marketing remained. Even when the company had unveiled its high-tech Stadium Club cards in 1991, it was done amid little fanfare. The quality of Stadium Club spoke for itself, and collectors had embraced the new product.

But after 1991, when the National had been transformed from a hobby card show into a corporate trade event dominated by Upper Deck, Topps had changed its approach, spending millions on advertising and marketing. When it signed a deal with NBA Properties to produce basketball cards again for 1992—after giving up on basketball cards in 1982—it came under the condition that Topps take an aggressive approach to marketing basketball cards.

That meant a strong presence at the National, and while Topps chairman Arthur Shorin stayed in Brooklyn, he sent his second-in-command, president John J. Langdon, along with vice presidents Ron Boyum and Bill O'Connor, and representatives from Lesnik PR, the company's Chicago-based public relations firm.

The increased marketing and advertising budget for Topps was a direct result of Upper Deck. In 1989, according to *Advertising Age*, cardmakers spent just over $1 million in advertising. That figure jumped to $3.3 million in 1990, climbed to $7 million in the first nine months of 1991, and had grown to $10 million in 1992. No longer did card companies advertise just in hobby magazines. There were television spots on ESPN and full-color ads in *Sports Illustrated*. The advertising and marketing of sports cards, like the industry itself, had become big business.

The Topps executives had gathered at the Sundial, along with members of the media, to choose the grand prize winners of Topps's "Match the Stats" promotion. For the previous five months, collectors opening packs of Topps cards received a scratch-off game card. If the card read "Topps Card Show Buying Spree," the collector won a trip to Atlanta for the National and at least a $10,000 shopping spree at the show. The night before the show, the names of the $10,000 winners would be put in a hat to determine the winner of the grand prize: a $100,000 buying spree.

Only two winners had come forward: Dan West, a 25-year-old warehouse receiving clerk from Brockton, Massachusetts, and Bert Price, 39, an auto worker from Sandusky, Ohio.

Before the grand prize drawing, Topps officials put the names of the assembled media in a hat. Bob Ibach, vice president of Lesnik Public Relations, put his hand in to determine which media member would make the grand prize drawing. He drew James Beckett, the publisher of Beckett Publications.

Next, Ibach placed the names of West and Price in the hat. As Beckett got up to make the selection, Price embraced his wife and daughter while West grabbed his girlfriend's hand. Beckett carefully reached into the hat, drew a paper slip and handed it to Ibach, who unfolded it and announced the name Bert Price.

The next morning, a camera crew trailed Price as he made his way through the Georgia World Congress Center. In the afternoon, his prizes were displayed for the press at the Topps hospitality suite in the Omni Hotel. When The Hobby media gathered, they were photographed for their very own Topps baseball cards. Even Sy Berger, the 69-year-old grandfather of the card industry, was on hand, spinning tales of the card industry's early days.

All told, the promotion cost Topps $110,000, along with travel expenses for Price and West. It was a modest promotion, just one of many among the cocktail receptions and product debuts at the National. But the company that had fallen behind when Upper Deck launched its new cards in 1989 now had rebounded behind Stadium Club and a glitzy new ad and promotion campaign.

Berger worked the Topps suite, conducting wave after wave of interviews with The Hobby media. Topps, it seemed, was back on top.

But the industry itself was struggling. While 100,000 collectors had attended the 1991 National in Anaheim, only 30,000 came through the turnstiles in Atlanta in 1992.

■ ■ ■

Unlike 1991, Upper Deck had only a modest presence at the Atlanta National. Instead, its promotional efforts were targeted at the All-Star game, which was scheduled for July 14, just two days after the National ended.

For Upper Deck, the All-Star game was much more than the Tuesday night exhibition between the American and National Leagues. Upper Deck had signed on as the title sponsor of "All-Star FanFest," which began the Thursday before the game and ran through the final out.

FanFest debuted in 1991 at the All-Star game in Toronto. Sponsored by Coca-Cola of Canada and held at the Toronto Convention Center, the event was a combination baseball theme park and merchandise store. Fans could hit in batting cages, see how baseball cards were made, and, of course, buy official merchandise featuring the logos of the 26 baseball teams. Originally designed to pacify fans who could not obtain tickets to the game, FanFest became a smash hit, drawing 100,000 fans over four days. One major attraction was a card show area that drew many of the top dealers from the U.S. and Canada.

Tony Loiacono saw the success of FanFest, particularly the popularity of the card show, and made a proposal to Major League Baseball for the 1992 All-Star Game. In addition to FanFest, Upper Deck would put on a Heroes of Baseball exhibition the day before the All-Star game. The Heroes, who would come from Upper Deck's stable of ex-players who traveled the country playing in its Heroes series, would be available to sign free autographs during FanFest. In return, Upper Deck would be prominently displayed in all marketing efforts, including advertising, flyers, and brochures. Its blow-up baseball cards would be posted throughout the FanFest facility.

It was an attractive offer for Major League Baseball. The 1992 All-Star Game would take place at Jack Murphy Stadium in San Diego, just 20 miles south of Upper Deck's headquarters in Carlsbad. Upper Deck would have a full support staff on hand, and agreed to pay Major League Baseball $400,000 for the rights to FanFest. A three-year agreement was signed.

"This is a perfect fit for Upper Deck and Major League Baseball," McWilliam announced. "We will use the same vigor and enthusiasm demonstrated in how we have revolutionized the sports card world to benefit Major League Baseball's All-Star FanFest.

"Upper Deck will further ensure the event remains a part of the fabric of baseball and an All-Star week tradition for this year and in the future."

The four-day affair went perfectly for Upper Deck. Its logo, it seemed, was everywhere. Blown-up versions of Upper Deck cards dominated the San Diego Convention Center, the site of FanFest. Collectors received thousands of autographs from former stars decked out in Upper Deck caps and knit shirts. Upper Deck even produced a special FanFest set of baseball cards that would be sold exclusively to hobby dealers attending the show. Loiacono figured the profits from the set would pay for the $400,000 FanFest rights, in effect giving Upper Deck four days of exposure for free.

Upper Deck made the most of the four days. Upper Deck banners blanketed Jack Murphy Stadium for Monday's Heroes of Baseball game. The players wore Upper Deck caps. Reggie Jackson was on hand in a dual role: as an Upper Deck employee and the cleanup hitter for the American League All-Stars.

Jackson came to bat in the top of the first inning with the bases loaded. With Hall-of-Famer Bob Gibson on the mound, Jackson stepped in, clad in an Upper Deck Heroes uniform.

Jackson took the first pitch for a ball, then belted the next pitch over the center-field wall for a grand slam. As Jackson rounded the bases, the crowd erupted in a chant of "Reg-gie! Reg-gie!"

Loiacono surveyed the scene and smiled. The $400,000 Upper Deck had spent on FanFest had been repaid many times over. The company had received national exposure and, perhaps more importantly, demonstrated again why it was part of the fabric of baseball.

■ ■ ■

The 1992 FanFest baseball card set was a smash hit. As word got around the San Diego Convention Center that the set had been produced in limited quantities, and only for FanFest, dealers and collectors scrambled to acquire sets for investment.

The 54-card set included established stars such as Barry Bonds, Cal Ripken, Jr., Bobby Bonilla, and Roger Clemens along with up-and-coming players such as

Jeff Bagwell and Ivan Rodriguez. It also featured ten "All-Star Heroes"—all Upper Deck regulars—such as Reggie Jackson, Lou Brock, Bob Gibson, and Gaylord Perry.

On the night of the All-Star Game, Mike Berkus set up a show on the Home Shopping Network that featured Upper Deck's FanFest set. Upper Deck had produced 3,700 cases of the set, each containing 60 sets. All told, there were 220,000 sets. Upper Deck sold 60,000 sets to Home Shopping for $7.60 a set. The $456,000 the company made in return was more than enough to make back the $400,000 sponsorship fee.

Home Shopping broadcast live from the San Diego Convention Center during FanFest. It sold all 60,000 sets, at $14.70 apiece.

Berkus could not contain his excitement. Upper Deck and DeCinces Sports Productions could develop a line of products exclusively for the Home Shopping Network. Even die-hard collectors who normally shunned the station would be forced to buy from Home Shopping since the cards were not available anywhere else. Upper Deck could be the first to capture the television market.

■ ■ ■

As FanFest ended, Upper Deck dealt with its first major crisis. Sales projections had fallen since the end of 1991, forcing Upper Deck to slash production. On July 20, with less work available, Upper Deck laid off 170 plant workers, 21 percent of the company's entire workforce of 800. Two members of the executive staff received permanent vacations.

For Brad Maier, Upper Deck's art director, the news was shocking. He not only considered McWilliam his boss; he also thought of him as a close friend. He had known McWilliam for years, leaving his graphic design business in Hawaii to come work for Upper Deck in 1990. McWilliam had done accounting work for Maier's company and the two frequently had socialized in Hawaii. One time, Maier introduced him to a young woman from Grosse Point, Michigan, named Lisa Andrus, who was now McWilliam's fiancée.

"Brad, your position's being eliminated," McWilliam told him. "You know how it is, business is business."

McWilliam laid out a severance package and gave Maier three weeks to decide. Maier accepted on the spot. Word around the office was that this would not be the last layoff, and Maier wanted to return to Hawaii with something.

For Dennis Sienicki, his dismissal came as no surprise. For six months, he and McWilliam had argued over the financial direction of the company, clashing on everything from dividends to corporate investments. Plus, as a member of the executive bonus plan, Sienicki knew he was among a group of vice presidents who could be replaced by younger, lower-salaried employees.

The executive bonus plan was the brainchild of Adrian Gluck. Since Upper Deck was not a publicly held company, but nonetheless became a very prosperous firm quickly, there had to be a mechanism to reward the management team. Normally, a company would go public, and the managers would reap the rewards. But McWilliam had no desire to go public, at least not yet. So Gluck put the bonus plan in place. Each March, the executive staff would get a bonus for the preceding year. It was based on service time and position, but it was generous for everyone involved. Vice presidents typically received between $100,000 and $200,000. For senior staff, bonuses of $400,000 were not unheard of.

In March, the board of directors announced that the bonus plan had been greatly reduced and that bonus compensation would have to be deferred. Sienicki thought the deferment also applied to McWilliam. But McWilliam, who had a base salary of $750,000 and received annual bonuses of between $1 and $2 million, said, "It doesn't apply to me. I'm a cash kinda guy."

In the summer of 1992, Upper Deck began receiving millions of dollars in returned sports cards that would require the company to give credit to retailers and distributors. For the first time in the company's four-year history, its products were failing to sell through completely.

Upper Deck was facing its first crisis. Cuts had to be made, at least to maintain the company's dividend distribution plan. That meant the members of the executive staff would be the first to go, and Bodow had led the parade out the door in March.

Sienicki had left a message with Boris Korbel before he got fired. That evening, Korbel reached Sienicki at home.

"How's everything going?" Korbel asked.

"Under the circumstances," Sienicki said, "fine."

"What do you mean, circumstances?"

"I was released from your company today."

Korbel became livid. "McWilliam cannot do that without board approval. You are still a member of this company."

Korbel asked Sienicki to meet with him the following day. When Sienicki arrived, Sumner also was there. "Would you be willing to come back if I straightened this out?" Sumner asked.

"Only under the circumstance that I would have full authority over accounting," Sienicki said. "As it is, he second guesses everything."

"I'll see what I can do," Sumner said.

But Sumner could do nothing. Later, after Sienicki negotiated a severance package, he received a call from Don Bodow, who lived nearby in Poway.

"Dennis!" Bodow said. "Welcome to the Upper Deck alumni club!"

■ ■ ■

Late in July, Upper Deck and Score Board tried one last time to strike a deal to market autographed sports memorabilia together.

On July 24, 1992, after a conversation with Ken Goldin, Richard McWilliam again wrote to Score Board, expressing interest in having the two companies market autographed sports memorabilia together. He said he could not specify the projects—other than "various Mickey Mantle products"—because Upper Deck's "product mix" was not yet set. McWilliam also offered to sell Score Board certain 1992 basketball sets and a commemorative sheet. "In return," McWilliam wrote, "we appreciate your efforts in putting a cap on the escalation of salary contracts and fees."

This is bullshit, Goldin thought to himself. *Upper Deck not only knew about its "product mix," it had been negotiating with athletes under contract to Score Board. They just wanted to find out what Score Board was paying its athletes and how the memorabilia business was run.*

They weren't going to find out, Goldin decided, because Score Board was not going to do business with Upper Deck. (The entire episode had soured the relationship between the two companies, and the '92 factory basketball sets would be the last product Score Board bought from Upper Deck.)

Goldin reread the last line of McWilliam's letter. Score Board certainly wasn't trying to set a limit on compensation for autograph contracts. He wondered how player agents would feel if they knew Upper Deck had been working to put "a cap on the escalation of salary contracts and fees." The baseball owners had tried that once, and got slapped with a collusion suit.

Fortunately for the athletes, Goldin realized later, there would be no cap on contracts and fees. Upper Deck, in its haste to compete with Score Board, would send salaries soaring.

■ ■ ■

On July 27, Robert Pelton responded to his firing nearly two months earlier.

> **MEMO**
>
> **To: Richard McWilliam**
>
> Dear Richard:
>
> It was quite a shock to get my termination notice via fax in the jungles of Borneo. It made enduring my plane crash, arrest, rapids and leeches seem like a cakewalk!

After celebrating my 37th birthday I realized that the major focus for four years of my life has been making Upper Deck the most successful card company in the world. You can understand why it is a major change in my life (and my employees) to be told thanks for nothing and don't let the door hit you on the way out.

It also made me sit down and think what I have accomplished over the last four years. I think we can be proud of what we have done. . . . We have never accepted the status quo and we have lost a lot of money resigning business when we didn't feel right about where Upper Deck is going or where your employees were forcing us to go. We have pushed for concepts that we think are beneficial, even when there is no benefit to us.

We are not arrogant, we are just infuriatingly correct. Our marketing plans are dead nuts on. Ever since the first plan in 1988. When we create a product, it sells like hell. When we design a card, it is usually card set of the year. When we create advertising it sets trends that others try to follow. Pelton & Associates can take direct credit for re-inventing the card market and creating the way card products are marketed today. Upper Deck gets credit for letting us do it. Or I should say, USED to let us do it.

Upper Deck used to be smart. They used to listen. We used to work with top management to create ideas and programs based on our analysis and temper it with Upper Deck's knowledge of the market. Now we are ordered around like waiters who can't speak English. By people who have worked there less than a year. You'd almost think we did something wrong.

I would agree that I would be a fossil if Upper Deck did something radically different in the last four years, but it seems you are still trying to outdo what we started. Actually the latest round of products look an awful lot like you are starting to copy people who once copied Upper Deck.

. . . I do not think that we deserved to be treated as an agency the way we have and wish to state that for the record. Now that we have been stomped to death and there is no more dissension, you may find the silence deafening.

Sincerely,

Robert Young Pelton

■ ■ ■

On July 31, Dennis Sienicki sent a letter to Upper Deck's chairman of the board, Richard Kughn, at the request of Boris Korbel and Paul Sumner. Sienicki wrote that he had advised McWilliam on several occasions that the company should abandon its practice of making monthly dividend payments to shareholders according to a schedule set at the beginning of the year. Starting in 1990, Sienicki stated, he asked for permission to propose "a more prudent policy" to the board. He wanted to make shareholder distributions quarterly, or at least wait until the fifteenth day of each month to pay distributions, so that the company could determine how much cash would be available in light of its actual revenues and financial covenants. But McWilliam had told him that the board wanted to maintain the fixed schedule of shareholder payments.

The letter went on to inform Kughn: Sienicki had asked McWilliam to reduce or delay two particular distributions (November and December 1991), but McWilliam had instructed him that the distributions to the board could not be changed. As a result, Sienicki said, the company broke financial covenants with its bank and the lessors of its equipment and premises—with McWilliam's "full and willful knowledge"—and it was only through hard negotiations that he was able to avoid default. Sienicki warned Kughn that three leasing companies would no longer do business with Upper Deck and that the company's "apparent disregard for covenants" made it difficult for him to get the best interest rates for Upper Deck.

Sienicki also noted that, while the company had managed to meet its financial covenants and make distributions to shareholders during the first half of 1992, problems loomed. Sienicki said he had not been informed of significant downward revisions in the company's projected revenues until June. The dramatically decreased revenues for the second half of 1992 would have serious implications for the company's ability to maintain its schedule of shareholder distributions and meet its other financial obligations.

Sienicki never received a response to his letter. But the document ignited an internal investigation by the board of directors, a probe that would include McWilliam.

16

La Costa

In the summer of 1992, before the July layoffs and firings of Brad Maier and Dennis Sienicki, Upper Deck began receiving massive returns of sports cards. For the first time since the company began producing cards in 1989, the market had softened, and distributors which supplied retail outlets with Upper Deck products were sending significant quantities of cards back to Carlsbad. Unlike hobby dealers, who did not have the option of returning their leftover cards to Upper Deck, retail stores and wholesalers could send unsold product back to Upper Deck in return for credit toward future products. So if a customer returned $2 million of Upper Deck's 1991 baseball, it could apply the credit to 1992 baseball or any other upcoming product.

For Upper Deck, which had grown accustomed to virtually selling through on all its products, the returns were particularly troublesome. During the company's first three years, the market had been able to bear however many cards it produced.

Monthly dividend checks were based on sales forecasts that provided for minimal returns. Now that credit had to be issued for returns on a grand scale and sales forecasts dipped, the dividend schedule had to be readjusted. For the first six months of 1992, Upper Deck's forecasts and production schedule were in a constant state of flux. The sales and marketing departments recommended changes to Sienicki and Brian Burr, now vice president of operations, who instructed the production room to alter its schedule.

But the major problem was the returns. In the summer of 1992, according to sources familiar with the situation at the time, Upper Deck received $16 million in returned product. For the first several months of the year, the owners of Upper

Deck had been splitting an average of $8 million in monthly dividends. At the end of June, with returns pouring in and Sienicki facing pressure from the company's bank and lessors, he cut off distributions.

Paul Sumner was vacationing in the South Pacific when he heard the news from Boris Korbel.

"We're not getting our July distributions," Korbel said. "In fact, we may not get any more distributions for the rest of the year."

"Why is that?" Sumner asked.

"Because a lot of product is coming back in and we have to credit people for the product. It's millions of dollars."

Sumner couldn't believe it. For three years, they had routinely received monthly dividend checks. His share of an $8 million monthly dividend came to $1.17 million. Now the dividends had gone from $8 million to nothing?

Sumner returned from the South Pacific and along with Korbel, Richard Kughn, and Adrian Gluck held a series of board meetings in August. "We decided in the absence of Richard, to interview the executives in the company to find out why all this product is coming in and we don't know anything about it," Sumner recalled. "How can you have several million dollars of something and all the sudden it appears on your doorstep? This is impossible to happen."

According to Gluck, the meetings were held for a second reason: to investigate McWilliam. "Something was drastically wrong with the company," he recalled. "Two things made us feel that way. One of them was that sales had slowed down considerably. We were told by Richard that it was an industry slowdown, but since it was so sudden we had to consider the fact that maybe it was our fault; not an industry thing, but an Upper Deck thing. We were not happy with the high level of turnover. It had gotten to the point where nobody could say it was normal. People were increasingly critical of Richard's handling of personnel and were wondering why these respected people were being forced to leave the company."

When asked about the returns and why he allowed such meetings to take place without his being present, McWilliam did not comment. According to those involved in the sessions, McWilliam was aware of the interviews of the executive staff and expressed no reservations about them taking place.

■ ■ ■

The meetings were held at La Costa, the world-renowned resort and spa four miles east of Upper Deck. One by one, Upper Deck executives were called to La Costa to testify before the board.

Bob Bove and Jay McCracken were on the East Coast the weekend of August 8–9 when they were summoned back to Carlsbad. McCracken was in Philadelphia overseeing the Phillies' Heroes of Baseball game, while Bove was 120 miles south at Baltimore's new Oriole Park at Camden Yards, supervising the Orioles' Heroes game.

McCracken and Bove drove to La Costa together the following Tuesday morning, knowing full well that the meeting had to do with the returns. As the vice president of sales and the national sales manager, they knew they would be held largely responsible. But it wasn't their fault, they felt. They had advised the board of the prospect of returns as far back as January. Bove had told the board that, although the 1991 baseball had sold through better than the 1990 product, it could be a false sense of security since a lot of it was still sitting in retail stores across the country. Just because it was sold did not mean there would be no returns. After all, baseball card production alone had increased in 1991 to 364,913 cases, up from 273,779 cases in 1990. The market might not have been able to support a 33 percent increase in Upper Deck baseball cards.

McCracken went into a conference room at 8:30 A.M. and sat down with Gluck, Korbel, Kughn, and Sumner. Attorney Ben Frydman of Stradling, Youcca, Carlson & Rauth, Upper Deck's outside counsel, was also there. (Frydman had a long-standing relationship with McWilliam dating back to the summer of 1988, when he wrote the letter informing Upper Deck's board of directors that McWilliam would surrender his stock in return for the $70,000 he had advanced the company along with an additional $150,000.)

Gluck took notes and led the questioning. "Jay," he said, "the first thing we want to say is that this is not a witch hunt."

Not a witch hunt? McCracken thought to himself. Clearly someone was going to get blamed for this. Since McWilliam wasn't there, it had to be either him or members of the executive staff.

For the next hour, McCracken outlined his concerns. The returns were bound to happen sooner or later, especially now that the market had softened. He also expressed his frustrations with McWilliam and his outrage over the French hockey incident.

At 9:30, McCracken was excused and Bove brought in.

"Look," Bove said, "we're in better shape than any other company out there. We have fewer returns than anyone and we're taking measures to prevent returns in the future."

After an hour, Bove was dismissed. As the two executives drove back to Sea Otter Place, they discussed the hearings. "I thought it went pretty well," Bove said. "But I would have liked to have had more than an hour to explain this mess."

McCracken nodded. This indeed had become a mess.

■ ■ ■

During Labor Day weekend, Upper Deck went back to Iowa for a second "Field of Dreams" extravaganza. In 1991, Upper Deck had found, like Ray Kinsella, that if you build it, they will come. And just as the company strove to be the leader in innovation with its cards, so too did it look to remain at the forefront in marketing. That meant improving upon Field of Dreams.

Tony Loiacono and Andy Abramson, Upper Deck's manager of sports marketing and promotions, knew the event could be their last hurrah as members of Upper Deck. For months, rumors had circulated at Sea Otter Place that they would be getting fired. A scapegoat had to come out of the La Costa hearings, and they realized it was either going to be McWilliam or the group of executives that frequently clashed with him. McWilliam, they figured, was going nowhere.

So with their days numbered, the two executives took refuge at the magical baseball field in Dyersville amid the farms of Al Ameskamp and Don Lansing. Abramson had spent the better part of the previous six months working as the advance man for the event, traveling to Dyersville and making sure everything was perfect.

It was. Once again, Upper Deck put together a heavy schedule of events, complete with an autograph signing, baseball clinic, golf tournament, and media workout. Unlike 1991, when the game was played on Labor Day in the afternoon, the '92 game was scheduled for Sunday night. For the first time since the filming of the movie, the lights would be turned on for a competitive game.

At 6 P.M., buses filled with 2,000 spectators began leaving downtown Dyersville for the Ameskamp and Lansing farms just northeast of town. At the field, Ron Paxton, a member of Upper Deck's creative services department, tracked down Abramson.

"Richard's trying to reach you."

"What for?" Abramson asked.

"He wants you to move the time of the game up from 8 o'clock to 7. He and Reggie want to get out of here earlier."

That's ridiculous, Abramson thought to himself. McWilliam and Jackson had flown in on a private charter and could leave the moment the game ended. It's not like they were catching an earlier flight. Besides, there was no way he could move the time of the game now. The entire evening was planned to begin at 8:00—sundown. Even if he wanted to move the starting time up, there was no way he could. There were too many people to inform. Besides, most of the fans would miss the start of the game.

"Tell him I can't do it," Abramson told Paxton.

"I'm not going to tell him that."

"All right, then just tell him you couldn't find me."

Shortly before 8 o'clock, as the sun set over the farm, the Upper Deck Heroes of Baseball team walked out of the corn in center field. In addition to Jackson, there were Hall of Fame pitchers Bob Gibson and Ferguson Jenkins, along with Vida Blue, Randy Hundley, Joe Rudi, Joe Hoerner, Jose Cardenal, Jay Johnstone, Joe Pepitone, and Gene Oliver. The Heroes team also included Upper Deck executives McWilliam, McCracken, and Michael Merhab. Their opponent, the Upper Deck All-Stars, included *Saturday Night Live* star Jon Lovitz, Kelsey Grammer of *Cheers*, Candace Cameron of *Full House*, and Iowa governor Terry Branstad. The rest of the All-Stars consisted of actors who played Joe Jackson's White Sox team-mates in the movie *Field of Dreams*.

During pre-game warm-ups, Abramson looked into the outfield and spotted McWilliam, clad in his Upper Deck Heroes of Baseball uniform, playing catch with Reggie Jackson.

"I heard you wanted to move the game up an hour," Abramson said. "I couldn't do it. Everything is timed to begin at sunset."

"Fine," McWilliam said. "Don't worry about it."

Abramson didn't worry about it. After all, he figured he was working his last Upper Deck event. Why upset 2,000 fans if his job was history anyhow?

The festivities began with a stirring rendition of the National Anthem by Meat Loaf, the heavy, long-haired singer who had developed a cult following with his 1977 album "Bat Out of Hell." Later Meat Loaf reappeared at second base for the All-Stars and stole the show. He jovially argued with the umpires—even body-slamming one of them. At one point he handed his glove to an umpire and the game went on with the ump at second base and Meat Loaf serving as an official. He was ejected twice, but returned each time, much to the delight of the fans. When he threw out a runner at first, the fans chanted "Meat Loaf! Meat Loaf!"

Later he dropped a routine pop-up and the crowd erupted in a chorus of boos. When the inning was over, he ran to the foul line and knelt before the crowd. "I want to personally apologize to each and every one of you for dropping that fly ball," he bellowed. "It was the sixteenth most embarrassing moment of my life."

Vida Blue, who won 209 games as a major league pitcher, dazzled the fans with his bat, launching two home runs into the corn, including a grand slam. Gene Oliver, a 57-year-old former catcher, also hit a ball into the corn. Even McWilliam chipped in for the Heroes, singling and scoring the first run.

The All-Stars held their own against the former big leaguers. Steve Eastin, who played pitcher "Knuckles" Sittoci in the movie, threw four innings and held Jackson hitless. Chuck Noyes, Eastin's catcher in the movie and the game, homered for the All-Stars.

The Heroes won, either by a score of 10–3, 9–3, or 9–4. The true count was difficult to determine between Meat Loaf's antics and the extra pitches and outs that were generously allowed.

The day was a colorful display of Americana, right down to the ever-present corporate sponsorship. But even Upper Deck's numerous logos could not spoil the innocence and majesty of the Iowa cornfield. During the game, two rainbow-colored hot-air balloons hovered over the corn beyond center and right field. After the final out, fireworks were set off over the diamond and continued for 15 minutes. As the 2,000 fans boarded shuttle buses at 11:30 P.M. for the ride back to town, a cloud of smoke hung over the cornfields. It was a surreal scene; it looked like Shoeless Joe Jackson and a few ghosts really *were* lurking on the diamond.

For Abramson and Loiacono, their tenures at Upper Deck were over, although they wouldn't learn the news officially until later that week. Still, standing next to the deserted baseball diamond watching the smoke drift over the Lansing and Ameskamp fields, the two executives found themselves feeling very pleased with themselves; they had managed to top 1991.

And if this really were the end, they took great comfort in knowing that they had literally gone out with a bang.

■ ■ ■

Wednesday, September 9, 1992, was not a pleasant day to be working at 5909 Sea Otter Place.

Loiacono, who had returned from Dyersville a day earlier, had heard rumors about his firing for months. He had started to hear speculation, ironically, in July after he had been named by *Advertising Age* magazine as one of the top 100 marketing executives in the country. Now he was receiving phone calls from people who prefaced their remarks with: "Gee Tony, I really didn't expect you to answer the phone. I thought you had been fired."

He and McWilliam had squared off many times over the marketing department. Loiacono thought one of the reasons McWilliam respected him was because he wasn't afraid to speak his mind. McWilliam had hired him to get Upper Deck out of the hobby publications and into the mainstream press. He wanted to see Upper Deck mentioned in *The Wall Street Journal* and *The New York Times*, like Topps. So Loiacono fired Robert Pelton and his modest Redondo Beach Pelton & Associates firm and hired the high-profile ad agency Chiat/Day/Mojo. He stepped up the marketing department, cultivating Abramson and the sports and events marketing team. He had developed the brand management group, putting a junior executive in charge of each product. Before he arrived at Upper Deck, it seemed no one other than Bove and McCracken, with their experience at Nestlé, was familiar with the concept of brand management.

Loiacono had helped Upper Deck gain recognition for its charitable endeavors through events like celebrity all-star hockey and the *Field of Dreams* weekend. He had negotiated the contract with Major League Baseball that made Upper Deck the title sponsor for All-Star FanFest, and was the point man for the Heroes of Baseball program. All in all, he believed, he had done exactly what McWilliam hired him to do: increase Upper Deck's visibility. Loiacono figured he must have done something right, at least according to *Advertising Age*.

For two months, Loiacono had seen all the signs that he was being phased out. He knew them all too well, having seen it happen from the other side, as he took over Don Bodow's role. In the months before Bodow had resigned as senior vice president, his duties gradually were taken away. Nobody even spoke to him. It reached the point where the only thing Bodow did each day was come to work and talk on the phone to the media.

It had not gotten that bad for Loiacono, although he saw Steve Mitgang being given greater responsibilities in the marketing department. Loiacono had concentrated his efforts in the last two months on FanFest, which Upper Deck had hosted with the Padres in San Diego, and the *Field of Dreams* weekend. Now that those events were over, there wasn't much planned for him to do.

Late in the morning of September 9, Loiacono received another call from someone surprised to hear his voice. At the end of the conversation, he slammed down the phone. "I'm not going down like this," he said to himself.

Loiacono walked down the hall into McWilliam's office, where McWilliam was seated at his desk. Loiacono, breathing heavily, leaned forward at McWilliam. Normally not a man accustomed to swearing, Loiacono exploded. "Richard, have some fucking balls and fire me!"

McWilliam remained calm. "I was going to do it later today, Tony."

"Yeah, sure you were."

Loiacono went back to his office, grabbed his laptop computer, and headed home to his ranch in the eastern San Diego County suburb of Bonsall. He walked quickly past the executive offices, down secretary row, keeping his eyes glued straight ahead. He didn't have to look to know that they were all staring at him.

■ ■ ■

Word of Loiacono's firing spread quickly. An afternoon meeting of executives was scheduled. On the way to the meeting, McCracken stopped in at Bove's office.

"Tony's gone," McCracken said.

"Yeah, I heard," Bove said. "You realize that you and I are next."

"Why do you say that?"

"That's just what I've heard."

"That's ridiculous, Bob. They don't have anybody who can handle sales other than us."

"Maybe, but we both know anyone can be replaced and Richard can do whatever the hell he wants."

McCracken shook his head. "All right, but I still don't think we're getting fired. I always hear about firings beforehand and I haven't heard a word about this one."

"That's because *you're* the one getting fired!"

It was a good point, McCracken had to admit. He always marveled how surprised other employees had been when they had gotten a pink slip. Everyone in the entire building, it seemed, knew except the employee. How could they have been so clueless? Now he too was getting canned and, like the others, was the last to know.

Bove's phone rang. It was McWilliam's secretary. McWilliam wanted to see McCracken.

"I'm sorry, Jay," Bove said. "But I hate to say I told you so."

As McCracken walked over to McWilliam's office, he still didn't believe it. He knew Loiacono was gone, but him? He had been with Upper Deck since the beginning; before the beginning really, if one counted the time he spent at Bill Hemrick's Upper Deck card shop. In four years, he had put together a successful national sales force and placed Upper Deck product in every imaginable retail outlet in the country. Plus, perhaps more importantly, he had worked with Bodow and Loiacono to cultivate Upper Deck's image as The Hobby darling. Dealers raved about Upper Deck and The Hobby press could say no wrong about the company.

While he was not an owner nor even the president, McCracken had become the most visible person in the company. He did dozens of media interviews a week and spent the equivalent of four months of the year on the road. While representing Upper Deck at Heroes games, he had thrown out the first pitch at Major League ballparks across the country. In July, *Sports Card Trader* magazine had named him one of the "25 Most Powerful People in the Sports Card Industry." He was the only Upper Deck employee to appear on the list.

If this really were his last day at Upper Deck, he thought, the timing sure was strange. Just three days earlier, he was clad in an Upper Deck uniform playing on the Field of Dreams in Dyersville alongside McWilliam and Jackson. Playing baseball on that magical field, in the same lineup as three Hall-of-Famers, was the best moment of his professional life. Hell, it was one of the best moments of his life, period.

McCracken entered McWilliam's office, saw Sheryl Roland, Upper Deck's human resources director, and knew it was over. As with any firing, McCracken knew, the company always wanted a witness present. That way, if there was ever a lawsuit based on what was said during the termination, the person doing the firing would have a second party to confirm his side of the story.

"Jay, we're making some changes," McWilliam said. "You're not part of them."

McCracken thought of a thousand things to say, but remained silent. He took one last look around the room. On a shelf, there were three baseballs, representing Reggie Jackson's home runs No. 501, No. 502, and No. 503. There was the mammoth, framed, autographed print of all the living players who had hit 500 home runs. Scattered about were autographed photos, bats, and balls, many similar to the ones that would be unveiled shortly as part of Upper Deck's new line of autographed sports memorabilia. To think, McWilliam used to call *him* a jock sniffer. At least he knew the history behind these baseball players. This was a man who wasn't sure who Reggie Jackson was when he showed up at Upper Deck's doorstep.

McCracken's eyes came back to McWilliam. "Okay Richard, whatever."

■ ■ ■

Next it was Bove's turn. As the national sales manager took the long walk to McWilliam's office, he tried to convince himself that he was being summoned for a different reason. Maybe he had been wrong. Maybe only Loiacono and McCracken were getting fired. But when Bove entered the office and saw Roland already there, he knew it would be his last visit with McWilliam.

"How you doing today, Mr. Bove," McWilliam said.

Mr. Bove. It was McWilliam's way of being cute. "I'm just fine, Richard."

"Well," McWilliam said, smiling. "You won't be doing fine a few minutes after hearing what I have to say."

"Oh, what's that?"

"We're having a reorganization and I'm going to have to ask you to leave the company. We're scaling back and. . . ."

"C'mon Richard, tell me the real reason."

Roland spoke next, stressing that Upper Deck was going through a transitional period and changes had to be made. Bove looked at Roland incredulously.

"Sheryl, shut the fuck up!" Bove said. "This doesn't pertain to you."

"Look, Bob," McWilliam said. "We should have known about these problems earlier. The problems in the industry, well, they've affected all of us."

"You still don't get it, Richard. You still don't fuckin' get it."

"Get what?"

Bove looked at McWilliam, then at Roland, and shook his head. "Never mind," he said, and left to clean out his office.

Later, Greg Green was called to McWilliam's office. Like Loiacono, Green had felt he was living on borrowed time. As the manager of creative services, he felt his days were numbered when McWilliam had brought in Brad Maier as art director in October of 1990. Green had outlasted Maier, but now it had become apparent that Merhab was going to be in charge of the creative department. Like Loiacono, Green had seen all the signs. His duties gradually had been transferred over to Merhab. And people stopped talking to him.

Green knew too that, as one of the last "Paul Sumner people," he had to go, especially now that McWilliam had won the final battle over Sumner. After the investigation at La Costa, the board decided that McWilliam would stay and those executives who had questioned his authority in the past would have to go. Green knew that McWilliam blamed the La Costa investigation on Sumner. Now that the board had given McWilliam a vote of confidence, he was going to clean house of anyone who was not completely loyal to him. Green, who still kept in touch with Sumner, knew that group included him.

While Green was getting fired, the phone rang at Abramson's apartment in Del Mar. He had just gotten back from Dyersville that morning, having stayed behind two extra days to supervise Upper Deck's moveout. He already had received two calls about Loiacono. This one, from new vice president of marketing Mitgang, was about him.

"Andy, I need you to come into the office," Mitgang said.

It was 5 o'clock. Abramson was sitting on his couch in a T-shirt and shorts. "What for?" he asked.

"I just need you to come in, that's all."

"C'mon Steve, if you're going to fire me, be a man about it and just tell me now."

"I'll see you in 20 minutes, Andy," Mitgang said, and hung up.

Abramson got dressed and drove to Carlsbad. As he walked passed McCracken's office, he noticed him packing boxes.

"What's going on, Jay?"

"You know what's going on."

"Not you?"

McCracken picked up a box and walked through his office door. "Yes, me."

Abramson went to see Mitgang, who was waiting with Roland. The woman quickly was earning a reputation as the Grim Reaper of Upper Deck.

"Andy," Mitgang began. "You and Tony have your own way of communicating and doing things. That no longer fits in with the company."

Five minutes later, Abramson was driving back to Del Mar. There was no executive meeting at Upper Deck that day; there weren't enough executives left to have one.

The new executive staff would be introduced in the morning.

CHAPTER

17

Just a Souvenir

Mickey Mantle, on what St. Peter will say to him when he dies and arrives at the Pearly Gates: "Sorry, Mickey, but because of the way you lived on earth, you can't come in. But before you leave, would you autograph these bats for Him?"

The day after Jay McCracken, Tony Loiacono, Bob Bove, Andy Abramson, and Greg Green were fired, McWilliam gathered the office staff together to dispel rumors that Upper Deck was having financial difficulties.

As a privately held company, Upper Deck did not disclose its financial records. Even though it issued $66.6 million in dividends in 1991 (and, despite the temporary halting of distributions by Dennis Sienicki, would issue $45.7 million for 1992), the company continually had to fight rumors of financial troubles. News of Upper Deck receiving $16 million in returns had spread quickly through the industry, and Upper Deck was deluged with phone calls from dealers, distributors, and the media wanting to know if Upper Deck was going out of business.

Even Upper Deck employees, who outside of the executive staff knew little about the company's finances, grew concerned.

"We are definitely not having financial problems," McWilliam told his staff. "We recognize that the industry has changed and that it's necessary for us to stay on the cutting edge. We needed to promote people with new ideas."

Bruce Regis, who had been the assistant to the president, was promoted to vice president of sales. Steve Mitgang, as expected, became vice president of marketing. Reggie Jackson, who had taken over Don Bodow's office in March, received an official title: assistant to the president. With Green and Brad Maier now gone, their duties were combined into a new position: vice president of creative services, which Michael Merhab now assumed.

231

McCracken became livid when he heard McWilliam's statements. It was one thing to get fired. It was quite another to learn that you no longer had the ideas that would keep the company on the cutting edge. McCracken figured his dismissal had to do with the returns, which was ridiculous considering Upper Deck still stood to equal its 1991 sales figures. (For 1992, Upper Deck recorded $263.3 million in sales, slightly above the 1991 mark of $263.2 million.)

"So what if they took back some returns," McCracken recalled. "It's not like it was going to bankrupt the company. I mean, is it better to produce $100 million in cards and take back no returns or to do $130 million and take back $10 million? As a collector, you'd like to see the smaller amount produced. But as a businessman, that's a difference of $20 million for your company. That seems like a no-brainer. But the board of directors was not happy with the returns—any returns. They needed some scapegoats."

Loiacono, who as vice president of marketing shouldered less responsibility for the returns than vice president of sales McCracken or national sales manager Bove, felt the firings were more for philosophical reasons. McWilliam, he believed, could not handle dissension in any form.

"Richard couldn't handle anyone standing up to him and that's what we did," Loiacono said. "You look at a lot of the people who have been fired—me, Jay, Bove, Andy, Buzz [Rasmussen], and [Dennis] Sienicki—we were the only ones not afraid to get in Richard's face and tell him when he was wrong. And there's nothing wrong with that. You need to listen to various ideas in any company. If what he wanted was to surround himself with a bunch of 'yes men,' people who would agree with some of his bad ideas rather than try to improve the company, then he accomplished his objective."

According to Adrian Gluck, the Upper Deck board member who led the La Costa investigation, the firings were necessary because the five men were willing to stand up to McWilliam, who did not want to deal with conflict.

"I'm really torn over being critical of the guy," said Gluck, who stepped down from the board in January of 1993. "If I was to look at all the latest theories on leadership, I would say the guy is definitely wrong. You should not surround yourself with a lot of yes men. But it's like war. You can't have back talk in the heat of battle.

"At the same time, Richard has been much too quick to terminate people. He has a hard time dealing with people. It's sad and it bothers me. I'm not going to say it was a major reason why I quit the board, but it might have been a factor."

Asked about the firings for this book, McWilliam replied, in writing: "The experience and leadership you need to run a company that is in a highly competitive market share battle is different than that which faces an unlimited growth company. Fortunately, we had staff members at Upper Deck who had the experience to lead such a battle and they were promoted to the appropriate positions. Other executive staff members left the company at that time."

Regis moved into McCracken's office, and Mitgang set up shop in Loiacono's old digs. Regis explained the personnel changes to John Leptich of the *Chicago*

Tribune. "We evaluated our position and felt some changes were necessary," he said. "We needed to set up our organization in the best way to go forward. Changes were necessary and, unfortunately, there were no positions for these people."

As one group of executives moved out and another played musical offices, Upper Deck officials finalized plans to launch a sister company to market autographed sports memorabilia. The business would be called Upper Deck Authenticated, and be located in a building next door to Upper Deck at 5932 Sea Otter Place—the site of the French hockey repackaging in 1991.

The formation of Authenticated had been a gradual process, beginning with negotiations in 1991 to bring Ken Goldin and The Score Board, Inc., into a partnership with Upper Deck. That potential relationship had fallen through, but Upper Deck had discovered a more high-profile partner, one of the world's foremost collectors, named Bruce McNall.

■ ■ ■

There are collectors, and then there is Bruce McNall. To say that McNall is a collector is to say Alexander the Great liked to travel. But from early childhood McNall, unlike Alexander, never seemed to run out of worlds to conquer.

Until 1994, when McNall was charged with one count of conspiracy, two counts of bank fraud, and one count of wire fraud in connection with an alleged scheme to defraud six banks out of $236 million in loans, he had led a charmed life.

Bruce Patrick McNall was born in 1950, the son of a University of Southern California biochemistry professor named Earl McNall. His mother, Shirley, a lab technician, despised the idea of her children watching television all day and stocked the family home in suburban Los Angeles with games and collectibles for Bruce and his younger sister. At the age of six, McNall was collecting stamps, and by the third grade, he had immersed himself in coins. His behavior bordered on the obsessive; often he asked his mother to take him to banks, where he would ask to inspect coin rolls in search of rare pennies.

Soon McNall was trading coins through newspaper ads and by mail across the country. At 15, with the inventory he had stockpiled, he opened a numismatic shop called Coins of the World in Arcadia, California. A year later, he sold the business for $60,000 to enroll at UCLA and study ancient history, hoping one day to join his father as a professor.

While at UCLA, McNall found he could apply the knowledge of ancient history he had developed through coin collecting to his studies, and his vast expertise of early Rome made him an instant prodigy. Several of his professors were coin collectors, and it wasn't long before McNall was selling coins again. Among his clients were a number of Hollywood producers, including Sy Weintraub, who had made several Tarzan movies.

McNall graduated from UCLA in three years and received a prestigious Regent's Fellowship for graduate study in Roman history. Realizing that he was making more money in the coin business than he ever would as a professor, he dropped out of UCLA's doctoral program and founded Numismatic Fine Arts, a coin shop on ultra-chic Rodeo Drive in Beverly Hills.

In 1974, 24-year-old McNall purchased the Athena Decadrachm, regarded among collectors as the Mona Lisa of Greek coins. No coin had ever sold for more than $100,000 at auction, but McNall purchased the coin for $420,000, outbidding representatives of, among others, Aristotle Onassis. A week later, McNall sold the coin for $470,000.

The deal had a lasting effect on McNall, who realized that there was a world of undiscovered value to be had for the asking. Over the next 17 years, as he emerged as the nation's top dealer in antique coins, McNall branched out into the sports and entertainment businesses. He started a horse-racing syndicate with Texas oil baron Nelson Bunker Hunt, and purchased a film studio that produced *Wargames, Mr. Mom,* and *Blame It on Rio.*

McNall's involvement in sports began when he bought a minority interest in the Dallas Mavericks of the National Basketball Association in 1979 and sold it three years later. Later, he became friends with Jerry Buss, a coin and stamp collector who owned two Los Angeles sports teams, the NBA Lakers and the NHL Kings. Buss, recognizing that McNall was a huge hockey fan, sold him 25 percent of the Kings in 1986 and 24 percent the following year. In March of 1988, McNall purchased the rest.

When McNall bought into the Kings in 1986, the team had finished with a losing record 16 times in 21 seasons. As a Hollywood "producer," McNall recognized that there was one thing missing from the team: star quality. So in 1988, for $15 million and several players, McNall purchased the biggest star in hockey, the Athena Decadrachm of the sport, Wayne Gretzky of the Edmonton Oilers.

The team improved immediately and Hollywood embraced the Kings. Attendance shot up, and McNall suddenly wielded even more power in Los Angeles than he had as a movie producer and coin dealer. Despite being 5 foot 9, 250 pounds, McNall did not come across as a typical corporate tycoon. With a gregarious personality, a Babe Ruth–like moonface, and a tendency to chuckle at the end of each sentence, he seemed very much the little boy who had discovered a handful of rare coins. His private box at the Great Western Forum attracted regular guests such as actors James Woods and Michelle Pfeiffer.

McNall and Gretzky developed a partnership that transcended the Kings. McNall introduced Gretzky to coin collecting and horse racing, two fields in which the hockey star demonstrated, like McNall, a Midas touch. The two, together with the late actor John Candy, purchased the Toronto Argonauts of the Canadian Football League. In 1991, they lured Notre Dame wide receiver Raghib "Rocket" Ismail—the most coveted player coming out of college—away from the NFL. Attendance at Toronto's SkyDome soared, and Ismail helped the "Argos" win the Grey Cup, the championship of the CFL.

That same year, McNall and Gretzky stunned the sports card world by bidding $410,000 for a T206 Honus Wagner card at a Sotheby's auction in New York. Over the next year, as McNall lent the card to major memorabilia shows for display, he kept an eye on the growing sports collectibles field. Of particular interest was the autograph market. McNall could not believe how autographs soared in value even as athletes continued to sign thousands each weekend. The process of athletes traveling the country to appear at cattle-call style card shows seemed demeaning for both players and collectors—even if it did pay athletes thousands of dollars for a few hours' work.

McNall's idea was to contract with sports stars to produce a limited quantity of autographed items through a controlled process by which handwriting experts could assure the authenticity of the signatures. If a company had the exclusive right to market a player's autograph, through an undisputed authentication process, collectors could rest assured the signature they purchased was legitimate. By working with the athletes themselves, McNall figured, he could create products that not only maintained value, but possibly increased in worth.

Granted, it was not an entirely original idea. Score Board, by locking in athletes to exclusive contracts, had cornered the market on certain star players for three years. But McNall, with his bankroll and contacts in the sports world, figured he could do it on a grand scale. He could create a line of sports memorabilia that not only was collectible, but genuine. No longer would collectors who purchased autographs secondhand—as opposed to in-person—have to worry about whether the signature was a forgery.

The question was how such an authentication process would be developed. McNall wasn't sure, but he knew of a company that might, the same firm that had created the counterfeit-proof sports card: Upper Deck.

■ ■ ■

Upper Deck Authenticated was formed in June of 1992 as a partnership between Upper Deck and McNall Sports and Entertainment. Since the business was located in Carlsbad, next door to Upper Deck, it seemed more of an Upper Deck than a McNall production. That was fine with McNall, who wanted to capitalize on the Upper Deck name without putting too much of his own time and resources into the project.

But McNall wanted to keep a close eye on his investment and so he hired Al Thomas as the president of Upper Deck Authenticated. Thomas was the senior vice president/director of operations for the western region of the Sheraton hotel chain. He also handled sports promotions for Sheraton, which was a sponsor of the Los Angeles Kings. The two met in March of 1988 when McNall bought the final 51 percent of the franchise from Jerry Buss. At that time, McNall told Thomas he had big plans for the team.

"I trust you with this," he said in a hushed tone. "I'm planning to acquire Wayne Gretzky."

Thomas could not believe it. Gretzky, the most popular athlete in a sport dominated by Canadians, was going to go from Edmonton to Los Angeles. Yeah, right, he thought. The idea was so preposterous, Thomas didn't mention it to anyone.

Three months later, McNall called Thomas. "I need a ballroom to make an announcement. I think you know what it's for."

Thomas set up the Los Angeles Sheraton for McNall, and it was there that Gretzky was introduced to the media as the newest member of the Kings. Over the next four years, the relationship between Thomas and McNall grew, and when Sheraton wanted to transfer Thomas back to his native Boston, he turned to the Kings' owner for help. Thomas didn't want to go back east and was wondering if he could work for McNall.

McNall gave him a choice: Come to work for the Kings or become the head of Upper Deck Authenticated. Thomas chose the latter and reported to Carlsbad on June 5, 1992, as the chief operating officer of Upper Deck Authenticated.

When Thomas arrived, "UDA" consisted of two player contracts and an empty building at 5932 Sea Otter Place. McWilliam and Steve Mitgang had negotiated the two deals with Mickey Mantle and Reggie Jackson.

Mantle was to be paid $2.75 million a year. In return, Mantle would provide 20,000 autographs and make 26 appearances on behalf of the company. UDA also received exclusive marketing rights to Mantle, meaning they could manufacture anything with Mantle's image. Jackson's contract paid him $1 million a year in return for 30,000 autographs and 20 appearances. Both contracts were exclusives; neither man could appear at card shows or negotiate autograph deals with any other company. Of course, they were free to sign autographs for charity or when approached in public.

In New Jersey, Score Board vice president Ken Goldin learned of the contracts and laughed. He remembered the memo McWilliam had sent him, mentioning a cap "on the escalation of salary contracts and fees." Not only had Upper Deck not capped the contracts; it had sent prices through the roof. Score Board, which had a nonexclusive contract with Mantle through the end of 1992 that allowed him to appear at card shows, had offered Mantle a three-year contract extension for $1.33 million a year. Mantle told Paul Goldin, Score Board's president, that he was tired of the card show circuit and wanted an exclusive deal comparable to Joe DiMaggio's $3.5 million annual compensation from Score Board.

The Goldins refused, figuring Mantle's signature never would command the price of DiMaggio's, even if it were exclusively marketed through Score Board. Mantle did not have the magical allure of Joe DiMaggio, who had compiled a 56-game hitting streak in 1941, married Marilyn Monroe, and been immortalized in song by Simon and Garfunkel. Plus, DiMaggio, at 78, was 17 years older than Mantle. Collectors figured Mantle would be around much longer than the Yankee Clipper and thus would sign many more autographs.

But as outrageous as the Mantle deal was, Goldin thought, it paled in comparison to Jackson's. For years, Jackson had been one of the most prolific signers on the card show circuit. He frequently boasted that he could sign 2,500 to 3,000 autographs at a sitting before his hand grew tired. (Most athletes could do between 700 and 1,000.) As a result, the market was flooded with Jackson autographs. Goldin, who had Jackson under contract from July of 1989 through the end of 1992, had thousands of Reggie autographed bats, balls, and photos in his warehouse that he couldn't give away. It wasn't that Jackson wasn't popular; it was just that everyone who wanted a Jackson signature already had one.

Thomas would find out later how difficult it would be to earn back UDA's investment in Mantle and Jackson. His task at hand was to sign up more athletes for the company's initial catalog, scheduled to be released in September. The idea was to get the premier athletes from each of the four major sports—baseball, football, basketball, and hockey—locked into exclusive deals with UDA. If collectors knew they had to go to UDA for the autographs of certain star players, the company would flourish.

Through McNall, Thomas negotiated a deal with Gretzky that paid the Great One $500,000 a year for 12,000 autographs. San Francisco 49ers quarterback Joe Montana, who already was Upper Deck's football card spokesman, inked a deal to provide 30,000 autographs for $850,000. Miami Dolphins quarterback Dan Marino, whose agent, Marvin Demoff, had helped Upper Deck secure its license to produce football cards, came aboard for $500,000 for 20,000 signatures. McNall, through his contacts with the Los Angeles Lakers, landed former Lakers point guard Magic Johnson ($1 million for 12,000 signatures), who in turn put his friend Larry Bird in touch with UDA. Bird, unlike the others, did not have a set fee. He would sign photos for $20 apiece and jerseys and balls for $30 each.

Thomas, realizing the company needed one more hockey great, signed the legendary Gordie Howe—whose all-time goals-scored record Gretzky was close to breaking—for $100,000.

Dozens of other athletes signed on for lesser, nonexclusive, autograph-signing deals. Upper Deck drew heavily from its stable of baseball players who participated in the Heroes of Baseball series, including Hall-of-Famers Rollie Fingers, Billy Williams, Lou Brock, and Bob Gibson. Other Hall-of-Famers who signed on included Frank Robinson, Ernie Banks, Carl Yastrzemski, Stan Musial, Rod Carew, Yogi Berra, and Ted Williams. (Later, Williams would negotiate a more extensive deal that paid him $1 million annually.)

By September, Thomas had more than thirty top athletes under contract to sign autographs for Upper Deck Authenticated. Together, the players were responsible for providing the company with a half-million autographs.

Now Thomas just had to sell them.

■ ■ ■

The first Upper Deck Authenticated catalog, appropriately enough, was released as a collectible. Billed as "authentic signed collectibles for the ultimate sports fan," the catalog came in two versions, one with Mickey Mantle on the cover, the other with Magic Johnson. Each version was numbered one through 5,000 and came with a hologram affixed to the cover.

The memorabilia, as McNall had planned, was billed as counterfeit-proof. According to the catalog, each athlete's signature was witnessed by a UDA employee and assigned a number. A hologram with a corresponding number was then affixed to the item and packaged with a corresponding certificate of authenticity. The item numbers then were recorded in a databank at UDA to track ownership of each piece of memorabilia.

For dealers who sold autographed sports collectibles, Upper Deck Authenticated was a slap in the face. Who was UDA to say that their merchandise was any more authentic than theirs? (In early 1993, UDA began marketing its memorabilia under the slogan "If it's not Authenticated, it's just a souvenir.")

"I think that adding a hologram to a baseball defaces the ball," said Goldin. "All you're guaranteed of is getting an authentic hologram. I know that their stuff is real. However, what I would point out is that you can sign a Nolan Ryan baseball yourself and stick a hologram on it. It doesn't mean it's real. A certificate of authenticity is only as good as the company behind it. With Score Board and Upper Deck you know what you're getting. I don't think it was necessary on their part and I don't think it adds anything other than being a sales technique."

For each athlete, UDA acquired replica merchandise for autographing similar to that used by the player in competition. For Jackson, UDA ordered brand new bats from Rawlings identical in size and weight to the ones he used as a player. The company procured a quantity of baseball jerseys from Mitchell & Ness, an official licensee of Major League Baseball, similar to the one Jackson wore as a member of the 1971 Oakland Athletics.

As lucrative as the players' contracts were, what Goldin found hardest to believe was that Authenticated had actually agreed to be licensed by the four major sports leagues and their players associations. As a result, UDA had to pay royalties of between 5 and 13 percent on every item sold. If UDA bought jerseys or equipment from companies that were officially licensed by one of the four sports leagues or their players associations, they paid a royalty, even though the companies—as official licensees—had already done so. In the three years that Score Board had marketed autographed memorabilia, it had never paid a royalty. After all, Goldin figured, once you've purchased the item from an official licensee, you've already paid the royalty. Upper Deck Authenticated had willingly taken on an unnecessary cost of 5 to 13 percent!

"If I had to do it all over again, I never would have gotten the licenses," said Thomas, who was fired as UDA's chief operating officer in August of 1993 and was later embroiled in litigation with Upper Deck. "If I bought a jersey from Champion, what's the difference in me selling it or a retail sporting goods store? Either way, the league has gotten its money. The royalties were killing us, that's why our costs were so high."

Because of the royalties and the hefty salaries UDA doled out to athletes, the merchandise came at prices far beyond those seen at card shows. The first UDA catalog included a limited edition of 1,951 baseball bats signed by Mantle for a staggering $1,750 apiece. Although autographed bats that Mantle actually used as a player from 1951 to 1969 regularly sold at auction for more than $10,000, the notion of a freshly cut, autographed bat selling for $1,750 was a first.

In effect, Upper Deck and Mantle had manufactured rarity. In the late 1980s, Mantle and DiMaggio were among the first athletes to refuse to sign bats at card shows. Collectors and dealers had been purchasing their replica bats, approaching them for signatures at card shows, and selling them for hundreds of dollars. Mantle and DiMaggio, who at the time were receiving between $25 and $50 a signature, saw only the price they charged for an autograph.

Since both players had stopped signing bats, demand increased. And when Mantle cut his deal with UDA, it came under the condition that he would autograph bats. UDA could buy bats from Louisville Slugger for $25 apiece, have Mantle sign them, and place the items in catalogs for $1,750. Collectors who wanted a signed Mantle bat either had to purchase an existing one on the secondary market or go through UDA, since Mantle's contract prohibited him from signing bats through any other channels.

For purist collectors, the idea of paying $1,750 for a Mickey Mantle bat that had not come within miles of a baseball stadium was an outrage. Phil Wood, editor of "Diamond Duds," a newsletter on game-used uniforms and equipment, remarked: "I'd rather have Mantle sign a picture of one of his actual bats. To me, that's more of a collectible than a bat that was just manufactured last month. If you're going to buy that, why not just have Mickey sign a two-by-four? It's the same difference."

The UDA catalog also included signed replica jerseys of Montana ($269.95), Jackson ($399.95), Bird ($459.95), Johnson ($549.95) and Marino ($369.95). (Since Mantle was still under contract to provide signed balls, jerseys, and photos to Score Board through the end of the year, Mantle was restricted to signing bats and New York Yankees' replica jackets for UDA until 1993.)

UDA also offered signed baseballs, footballs, basketballs, and hockey pucks ranging in price from $49.95 to $499.95 (for a basketball signed by Bird and Johnson). There were signed football helmets, hockey sticks, and hockey gloves. There were framed signed photos and *Sports Illustrated* magazine covers. There were Upper Deck hats, golf shirts, and varsity jackets. There were even combination items, such as a jersey, basketball, photo, letter, and basketball card from Magic Johnson, all signed and packaged in a 4^1/$_2$-foot-square black lacquer and Plexiglas frame for $3,995.

In addition to the catalog, UDA planned to sell the merchandise through kiosks at sports arenas such as the Great Western Forum and Boston Garden. A UDA memorabilia and apparel store would open at Universal Studios in Hollywood. Mike Berkus and Doug DeCinces of DeCinces Sports Productions had begun setting up UDA kiosks in 25 shopping malls in southern California. And Berkus was lining up UDA-related shows for the Home Shopping Network.

By using the Upper Deck name and McNall's contacts, Thomas had put Upper Deck Authenticated together with astonishing speed. On September 22, 1992, Upper Deck and McNall officials, along with Mantle, Jackson, and Fingers, held a press conference at the Beverly Hills Hilton to publicly unveil the company.

McNall, ever the showman, had provided the most intriguing collectible for the first UDA catalog. On the inside back cover, McNall was pictured touting the "ultimate Kings collectible." For a mere $5 million, a collector could buy a Boeing 727-100 that had been used as the team plane for the Los Angeles Kings. "Now your company, family, or just 70 of your best friends can enjoy the same level of comfort and relaxation that helped Gretzky and the Kings perform to their highest potential," the catalog read. "This fine pre-owned airplane has extremely low hours. The previous owner was the President of Mexico, who used the jet only occasionally for official duties. A must-have for the ultimate Kings fan!"

The jet even came autographed by the entire Kings team. But although it had a state-of-the-art video system, on-board VCRs, and compact disc players, it was not an official UDA product.

Someone had forgotten to stick a hologram on it.

■ ■ ■

Late in September of 1992, Upper Deck summoned its photographers to Carlsbad. The gathering had been postponed for weeks, what with the shakeup of the executive staff and the launch of Upper Deck Authenticated.

Since its inception in 1989, Upper Deck's cards had featured the finest photography in the industry. The company employed about 30 freelance photographers whose work had appeared in the likes of *Sports Illustrated, Inside Sports, Sport* magazine, *The Sporting News,* and *USA Today.*

Many of them worked through The Lovero Group, a southern California stock photography agency headed by V. J. Lovero, a frequent contributor to *Sports Illustrated.* During Upper Deck's formation in 1988, Lovero—then a photographer for the California Angels—was approached to take photos for Upper Deck's upcoming baseball cards. The relationship had grown over the next four years, with nearly all of Upper Deck's photo requests going through Lovero, who in turn would assign them to his photographers. The photographer and Lovero would split the fee charged to Upper Deck.

Since Upper Deck needed thousands of photos a year, it was an exceptionally profitable relationship for Lovero and the photographers. Since most of them held press credentials to sporting events through newspapers or magazines, they could send their unused photos to Upper Deck; often, there were no additional costs involved to them.

For some of the more industrious photographers, Upper Deck—and the other card companies—provided them with up to $50,000 in annual income in addition to their regular clients. But since Upper Deck demanded the finest photography, they naturally paid the best.

Problem was, the photographers were not always paid on time. And in September of 1992, as rumors circulated of Upper Deck having financial difficulties, the photographers worried that they not only were going to lose future work, but would not get paid for some of the cards they had already done.

Two weeks after the executive firings, Upper Deck flew 25 of its top photographers to southern California and put them up at the Newport Beach Marriott. Over the course of their two-day stay, Lovero hosted a barbecue and softball game. As the photographers ate, drank, and played, they spoke about Upper Deck, the rumors of financial instability, and their haphazard compensation payments. They were under the impression that they had been summoned by Upper Deck in order to ease their fears and develop a better working relationship. At the very least, some of the photographers who knew the company only by phone would get to meet the people who used their film. Perhaps they would even receive a tour of the facility.

On the photographers' last day in California, hotel shuttle vans drove them to Upper Deck headquarters in Carlsbad, where they were led into a conference room and seated.

For an hour they waited. No one came to greet them. A luncheon had been planned, but when no one arrived, Lovero called Domino's Pizza. Finally, Michael Merhab, who as Upper Deck's new vice president of creative services was the executive who dealt the most with the photographers, poked his head in the door. After a brief hello, he left.

Another hour passed. The pizza arrived and was eaten. Still there were no signs of anyone from Upper Deck coming to talk to them. Then a secretary brought word that there must have been a misunderstanding; Upper Deck didn't have anything planned for them.

As the photographers rode the shuttle vans back to Newport Beach, two of the veteran Upper Deck shooters sat in the back of one van and talked.

"How can they say they didn't have anything planned for us? They flew us all in from all over the country, put us up, drove us down, and didn't tell us anything."

The other photographer looked out the window as the van turned off Palomar Airport Road onto the #5 Freeway heading North. "I don't know, man," he said. "But this is one fucked-up company."

■ ■ ■

Not long after Jay McCracken was fired, Upper Deck offered him a one-year severance package. The deal included a non-compete provision and other benefits relating to his four years of service to the company. McCracken had 30 days to respond.

On October 28, 1992, McCracken and Upper Deck reached an agreement. Under the terms of the deal, McCracken was to issue a press release through Upper Deck. Camron Bussard drafted a letter in which McCracken praised the company and wished it all the best for the future.

Initially, McCracken did not want the press release issued until changes were made in his statements. After all, he had not left Upper Deck on the best of terms. But after Steve Poludniak, Upper Deck's vice president of business and legal affairs, and McCracken's daughter, who was serving as his lawyer, reminded him of the otherwise acceptable terms of the settlement, McCracken agreed to Bussard's release, with minor alterations.

In the two-page document, McCracken announced plans to fulfill a "long-time wish" to open his own card shop in Carlsbad.

"I have a long association with Upper Deck, and I have confidence that the current management team will maintain Upper Deck's position of industry leadership," he said. "The current management team is responsible in large part for the company's success. I wish them well in the future, and look forward to working with them once again."

McCracken also stated that: "I was upset after my termination, and I reported things about Upper Deck that might have been misconstrued. But I want to make it clear that though my working relationship with Upper Deck may have changed of late, my belief in the company and its products has not.

"Upper Deck makes the best cards in the industry. The direction the company gets from its board of directors and current management should enable the Upper Deck Company to remain the leader in the trading card industry for years to come."

■ ■ ■

Although Tony Loiacono had been fired from Upper Deck in September, Richard McWilliam had not seen the last of his former vice president of marketing.

From the moment he walked out of Upper Deck on September 9, Loiacono remained in the card business. He spent little time reflecting on his 20 months at Upper Deck; nor did he take a vacation while the shock of his dismissal wore off.

Since the firing came as no surprise to Loiacono, he had his post–Upper Deck career already plotted out, turning to contacts he had made as vice president of marketing for job opportunities. One of his first calls went to Bill Hemrick, who no longer was on the board of directors, but still owned four percent of Upper Deck. The only time he came in contact with the company was when his monthly dividend check arrived. And even that had ceased temporarily when Dennis Sienicki cut off distributions in June.

Hemrick kept his home in the city of Orange, California, but spent much of his time in Nashville. There he started a company called Sterling Cards that manufactured cards of country music stars. A second business distributed the Upper Deck cards he received as part of his 1988 settlement with the company.

Shortly after Loiacono was fired, Hemrick invited him to join Sterling. The two men had much in common. Both were born-again Christians and both had played an integral role in the Upper Deck Company before being forced out. When Loiacono joined Hemrick in Nashville, it seemed like a perfect match.

But after two months, Loiacono grew restless. He wanted to remain in sports and create a product that could challenge Upper Deck. That brought him to a second acquaintance from Upper Deck, Ted Williams.

At 74, Williams was a heavy hitter in the sports card and memorabilia industry. Next to DiMaggio, his autograph was the most sought after among living Hall-of-Famers. He had signed a contract with Score Board to provide autographs and even appeared on the Home Shopping Network on Score Board's behalf.

Companies wishing to deal with Williams had to go through Grand Slam Marketing, a firm run by Williams's 24-year-old son John Henry Williams along with Ted's close friend Brian Interland. At 52, Interland had known Williams nearly his entire life. At the age of nine, Interland was attending a pre-game clinic being conducted by the Red Sox for kids when he was one of three youngsters selected to come onto the field and have their picture taken with Ted Williams. The next morning, the picture ran on the front page of the *Boston Globe*, and Interland became a Williams fan for life.

Nine years later, as a freshman at Northeastern University, Interland was working for a TV station when he was sent to Fenway Park as part of a team working on a piece on Williams. At the end of the session, he told Williams how he had kept statistics on him over the years. Williams invited him to come by his hotel and show him the stats. So began a lifelong friendship. Today, Interland's den houses what is probably the finest collection of Williams memorabilia.

After college, Interland went to work in the music business as a concert promoter and became so successful that he now has 100 gold records hanging on the wall of his home. But he always kept in touch with Williams, and when John Henry formed Grand Slam in 1991 to market his father, he turned to Interland for help.

One of the first endorsements Grand Slam negotiated for Williams came through Upper Deck. Loiacono, then Upper Deck's vice president of marketing, negotiated a deal giving Upper Deck exclusive rights to market cards of Williams from November 1991 through November 1993.

For its 1992 baseball cards, Upper Deck included a ten-card subset of "Ted Williams Heroes." In addition, Williams personally autographed 2,500 cards of himself, which were randomly inserted into packs of low-series cards. Don Bodow, who had come up with the autographed insert idea in 1990 with the Reggie Jackson inserts, traveled to Williams's Florida home where he and Interland supervised the signing. For the 1992 Upper Deck high series, Williams selected 20 of his favorite active players for a "Ted Williams Best" subset.

In the summer of 1992, Upper Deck approached Grand Slam to sign Williams to an Upper Deck Authenticated contract. John Henry Williams and Interland were interested, but also wanted to buy back the rights to produce cards of Williams. The two wanted to create their own card business to produce sports cards. The cards would come under the name of a new company, but could be manufactured and distributed through Upper Deck, which would share in the profits. To capitalize on Ted Williams's marketability, the operation would be called the Ted Williams Card Company.

Between October and December, John Henry Williams and Interland met with McWilliam on three occasions. Finally, they agreed on a deal that would pay Williams $1 million annually to provide signed memorabilia for Upper Deck Authenticated. Grand Slam also re-obtained the rights to produce cards of Williams, which Upper Deck otherwise would have held until November, 1993. Through the terms of the agreement, Upper Deck would have the right of first refusal to print and distribute cards for the Ted Williams Card Company.

During this period, Loiacono met with Interland and John Henry Williams about joining their new card company. The two men wanted to hire Loiacono, but wondered if the bad blood between him and McWilliam would ruin their chances of having their cards produced by Upper Deck. In each of their three meetings with McWilliam, they asked for his opinion of Loiacono without mentioning that they were considering hiring him. Each time, McWilliam spoke highly of his former vice president.

Shortly before Christmas, the two companies arranged a luncheon where the Ted Williams Card Company would unveil its new card product. The event was scheduled for the La Costa Resort and Spa, which only three months earlier had served as the site of Upper Deck's board "investigation" into McWilliam.

John Henry Williams and Interland spared no expense for the luncheon. A large conference room was rented out, with enough food for 30 people. Poster-sized versions of cards from the proposed Ted Williams card line were positioned throughout the room, along with packs of cards and marketing materials.

Upper Deck sent a six-man contingent to the meeting. McWilliam, Reggie Jackson, Mitgang, and Merhab attended, along with Mark Christenson and Stuart Ellis of the marketing department.

The Upper Deck executives seated themselves around a conference table facing Interland and Williams. A speakerphone was placed in the middle of the table, connecting Ted Williams himself to the meeting from Florida. John Henry and Interland stood, facing McWilliam. The rest of the Upper Deck executives sat along the sides of the table.

Williams and Interland outlined the marketing and distribution strategies for the Ted Williams Card Company. Since they would not be able to obtain a license to produce cards of active players, the card line would focus on all-time greats. Ted himself would have an active role in the selection of players.

After 15 minutes, Interland announced: "We'd like to introduce the rest of our management team."

A door that connected the back of the room to a kitchen opened and out walked Loiacono and Bob Mitchell, the chief financial officer of the Ted Williams Card Company.

McWilliam, with his back to the kitchen, did not see the two men come out. But the rest of his staff had watched in amazement as Loiacono stepped into the room.

Loiacono approached McWilliam from behind, put both hands on his shoulders and said "How you doin', Richard?"

McWilliam turned around and saw Loiacono. "Holy shit!" he said. Then, to Interland and Williams, "You've got to be kidding."

For a moment, the officials from both companies did not know if McWilliam was merely surprised or genuinely angry. Then, McWilliam got up, pointed at Interland, and said: "This is bullshit!"

McWilliam stormed out of the room. John Henry Williams followed. "What's going on?" Ted Williams asked via speakerphone.

"Uh, nothing, Ted," Interland said. "Richard's just gone out to take a breather."

As Interland continued the marketing and distribution presentation, John Henry and McWilliam could be heard arguing out in the hallway. By now, nobody was listening to Interland. Even he spoke softly so he could hear the argument.

After 20 minutes, Jackson got up and tried unsuccessfully to calm McWilliam down. Finally, the two left for Upper Deck.

When McWilliam got back to his office, Mike Berkus was waiting for a scheduled appointment. He could tell McWilliam was in a foul mood.

"You're not going to believe this bullshit," McWilliam said. "Ted Williams hired fuckin' Tony Loiacono!"

Berkus had driven down from Irvine and hoped to discuss the program whereby Upper Deck kiosks would be placed in shopping malls in southern California during the Christmas shopping season. Instead, he listened as McWilliam paced his office and fumed over the Ted Williams Card Company.

Meanwhile, back at La Costa, Loiacono was making his marketing presentation when a call came in for Mitgang. The remaining four executives were to return to Upper Deck immediately.

"That's okay," Loiacono said. "We're almost finished."

"Sorry," Mitgang said. "We have to go right now."

Mitgang, Christenson, Merhab, and Ellis got up and departed. The four executives of the new Ted Williams Card Company were left standing around looking at a room full of uneaten food. Ted Williams himself had hung up.

Loiacono turned to Interland. "I thought Richard was cool with this," he said. "So did I," Interland replied.

While the contract between Upper Deck and Ted Williams was honored, with Williams receiving his card rights back and $1 million a year for signing autographs for Upper Deck Authenticated, Upper Deck did not exercise its option to produce and distribute cards for the Ted Williams Card Company.

But Interland and John Henry Williams learned a lot from McWilliam's outburst. If the president of the world's largest and most successful company was outraged by the hiring of one former employee, maybe it would be a good idea to hire a few more Upper Deck alumni. There was, of course, an ever-growing pool of former employees looking for work.

Loiacono surveyed the room. It had been only three months since he had walked out of Upper Deck, but it already seemed like a lifetime had passed. Still, as he looked at the blow-up baseball cards perched on the conference table and the marketing materials that littered the room, he could not help but think of the Upper Deck influence on his new company. If Upper Deck would not cooperate with Ted Williams, then the business would move on alone.

Loiacono turned to Interland. "Whoever Richard fires, I'll hire," he said. "Upper Deck made a better baseball card. Now let's see if we can make a better Upper Deck."

Loiacono said good-bye to his new partners and headed for the parking lot. All in all, he felt much better than he had the last time he left La Costa, following his interrogation by Upper Deck's board of directors.

Loiacono got in his BMW, and as he began the drive back to his ranch in Bonsall, he pondered the luncheon. He had tried to extend an olive branch to McWilliam through the Ted Williams Card Company, but McWilliam threw it back in his face.

Now, just three months after Loiacono had been fired from the most successful card company in the world, his ties with Upper Deck had been completely severed. That was okay, he thought, now that he had become involved in a promising new company, one ready to swim with the card sharks at Sea Otter Place.

18

Slowdown

As 1992 ended, Upper Deck was not the only card manufacturer feeling the effects of a slowdown in the sports card industry. On January 25, 1993, Topps announced that it would suffer a financial loss for the fourth quarter of fiscal 1993, ending February 28, 1993. Its stock, traded on the NASDAQ exchange, immediately dropped from 12^{1}/_{4}$ to 8^{1}/_{2}$ a share.

The loss was Topps's first since the fourth quarter of 1981 and reflected an industry-wide trend. According to Action Packed Sports Cards, a Chicago-based manufacturer of football and auto racing cards that commissioned an independent research firm to monitor the industry, the sports card market shrunk from $2 billion in 1991 to $1.8 billion in 1992.

Like Upper Deck, Topps had begun to see large quantities of returned product late in 1992. "We see this development as a market contraction rather than a seasonal fluctuation," Topps chairman Arthur Shorin announced. "The speculative frenzy of the last few years is giving way to a hobby reflecting true collector interest."

Although the "contraction" could hardly be called a market crash, it did reflect a softening in the industry. The glory days of 1991, when 100,000 people descended upon the National Sports Collectors Convention and investors stockpiled any piece of cardboard with a sports photo, clearly were over.

In his letter to shareholders in Topps's annual report, Shorin wrote: "The sports card category has entered a period of contraction after the speculative frenzy of recent years—and there is a price to pay for it."

Sales at Topps had fallen to $263.2 million for the year ending February 28, ironically the exact figure Upper Deck had recorded for calendar 1992. But while Upper Deck only produced sports cards, Topps also produced candy and gum. Its sales of sports picture cards fell 15 percent from the previous year, dipping to $171.6 million from $202.1 million for fiscal 1992.

The decline in the market caused Topps to lay off over 300 people, including the entire third shift at its factory in Duryea, Pennsylvania. Shorin's comments seemed to reflect a feeling that the company no longer could rely on sports cards for further growth.

"Topps has other lines of business such as non-sport picture products, comic books, candy and direct marketing which, over the next few years, should begin contributing more meaningfully to our results."

It was a time of change at Topps, which could be seen each time a collector opened a pack of its cards. Gone was the familiar gum. Topps, which had fought for years to preserve its exclusive right to produce cards alone or alone with gum, had removed the gum in 1992 in response to a frequent complaint by collectors that it stained the cards.

■ ■ ■

Jay McCracken did not go far from Upper Deck. On March 15, 1993, he and his wife Jane held the grand opening of McCrackens' Sports Cards, located just four miles from Upper Deck headquarters.

Located at the corner of Palomar Airport Road and Paseo del Norte, just off the #5 Freeway in Carlsbad, McCrackens' sat in a high-traffic area that McCracken hoped would provide a steady flow of customers. The store shared a small strip shopping center with a 7–11, a Subway restaurant, and a dry cleaner's. With 1,800 square feet, the store was three times bigger than Bill Hemrick's old Upper Deck card shop.

Although it had been just six months since his bitter departure, McCracken made no attempt to downplay his former life at Upper Deck. The store contained framed photos of McCracken making appearances on behalf of Upper Deck at Heroes of Baseball games. A two-page feature article *Sports Collectors Digest* had done on Upper Deck vice president McCracken hung alongside a baseball locker that had been custom-built to hold his collection of Mike Schmidt memorabilia.

Over the next three months, McCracken put the final touches on the store, moving photos around and positioning displays. Upper Deck employees wandered in on their way to and from work, much to Richard McWilliam's dismay. Michael Merhab, Upper Deck's vice president of creative sports, walked in one day just as several customers were criticizing Upper Deck.

"Hey, don't talk to me, I just sell the stuff," McCracken said, tongue in cheek. Then, pointing at Merhab. "This is the guy you want."

One day, as McCracken went through an old box of Upper Deck mementos, he came upon a sheet of DeWayne Buice prototype cards. It was from Jack

Petruzzelli's Memorial Day card show at the Disneyland Hotel in 1988, one of hundreds Buice and Wally Joyner had autographed for collectors.

McCracken had the sheet framed. He hung it above a doorway that connected the store to the storage room and his office. Each time he went back to obtain cards, he caught a glimpse of five smiling Buice cards, autographed by the man himself.

"Hey, Jay," the sheet read, "let's make millions."

■ ■ ■

In April of 1993, Anthony Passante finally got his day in court. Passante, who served as Upper Deck's first corporate counsel from March to December of 1988, had filed suit against Upper Deck on December 14, 1990. In the suit, Passante alleged that he had been promised a 3 percent stake in the company that he never received.

It was a nasty dispute. Passante and Andrew Prendiville, former classmates of Richard McWilliam at Servite High School, contended that Upper Deck's board of directors had promised Passante 3 percent of Upper Deck's stock for arranging a $100,000 loan from Prendiville's brother, Kevin, in August of 1988. Since Andrew Prendiville was responsible for convincing his brother to make the loan, Passante had agreed to give him half of the 3 percent share.

Although Passante had never received anything in writing promising him ownership in the company, he contended that Boris Korbel had made a verbal promise to hold his shares in his name. Passante said he took Korbel at his word since he had known him both professionally and personally for nearly a decade. But when Korbel informed Passante in 1989 that he would not be receiving 3 percent of the company, Passante began preparation for the lawsuit. McWilliam, responding to the allegations in the February, 13, 1993, edition of *The San Diego Union-Tribune* said the lawsuit "is a fabricated lie" that "should have been thrown out of court years ago." Passante is "manipulating the legal system to get money."

The trial took place in Orange County Superior Court in Santa Ana, California. Passante testified for the better part of two days. His lawyers also called as an expert witness Paul Much, a senior vice president with Houlihan Lokey Howard & Zuvkin, a Los Angeles company that appraises the value of companies. While on the stand, Much testified that Upper Deck was the leader in the $1.8 billion trading card industry.

That came as no surprise, but Much stunned the courtroom when he estimated the market value of the Upper Deck Company, as of December 31, 1992, at a staggering $1.5 billion. Much's testimony was particularly significant since Judge James Cook was expected to allow the 12 jurors to determine the value of Passante's shares based on the figure. If they agreed with Much, then Passante's 3 percent stake would be worth $45 million.

Four of Upper Deck's five owners were called to the stand: McWilliam, Korbel, Paul Sumner, and Bill Hemrick. (Richard Kughn, who did not come into the company until after the alleged promise to Passante had been made, did not testify.)

After a day of deliberation, the jury ruled May 12, 1993, in favor of Passante and Prendiville, deciding that they should have been given a 3 percent ownership position in Upper Deck. The only question remaining was how much that 3 percent was worth.

For the next week, Upper Deck tried to disprove Much's claim that the company was worth $1.5 billion. The most intriguing testimony came from McWilliam, who for five years had managed to keep Upper Deck's financial records private. But in order to show that the company was not worth $1.5 billion, he had to reveal Upper Deck's sales and profit numbers. Those figures, listed in this book, showed that Upper Deck had been just as successful as Topps. Based on the selling price of Topps's stock and the number of outstanding shares, McWilliam estimated the value of Upper Deck at $250 million. (McWilliam, ironically, probably wished Much's $1.5 billion figure was accurate; as a 27.08 percent shareholder, his portion would have been worth $406.2 million.)

While on the stand, McWilliam said that Upper Deck had taken a $15 million loss when the Comic Ball line of cards had bombed with youngsters. The company also endured a "significant failure" when consumers failed to embrace a wall poster featuring the 1992 U.S. Olympic Basketball "Dream Team." Upper Deck took a $6 million loss when retailers returned 75 percent of the posters. Overall sales for the first quarter of 1993, McWilliam said, were $68 million, down from $103 million for the first quarter of 1992. The company had even stopped production for a month in mid-April, McWilliam said, to "give the market a breather."

Despite McWilliam's testimony that portrayed Upper Deck as a struggling company, the jury came close to agreeing with Much. On May 21, 1993, it awarded Passante and Prendiville a staggering $33.1 million for their three percent stake in the company, which meant Upper Deck was worth—at least according to the jury—a whopping $1.1 billion. The jury also ordered Korbel to pay the two attorneys $1 million.

Passante and Prendiville were elated. More than four years after being fired by Upper Deck, they now were going to receive what they thought had been promised to them all along.

Upper Deck responded quickly. Camron Bussard, a friend of Reggie Jackson's and former magazine editor who had been hired as the company's director of communications in the fall of 1992, told the *Los Angeles Times*: "We think [the award] is unbelievable and ridiculous. We find it incomprehensible that Mr. Passante could perpetrate a fraud on the company and still receive the award. We think it is a sad state of affairs that the jury was so unintelligent and unsophisticated that it could not distinguish between reality and fiction."

Unfortunately for Passante and Prendiville, Judge Cook agreed with Upper Deck. On July 2, 1993, he ruled that the jury's decision could not stand because there was "insufficiency of the evidence to justify the verdict and the verdict is against the law."

Cook ruled that Passante's lead counsel, San Diego lawyer Vincent J. Bartolotta, won the case by introducing disputed evidence against court rules and continually asking questions that the judge had ruled inadmissible. "The misconduct of counsel was persistent and pervasive," Cook wrote. "It prevented the defendants from having a fair trial."

Cook also wrote that there was no basis for the verdict. Passante's ownership claim came from an August 1988 telephone conversation with Korbel, Cook ruled, in which the two men decided to withhold Passante's interest from McWilliam. "The agreement was in fact an agreement to defraud by concealment," Cook wrote. "The agreement was unlawful and void."

Both sides argued the merits of Cook's decision in the press. "My client was an absolute, downright victim," Bartolotta told the *Los Angeles Times.* "Those twelve jurors saw that."

In the same article, McWilliam said: "I think we are entirely vindicated."

Passante and Prendiville have appealed the case. As of September 1994, the appeal was pending.

■ ■ ■

For Reggie Jackson, the first eight months of 1993 were one big, magical victory tour. Wherever he went, he was honored for his 21-year career. And wherever he went, he made it a point to mention Upper Deck.

In January, after the Baseball Writers Association of America made him a near-unanimous selection into the Baseball Hall of Fame in his first year of eligibility, he and Richard McWilliam visited outgoing president George Bush at the White House. Clad in Upper Deck varsity jackets, the two presented Bush with Upper Deck baseball cards.

In March, New York Yankees owner George Steinbrenner named Jackson a "special adviser." Jackson and Steinbrenner, who endured a tumultuous relationship during Mr. October's five years in New York, appeared together at a press conference to announce the new arrangement. Among the first things Jackson said was: "most of my time will be spent with the Upper Deck Company."

And why not? In January, Jackson had replaced Adrian Gluck on the company's five-man board of directors. He had a $500,000 salary and a $1 million contract to sign autographs for Upper Deck Authenticated. He was to provide the company with 30,000 autographs and 20 appearances annually.

But even in his Hall of Fame induction year, Jackson autographs were a tough sell. In the first UDA catalog, Jackson's autographed bats were offered at $699. Over the next six months, according to UDA sources, the company sold exactly one bat. In the spring '93 catalog, the same bat was offered for $399.

Through the years, Jackson had signed thousands of autographs. But that was only half the problem. Jackson's arrogance rubbed many collectors the wrong way.

"I can remember going into a department store in Newport Beach," recalled Al Thomas, UDA president from June of 1992 until he was fired in August of 1993. "We wanted to do a promotion with Reggie in the store. The manager immediately says, 'We will not do a promotion with Reggie.' I asked why. After all, the guy was going into the Hall of Fame. He said, 'That guy is the most arrogant customer we've ever had in this store. We don't want to sell any of his stuff.' It was amazing how many times we'd run into something like that."

According to Thomas, Authenticated had a difficult time getting Jackson just to sign the items he was responsible to sign under his contract—even though he had an office next door at Upper Deck.

"We tried to renegotiate Reggie's contract before we left because it was a disaster. He's the worst guy I've dealt with for anything in my life."

Jackson could not understand why his memorabilia did not sell. After he homered off Bob Gibson during the celebrity home run contest the day before the 1993 All-Star Game in Baltimore, he circled the bases and turned to a group of Upper Deck executives standing in the dugout. "There are 50,000 people chanting my name," he yelled. "And you guys can't sell any of my fuckin' stuff."

Three weeks later, Jackson flew a contingent of Upper Deck employees to Cooperstown, New York, to witness his Hall of Fame induction August 1. He rented a house outside of Cooperstown and rehearsed his speech with McWilliam. Like the rest of his public remarks, his speech included references to Upper Deck.

Afterwards, Phil Mushnick, a columnist for the *New York Post,* wrote: "Reggie Jackson, an Upper Deck shill, used the occasion of his Hall of Fame induction speech Sunday to praise Upper Deck for endeavoring to return baseball to America's children. What garbage! Upper Deck sells Reggie Jackson autographed jerseys for $500, autographed Reggie bats for $700. What kid can afford these—Richie Rich?

"Upper Deck has fed the sickening reality that has turned the just-for-fun kids' hobby of collecting baseball cards into the scam-infested, greed-driven industry that sports collectibles has become. Upper Deck sells baseball cards to children the same way lottery tickets are sold to adults—buy a pack, kid, not to embrace baseball, but because maybe you'll strike it rich.

"Now where in hell is the love of either baseball or children in these sells, Reggie? Upper Deck is motivated by profit, not by the love of children. Upper Deck is as friendly to children as a vulture is to a wounded fawn. And if Reggie's regard for children and baseball is so great, why then does he charge kids for his autograph? Why, if not the quest for money, did he change teams three times as a free agent? Then, this man stands before his Cooperstown audience and warns against the greed that's ruining baseball. What a phony."

Jackson's Upper Deck promotional tour wasn't over. On the afternoon of August 14, he appeared at Yankee Stadium, where his uniform number 44 was retired in a pre-game ceremony. He then traveled to West Chester, Pennsylvania, where later that night he appeared on the QVC shopping network selling his memorabilia, including a signed replica Yankees jersey—billed as "just like the one retired this afternoon"—for $359.95.

Although Jackson wore No. 9 for the Kansas City/Oakland A's from 1967 to 1975, he had taken up the practice of signing everything—including A's No. 9 jerseys sold by Authenticated—with No. 44 following his signature. This confused at least one QVC viewer, who called asking if the items were signed by accident.

"No," said Jackson, who noted he wore No. 44 during his final season in 1987, which he spent with Oakland.

"People talk about tradition," Jackson had said earlier in the day in New York. "I believe it started right here. No offense to the Red Sox, Dodgers, Cardinals, Cubs, Celtics, Packers, and Cowboys. But anywhere you go in the world, the greatest name in sports belongs to the Yankees."

And certainly the greatest marketing name, which Jackson was quick to note on QVC. "The Yankees are the No. 1 team in brand name value in the world," he said.

Jackson realized that, from a marketing perspective, it was important for him to be seen as a New York Yankee—even if he only spent five of his 21 years in the major leagues there. Memorabilia of Yankee greats Babe Ruth, Lou Gehrig, Joe DiMaggio, and Mickey Mantle dominated the industry, and Jackson hoped that by linking himself to the Yankees through his memorabilia, he would be linked to the Yankees in the minds of baseball fans.

Jackson, appearing on the show in jeans and a blue, short-sleeved shirt, was in prime form. He said that while he could only compete in Upper Deck's Heroes of Baseball games, he was still the best "lobby man" in the game. "In hotel lobbies, I have my gold watch, nice clothes, fancy shoes. I'm a good lobby man."

A viewer from Chapel Hill, North Carolina, called and said he had approached Jackson at the All-Star game, hoping to get a lithograph signed. "Yeah, you told me you were busy," the caller said. "Would you sign it if I sent it to you?"

"Sure," said Jackson, pausing at the irony that he had agreed to a free autograph on a shopping show. "Just send it to the Upper Deck Company."

Jackson returned to Carlsbad after the show. But the Jackson tour was not over. In September, Upper Deck, in conjunction with the D. L. Clark Candy Co. of Pittsburgh, re-released the Reggie! candy bar.

Like the 1977 Reggie! bar, the '94 version was a peanut butter and caramel concoction that only a dentist could love. But this time, each candy bar came with one of three Upper Deck cards picturing Jackson.

■ ■ ■

Never was the growth and importance of the sports card industry, particularly the baseball card market, more evident than on August 12, 1994. It was on that day that the baseball card business helped shut down Major League Baseball.

On that day, in the midst of one of the most exciting seasons in the history of the sport, the Major League Baseball Players Association went on strike. As players packed up their belongings and headed for home, locks were placed on the gates of the 28 stadiums in the U.S. and Canada.

The dispute was a simple one, but a seemingly impossible one to solve. The team owners wanted to impose a cap on player salaries, which had grown from an average of $185,000 in 1981 to $1.2 million in 1994. The players, naturally, were opposed to such an idea, and walked off the job rather than run the risk of the owners unilaterally imposing a cap at the end of the season.

The owners contended that a salary cap was the only way to restore competitive balance to the game. The amount of money a team could spend on salaries varied widely, from the $15 million payroll of the San Diego Padres to the $52.1 million the Atlanta Braves were scheduled to shell out for 1994. Since teams such as the Braves, New York Yankees, and Chicago Cubs enjoyed greater revenues through a combination of lucrative local television contracts and larger attendance figures, they had more money to spend on top-quality players. This, the owners maintained, kept clubs in small media markets—such as Milwaukee, Pittsburgh, San Diego, and Montreal—from competing with the big city clubs. And because they could not compete, according to this reasoning, they could not draw big crowds to the ballpark. According to the owners, at least 12 teams were on pace to lose money for 1994.

The players, meanwhile, said that baseball was as financially healthy as it had ever been. The fact that the wealth was not spread evenly was not their fault. If the owners wanted a system of revenue sharing, they merely had to come up with an equitable means of distributing the greater proceeds the "larger market" teams received from their increased attendance and local television money. Besides, the system that allowed major leaguers to make an average of $1.2 million had come about through 25 years of hard-fought labor negotiations. Why give that back and risk future earnings by conceding to a salary cap?

By striking, the players risked the possibility of losing nearly two months' salary. Bobby Bonilla of the New York Mets stood to lose $31,000 each day the strike continued. Of course, with the minimum salary at $109,000, no player and his family was going to starve even if the strike continued for the rest of the season. Unlike the 50-day strike of 1981, when then–Chicago Cubs pitcher Lee Smith took a job driving a garbage truck, no one had to worry about paying bills.

Still, lost money was lost money—even among multimillionaires. But if the owners hoped to use the lost salaries as a means to break the union, they would have a difficult time. The players had additional leverage in the form of a $175 million "strike fund" built from royalties received from the sale of officially licensed merchandise depicting player images.

Of that money, which in 1991 alone generated more than $80 million for the Players Association, 90 percent came from the sale of baseball cards.

Normally, in a year in which the prospect of collective bargaining did not loom between the players and owners, each player would receive a check in spring training as his share of the licensing royalties. The shares, called "Marvin Money" after former Players Association executive director Marvin Miller, had grown from $100 a man in 1968 to $80,000 a player in 1991.

But after the 1991 season, the licensing checks were decreased in anticipation of a possible work stoppage brought about by the expiration at the end of the season of the Basic Agreement, the labor accord between the leagues and the PA. Over the next three spring trainings, as PA executive director Donald Fehr made his way through Florida and Arizona, players received increasingly smaller checks. In 1994, they got only $5,000 in spring training.

None of which was a problem for the players, who knew that this deferred money went into the strike fund. By August of 1994, the war chest had grown to $175 million.

With an average salary of $1.2 million, the average loss per player stood to be about $7,000 a day. If the strike fund were dispersed at that rate, it would last 30 days. Each player, therefore, would receive $210,000. Enough, in short, to make up for two months' lost salary. (In practice, the Players Association issued several payments of $5,000 a player during the first months of the strike. The licensing revenue became a point of negotiation during the conflict, with both sides targeting the licensing money as a means toward a settlement. During the strike, the Associated Press obtained information related to the PA's licensing fund that illustrated the decline in the baseball card market. In 1992, the union received $79.5 million in licensing revenue. In 1993, the figure decreased to $49.3 million. Through August of 1994, the '94 revenues were on pace to fall further.)

The strike fund represented an awful lot of baseball card sales. In 1991, the Players Association signed three-year contract renewals with its five licensed card manufacturers: Topps, Fleer, Leaf/Donruss, Score (now Pinnacle Brands), and Upper Deck. In 1993, the PA signed up a sixth card manufacturer, Pacific Trading Cards of Lynnwood, Washington, to produce baseball cards in Spanish. The PA required each company to pay a royalty of 13.2 percent of sales, up from 11 percent under the pre-1991 agreements.

Of the $175 million in the strike fund, 90 percent, or $157.5 million, came from baseball card royalties. At the 13.2 percent royalty rate, the $157.5 million represented baseball card sales of $1.2 billion. That just represented the wholesale price. With a 40 percent retail markup, the $157.5 million in royalties represented $1.68 billion spent by consumers on baseball cards.

By buying baseball cards, collectors unwittingly provided the players with leverage for the baseball strike. Each time they bought a pack of cards at $1 retail, 13.2 percent of the wholesale price of 60 cents—roughly 8 cents—went to the strike fund. Ironically, collectors were helping to bring about a work stoppage in the game that had inspired them to collect cards.

That fact was not lost on Dennis Prochaska, owner of the Hot Card Connection sports card store in Wheeling, West Virginia. When the strike began August 12, Prochaska hung a sign in his store window that read: "The Hot Card Connection is on Strike."

Prochaska vowed not to sell baseball cards or anything licensed by the Players Association as long as the players remained on strike. Asked by the Associated Press why he did so, Prochaska replied: "They're getting so much money even while they're on strike from royalties on team merchandise. They're still getting paid even when they don't play."

Which, of course, they owed to the generosity of millions of baseball card collectors.

■ ■ ■

For Bruce McNall, 1994 was a terrible year. The gregarious owner of the Los Angeles Kings who had combined with Upper Deck in 1992 to create Upper Deck Authenticated saw his financial empire crash amid allegations of impropriety.

McNall's troubles came to a head in April when *Vanity Fair* published a 10,000-word exposé on his business dealings. Written by Bryan Burrough, co-author of the bestseller *Barbarians at the Gate*, the story chronicled McNall's storybook life and how he parlayed a coin business as a teenager into a personal fortune that included sports franchises, a movie studio, and a horse-racing syndicate.

But that wasn't all of the story. Burrough traveled the world investigating McNall, finding that his entire financial empire was built on art and coin smuggling. Since the age of 18, Burrough found, McNall had journeyed through Europe, engineering deals with smugglers and grave robbers to acquire coins. The story had all the overtones of Indiana Jones and, indeed, the headline of the story read "Raider of the Lost Art."

Presented with evidence that his main company, Numismatic Fine Arts (N.F.A.), had sold smuggled artifacts for years, McNall acknowledged the practice, admitting that N.F.A. had routinely broken the export laws of Turkey, Italy, Greece, and other Mediterranean countries. "It was illegal in those countries, yes," McNall told Burrough. "But until '83, there were no laws in this country, not really."

The coin market that was responsible for McNall's rise to prominence softened during the mid-1980s. By 1994, there was little left. Two coin-trading partnerships McNall had put together called the Athena Funds were forced into liquidation.

In the spring of 1994, 45,000 coins were put up for auction in Zurich. When they sold for only a fraction of what McNall hoped, he told Burrough: "I'm fucked. I will lose millions in this thing. I'm taking a big hit. This [coin] business is finished. There may come the point when I go under. I can't go on financing negative cash flow. With the coin business and the Kings both negative—it's not going to happen today or tomorrow, but I will go under. If something doesn't change, I'm finished."

McNall, as it turned out, did go under. In April, shortly after the article was published, a federal grand jury launched an investigation into McNall's business dealings over the previous 10 years. In May, McNall—facing negative cash flow—sold 72 percent of the Kings for $60 million to help pay off a $92 million business loan made by Bank of America. Shortly thereafter, McNall was forced into bankruptcy proceedings, with published reports indicating he was between $200 and $300 million in debt. He resigned his position as chairman of the National Hockey League's Board of Governors, saying he was doing so "in the best interests of hockey." Even the Los Angeles Kings' plane that McNall once placed in the Upper Deck Authenticated catalog was seized by federal authorities and was put up for auction.

On August 22, 1994, Joanna Orehek, a former vice president and controller of McNall Sports and Entertainment—the company that created Upper Deck Authenticated with Upper Deck—pleaded guilty to one count of conspiracy and one count of wire fraud in connection with a scheme to defraud four financial institutions of more than $138 million in loans.

Orehek, along with unidentified conspirators, was charged with creating false financial statements overstating McNall's net worth to persuade banks to make loans. A 15-page criminal complaint detailed how Bank of America fell victim to the fraud when it began loaning money to McNall and his company beginning in 1990.

The activity even included the sports card industry. In 1992, according to the complaint, Orehek and others told Bank of America officials that the collateral for a $20 million personal loan to McNall, $15 million in rare coins, had been traded for a collection of sports memorabilia.

The complaint stated that there was neither a collection of coins nor sports memorabilia, and that Orehek bought about one million sports cards that were nearly worthless and told the bank officials they were worth millions. Later, she obtained cards on consignment from sports card dealers and told the bank that McNall Sports and Entertainment owned them. When the dealers asked for the cards back, according to the complaint, Orehek bought replicas and tried to age them, passing them off as the real cards. Orehek allegedly told the banks the replica cards were worth $300,000 when they cost only about $200.

On November 14, 1994, McNall was charged with one count of conspiracy, two counts of bank fraud, and one count of wire fraud for allegedly defrauding banks out of more than $236 million from January 1983 to April 1994.

McNall's attorney, Tom Pollack, issued a statement in which he said his client's downfall was accelerated by becoming a partner in a motion picture company and giving his personal guarantee for loans. When the company could not repay the loans, McNall became personally liable for $120 million.

"The false loan applications to the banks, and the diversion of monies from the funds, were part of an effort to keep the businesses afloat in the face of this unexpected liability and a deteriorating market for collectibles, coins and horses," Pollack told the Associated Press.

McNall and several alleged co-consipirators were accused of using false and fraudulent financial statements, inventory lists, tax returns, and invoices to support the loan applications and had allegedly diverted loans from sham companies to pay operating costs of McNall Sports and Entertainment, Inc., repay loans, and cover personal expenses of McNall.

By December 14, 1994, seven people had been charged in the government's investigation into McNall's businesses, including three officials of McNall Sports and Entertainment. Of the group, six had entered guilty pleas.

According to a 44-page affidavit filed by prosecutors, McNall and others created a sham company, U.S. Coin Enterprises, and claimed it had an inventory of $15 million in rare coins in order to obtain bank loans of $14 million. "In fact, the company had no assets at all," the government charged, "and it was created solely for the purpose of obtaining loans."

In an interview published November 27 in the *Toronto Sun*, McNall said he was ready to accept a jail term.

"If the judge thinks it's appropriate, if that's what he thinks is the right thing to do, I'll live with that and try to make the best of that time," he said. "All I can do is be sorry and remorseful for what went wrong.

"I was never a good businessman. I never viewed myself as a businessman ever and that's probably why I got myself in all this trouble. A tough, hard businessman doesn't do all the stupid things I did."

On December 14, McNall pleaded guilty to all four counts. After he entered his pleas, Assistant U.S. Attorney Peter Spivak spent a half hour recounting McNall's illegal acts over the previous decade. When he was done, U.S. District Court Judge Richard Paez said, "That was a lot Mr. Spivak had to say. Is everything that Mr. Spivak said about you true and correct."

"Yes it is," McNall responded.

McNall, who earlier in the day resigned as president and governor of the Los Angeles Kings, was freed on $100,000 bail posted by Kings executive and former goalie Rogie Vachon. McNall was facing maximum penalties of 45 years in prison, at least $1.75 million in fines, and up to the full amount of the losses caused by his conduct. Sentencing was scheduled for July 6, 1995.

In a statement released by Pollack, McNall said, "I knew that my actions were wrong, but I proceeded anyway in a misguided effort to try to resolve the increasingly severe financial problems resulting from businesses in which I participated. My intentions have always been to repay the debts which these businesses and I have incurred. In my own naive thinking, I was hoping to buy enough time to pay back the loans, but it was a race that I ultimately lost."

■ ■ ■

Even before his troubles began, McNall had distanced himself from Upper Deck Authenticated, which, according to sources, lost more than $5 million in its first year. It had been difficult for the company to recoup the tremendous outlays it had made in player contracts. There was no way, for instance, the company could make back $2.75 million a year from the 20,000 autographs Mickey Mantle was contractually bound to produce. Each autograph, under the contract, cost Upper Deck Authenticated $137.50—far more than the going rate for Mantle's signature. But since Mantle also owed UDA 26 appearances a year, the company sold the appearances to show promoters. For $50,000, a promoter could have Mantle appear at a card show. To make back the $50,000, promoters—such as *Tuff Stuff* magazine, which brought Mantle to its "Summer Classic" card show in Richmond, Virginia, in July of 1994—charged a whopping $80 per signature.

Other contracts had also become huge burdens for Upper Deck Authenticated to bear. In addition to the Reggie Jackson contract, Upper Deck had entered into a 10-year contract with Michael Jordan that would pay him $1 million annually. In the months leading up to Jordan's surprise retirement from the NBA in October of 1993, his agent, David Falk, shopped the exclusive rights to Jordan's autograph.

His first stop was in Cherry Hill, New Jersey, where he met with Score Board vice president Ken Goldin and John Thompson III, the son of Georgetown basketball coach John Thompson, Jr. Thompson III handled basketball contracts for Score Board.

Falk told the Score Board officials that Jordan planned to retire within one to five years. He was looking for a 10-year deal. That was fine with Goldin and Thompson.

Then Falk said that, as part of the deal, Jordan would sign a quantity of the book *Rare Air*, a picture book of Jordan's career featuring photos by the renowned sports photographer Walter Iooss, Jr. To sign the books, Jordan would require $200 an autograph. A line of 2,500 books would cost Score Board $500,000.

Goldin and Thompson looked at each other, both thinking the same thing. *Autographed books? No one wants an autographed book. People wanted signed balls and photos. No one wants a book.*

When Falk was adamant that the book be included as part of the deal, discussions broke off. On October 12, 1993—just days after Jordan announced his retirement—Upper Deck Authenticated announced that it had signed Jordan to an exclusive contract to sign autographs.

Jordan was quoted in a UDA press release saying, "Other than for charities, I have not signed memorabilia because there was just too much counterfeit product on the market. But with Upper Deck Authenticated, I know and my fans will know they're getting a real Michael Jordan autograph when the UDA hologram is attached. This was the only company that can offer that assurance to the athlete and the buyers."

Upper Deck Authenticated was also, of course, the only company that would pay Jordan $1 million a year for 10 years for signing autographs and agree to market signed copies of *Rare Air*.

In April of 1994, Authenticated issued a new catalog. For the first time, it included Jordan memorabilia. There were autographed basketballs for $699 and signed photos for $499. By this time, Jordan was an aspiring baseball player, and UDA offered signed baseballs for $299—twice the going rate of any active baseball player and more than any living baseball player except Joe DiMaggio. And, naturally, there were 2,500 autographed copies of *Rare Air*, available for $499 apiece.

■ ■ ■

In July of 1993, during the National Sports Collectors Convention in Chicago, Bruce McNall hosted a luncheon for a dozen members of the Hobby media at the Hilton and Towers on South Michigan Avenue.

For two hours he listened, as the editors and reporters commented on Upper Deck Authenticated. The memorabilia was fine, they said, for display in sports bars and for people who were not serious collectors. But the sports market was driven by investors, and UDA's high-priced merchandise would never appreciate in value because UDA could always make more of it. Since the signed bats and balls had never been used in a game, they told McNall, they were worthless as collectibles.

McNall listened intently, and over the next nine months he worked to divest himself of Upper Deck Authenticated. McNall, according to sources at UDA, had a clause in his partnership agreement with Upper Deck that allowed him to relinquish much—but not all—of his commitment to UDA after one year. His remaining involvement in Upper Deck Authenticated was unresolved as of August 1994, as the federal investigation unfolded.

In the February 1994 issue of *Inside Sports* magazine, McNall was asked what he thought the overall state of the sports memorabilia industry was. His comments reflected what the Hobby media had told him in Chicago seven months earlier. He said the market for true, game-used memorabilia would always be there. But manufactured memorabilia—such as, ironically, that produced by the company he helped create, Upper Deck Authenticated—was destined to fail.

"Well, there always will be memorabilia," McNall said. "You have to divide the two categories between what I call 'real memorabilia'—things that actually were used by people of the past—and that which was made for collectors. They are two different markets, in a way, and I do think that real memorabilia will always be there.

"Those things that are made for collectors and the general public, I think people should look at as just that and nothing more. Don't view that kind of memorabilia as a marketplace that's going to grow in value or be a good investment because it probably isn't. I think what has happened in the past—and it's true of all collectibles and memorabilia—is that people forget what they had that for, and they started to get into this investment mentality: 'Wow, I have this to make money.' Well, if that's the way you view it, that probably isn't going to happen. I collected coins not to make money but because I enjoyed it. And because I enjoyed it and learned a lot about it and understood what I was doing, it ended up becoming very profitable."

Los Angeles Kings star Wayne Gretzky, whose partnerships with McNall included ownership of the Toronto Argonauts of the Canadian Football League, was left partners with a bankruptcy trustee. The T206 Honus Wagner card that he and McNall purchased in 1991 was now 50 percent controlled by the trustee.

Asked by *USA Today* if he would buy the other "half of the card" that had belonged to McNall, Gretzky said he had not decided. "Right now," he said, "the market is down."

But not as down as McNall, who remained cheerful even as he faced the prospect of a prison term. On August 25, he told the *Los Angeles Times*: "I don't know what will happen, but there's nothing to do but take things as they come. . . .You wish you hadn't done certain things. I know that I need to make restitution from a greed standpoint and from the city's standpoint and I will. That's all I can do. Whatever my personal future is, it is."

Even as McNall endured a federal investigation, collectors purchasing autographed memorabilia from Upper Deck Authenticated received a letter of authenticity that had two signatures at the end, one of which belonged to McNall.

The letter read: "We are proud to introduce this Upper Deck Authenticated hand-signed collectible. The identification number below has been recorded at our headquarters and corresponds to the holographic marking on the actual item. Through this process, the authenticity of Upper Deck Authenticated memorabilia and the signature it bears is fully guaranteed."

Below McNall's signature was the autograph of the other key figure in Authenticated, who like McNall was becoming less involved with Upper Deck. That signature read Richard McWilliam.

■ ■ ■

On August 15, 1994, Upper Deck announced the creation of the "office of the CEO." Richard McWilliam stepped down as president, but remained chief executive officer. Brian Burr and Steve Mitgang, who held the titles senior vice president of operations and senior vice president of sales and marketing respectively, were promoted to president of operations and president of sales and marketing. Sal Amatangelo, Upper Deck's chief financial officer, also became part of the office of the CEO.

In a press release issued by the company, McWilliam cited a desire to build Upper Deck International, the company's foreign expansion division. "I wished to put more of my efforts into the growth opportunities for The Upper Deck Company for some time, and these changes will allow that to happen. I will remain CEO and concentrate on international expansion and long-term growth plans for the Company. Brian [Burr] and Steve [Mitgang] will be responsible for running the company. They will be joined by Sal Amatangelo, our CFO, as a three-member team running day-to-day business."

Of course, no one at Upper Deck actually believed that McWilliam, as CEO, would not have final say on all "day-to-day" matters. But it was important, according to company sources, to place Mitgang and Burr as the leaders of the company. Some of the licensing officials from the four major sports leagues, as well as their respective players associations, had grown weary of dealing with McWilliam, his negotiating tactics, and the persistent allegations that Upper Deck had reprinted sports cards.

"Whenever we come to Richard with a problem or allegation, the first thing he does is he claims he doesn't know," said one high-ranking licensing official. "Then he makes someone a scapegoat and fires him. Then he comes back to us, apologizes, blames that person and says it will never happen again. He then puts someone new in his place. You see it time and time again. Look how many people are no longer there.

"He's very tough to deal with because you never know what he's thinking about. You might think you're getting a good deal, but in actuality he's thinking about something completely different down the road. You have to constantly figure out where he's going with it."

Beginning in 1993, certain licensing directors insisted on dealing with Mitgang. Before coming to Upper Deck in 1991, Mitgang had worked for three years as general manager of business development for Reebok. From 1984 to 1989, Mitgang worked for Chiat/Day/Mojo, the advertising agency that later succeeded Pelton & Associates as Upper Deck's top ad firm.

Just 33 when he became co-president, Mitgang was very different than McWilliam. A soft-spoken man with a slight build and brown curly hair, Mitgang still looked like a student from the University of California at Berkeley, where he earned his undergraduate degree. Unlike McWilliam, whose temper was legend-ary, Mitgang took a laid-back approach to managing people.

But there were similarities. Mitgang, like McWilliam, did not have a vast background in sports. Just as McWilliam had to discover that Tony Gwine was really Tony Gwynn, so too did Mitgang have to educate himself regarding sports. One oft-repeated story about Mitgang took place in 1992, when Upper Deck was scheduling an appearance by Mickey Mantle in Seattle at one of its Heroes of Baseball games.

"This will be great," Mitgang said. "People haven't seen Mickey play in Washington in years."

Someone pointed out that Mantle had retired after the 1968 season. The Seattle Pilots played one year—1969—in the city before moving to Milwaukee, where they became the Brewers. The Seattle Mariners joined the American League as an expansion team for 1977.

Mitgang looked puzzled. "Yeah, but wouldn't he have played against the Washington Senators?"

Burr, who joined Upper Deck in July of 1990 as assistant to the president, would now oversee the entire physical plant operation of Upper Deck. In the release announcing the "office of the CEO," Burr was credited with directing "the company's relocation to its new facilities in Carlsbad, CA," and with "head[ing] the company's investment in state-of-the-art printing equipment and technologies."

The release did not mention Burr's involvement in the repackaging of the 1990–91 French hockey cards.

■ ■ ■

By the fall of 1994, Upper Deck was involved in at least half a dozen major lawsuits. Although the two-year-old battle with Robert Pelton and Pelton & Associates had been settled out of court, the Passante case still loomed on appeal. There were also breach-of-contract suits and countersuits still pending with Doug DeCinces and his former company, DeCinces Sports Productions; Mike Berkus and his company, All-Sport Hobby Sales; and Bob Cohen, the sports agent and attorney who had negotiated card licensing agreements on behalf of Upper Deck.

On November 3, 1994, Mickey Mantle filed suit against Upper Deck. Mantle claimed the company refused to abide by the terms of his July 2, 1992, contract that called for him to sign autographs and make appearances on behalf of the company for $2.75 million annually.

Mantle claimed Upper Deck told him that unless he agreed to a reduction in the payments due him, it was the company's intention to attempt to escape the payment obligations to Mantle by claiming that his January rehabilitation and public acknowledgment of his alcohol problem diminished its ability to market him.

Early in 1994, Mantle's battle with alcoholism captured the attention of the entire country. In January, he entered the Betty Ford Center in Rancho Mirage, California, and stayed 32 days. When he left, he wrote a gripping account of his 42 years drinking that was published in the April 18 issue of *Sports Illustrated.*

As a player, Mantle was known for his prodigious athletic feats on the baseball field. But although he hit 536 home runs, he also was known for not taking care of his body. Injuries were largely responsible for cutting his career short at age 37, but as Mantle admitted in *Sports Illustrated,* alcoholism was also a factor. Now, 26 years after his retirement, he worried that alcohol would soon kill him if he did not stop drinking.

"I was worried that fans would remember Mickey Mantle as a drunk rather than for my baseball accomplishments," he wrote. "I had always thought I could quit drinking by myself, and I'd do it for several days or a couple of weeks, but when I got to feeling good again I'd go back to getting loaded. I was physically and emotionally worn out from all the drinking. I'd hit rock bottom."

In a seven-page complaint filed in Dallas district court, Mantle alleged that from July through December of 1993 his attorney, Roy True, had had ongoing discussions with Upper Deck regarding the company's "cash flow and financial problems" and the "difficulties Upper Deck was encountering in creating a marketing plan to generate income to pay Mantle" the sums due under the terms of the agreement.

In December of 1993, according to the complaint, True met with three Upper Deck officials to discuss the prospect of Mantle entering the Betty Ford Center. The complaint said that they all agreed that Mantle's decision was a wise one and they agreed to reschedule two events Mantle was to appear at in January of 1994. "Upper Deck expressly consented to Mantle's decision to check into the Betty Ford Clinic and sent out a press release announcing Upper Deck supported Mantle in his efforts to seek treatment."

On October 7, 1994, Upper Deck informed Mantle that it was unable to perform its obligations under the agreement, alleging that their nonperformance was a result of the labor disputes that had shut down Major League Baseball and the National Hockey League. The company also told Mantle that it was going to claim a right to terminate the contract based on Mantle's decision to enter the Betty Ford Center unless Mantle agreed to a "substantial reduction" in pay.

Steve Mitgang, Upper Deck's president of sales and marketing, addressed the Mantle suit in a press release. "The discussions regarding restructuring Mr. Mantle's contract were the product of his disability and other performance-related concerns. In short, Mr. Mantle has failed to live up to his commitments as effective spokesperson for the company."

Neither side said how much of a pay cut Mantle was to take, but the complaint claims damages of $4.54 million plus attorneys fees. The three-year contract, which continued through January 31, 1996, included two additional one-year options.

Upper Deck's contention that Mantle's admission of alcoholism diminished his marketability came at a curious time. Two days before the suit was filed, the company unveiled a special Upper Deck Master Card that pictured Mantle. The Upper Deck Authenticated holiday gift catalog, released the same week, was heavily weighted toward Mantle. It included Mantle-autographed bats ($1,750), jerseys ($899), baseballs ($119), photos ($399), and magazine covers ($299).

Upper Deck Authenticated gift certificates, which pictured Mantle, could be purchased in $25 increments. There were Mantle golf balls and even Mantle Waterford crystal baseballs.

"Clearly Upper Deck is not having any trouble marketing Mickey Mantle," True said.

In its five-year existence, Upper Deck also had been involved in lawsuits with founders of the company (Bill Hemrick and DeWayne Buice); former executives such as Bob Bove and Buzz Rasmussen, who later settled breach-of-contract suits after being fired; and a former public relations firm, Burson-Marstellar. Upper Deck had squared off with Topps, in 1991, over the rights to use certain hockey players—the suit was settled out of court—and took on the NFL Players Association over licensing arrangements. (It too was settled.)

The lawsuits have not kept Upper Deck owners from investigating the prospect of taking the company public. While they had considered the idea since 1990 and seriously pursued it since late in 1991—when the sports card market was at an all-time high—the idea was stalled by the uncertainty of the industry. According to investment bankers who have worked with Upper Deck, the financial performance of Topps—the only publicly traded sports card company after Fleer was sold to Marvel Entertainment in 1992—will dictate whether Upper Deck goes public.

That seems unlikely. While Topps's stock sold for 12^1/_4$ a share in January of 1993, it sold for between $6 and 8^1/_2$ during the next 20 months.

One investment banker who has worked with Upper Deck said that even if the trading card industry were healthy, it would be difficult to take the company public.

"Look at the five owners involved," he said, referring to Richard McWilliam, Richard Kughn, Boris Korbel, Paul Sumner, and Bill Hemrick. "You have one guy [Hemrick] who has sued the company and you have two others [McWilliam and Sumner] who have never gotten along. Getting all these guys to agree on what day of the week it is is next to impossible, let alone trying to get them to agree on how best to take the company public."

For now, the company will remain private. While the U.S. card market has peaked, Upper Deck has turned its attention to the international arena. It signed on as a title sponsor to the World Cup for 1994, and produced a line of soccer cards. It also issued a line of basketball cards in Italy. At home, it manufactured "Upper Deck Racing" cards focusing on the NASCAR circuit and a 225-card "Heroes of Baseball" set featuring all-time baseball greats.

The set was a direct response to the Ted Williams Card Company, which in the summer of 1993 debuted with a set of all-time stars. Tony Loiacono, the former Upper Deck vice president of marketing, made good on his promise to hire "whoever Richard [McWilliam] fires." As the chief operating officer of Ted Williams, Loiacono brought on former Upper Deck manager of sports marketing and promotions Andy Abramson to handle public relations. Bob Ruggieri, Upper Deck's former assistant plant manager, has worked as an outside consultant while Jay McCracken, Upper Deck's former vice president of sales, sits on the board of directors.

Brian Interland and John Henry Williams, whose Grand Slam Marketing Company reacquired the rights to produce cards of Ted Williams himself in 1992, had a difficult time working with Upper Deck following the introduction of Loiacono at the La Costa Resort and Spa. Even Topps found itself caught in the middle of the ongoing dispute.

In May of 1994, Topps issued a reprint set of its 1954 baseball cards. Unlike the reprinting conducted by Upper Deck, the 1954 Topps set was marketed as a reproduction series and could be easily distinguished from the originals. The cards themselves measured $2^1/2$ by $3^1/2$ inches, unlike the originals, which measured $2^5/8$ by $3^3/4$. Because of the contractual relationship between Williams and Upper Deck, Topps could not include Williams in the reproduction set, even though he appeared in the 1954 set. The "missing card" of Williams was produced by Upper Deck and included as an insert in the Heroes series. Collectors hoping to complete the Topps set had to purchase Upper Deck cards to obtain the Williams card.

"At times, it seems like a bunch of schoolgirls arguing," Loiacono said, noting the ongoing feud between Upper Deck and the Ted Williams Card Company. "But this is how the card business operates in 1994. Some hobby we have, huh?"

Indeed. Early in 1994, the Ted Williams Card Company signed a contract with a former NFL star to sign 3,000 cards that would be randomly inserted into packs of its 1994 football cards. Like its baseball cards, the Ted Williams football cards pictured retired stars.

The athlete had been paid and the company was all set to have him sign the cards. Then, during the summer of 1994, a series of events unfolded that captured the attention of the entire country. Ted Williams executives wondered if they should still include the cards as planned.

In the end, they opted to do so, and in September, 3,000 cards were delivered to the Los Angeles County jail, where they were autographed by O. J. Simpson.

At one point during the summer, the executives of the company were divided over whether to have Simpson sign the cards. McCracken did not want the company to be perceived as capitalizing on the situation. But it was Simpson himself, ironically, who made the decision a no-brainer for the company.

When the first Ted Williams football cards—entitled "Roger Staubach's NFL Football"—were released in February of 1994, each ex-player who appeared in the set was given 200 of his own card. After Simpson was jailed in June for allegedly murdering his ex-wife Nicole and her friend, Ronald Goldman, he autographed the cards and sold them to a California sports memorabilia dealer to help defray his legal expenses. By Labor Day, the cards were reselling at card shows for $1,500 apiece.

Collectors already thought the Ted Williams Card Company was capitalizing on the situation. If Simpson himself was going to use the cards for his own benefit, Ted Williams executives figured, then why not go forward with the autographed inserts as planned?

■ ■ ■

In 1993, *Collector's Sportslook* magazine asked Richard McWilliam: "What are the keys to your success?"

McWilliam responded: "Being fair and honest. I believe in creating relationships with people and bending to what the consumer wants."

Others have a different read on the chief executive officer and former president of Upper Deck.

"Richard is a paranoid person who has to be in control of everything," Tony Loiacono said. "He wants to win all the time and at all costs. It doesn't matter how he does it: backhanded, underhanded—any way that he can win. But he's got a passion for greatness. It's misdirected sometimes, but he has a passion to be number one that I've never seen in anyone else."

Lisa Andrus, who was engaged to be married to McWilliam for more than two years when their engagement broke off in 1992, said, "There is a good side deep down to him, but I don't think he believes that. He has a wonderful soft side that I saw often enough that I stayed in the relationship. But there's this internal fight going on inside of him. And the bad part always wins. He can't sit back and enjoy it and say 'Hey, I've accomplished something here.' There always has to be more—at any cost."

"The bottom line was that he wanted to make a couple million dollars and have his own card company," said Brad Maier, Upper Deck's art director from 1990 to 1992. "He found the opportunity to capitalize on the idea of developing a high quality baseball card. The actual handling of a company got to be more than he expected. But he must be doing a pretty good job if they're making so much money."

Robert Pelton, whose Pelton & Associates agency worked for Upper Deck from 1988 to 1992, said: "If you think about who is responsible for Upper Deck, you would have to say Paul Sumner. It was his concept. Without him, there is no Upper Deck. Richard was a bean counter who became an opportunist. Now he's positioned himself as the man responsible for the success of Upper Deck."

Which may, of course, be an accurate assessment. Richard McWilliam and Upper Deck are now inextricably linked, so much so that card dealers, distributors, rival card company executives, and licensing officials, as well as former employees, refer to both the company and its chief executive officer by the same name.

Upper Dick.

Andy Abramson—is a public relations and media consultant to several card manufacturers, including the Ted Williams Card Company—where he works with fellow Upper Deck alumni Tony Loiacono and Jay McCracken—and Press Pass, a Dallas-based card manufacturer which employs Bob Bove, formerly Upper Deck's national sales manager.

Dr. James Beckett—is chairman and publisher of Dallas-based Beckett Publications, the sports card industry's most followed line of price-guide magazines. In July of 1994, Beckett unveiled his seventh magazine, dedicated to auto racing and collectibles.

Seymour "Sy" Berger—is vice president of sports and licensing for The Topps Company and is a member of its board of directors. Berger owns 460,768 shares of Topps stock, 1 percent of outstanding stock.

Mike Berkus—split with Doug DeCinces, his partner in DeCinces Sports Promotions, early in 1993. He formed a new company, All-Sport Hobby Sales, and signed an agreement to do consulting work for Upper Deck. In June of 1994, Berkus filed suit against Upper Deck, claiming breach of contract. Upper Deck filed a countersuit, and the matter remains unresolved. Berkus now works for The Score Board, Inc., commuting between Cherry Hill, New Jersey, and his home in Irvine, California, and arranging the sale of memorabilia on home shopping shows. He remains on the National Convention Committee, which governs the National Sports Collectors Convention.

Don Bodow—is president and CEO of Merlin Editions, Inc., a subsidiary of Merlin Publishing of Great Britain. Bodow's Poway, California, business manufactures stickers and sticker albums.

Bob Bove—is the vice president of sales for Press Pass, a Dallas-based manufacturer of stock car racing cards.

DeWayne Buice—is retired and lives in Incline Village, Nevada, with his wife and two sons. Buice was scheduled to receive the final payment ($4.25 million) of his $17 million severance package from Upper Deck in January 1995.

Brian Burr—was promoted from senior vice president of operations to president of operations for Upper Deck on August 15, 1994. He shares the presidency with Steve Mitgang, who on the same day became president of sales and marketing.

Bob Cohen—is a sports attorney in Los Angeles. He represents Mark McGwire of the Oakland Athletics and approximately 30 minor league baseball players. On August 3, 1994, he filed suit against Upper Deck, alleging that the company had breached his contract stemming from his negotiations on their behalf for licenses to produce baseball, football, and basketball cards. The suit is unresolved.

Doug DeCinces—is president of DeCinces Properties, a real estate development company, in Newport Beach, California. In 1993, DeCinces Sports Productions and Upper Deck filed dueling lawsuits against one another, each claiming breach of contract. The matter is unresolved.

Tom Geideman—left Upper Deck in October of 1994 to become football and hockey card brand manager for Classic Games.

Adrian Gluck—resigned from Upper Deck's board of directors in January of 1993. In August of 1994, he launched a new sports card company called Super Slam at the National Sports Collectors Convention in Houston.

Ken Goldin—became chairman, president, and chief executive officer of The Score Board, Inc., after his father, Paul, died of a heart attack on May 21, 1994.

Greg Green—lives in Vista, California, where he works as a West Coast sales representative for Panel Prints, a manufacturer of supermarket "point-of-purchase" displays.

Bill Hemrick—maintains a 4.2 percent stake in Upper Deck, but is not involved in the company. He splits his time between his home in Orange, California, and Nashville, where he owns Sterling Cards, a manufacturer of cards depicting country music stars.

Bob Henry—who helped repackage the reprinted French hockey cards in May of 1991, is a partner in a card packaging business called Bear Instincts International in Huntington Beach, California. His partner is Buzz Rasmussen, the former Upper Deck plant manager who supervised the reprinting of the French hockey.

Reggie Jackson—maintains an office at Upper Deck, where he remains on the board of directors. He also serves as a special assistant to George Steinbrenner, chairman of the New York Yankees.

Wally Joyner—is in the final year of a three-year contract with the Kansas City Royals.

Boris Korbel—sold Orbis Graphic Arts and pursues several business endeavors through a company called Orbis International. He owns 27.08 percent of Upper Deck and is on its board of directors.

Richard Kughn—is chairman of the board of Upper Deck and owns 27.08 percent of the company. He also is chairman of Lionel Trains and lives in Detroit.

Tony Loiacono—is part owner of the Ted Williams Card Company and runs the creative end of the business from his ranch in Bonsall, California. He still owns Celebrity All-Star Hockey, and promotes several charity exhibitions annually.

Brad Maier—is the creative director for Crazy Shirts, a T-shirt manufacturer in Honolulu, Hawaii.

Mickey Mantle—entered the Betty Ford Clinic in January of 1994 and spent 32 days there for the treatment of alcoholism. He filed suit against Upper Deck November 3, 1994, claiming the company would not fulfill its contract with him because of his past problems with alcohol.

Jeff Marx—is president of the National Trading Card Company, a sports card distributor in Orange, California.

Jay McCracken—owns and operates McCrackens' Sports Cards, a card shop located just four miles south of Upper Deck in Carlsbad, California. McCracken also sits on the board of directors of the Ted Williams Card Company and writes a regular column for *Sports Collectors Digest.*

Bruce McNall—pleaded guilty December 14, 1994, to defrauding several banks of more than $236 million. McNall pleaded guilty to one count of conspiracy, two counts of bank fraud, and one count of wire fraud. McNall faces maximum penalties of 45 years in prison, $1.75 million in fines, and restitution up to the full amount of the losses caused by his conduct. Sentencing was set for July 6, 1995.

Richard McWilliam—is CEO of the Upper Deck Company. On August 15, 1994, he stepped down as president of the company, citing a desire to turn his attention to Upper Deck's International division. He owns 27.08 percent of Upper Deck and lives in Encinitas, California.

Michael Merhab—resigned from Upper Deck in June of 1994 after being told his job as vice president of creative sports would be eliminated and that he would be demoted. He now works as a consultant to the National Hockey League Players Association and lives in Oceanside, California.

Steve Mitgang—joined Brian Burr as co-president of Upper Deck on August 15, 1994. Mitgang, who formerly was senior vice president of marketing, was fired from his position as president of sales and marketing in January 1995 as this book went to press.

Anthony Passante—is an attorney in San Diego. His lawsuit against Upper Deck, in which a Santa Ana Superior Court judge ruled in 1993 that he was not entitled to 3 percent ownership of the company, is under appeal.

Don Peck—is retired from The Fleer Corporation. He lives in Ocean City, New Jersey.

Robert Pelton—and his Pelton & Associates advertising and marketing agency filed a $1.6 million suit against Upper Deck September 22, 1992, for nonpayment of products and designs. Upper Deck filed a countersuit for $20 million for "attempts to intimidate Upper Deck's customers and vendors." After nearly two years of legal wrangling that included press releases from both sides denouncing the other, the parties reached an undisclosed settlement during the summer of 1994. Pelton & Associates continues to do design work for several card manufacturers, most notably Topps. Pelton also is a 10 percent owner of Donovan Publishing, a Newport Beach, California, business owned primarily by Upper Deck board member Paul Sumner.

Jack Petruzzelli—is retired from the Fullerton, California, police force and promotes sports card shows in southern California. In July of 1994, he hosted the first annual International Sportscard Expo at the Anaheim Convention Center. He also has remained in the National Sports Collectors Convention as a member of its organizing committee. In August of 1994, he and his wife Patti won the rights to host the 1996 National in Anaheim.

Andrew Prendiville—is a personal injury attorney in Dana Point, California.

Bruce Regis—was replaced as vice president of sales of the Upper Deck Company in August 1994. He remains the company's special projects manager. According to an interoffice memo announcing the move, Regis "will focus on our new go-to-market strategy which is designed to improve retail distribution and sell-through of our products."

Bob Ruggieri—was fired as Upper Deck's assistant plant manager in October of 1992. He is now the owner of Graphic Strategies, Inc., in Oceanside, California. He works as a consultant to several card and pre-press companies.

Arthur Shorin—is chairman of the board and chief executive officer of The Topps Company. Shorin owns 2,183,989 shares of Topps stock, 4.6 percent of outstanding shares.

Dennis Sienicki—is a regional owner of Ledger Plus, an accounting and tax franchise in Rancho Bernardo, California.

Paul Sumner—is president and majority owner of Donovan Publishing in Newport Beach, California. He owns 14.6 percent of Upper Deck and remains on its board of directors.

Al Thomas—was fired as president of Upper Deck Authenticated in August of 1993. He is now president of Back Bay Merchandising in Culver City, California. The company markets autographed memorabilia for professional sports teams, including the Anaheim Mighty Ducks, Boston Celtics, and Pittsburgh Penguins.

I N D E X

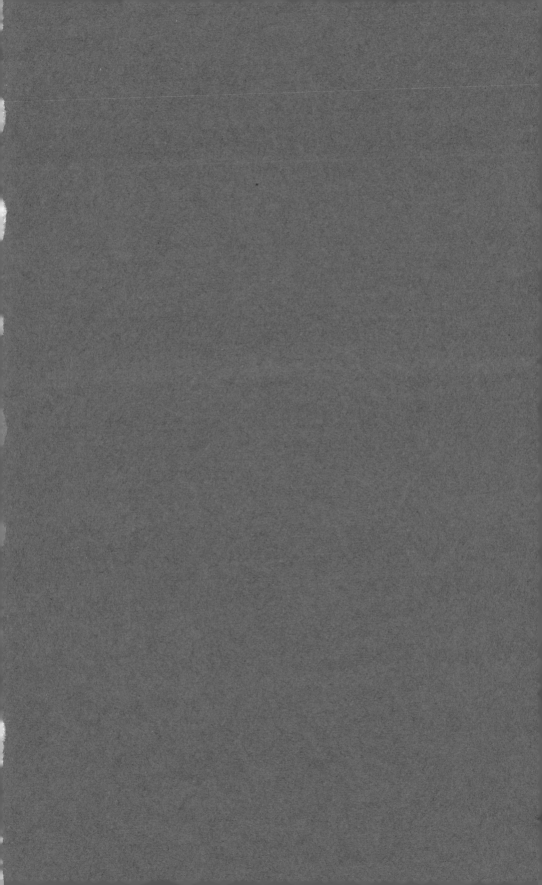